Cemeteries and Remote Burials in Larimer County, Colorado Volume III:

Estes Park Area and Rocky Mountain National Park, Including Park Property in Grand County

by

Duane V. and Susan B. Kniebes

Cemeteries and Remote Burials in Larimer County, Colorado, Volume III:

Estes Park Area and Rocky Mountain National Park, Including Park Property in Grand County

by Duane V. and Susan B. Kniebes

Published by:

Iron Gate Publishing
P.O. Box 999
Niwot, CO 80544

All rights reserved. No part of this book may be reproduced or transmitted in any form or by any means, electronic or mechanical, including photocopying, recording or any information storage and retrieval system without written permission from the authors, except for the inclusion of brief quotations in a review.

The authors have used their best efforts in collecting and preparing material for inclusion in *Cemeteries and Remote Burials in Larimer County, Colorado, Volume III: Estes Park Area and Rocky Mountain National Park, Including Park Property in Grand County*, but do not warrant that the information herein is complete or accurate, and do not assume, and hereby disclaim, any liability to any person for any loss or damage caused by errors or omissions in *Cemeteries and Remote Burials in Larimer County, Colorado, Volume III: Estes Park Area and Rocky Mountain National Park, Including Park Property in Grand County*, whether such errors or omissions result from negligence, accident or any other cause.

Copyright © 2015 by Duane V. and Susan B. Kniebes
Printed in the United States of America
    ISBN 13 978-1-68224-014-4 (softbound)
    ISBN 13 978-1-68224-015-1 (hardbound)
    LCCN 2015944771

Publisher's Cataloging-in-Publication Data

Kniebes, Duane V., 1926–

Kniebes, Susan B., 1943–

    Cemeteries and Remote Burials in Larimer County, Colorado, Volume III: Estes Park Area and Rocky Mountain National Park, Including Park Property in Grand County
by Duane V. and Susan B. Kniebes.

        p.   cm.
    Includes index.
    ISBN 978-1-68224-014-4 (softbound) $23.95
    ISBN 978-1-68224-015-1 (hardbound) $33.95

    1. Cemeteries—Colorado—Larimer County.
2. Inscriptions—Colorado—Larimer County.
3. Larimer County (Colo.)—Genealogy.   I. Title.

F782.L2 K54 2015—Larimer County Cemeteries
929.5.0978868

Cover Photo: Hupp Family Cemetery, Rocky Mountain National Park

Dedicated to the memory of

Dr. D. Ferrel Atkins

Jackie Jaye Johnson

both of whom provided extensive assistance to our efforts
to find and document graves and cemeteries
in Rocky Mountain National Park and in the Estes Park area
of Larimer County

Colorado cemeteries often whisper the long silent stories of history.

"The Ghosts of Colorado Past," written by Donald MacDonald, *5280: Denver's Mile-High Magazine*, Vol. 14, No. 5, November 2006, pages 108-115.

Like a museum, a well-maintained cemetery makes the past available to the present.

To come upon a grave in what we think of as wildlands and natural landscapes is eerie. These human traces are like messages, calling attention to the action of time, to the recession of the past. They make tangible the discord of great forces, of decay and endurance.

Sometimes I think it is the dead who seek me out rather than vice versa.

From the "Epilogue" of *Rabbit Creek Country: Three Ranching Lives in the Heart of the Mountain West*, written by Jon Thiem with Deborah Dimon and published in 2008 by the University of New Mexico Press, Albuquerque, New Mexico.

To be remembered and nothing more—that may be the secret of immortality.

The last words of a National Geographic Special on KRMA Channel 6, Denver, 25 October 2001.

ABOUT THE AUTHORS

Duane Kniebes was born and raised in Michigan. After graduation from high school, he was able to attend two terms at Michigan State University before being called up by the U.S. Army Air Forces to serve his enlistment in the World War II pilot training program. While waiting for a class to become available, he served as the base aerial photographer at Keesler Field in Biloxi, Mississippi. However, the war ended before a pilot training slot became available. He then finished his education at Michigan State University, from which he graduated in 1948 with a B.S. degree in chemistry.

In January 1949 Duane joined the staff as a chemist at the Institute of Gas Technology (IGT) on the campus of the Illinois Institute of Technology in Chicago. He remained at IGT until he retired in 1984, with his last position there being as an Assistant Vice President. In 1954, he received an M.S. in physics from the Illinois Institute of Technology by going to night school. Duane is the author of 47 technical publications including 5 patents.

Following his retirement, he served as a consultant and expert witness on a large number of law suits in which natural gas or propane odorization played a part. In 1985, Duane and Susan moved to Boulder, Colorado, where Duane continued his consulting activities and spent time researching his family tree, which led to his becoming President of the Colorado Chapter of Palatines to America, an organization for individuals researching their German-speaking ancestors. So that he could format this book for publication, he learned and used InDesign's desktop-publishing software.

Susan Briles Kniebes was born in Massachusetts and grew up in College Station, Texas, and DeKalb, Illinois. She graduated from the University of Illinois in Champaign-Urbana in 1966 with a B.A. in English with minors in French and library science. After graduation, she began working for the Institute of Gas Technology as a Technical Editor and ended her time there in 1982 as Associate Director of Technical Communications. Between 1982 and 1985 she served as the Director of Technical Services for a large Chicago law firm. Then in September 1985 Susan and Duane moved to Boulder, Colorado, where Susan worked as a Senior Support Planner for a technology company in Boulder, a Senior Communications Specialist for a medical equipment company in Lakewood, and finally as a Project Manager for several translation agencies in Boulder before her retirement in December 1999.

In addition to making numerous internal presentations and creating a wide variety internal or customer documents for her employers, Susan also published and/or presented over 20 papers or articles, 4 of which received Outstanding Paper or Outstanding Article awards from the Society for Technical Communications.

Like Duane, Susan has long been interested in researching the genealogy of her ancestors, all of whom were early settlers in Texas, some arriving there from the U.S. when Texas was still part of Mexico.

CONTENTS
VOLUME III

Title	Page
Preface	1113
Introduction	1115
Maps	1123
Aspenglen Campground Cemetery	1126
Edwin Bradt Grave	1131
J. P. Chitwood Grave	1133
Cleave-Griffith Family Cemetery	1142
Community Church of the Rockies Columbarium	1153
Elkhorn Lodge Cemetery	1155
Joel Estes Memorial	1171
Estes Valley Memorial Gardens	1176
F.H.R. Cemetery	1177
Carrie Cassedy Fuller Grave	1180
Gaskill Cemetery	1186
Bruce William Gerling Memorial	1194
Grand Lake Cemetery	1196
Lillian Georgina Fearnly Haines Cremains	1200
Horseshoe Park Graves	1202
Hupp Family Cemetery	1225
Mary Jane James Grave	1239
Ransom S. Kendall Grave	1243
Leo J. Kerstien Grave	1247
Louis R. Levings Grave	1250
Lulu City Graves	1259
Lumpy Ridge Skeleton	1267
MacGregor Family Cemetery	1269
Charles D. Miller Grave	1284
Mills and Kiley Grave and Scattered Cremains	1286
Julia Ann Morrissey Grave	1292
Bob Ozmen Grave	1297
Herbert Richards Grave	1302
Rocky Mountain National Park Scattered Cremains	1307
Cemetery of the Episcopal Church of St. Bartholomew the Apostle	1328
St. Francis of Assisi Anglican Church Cemetery	1332
Reverend Thornton R. Sampson Grave	1334
Donald and Dorothy Sandburg Scattered Cremains	1341
Sundance Mountain Graves	1343
Tuxedo Park Cemetery	1353

LARIMER COUNTY CEMETERIES

Title	**Page**
Unknown Adult Graves	1360
Unknown Child Graves	1361
Unknown Child No. 3 Grave	1362
Carl Wilbur Weaver Grave	1364
Harris P. Wellcome Grave	1366
Clement Yore Headstone	1371
Graves and Cemeteries Not Found	1374
Acknowledgments	1378
Bibliography	1384
Index	I-1

PREFACE

Little did we know when we began our grave-search efforts in Larimer County in late 1999 that we would encounter so many unexpected adventures, remarkable sights, and many friendly, knowledgeable, interesting, and sometimes even colorful individuals.

However, as exhilarating as many of our grave-search efforts were, we undertook this project because our personal experiences with researching our own families' genealogies had made us aware of the importance to families of knowing the burial locations of their family members and of learning the histories of both those individuals and their extended family members. Thus, we felt that not only the families of those buried in Larimer Country graves and cemeteries but also other Larimer County residents interested in their county's history would appreciate a book that recorded the locations of burial sites in Larimer County and reported the histories of those sites, those buried there, their families, and the property on which the burial sites were found. Indeed, as the books listed in the "Bibliography" make clear, Larimer County residents have long shown an interest in their county's history, especially the history of the county's burial sites.

During our grave-search efforts, we encountered a number of situations in which our search and research endeavors allowed us to help family members learn of the burial locations of their ancestors or property owners learn the identities of the occupants of remote graves on their property. The most gratifying of these situations occurred when an article on our efforts to find "where past is buried in Larimer County" in the 12 May 2000 issue of the *Fort Collins Coloradoan* was picked up by the *Denver Post*. One of the burial sites discussed in that article was the Lass Family Cemetery on the Tip Top Guest Ranch on the south side of Buckhorn Mountain.

The *Denver Post* article was seen by Kathleen Lass Wacker of Fort Morgan, who is the granddaughter of the Wilhelm Lass who is buried in the Lass Family Cemetery along with two of his sons. Kathleen had last visited the cemetery in 1951 when the decaying wooden fence around the cemetery was replaced by the current metal and wire one, but she could not remember where the cemetery was. Thus, she was most eager to return. On 16 July 2000, Kathleen and members of her family met us and Terry and Glenda Anderson, the owners of the Tip Top Guest Ranch, at the top of Buckhorn Mountain where Terry took her to the cemetery for the first time in 49 years and showed us the parts of the Tip Top Guest Ranch on which the Lass family's buildings had been located. On 8 July 2011, Kathleen and her family had a formal, inscribed headstone placed at the cemetery, which had previously been marked by only a fence and uninscribed local rocks. (For more about the Lass Family Cemetery, the Lass family, and the Anderson family, see the chapter on the Lass Family Cemetery in Volume II.)

We also encountered a number of mysterious deaths, one of the most intriguing being the death of Isaac Farrar, who was shot by the man who later married his widow. While the jury for Coroner's Inquest, which even included two of Isaac's relatives, found that his shooting was accidental, one can help but wonder. Indeed, one of Isaac's descendants reported that her grandmother had told her that "some people thought he had been killed by his wife's boyfriend." (For details of this incident, see "Death of Isaac Farrar" in the chapter on Black Mountain Ranch Cemetery and the Grave of Isaac Farrar in Volume I.)

Of the many friends we made during our years of looking for graves and cemeteries in Larimer Country, we could write many paragraphs. These remarkable individuals not only allowed us to find and document the burial sites we discuss in this book, they have truly

LARIMER COUNTY CEMETERIES

changed our lives. (For more about them, we refer you to the "Acknowledgments" section at the end of each volume of this book.)

So how did we get started on our grave-search efforts in the first place? It all began back in the fall of 1999 when author Duane Kniebes attended a meeting of the Colorado Council of Genealogical Societies (CCGS). He was at the meeting because he was then the President of the Colorado Chapter of Palatines to America, one of the numerous Colorado genealogy societies that belong to CCGS. (Palatines to America is an organization of individuals researching the genealogy and history of their German-speaking ancestors.)

At that CCGS meeting, Pat Kemper, then the Chair of the Colorado Cemetery-Location Project, announced that she was looking for county-specific volunteers for the joint effort of CCGS and the U.S. Geological Survey to find, GPS pinpoint, and document graves and cemeteries in all Colorado counties. Since Boulder County, the county in which we live, was already taken, Duane volunteered for Larimer County. Occupying 2,640 square miles, Larimer County is in north-central Colorado just south of Wyoming. It is bordered by Boulder County on the south, Weld County on the east, and Jackson and Grand Counties on the west.

The starting point for our grave-search efforts in Larimer County was the Larimer County pages from CCGS's 1985 *Colorado Cemetery Directory*, which consisted of tables that provided the following information for 69 Larimer County graves, cemeteries, and memorial markers: Cemetery Name, Location, Type (Public, Private, Family, etc.), History, Status (Active, Occasional Use, Abandoned, etc.), Record Custodian, Published Records, and Where Available (the source of CCGS's 1985 information on the burial site).

Unfortunately, for many of the burial sites we needed to locate, that table included only some of this information, making it especially difficult to find those sites. Indeed, even when the *Colorado Cemetery Directory* did provide fairly complete Location information, it still required a great deal of research and searching to locate many of the original 69 burial sites. Ameliorating this difficulty is why CCGS and the U.S. Geological Survey recruited volunteers to obtain GPS data (latitude and longitude) for each burial site included in the 1985 *Colorado Cemetery Directory*.

Duane and Susan Kniebes
Boulder, Colorado

INTRODUCTION

We began the effort that eventually resulted in this book working mostly on weekends because author Susan Kniebes was still employed full time, although author Duane Kniebes made some solo grave-search trips. But when Susan retired in December 1999, we began working on the project any day of the week we felt like it.

About a third of the way through the 14-year effort that resulted in this book, we became so interested in the history of the folks buried in the graves and the history of their property, which included many of Larimer County's most historic ranches and farms, that we decided to research and write up the history of the graves, cemeteries, and memorials we located.

This effort resulted in this three-volume book, which includes chapters for each of the 158 graves, cemeteries, or memorials that we found in Larimer County between 1999 and 2013, with a cemetery defined as more than one grave in generally the same location. We learned about 43 additional graves, cemeteries, or memorials that we were not able to find. (For what we were able to learn about these sites even though we were not able to find them, see Graves and Cemeteries Not Found, the last chapter in each volume.) And, of course, there are surely many, many more remote burials in Larimer County that we never learned about!

The 158 burial sites that we found and document in this book represent 89 more sites than the original 69 listed in the Larimer County section of the 1985 edition of the *Colorado Cemetery Directory*. So how did we learn of these 89 additional sites? Typically, when we were asking local inhabitants how to find one of the original 69 sites, some of our informants told us about one or more additional sites not part of the original 69. This happened over and over again.

In addition, when the *Fort Collins Coloradoan* published an article on our Larimer County grave-search efforts on the front page of its 12 May 2000 issue, at our request, they included our phone number so people could contact us about any remote graves or cemeteries of which they were aware. Those calls helped us find some of the burial sites on the original list of 69 as well as a number of the 89 additional sites.

However, as Jon Thiem expressed it in the third quote from his *Rabbit Creek Country* on the epigraph page, we have felt that the frequent coincidences that led to our finding some of Larimer County's remote burial sites had as much to do with serendipity as with diligent research or pure chance. For some examples of this, see the "Finding the Grave/Cemetery" sections of the following chapters: In Volume I, the Buckeye Ranch Cemetery, Holley Ranch Graves, Lamb Family Cemetery, and Ludwig Ranch Cemetery; in Volume II, Indian Cemetery No. 2 and the Rhodes Family Cemetery; and in Volume III, the Mary Jane James Grave and Tuxedo Park Cemetery.

Organization of This Book

Volume I of this book covers northern Larimer County, from the Cache la Poudre River north to Wyoming, including the Laramie River Valley and Livermore. Volume II covers Larimer County south of the Cache la Poudre River, including Berthoud, Fort Collins, and Loveland. Volume III covers the Estes Park area and Rocky Mountain National Park, including the part of the Park in Grand County.

The "Maps" section of each volume, which follows this "Introduction," contains a map of Larimer County showing the graves, cemeteries, and memorials discussed in the chapters of that specific volume. Volumes I and II also contain a map of "Early Northern Colorado Trails" that shows the location those trails and the stage stations and forts associated with them.

Private Property

Unless a grave, cemetery, or memorial is on public land (city cemeteries, public rights-of-way, public parks, Rocky Mountain National Park, national forests, wilderness areas, natural areas, etc.), it is on private land. Indeed, in the "Location" section of each chapter, we have specifically noted if the grave, cemetery, or memorial discussed in that chapter is on private land. **To visit any location on private property, you need the permission of the property owner.**

To learn the name and contact information for the current owners of all property in Larimer County, you can consult the Larimer County Assessor's Office land ownership website at http://larimer.org/assessor.

Respect for Remote Graves

It is not only morally wrong to disturb a remote grave or cemetery (indeed any grave or cemetery) or any inscribed headstones found there, it is also illegal! Once you have permission to visit the site, you can take photographs and get GPS readings, but you cannot disturb the grave or remove its headstone or other grave markers!

GPS Readings

The purpose of this project was to locate Larimer County cemeteries and remote burial sites so they could be easily found again by family members, genealogists, and historians. The best system available to the layman for determining and reporting geographic locations was and still is the Global Positioning System (GPS), of which the first was operated by the U.S. Department of Defense. It consists of at least 24 satellites orbiting the earth and transmitting position data. Initially, a "fuzz" signal was applied to make civilian use less accurate than that of the military. However, that signal was removed in May 2000.

When a receiver on the ground, in our case, a hand-held GPS device, obtains signals from at least three satellites, it triangulates them to provide the latitude and longitude information, which it then displays for the user. This measurement can be expressed in several ways. We have used degrees, minutes, and seconds (DMS), conforming to the method used by the Geographic Names Information System (GNIS), part of the United States Geological Survey (USGS).

There are two DMS measurements used, based on two measurements of the location of the center of the Earth, one made in 1927 and the other in 1983. The first is called NAD 27 and the second NAD 83, with NAD standing for "North American Datum." NAD 27 is used for all of the USGS's Quadrangle Maps since the USGS produced most of these maps before 1983. The GNIS, however, has converted all of its measurements to NAD 83 because it is the more accurate of the two. Thus, all DMS readings in this book are based on NAD 83. The difference between NAD 27 and NAD 83 readings in Larimer County is less than a second of latitude and about two seconds of longitude.

Note that one second of longitude equals about 80 feet and one second of latitude about 100 feet. We consider this to be close enough to find the burial sites described in this book.

Concerning Amount of Research Done

With more research, many of these chapters in this book could have been turned into entire history books or biographies. In fact, books have been written about some of the individuals or families we cover in this book. Some examples are Zethyl Gates's *Mariano Medina: Colorado Mountain Man*; Jon Thiem's *Rabbit Creek Country: Three Ranching Lives in the Heart of the Mountain West*; and Dan Rottenberg's *Death of a Gunfighter: The Quest for Jack Slade, the West's Most Elusive Legend*. (See the "Bibliography" for citations for these books.)

As it stands, some of our longer chapters cover well-known graves and cemeteries or discuss well-known individuals for whom a considerable amount of published historical information is available and/or for whom descendants of an individual or family provided significant information.

INTRODUCTION

Since our intention was to write a book that covered all of the 158 burial sites and memorials we found, history researchers will undoubtedly feel that some of the chapters would be improved with additional research. However, if we had done more exhaustive research, we would never have had the time to write this book. So we hope the occasional holes in our research will be excused. Maybe if we had started this project when we were younger . . . .

Biographical and Genealogical Information

Many of the chapters in this book include biographical and genealogical information on the individuals buried in the graves and cemeteries and their family members and on the owners of the property containing the graves, cemeteries, or memorials and their family members.

When any of those individuals are, as far as we know, still alive, we provide only the year of their birth and marriage to keep identity thieves from obtaining complete dates.

Ghosts

In the two "ghost stories" informants told us (the Campbell Cemetery in Volume I and the Elkhorn Lodge Cemetery in Volume III), it is of interest that, in both cases, a number of individuals without previous knowledge of earlier reports about a ghost on the property reported similar encounters.

Legal Land Descriptions

As discussed above, the primary reason for our grave-search efforts in Larimer County was to obtain GPS readings for the 69 graves, cemeteries, and memorial markers listed in the Larimer County section of the 1985 edition of Colorado Council of Genealogical Society's *Colorado Cemetery Directory*. Those readings provided the latitude and longitude information for each site, which then allowed us to determine where each site was located within the legal land description system used in the U.S.A.: the Public Land Survey System (PLSS), also known as the "rectangular survey system."

For example, the GPS reading for the Robinson Ranch Cemetery (covered in Volume I) yields the following latitude and longitude information: Latitude 40° 44' 39" North, Longitude 105° 32' 04" West. Armed with this information and the U.S. Geological Survey's Quad Maps for Larimer County (donated by the USGS), we were able to determine that this cemetery is in the Southwest Quarter of the Northwest Quarter of Section 15 of Township 9 North, Range 73 West, 6th Prime Meridian, which is the legal description for the land containing that cemetery.

Using this legal land description, we were able to learn that the 40 acres on which the Robinson Ranch Cemetery is located were originally bought from the U.S. Government in 1888 by David Frank Smith and that that same land later belonged to "Lady" Catherine Moon before eventually being purchased by Elbert Robinson. (See the chapter on the Robinson Ranch Cemetery in Volume I.) Even today, when rural land is sold and bought, PLSS legal land descriptions are still used to describe the land changing hands.

Throughout this book, you will see references to PLSS legal land descriptions when we are discussing the original owners of land obtained from the U.S. Government via any of the Unoccupied Land Acquisition Acts discussed below, the transfer of land between owners, and the current owners of land containing one of Larimer County's graves, cemeteries, or memorial markers. Consequently, we are providing brief definitions of relevant aspects of the Public Land Survey System below. For more detailed information on the PLSS, see:

1. http://www.glorecords.blm.gov/reference/default.aspx
2. http://en.wikipedia.org/wiki/Public_Land_Survey_System

LARIMER COUNTY CEMETERIES

3. The "Foreword and Acknowledgments" to the Revised Second Edition of the Livermore Woman's Club's *Among These Hills*. (See the "Bibliography" for a complete citation.)

Principal Meridian

A Principal Meridian is a principal north-south line (line of longitude) used in the PLSS system. The 6th Principal Meridian is used for surveys in Colorado, Kansas, Nebraska, South Dakota, and Wyoming and begins at Latitude 40° 00' 07" North, Longitude 97° 22' 08" West and is thus the principal meridian used in all legal land surveys and the resulting legal land descriptions in Larimer County. (The 6th Principal Meridian runs through eastern Nebraska and Kansas.)

Baseline

A Baseline is an east-west line (line of latitude) used along with a principal meridian to establish the "initial point" upon which a legal land survey is based. The baseline used for surveys in Larimer County runs along Baseline Road in Boulder, Colorado.

Township

A Township is a square parcel of land that measures 6 miles on each side and contains approximately 23,040 acres or 36 square miles. Townships are identified in relation to a baseline and a principal meridian. Thus, "Township 9 North, Range 73 West, 6th Principal Meridian" would be nine tiers north of the baseline (Baseline Road in Boulder) of the 6th Principal Meridian, with one "tier" being 6 miles high.

Range

A Range is used along with the township to identify the number of tiers that the parcel of land in question is east or west of that township's principal meridian. Thus, "Township 9 North, Range 73 West, 6th Principal Meridian" indicates that the township in question is 73 tiers west of the 6th Principal Meridian, with one "tier" being 6 miles wide.

Section

Each township is divided into 36 sections, each of which is 1 mile square and contains 640 acres. The location of these 36 sections appears in the same location in each township. For example, Section 1 is always in the northeast corner of each township. (For a diagram showing the location of each of the 36 sections in a township, see Source Nos. 2 and 3 above.)

Aliquot Parts

Since every parcel of land originally obtained from the U.S. Government or later sold between private parties does not necessarily contain an entire 640-acre section, surveyors have to be able to describe parcels of land smaller than one section. Thus, each section can be divided into "aliquot parts," as described below:

A half section equals 320 acres, half the 640 acres in a section.
A quarter section equals 160 acres.
A half of a quarter section (an 8th of a section) equals 80 acres.
A quarter of a quarter section (a 16th of a section) equals 40 acres, etc.

Halves of a section are identified as N, S, E, or W, such as the N Half of Section 15. Quarters of a section are identified as NW, SW, NE, and SE, such as the NW Quarter of Section 15. Following this pattern, the North Half of the Northeast Quarter of Section 15 is identified as NNE Quarter of Section 15, and the Northwest Quarter of the Northeast Quarter of Section 15 is identified as NW Quarter of NE Quarter of Section 15.

INTRODUCTION

Unoccupied-Land Acquisition Acts

The original owners of the land in Larimer County nearly always obtained it via one of the following U.S. Government's unoccupied-land acquisition acts.

Land Ordinance of May 20, 1785

This law established that Section 16 of every township (meaning "township" as defined by the Public Land Survey System discussed above) was to be used "for the maintenance of public schools within said township." This did not necessarily mean that a school had to be built within Section 16. Instead, the land in Section 16 could be sold, with the resulting profits being used to support public education.

Preemption Act of 1841

The Preemption Act was passed by the U.S. Congress in 1841 in response to the fact that pioneers in the Western states frequently settled on public land before that land could be surveyed and then auctioned by the U.S. Government. The purpose of this law was to allow those who were squatting on public land to "preempt" that land, meaning that by settling on the land they acquired a conditional right to buy the land before it was offered to sale to others. Specifically, the Preemption Act of 1841 allowed settlers to stake a claim on 160 acres (the equivalent of one quarter of a section) and then, after about 14 months, to buy it from the U.S. Government for as little as $1.25/acre before it was offered for public sale.

After the passage of the Homestead Act in 1862, Congress repealed the Preemption Act of 1841.

Homestead Act of 1862

A great deal of the land in Larimer County was originally obtained via the Homestead Act, which was signed into law by President Abraham Lincoln on 20 May 1862. The law provided for the transfer of 160 acres (a quarter of a section) of unoccupied public land west of the Mississippi River to U.S. citizens, or intended citizens, who had never taken up arms against the U.S. and were 21 years old or the head of a household.

Before gaining possession of the land, the potential land owner had to first file an application, improve the land ("prove it up"), live there for 5 years, and then file for a deed of title, referred to as a "land patent." (Recent immigrants had to become U.S. citizens before applying for their land patents.) Alternatively, a homesteader could live on the land for just 6 months and then pay $1.25/acre to obtain a land patent. Women were also able to obtain "land patents," and many did, including in Larimer County.

If the original homesteader left the land before the 5 years were up or without "proving it up," he relinquished his right to the claim. Someone else could then file a claim on the land, and the whole process would start over. Sometimes a second homesteader would actually pay the first homesteader to relinquish his claim to the land.

Timber Culture Act of 1873

The Timber Culture Act, which was passed by Congress in 1873, allowed homesteaders to get a second 160 acres if they set aside 40 acres of that land to grow trees. The purpose of the act was to solve the problems caused by the lack of wood on the Great Plains. After planting at least 40 acres of trees, the homesteader would be issued a land patent only if he had first occupied the land for at least 5 years. Later the amount of land that had to be planted in trees was reduced to 10 acres.

LARIMER COUNTY CEMETERIES

Desert Land Act of 1877

The Desert Land Act, which was passed by Congress on 3 March 1877, allows a married couple to buy up to 640 acres (an entire section) for $1.25/acre if they promise to irrigate and cultivate the land within 4 years. A single person can receive only 320 acres at the same price per acre. The purpose of the act is to promote the economic development of arid and semiarid public lands in the Western states. We use the present tense rather than the past tense in describing this act because, according to the website of the Bureau of Land Management (http://www.blm.gov/nhp/landfacts/DesertLand.html), this act is still in effect.

Stock-Raising Homestead Act of 1916

The Stock-Raising Homestead Act, which was enacted by Congress in 1916, allowed homesteaders to acquire 640 acres (a full section) of land that was deemed suitable for grazing but not for cultivation. The "proving up" of such land required some range improvements. Unlike the other unoccupied-land acquisition acts discussed above, the Stock-Raising Homestead Act separated surface rights from subsurface (mineral) rights, with the Federal Government retaining the ownership of the mineral rights.

Native American Graves

We were told by a number of archaeologists and Larimer County old timers that Native American in-ground burials in Larimer County were typically covered by fist-size local rocks that were mounded up over the graves, which generally had more of an oval shape than the rectangular shape typical of the remote graves of early European settlers. This is exactly the way the Native American graves we found in Larimer County looked. We assume that since the Native Americans typically would not have had metal digging tools, they were not able to dig graves that were sufficiently deep to keep predators from digging up the deceased and thus mounded up rocks over the graves. Some Native Americans in Larimer County practiced tree or rock cleft "burials" instead.

For information on the Native American graves that we have found in Larimer County and in the part of Rocky Mountain National Park that is in Grand County, see the following chapters: Buckeye Ranch Cemetery, Dowdy Lake Grave, Holley Ranch Graves (Grave No. 3), Indian Cemetery No. 1, Joe Wright Reservoir Grave, Trail's End Ranch Cemetery, Unknown Adult No. 4 Grave (on the Roberts Ranch), and the Worster Cemetery in Volume I; Indian Cemetery No. 2, the Langston Family Cemetery, and the Thomson Ranch Cemetery in Volume II; and the Gaskill Cemetery in Volume III.

Use of Dowser Rods to Confirm Burials

Dowsing has been used for many years, primarily to locate underground water. Although conventional science has no explanation for why dowsing should work, many people have used it with success. Albert Einstein was convinced of the authenticity of dowsing. He said, "I know very well that many scientists consider dowsing as they do astrology, as a type of ancient superstition. According to my conviction this is, however, unjustified. The dowsing rod is a simple instrument which shows the reaction of the human nervous system to certain factors which are unknown to us at this time."

Author Duane Kniebes, who has degrees in both physics and chemistry, knew nothing about dowsing until he went to the office for the Loveland Burial Park and Lakeside Cemetery to ask whether they had ever moved the remote burial of "Grandpa Langston" to either cemetery. Duane had encountered a spot that had recently been dug up and refilled while looking for Grandpa's grave and knew that the remote burials of H.L.W. Peterson and "Mexican Joe" had been moved to Lakeside Cemetery. (See the chapters on the Langston Family Cemetery and on the Loveland Burial Park and Lakeside Cemetery in Volume II.)] The manager there then asked if Duane had used "witch sticks" to check the spot. They then went out the door of the cemetery office to a set of graves where the manager demonstrated how his L-shaped dowser rods detected both burials and underground flowing irrigation water and then taught Duane how to use them. Since then, we have used a pair of dowser rods to confirm and find burials.

We make our own rods out of 1/8-inch welding rod. They are 23-inches long with a 5-inch handle bent at a 90-degree angle. Dimensions are not critical. Two rods are used, one in each hand held loosely like pistols, with the long part of the rods parallel to the ground. Keep your arms slightly away from your body, and your thumbs off the rods. When you slowly walk over a burial, the rods will cross, then uncross when you are past the burial. They also work over buried ashes, but the target area is, of course, much smaller. Note that a male or a female can be identified with the use of one rod. Usually the rod will swing right for a male, and left for a female.

The two largest cemeteries in Larimer County (and numerous other cemeteries around the country) were founded before they had much of a staff. Thus, when a family bought a plot of, say, five graves, they often buried relatives in those graves without telling the cemetery and without providing a grave marker. Therefore, a cemetery's records might show that there were two unused graves in a family plot when actually all of the graves were occupied. Consequently, the employees of these cemeteries use dowser rods before they dig in old family plots to avoid inadvertently digging up family members buried long ago without a grave marker.

We have encountered several situations during which our use of dowser rods indicated that we had found a remote grave with no formal marker and then an individual who remembered the location of the grave or an old photo of the grave confirmed that the dowers rods were right.

For discussions of several specific grave-search situations in which our use of dowser rods to identify the location of remote graves was later confirmed by other sources, see the "Finding the Grave/Cemetery" sections of the following chapters: the Cabin Creek Grave in Volume I and the Hupp Family Cemetery and the Reverend Thornton R. Sampson Grave in Volume III.

In the process of finding the 158 graves and cemeteries that we have located in Larimer County, we have used dowser rods to help confirm the location of graves that are not marked by formal, inscribed grave markers. While doing that, we have taught numerous property owners and others helping us with our grave-search efforts how to use dowser rods and have given them a pair of rods for their own use.

Methods of Documentation

We have included the sources of information used in a specific chapter (and sometimes within specific sections of a chapter) toward the beginning of many chapters or chapter sections rather than in a separate "Notes" section at the end of each volume. These in-chapter sources are listed in order by either the date they were gathered (census data), the date they were published, the date we received an email or letter, or the date the cited information was found in an online database or other online source.

At the end of each volume of this book, we have included a "Bibliography" that provides an alphabetical list of all of the books and frequently cited online databases used in all three volumes of this book. When the same source is included in both an in-chapter source list and in the "Bibliography," the citation in the in-chapter source list is an abbreviated version of the complete citation in the "Bibliography."

LARIMER COUNTY CEMETERIES

Larimer County Requirements Concerning Burials on Private Property

Since a number of the graves and cemeteries we found in Larimer County are on private, rural land, one of the questions that we are most frequently asked when we make presentations on our grave-search efforts is, "What rules does Larimer County have concerning burials on private land?"

We called a number of Larimer County offices to find out which office could answer that question. It turned out that, at least as of October 2007, Larimer County had vested the power to control burials on private land in the Environmental Health Services Division (970-498-6790) of the Larimer County Health and Environmental Department. When we talked to Rick Grossmann at the Environmental Health Services Division in October 2007, he provided the following information:

In all cases, including cremations:

- The body must go through a funeral home, which can help the family of the deceased with all of the requirements discussed below. This also applies to a body that is going to be cremated, no matter whether the ashes are going to be scattered or buried.
- A death certificate must be obtained from the Larimer County Vital Statistics Division (970-498-6710), which is also part of the Larimer County Health and Environmental Department.
- For body burials, a burial permit must be obtained from the Environmental Health Services Division and the location of the grave or cemetery must be put on the Larimer County Plat. To arrange for this latter requirement, contact the Larimer County Planning Department (970-498-7683).

Requirements concerning the grave itself are as follows:

- The body must be buried in a vault as well as a casket.
- Grave must be covered by at least 2 feet of earth.
- The bottom of the grave must be at least 4 feet above ground water.
- The grave cannot be in a ravine, must be at least 100 feet from a stream or lake, and must be at least 300 feet from any water wells.
- The county has no requirements concerning the distance that a body burial must be from a public road.

Larimer County's rules for establishing cemeteries are as follows: A small cemetery of three or fewer body burials does not require the permission of the Larimer County Commissioners. However, before establishing a cemetery that contains four or more body burials, you need to get the approval of the Larimer County Commissioners (970-498-7010).

MAPS

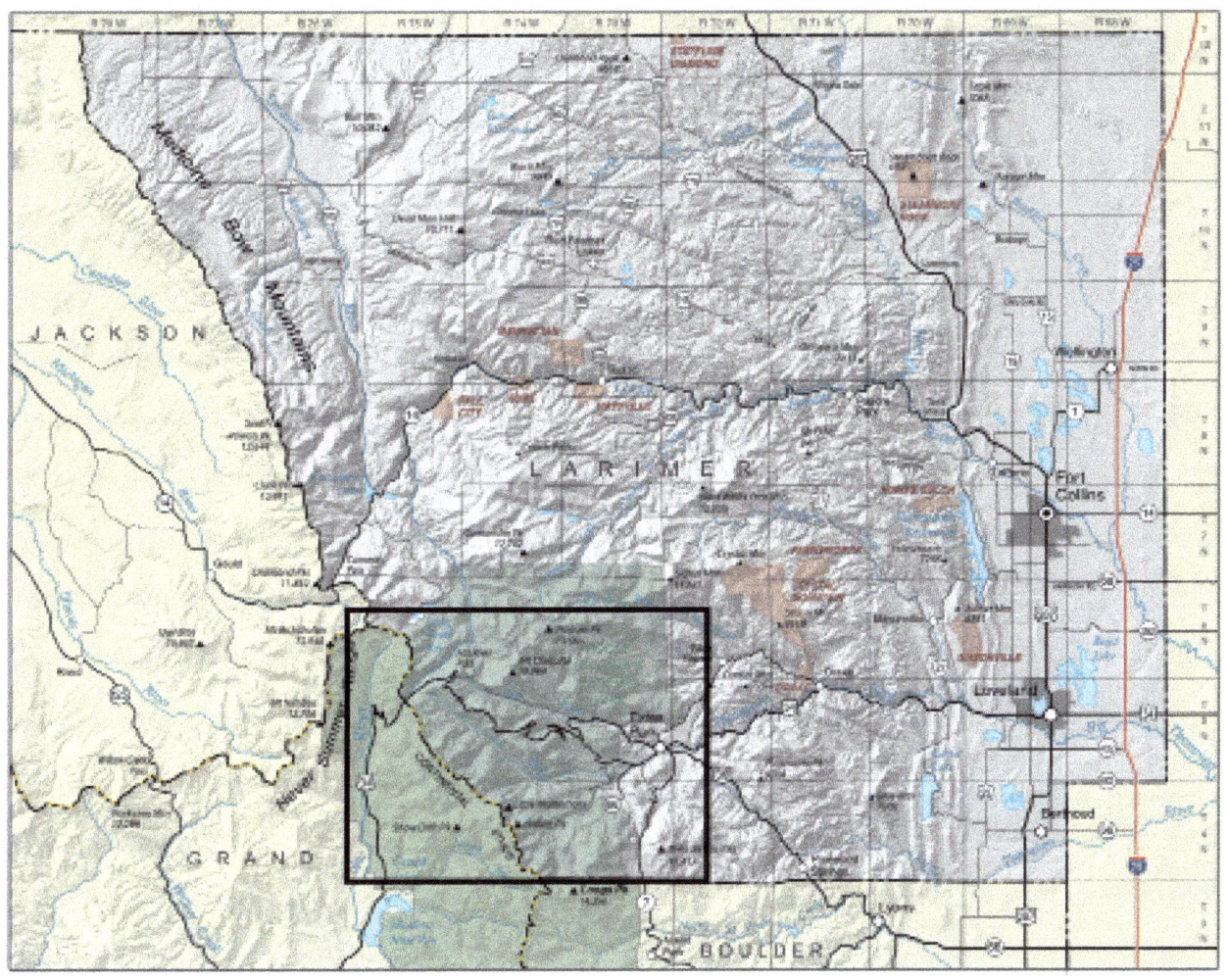

Portion of Larimer County Covered in this Volume

KEY TO MAP NUMBERS

118. Aspenglen Campground Cemetery
119. Edwin Bradt Grave
120. J. P. Chitwood Grave
121. Cleave-Griffith Family Cemetery
122. Community Church of the Rockies Columbarium
123. Elkhorn Lodge Cemetery
124. Joel Estes Memorial
125. Estes Valley Memorial Gardens
126. F.H.R. Cemetery
127. Carrie Cassedy Fuller Grave
128. Gaskill Cemetery
129. Bruce William Gerling Memorial
130. Grand Lake Cemetery
131. Lillian Georgina Fearnly Haines Cremains
132. Horseshoe Park Graves
133. Hupp Family Cemetery
134. Mary Jane James Grave
135. Ransom S. Kendall Grave
136. Leo J. Kerstien Grave
137. Louis R. Levings Grave
138. Lulu City Graves
139. Lumpy Ridge Skeleton
140. MacGregor Family Cemetery
141. Charles D. Miller Grave
142. Mills and Kiley Grave and Scattered Cremains
143. Julia Ann Morrissey Grave
144. Bob Ozmen Grave
145. Herbert Richards Grave
146. St. Bartholomew Episcopal Church Cemetery
147. St. Francis of Assisi Anglican Church Cemetery
148. Reverend Thornton R. Sampson Grave
149. Donald and Doris Sandburg Scattered Cremains
150. Sundance Mountain Graves
151. Tuxedo Park Cemetery
152. Unknown Child No. 3 Grave
153. Carl Wilbur Weaver Grave
154. Harris P. Wellcome Grave
155. Clement Yore Headstone

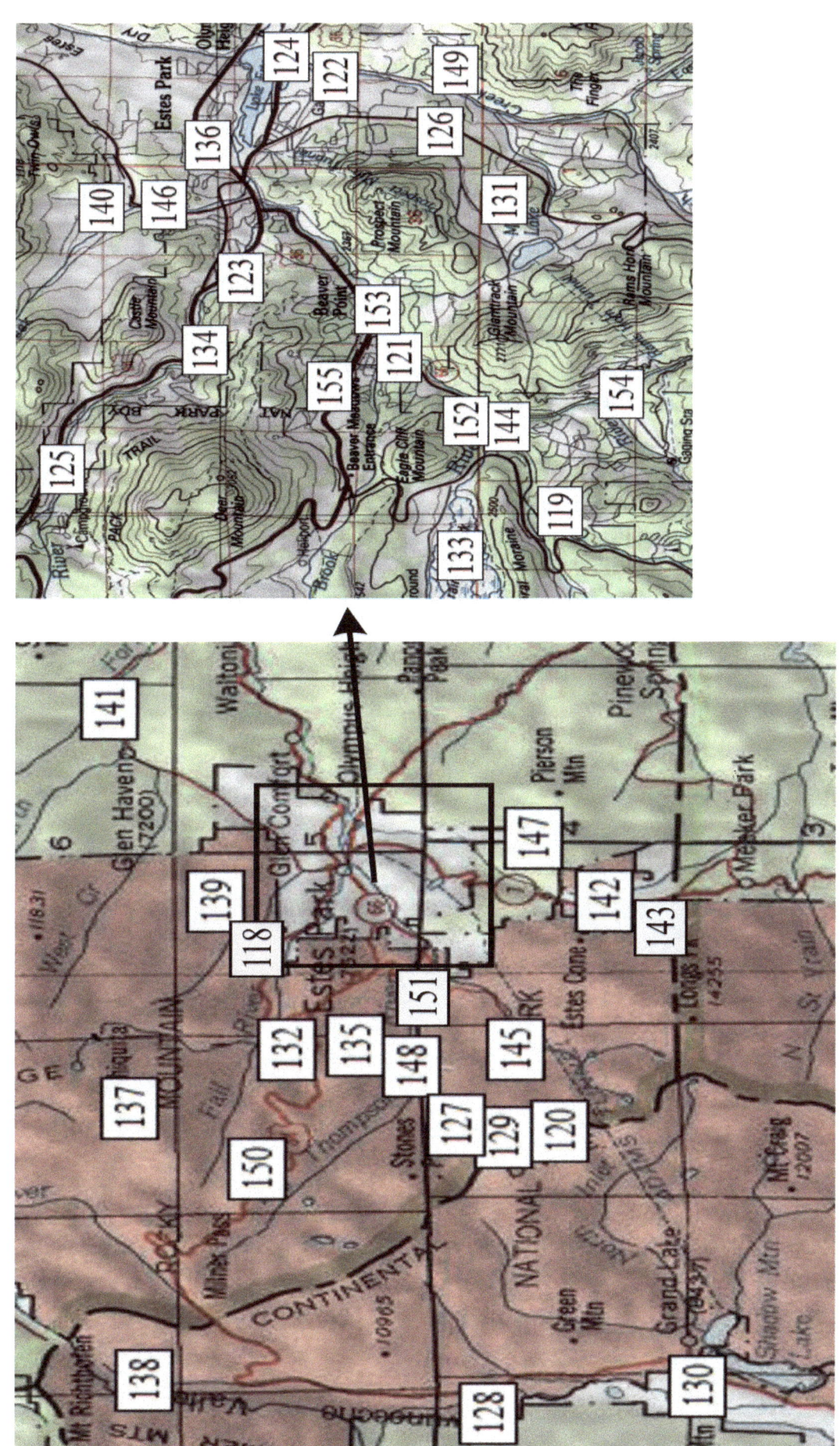

LARIMER COUNTY CEMETERIES

ASPENGLEN CAMPGROUND CEMETERY

Location: Latitude 40° 24' 01" N, Longitude 105° 35' 31" W

As the name of this cemetery implies, the Aspenglen Campground Cemetery is located in the Aspenglen Campground, which is in Rocky Mountain National Park.

Aspenglen Campground is almost immediately south of the Fall River entrance to the Park. The two graves are located west of a footpath that goes from the campground's amphitheater to a bridge over the old river bed of Fall River to the campground's walk-in campsites. The graves are on the south bank of the old river bed. One grave is immediately east of a big pine tree, and the other is south of a big boulder that is immediately west of the same pine tree. It was probably the tree and boulder that kept the two graves from being completely swept away by the Lawn Lake Flood. (See the fifth paragraph of "Finding the Graves" below for more information on this flood.)

Description of Graves

The two graves are sufficiently small to be the graves of children. Our use of dowser rods confirmed the presence of the burial of a child in each of the two graves.

Photo A: Two Child Burials in Aspenglen Campground in Rocky Mountain National Park

Finding the Graves

We were looking for graves in the Aspenglen Campground area because of information provided us by Dr. D. Ferrel Atkins during the late summer of 2000. (For more information about Ferrel, see the "Acknowledgements" section.)

In the late summer of 2000, Ferrel provided us with two items concerning a possible grave in the vicinity of Aspenglen Campground:

1. A copy of a "Memorandum of Call" for a call received by Park "Dispatch" at 12:30 (assumedly p.m.) on May 27. The year was not recorded, but because of the date on Item 2 below, we

can assume that the year had to be 1986 or earlier. This "Memorandum of Call" provided the following information:

- Message was for Glen Kaye.
- The call was from Chuck Kline.
- Subject of Message: Aspenglen Campground
- The message was as follows: "Chuck found an old tombstone in the 'old area' of the campground, near the old power line. Incscription reads: 'F.A.J. July 1883-May 1886.'"

2. Ferrel's "Report on FAJ Tombstone Found at Aspenglen Campground," dated 3 June 1986. This report is quoted in its entirety under "Search for Identity of FAJ" below.

Based on the information that Ferrel provided us, on Monday, 2 July 2001, we finally found time to visit the Aspenglen Campground to look for the grave that the FAJ tombstone had marked. We immediately encountered Ira Golfarb, a first-year Ranger, making his morning rounds of the campers. We explained our grave-search efforts and asked him where the "old area" of the campground might be. He thought it may be near the old, pre-flood bed of Fall River and directed us there. In particular, we and he both wondered if the walk-in camp sites in Aspenglen Campground might be part of the "old area" of the campground and if these sites are only walk-in now to eliminate the need to rebuild any road bridge that might have been destroyed by the Lawn Lake Flood described below.

Ira Goldfarb ended up providing considerable help with our efforts to locate, GPS-pinpoint, and photograph remote graves in the Park that were at too high of an altitude for us to visit. (For details on the assistance that Ira and his wife Joan provided, see the "Acknowledgements" section.)

The website for Rocky Mountain National Park provides the following information on the "Lawn Lake Flood":

> "At approximately 0530 Mountain Daylight Time on the morning of July 15, 1982, Lawn Lake dam [an earthen dam at Lawn Lake at the foot of Mummy Mountain], located in Rocky Mountain National Park, Colorado, failed.
>
> "The dam released 674 acre-feet (219,724,000 gallons) of water at an estimated peak discharge of 18,000 cubic feet (134,640 gallons) per second down the Roaring River valley. Three people were killed and damages totaled $31 million. The Colorado State Engineer determined that the probable cause of failure was deterioration of lead caulking used for the connection between the outlet pipe and the gate valve. The resulting leak eroded the earthfill, and progressive deterioration led to failure of the embankment.
>
> "Flood waters from Lawn Lake overtopped a second dam at Cascade Lake, 6.7 miles downstream, which also failed. Cascade Lake dam, a 17-foot high concrete gravity dam with a capacity of 12.1 acre-feet (3,944,600 gallons), failed by toppling with 4.2 feet of water flowing over its crest. The flood continued down the Fall River into the town of Estes Park, which suffered extensive damage from the overbank flow."

The Lawn Lake Flood changed the bed of Fall River in the vicinity of Aspenglen Campground. (A large alluvial fan that also resulted from this flood can be seen north of the road that connects Highway 34 with the Old Fall River Road just west of Sheep Lakes.) It could well have been that flood that dislodged the FAJ headstone from its original resting place and deposited it where Chuck Kline found it. Remember that the two children's graves that we found are on the south bank of the old bed of the Fall River, not on the bank of its current bed.

After searching in the area where Ira directed us, we located the two children's graves described above. However, we have no way of knowing if either of these graves is the grave of almost-3-year-old FAJ.

Search for the Gravestone

The information provided by Ferrel gave no indication of what happened to the FAJ headstone that Chuck Kline found in the "old section" of Aspenglen Campground. One of many Estes Park residents who has been a big help to us in our grave search in the Park and in the Estes Park area is Sybil Barnes, who was then the Local History Librarian at the Estes Park Public Library and the Librarian of the Rocky Mountain National Park Library. When we told her that we wondered what had happened to both the FAJ headstone and a headstone found north of Glacier Livery, she asked Christy Baker, who was then in charge of the Park's Museum Storage Facility, to see if she could find the two headstones for us. (For information on the headstone found north of Glacier Livery and its corresponding grave, see the chapter on the Herbert Richards Grave. For more information on Sybil, see the "Acknowledgments.")

On 30 July 2001, Christy got back to us to let us know that she had found the headstone of Herbert Richards, but that, as far as she could ascertain, the FAJ headstone either never was or was no longer in the possession of the Park.

Search for Identity of FAJ

Immediately following is a verbatim quote from Ferrel Atkins's 3 June 1986 "Report on FAJ Tombstone at Aspenglen Campground," with bracketed inserts containing relevant information from our research:

> "Since the child was born in 1883 and died in 1886, one would not expect to find the child in the censuses. [However, since Ferrel wrote this report, the Larimer County Genealogical Society published (in September 2000) a book containing a transcript of the Larimer County, Colorado, 1885 State Census. We searched through this book for a child with the initials FAJ who was born in 1883. We did not find one.
>
> However, it has been our experience that the census takers for the 1885 State Census did not find every resident of the county. In addition, FAJ could have been the child of someone traveling through the county in 1886 or who took up residence in the county after the 1885 census was taken.]
>
> "According to a phone call to the County Clerk's office, birth records in Larimer County start in 1900, too late to resolve our problem.
>
> "I turned next to the homestead tract books. Aspenglen lies on the boundary between Sections 16 and 17, T5N, R73W. The only homestead in those sections prior to 1886 was that of Lyman A. White in 1880.
>
> "I then searched the adjoining sections for a family name beginning with the letter 'J' dated before 1886. Arthur W. Jennings homesteaded in 1879 in Section 14. But the homestead (SW/4 SE/4 and SE/4 SW/4) lies in the Cow Creek drainage, so it is possible, though unlikely, that they would have taken a child over the ridge for burial. [There is no "Jennings" in the 1885 Larimer County Census. There is an Ed Jenning, but he was a single salesman who boarded with the Theodore Van Brunt family in Fort Collins.]
>
> "Homesteads in the sections adjacent to Aspenglen reminded me that the

James family was here very early—William homesteaded in Section 26 in 1876. But it was generally the practice to bury family members on land owned by the family, so I doubt they would have taken the body that far from home. [The 1885 Larimer County Census lists all of the members of the William Edwin James family living in the Estes Park area as of the date of the census. There is no child listed with the initials FAJ. For a list of what the 1885 Census has to say about the William Edwin James family, see "History of James Family and Elkhorn Lodge" in the chapter on the Elkhorn Lodge Cemetery. However, in later years, William's son Homer and his wife Jeannie did bury a baby daughter, Mary Jane, along Fall River Road. See the chapter on the Mary Jane James Grave.]

"Since the stone may have been washed down by the stream, I searched the sections west of the campground in the Fall River drainage, but found no family meeting the criteria.

"I turned next to the 1880 census. Unfortunately, the census does not give one a clue as to where the people lived, so one cannot specifically search the Aspenglen area. However, Jennings does not appear in the 1880 census, even though he homesteaded in 1879, so it appears they were not permanent residents, though of course they may simply have been missed by the census. The William James family is in the census, and they are—barely—of child-bearing age.

"Conclusion: I doubt we will ever know.

"Jennings is a possibility but (1) it seems unlikely they would cross the ridge to bury a child and (2) the census hints that they may not have been permanent residents.

"James is a possibility, but it seems unlikely they would go so far from home to bury. [Also, the 1885 Larimer County State Census lists all of the other known members of the William Edwin James family so it is unlikely that it would have missed this child.] The homesteads which reminded me of the James family were on the northeast slope of Deer Mountain and were homesteaded after 1890—so they owned no land in that vicinity on which to bury in 1886. [Also, our research shows that ALL of the other members of the William Edwin James family except Mary Jane James are buried in organized cemeteries—Mountain View in Longmont and, for Homer James, in Pasadena, California.] One cannot discount the fact that people lived on the land without homesteading and sometimes disappeared without ever having their names appearing on the records."

While one of the two graves we found could be the grave of FAJ, it could just as easily not be his or her grave.

History of Aspenglen Campground

In July 2001, Sybil Barnes sent us a copy of a page from *Historic Structures Volume II* from Ferrel Atkins's files in the Park Library that provided some historical information on Aspenglen Campground. A summary of that information follows:

- The Fall River Valley became such a popular spot for camping by tourists that, by 1922, owners of private property in the area had "fenced most of their property heretofore used by campers." Source: Superintendent's Monthly Report (S.M.R.), 31 August 1922.

- The S.M.R. dated 31 July 1922 mentions some camps that were under private ownership, specifically camps owned by Charles E. Bryson and Daniel March.
- Since the right-of-way along Fall River Road was the only place left for tourists to camp in the Fall River area, the S.M.R. dated 31 July 1923 indicates that the Park realized that it was necessary to develop a campground in that section of the Park. To that end, the S.M.R. dated 30 September 1923 says that the Park purchased 41 acres 4.5 miles west of Estes Park from Pieter Hondius. The S.M.R. dated 31 October 1924 mentions that, during that month, some additional land was purchased from Mrs. Minnie E. March. [The wife of the Daniel March mentioned above?]
- The Park's Photographic File #4007 indicates that, as early as the fall of 1923, the name Aspenglen was being associated with the land purchased from Pieter Hondius.
- Accordingly to the S.M.R. dated 30 June 1924, an access road was built across the Fall River in the spring of 1924. The S.M.R. dated 31 July 1924 states that Aspenglen Campground was first opened to visitors at the beginning of that month.
- Ferrel says in his notes that "little was said in the reports regarding the facilities provided the campers." He then goes on to point out that the 31 July 1924 S.M.R. does tell us that the campers did have running water, although not in a way that would be considered satisfactory today! "A small portion of the Fall River was diverted so as to run through this campground and give the visitors the advantage of running water."
- Page 14 of the 1938 Superintendent's Annual Report mentions the approval of a lecture circle, which Ferrel felt showed "an increase in both campground use and interpretive activities."

EDWIN BRADT GRAVE

Location: Latitude 40° 20′ 29″ N, Longitude 105° 35′ 20″ W

The grave of Edwin Bradt is located near the top of the 8,660-foot Bible Point at the Estes Park Center of the YMCA of the Rockies south of Estes Park. The hiking trail to the top of Bible Point starts at the northwest corner of the YMCA's livery stable.

Description

Edwin Brandt's grave is marked by a rock-cement cairn with a bronze marker cemented on its east side. That marker reads as follows:

> **EDWIN BRADT**
> Born October 3, 1899
> Died June 12, 1918
> A Normal Life
> He advanced in wisdom and stature
> and in favor with God and men.
> His Chosen Text
> "All things work together for
> good to them that love God."

On top of Edwin's grave is a pile of rocks and pine cones, each one left there by a visitor to his grave. Our use of dowser rods confirmed an adult-size burial at the site.

Photo A: Grave of Edwin Bradt at the Top of Bible Point

Finding the Grave

We are not sure who told us about "the grave at Bible Point," but believe it was Sybil Barnes, then the Local History Librarian for the Estes Park Public Library. (For information on all of the help that Sybil provided to our grave-search efforts in Rocky Mountain National Park and in the Estes Park area, see the "Acknowledgments" section.)

On 17 September 2000, we visited the Estes Park Center of the YMCA of the Rockies with the intention of climbing the trail to Bible Point to view the grave there. We did not then know who was buried in the grave at Bible Point. We were directed to the Lula W. Dorsey Museum at the Estes Park Center of the YMCA of the Rockies.

A museum staff member told us that Edwin Bradt was buried in "the grave at Bible Point," told us how to find the trail to the grave, and suggested that we also visit the YMCA's bookstore, where we could purchase Jack R. and Lulabeth Melton's *YMCA of the Rockies; Spanning a Century* (published in 1992 under the auspices of the Lula W. Dorsey Museum at the YMCA of the Rockies), which contains information about Edwin's life, death, and burial.

Following the staff member's instructions, we made the climb to the grave. Once we reached the top of Bible Point and Edwin Bradt's grave, we could see why his parents wanted him to be buried there, for the view was spectacular.

History of Edwin Bradt and Bible Point

Those interested in a complete and very readable account of the history of the YMCA of the Rockies should consult the Meltons' *YMCA of the Rockies; Spanning a Century* referenced above. The information below is summarized from pages 75 and 76 of that book.

Bible Point was originally known as "Buena Vista" and was not referred to as "Bible Point" until after Edwin Bradt was buried there and his family placed nearby a mailbox containing a Bible and a register for those visiting Edwin's grave. The Bradt family chose this location for Edwin's burial because they had a summer cottage at the foot of Buena Vista.

Even though the marker on Edwin's grave refers to "A Normal Life," Jack and Lulabeth Melton, the authors of *YMCA of the Rockies*, rightly point out that his life was, in fact, anything but normal:

- At 12, he accompanied his family on a trip around the world during which they visited "missionaries and world-renowned places."

- In 1914, when Edwin was 15, he visited Estes Park for the first time. During this visit, he climbed several mountains, including Longs Peak.

- In 1916, he returned to Estes Park to attend the YMCA Student Conference at the YMCA of the Rockies with his father Gordon Bradt. The Bradts remaine d in Estes Park after the conference to build a summer cottage at the foot of Buena Vista on land given them by A. A. Hyde. Hyde was a successful businessman from Wichita, Kansas, who, according to page 41 of *YMCA of the Rockies*, made the YMCA of the Rockies one of a number of charitable organizations to which he donated 90% of the profits from his "highly successful Mentholatum Company."

  Building the Bradts' cottage was not easy, for water for the cement had to be hauled from the YMCA to the building site.

- In June 1918, Edwin and a college friend were driving from Chicago to Seattle to attend the wedding of Edwin's brother. Unfortunately, in Nebraska, they were involved in an automobile accident, and Edwin was killed.

- At the request of Edwin's father, Edwin's body was taken to Estes Park, where funeral was held at what was then the YMCA's Assembly Hall and is now the Hyde Memorial Chapel. Dr. John Timothy Stone conducted Edwin's funeral service. Following the service, employees of the YMCA carried Edwin's casket to its current burial place.

(For information on a second grave on the property of the YMCA of the Rockies, see the chapter on the Bob Ozmen Grave.)

J. P. CHITWOOD GRAVE

Location: The latitude and longitude of this grave are not provided for the reasons discussed below.

The grave of J. P. Chitwood is located in Rocky Mountain National Park on the east side of the Continental Divide.

Finding the Grave

We began looking for information on this grave because it was on a list of graves in Rocky Mountain National Park provided us by Dr. D. Ferrel Atkins. (For more information on Ferrel, see the "Acknowledgments" section.) The typewritten information on Ferrel's list concerning J. P. Chitwood's grave follows:

> "Chitwood's body was found—and buried—in June 1921. In 1923 the remains became disinterred and were reburied by Moomaw."

Below this typewritten text is the following handwritten notation:

> "See 'Estes Park Trail' Friday, July 13, 1923, p. 16, column two. Chitwood caught in blizzard during October 1921. Body found next spring."

Ferrel's list of Rocky Mountain National Park graves is kept in the Park's Museum Storage Facility.

The text in the issue of the 13 July 1923 *Estes Park Trail* (Source No. 5 below) cited above provides the following information about the location of this grave:

> "Considerable excitement was created Monday [9 July 1923] when a party of Boulder people who had been on the top of Flattop Mountain the day before [Sunday, 8 July 1923] returned to the village and reported the finding of a body buried under a pile of rocks near the Flattop trail. Rangers were dispatched to investigate and discovered that the party reporting the find had come upon the grave of J. P. Chitwood, who lost his life in a blinding snow late in October two years previously and whose body was found the following spring and buried near where it was found. And thus ended wild rumors of foul play among the peaks of the Rockies."

The information provided below in the section titled "The Death, Discovery, Burial, Rediscovery, and Reburial of J. P. Chitwood" indicates that Chitwood's body was found on Tyndall Glacier. So, if his body was buried near where it was found, we assumed that Chitwood's grave should be on or near Tyndall Glacier.

Using the above location information from the 13 July 1923 issue of *Estes Park Trail* and additional location clues from the 15 July 1921 issue (Source No. 3 below), Rocky Mountain National Park Rangers Ira Goldfarb and Joan Feder made three trips to Flattop Mountain to try and find Chitwood's grave during the summer of 2001. Their first two trips were unsuccessful because of bad weather. The weather cooperated for their third trip, during which their use of dowser rods indicated that they might have found a grave exactly in the location described in the letter and report of Ranger Guild quoted in the "The Death, Discovery, Burial, Rediscovery, and Reburial of J. P. Chitwood" section below. However, at the time Ira and Joan found this possible location for Chitwood's grave, we had not yet discovered the 8 July 1921 article in the *Estes Park Trail* (Source No. 2 below) that contained the just-mentioned letter and report!

LARIMER COUNTY CEMETERIES

Ira and Joan did not take a photograph of the grave site because, at the time, they were not very confident that they had found it. However, the GPS location that they recorded almost exactly matched the location of the grave described by Ranger Guild in Source No. 2 below. Thus, in the spring of 2009, we asked Larry E. Carpenter of Estes Park and Fred S. Henkin of Westerville, Ohio (but an habitual summer visitor to Estes Park) if they might want to include a trip to Flattop Mountain to try to refind, GPS pinpoint, and photograph Chitwood's grave in their hiking plans for the summer of 2009. (See the entry for "Carpenter, Larry" in the "Acknowledgments" section for information on previous grave-search help that Larry, Fred, and Fred's wife Sharon had provided in finding graves on Sundance Mountain in the Park.)

(For additional information on Ira and Joan, who were immensely helpful to us in our search for graves and memorials in parts of the Park that were at heights beyond our ability to reach, see the entry for "Goldfarb, Ira and Joan Feder" in the "Acknowledgments" section.)

On 28 August 2009, we received an email from Larry Carpenter (Source No. 8 below) in which he told us that the grave of J. P. Chitwood had definitely been found but that it was in such a deteriorated condition that the exact location of the grave must remain known only to the National Park Service. Below we provide as much as we can of Larry's original email on the successful location of Chitwood's grave without reporting the grave's exact location:

On the morning of 6 August 2009, Larry Carpenter accompanied by Fred and Sharon Henkin and their daughter Jennifer left the Bear Lake parking lot for the trail to Flattop Mountain to search for the grave of J. P. Chitwood. As had been the case for Ira and Joan Goldfarb on their first two attempts to find Chitwood's grave, the winds "moving west to east across the Continental Divide were difficult to endure" so Larry and Fred searched the area above Tyndall Glacier where Ira and Joan thought they might have found the grave in 2001 while "the women retreated to calmer conditions below the hitching post on the Flattop Trail." The men had an old photo of Chitwood's grave to help with their search, but found nothing even "closely resembling the rocks surrounding the grave in the photo." Consequently, they gave up their search for that day, rejoined the two women, and headed for the parking lot.

During the summer of 2009, Larry was spending 60-80 hours a month in a volunteer position as a police auxiliary member of the Estes Park Police Department. When Larry returned to "work" during the week following his and the Henkins' unsuccessful effort to find Chitwood's grave, he mentioned the search to Detective Rick Life, under whose supervision he volunteered. Larry reported that "Rick expressed an interest in the matter and a return visit to Flattop was planned."

Consequently, on Saturday, 22 August 2009, Larry, Rick, and Rick's father Richard Life of Fort Collins made the 3-plus-hour hike to the top of Flattop Mountain. Thankfully, it was a cloudless day that was warmer and less windy than Larry's previous visit on 6 August. The three men spent 4 hours searching the area at the head of the Tyndall Glacier where the Goldfarbs thought they might have found the grave in 2001, but they found nothing matching the rocks in the old photo of Chitwood's grave.

They then expanded their search in a direction we will not disclose. After some additional searching, Larry reports the following:

> "Rick Life and I were speaking of the rocks upon which we were walking, commenting on whether we could discern a difference between rocks that had been in place since the last glacier had melted away and any that might have been moved and used to cover a grave.

"At 2:40 p.m. I happened to look down at my feet and noticed that a cross consisting of small parallel striations had been scratched into the granite surface of the flat rock upon which I was standing. Rick Life was just 10 feet east of me. . . .

"When I excitedly called out my discovery, it turned out Rick was practically standing on the grave. We called out for his father and immediately began matching nearby rocks with the photo [the old photo of Chitwood's grave] and were certain we had located the grave, [which was in a badly deteriorated condition] . . . .

"GPS readings and photos were taken and approximate reference points noted so that the site could be located again. NOTE [as will also be important later]: There was no evidence of a concrete vault!"

The very next morning a party of rangers visited the site. Based on their findings, the Park determined that, as noted above, due to the deteriorated condition of Chitwood's grave, its location should not be made public.

Description of Grave

The 13 July 1923 issue of the *Estes Park Trail* (Source No. 5 below) quoted above under "Finding the Grave" states that Chitwood's body was buried under "a pile of rocks." This agrees with the description of the grave found by Larry Carpenter and his team on 22 August 2009.

Sources of Information on Grave of J. P. Chitwood.

1. Death Certificate for J. P. Chitwood originally signed by H. M. Balmer on 6 July 1921 and issued by Colorado Department of Public Health and Environment on 11 September 2009. Larry Carpenter obtained this death certificate for us.

2. "National Park Rangers Find Corpse on Flat Top Mountain," *Estes Park Trail*, Vol. I, No. 13, 8 July 1921, page 1.

3. Follow-up paragraph on the above article identifying the body as J. P. Chitwood's, *Estes Park Trail*, 15 July 1921.

4. "Chapter Two of Flattop Mystery Discovered by Clifford Higby," *Estes Park Trail*, Vol. I, No. 22, 9 September 1921, page 1.

5. "Hikers Discover Grave on Flattop," *Estes Park Trail*, 13 July 1923, page 16, column 2.

6. Oral Interview of Jack Moomaw by William Ramaley conducted on 22 January 1972 as part of the Estes Park oral history project, which is jointly sponsored by the Estes Park Area Historical Museum and the Estes Park Public Library. The tape and its transcription are available in the Local History Section of the Estes Park Public Library. Pages 14 and 15 contain a reference to what is most likely Chitwood's burial on Flattop Mountain in Rocky Mountain National Park.

7. "The Saga of J. P. Chitwood," chapter on pages 23-25 of *The Way of the Mountains*, written by James H. Pickering and published in 2003. (See the "Bibliography" for a complete citation.)

8. Email received from Larry E. Carpenter on 28 August 2009 reporting on the rediscovery of the grave of J. P. Chitwood.

The Death, Discovery, Burial, Rediscovery, and Reburial of J. P. Chitwood

The first written record we were able to find concerning the death and burial of J. P. Chitwood occupied two complete columns and about half of a third column on page 1 of the 8 July 1921 issue of *Estes Park Trail* (Source No. 2). This article indicated that on 28 June 1921

LARIMER COUNTY CEMETERIES

Superintendent Way of Rocky Mountain National Park received the following letter, mailed from Denver on 27 June 1921 from "A Tourist":

> "Dear Sir:
>
> "A little time ago, just north of the Tyndall Glacier at the head of the cliff where the flat-top trail [sic] goes nearest to it, I came across what was evidently the luggage of a miner: saddle bags, provisions, a **rifle and revolver**, an overcoat, sock, coat, vest, etc. Same seemed very strange and after some thought I concluded that the owner of them had evidently fallen over a cliff into the glacier below. Feeling that notifications should be made in case of any names or addresses in his pockets, or in the saddle bags, I went through them and found 2 letters address to J. P. Chitwood—at Grand Lake and at Cheyenne. There were also several cards and names, one of them being J. A. Grout, 1311 South University, which I supposed to be of Denver.
>
> "Just before leaving, I made a wider search and came across the body of an old man, perfectly preserved except that the skin had shrunken somewhat and grown black. He had evidently fallen and hit his head on a rock. As the last letter in his pocket was dated sometime in Oct. 1920, I take it that he must have perished last fall and been preserved in the snow since.
>
> "The shock to me was tremendous. Of course I touched neither him nor the clothing upon him. And I left immediately as it was growing dark and I was not familiar with the trail or the country. I am notifying J. A. Grout and you so that what ever should be done will be done.
>
> "A Tourist"

We bolded the indicated text in the above letter.

When Superintendent Way received this letter, he dispatched a ranger to Flattop Mountain to try to find the body and the effects mentioned in the letter. However, the ranger found neither Mr. Chitwood nor any of his belongings.

Then, on 29 June 1921, Park Rangers Eugene R. Guild and Richard E. Wagner, who were stationed at Grand Lake, were out doing some scout duty and working on telephone lines when they found the body of a man lying in the snow at the "head of Tyndall Glacier." Ranger Guild's official report on their discovery follows:

> "On June 29, Ranger Wagner and I, while on telephone work on the summit discovered the body of a man who evidently lost his life through a fall about last October. The body is black and some what decomposed.
>
> Age—about 50 years
>
> Height—5 ft. 6 in.
>
> Full beard and hair—brownish gray
>
> "He was dressed as follows: no hat, blanket lined canvas coat, brown corduroy vest, gray trousers, blue flannel shirt and badly worn tan shoe [no ending "s"]. A yellow slicker with the bottom edge burned off lay nearby. He wore a cartridge belt and knife sheath, **but neither gun nor knife were found.** No papers or other marks of identification were found. The contents of his pockets were as follows: two pencils, one pair of steel rimmed spectacles, one pipe with porcelain rimmed bowl, one comb—small black rubber, six 32-40 soft nose rifle cartridges, one piece of one [sic].

"Location: The body was found about 250 yards south of the Continental Divide sign, near the Flat top trail, and on the brink of the cliff above Tyndall Glacier.

"The body lay face down, pointing toward the Glacier, with his head against a rock. The head was crushed on one side where he had evidently tripped and fallen on the rock. He had never moved after he had fallen.

"Your attention is called to my letter, File 128 dated October 14, 1920. I believe this man to have met his death a day or two before I came upon the Divide on Oct. 14. The snow at that time was a foot deep in this locality and had fallen the night before. I made a search at that time for some one, but without results. The dog's tracks were of that same day, and came from south along the Divide past Hallet's [sic] Peak, which led me to believe he [the dog?] had wandered up the Divide unaccompanied by any one.

"Disposition of body: I have covered the body with a slicker and placed rocks around the edges of it, awaiting instructions for final disposition. Technically, the body is in Larimer county, and I supposed it is a matter for the county coroner.

Signed, Eugene R. Guild
Nah'l Park Ranger
Grand Lake District"

We bolded the indicated text in the above report.

It turned out that the place that the two rangers found the body was about a mile from the location described by "A Tourist." While reporting this discrepancy, the 8 July 1921 issue of *Estes Park Trail* makes no comment about it. However, it probably resulted from the tourist's self-proclaimed unfamiliarity with "the country" because both the tourist and the rangers found that Chitwood's skull had been crushed on a rock, on which they all assumed he had fallen. Consequently, it is unlikely that Chitwood's body was moved between the times the tourist and the rangers encountered it.

The 14 October 1920 letter that Ranger Guild referred to contains his report of finding both fresh tracks of a dog and then the dog himself on the Divide in the Flattop area earlier that day. He took the dog to the ranger station. As the paragraph immediately below indicates, this dog was later determined to be Chitwood's dog. Consequently, Chitwood must have died either on or before 14 October 1920.

The 8 July 1921 issue of *Estes Park Trail* then goes on to report that Chitwood had been employed during the summer of 1920 on the road crew of Dick McQuery, who was a contractor on the Fall River Road. About 1 October 1920, Chitwood received about $400 in pay and left McQuery's employ, accompanied by his dog.

The July 8th article concludes by saying "Coroner H. M. Balmer and Undersheriff Ira Knapp, of Fort Collins, and Rangers McDaniel and Stephens went to the place Wednesday [6 July 1921] where the body was lying, for the purpose of holding an inquest and burying the corps [sic]."

In the death certificate he issued after examining Chitwood's body (Source No. 1), Coroner Balmer reports the following:

- Age: About 65-68
- Occupation: Prospector
- Birthplace, names of parents, etc.: Unknown

LARIMER COUNTY CEMETERIES

- Date of Death: Supposed to be in Oct. 1920
- Cause of Death: Found dead on Flattop Mt the 28th of June 1921. Died from exposure in storm [What about the reports of "A Tourist" that "he had evidently fallen and hit his head on a rock" and the report of Ranger Guild that "the head was crushed on one side"? Also, since "A Tourist" mailed his letter to Superintendent Way on 27 June 1921, he obviously found Chitwood's body *before* that date.]
- Place of Burial: Flat Top Mountain
- Date of Burial: Jul 6, 1921

The second mention that we found of J. P. Chitwood's death and burial occurred in the 15 July 1921 issue of the *Estes Park Trail* (Source No. 3) and is evidently the result of the formal Corner's Inquest:

> "The body found near the top of Flap Top mountain by Colorado rangers has been identified as that of J. P. Chitwood, formerly a ditchworker employed by the Water Supply and Storage Company, according to an announcement made in Fort Collins by Coroner H. M. Balmer."

If the Corner had suspected that J. P. Chitwood's death was caused by anything other than an accident, one would think that his suspicion would have been mentioned in the above brief statement or on Chitwood's death certificate.

However, several factors make one wonder if either Chitwood's death could have been the result of "foul play" connected with a robbery or if "A Tourist" or someone else had helped themselves to some of Chitwood's belongings following his death:

- The tourist's letter mentions a rifle and a revolver. (See bold text in the tourist's letter above.) The ranger's report does not. In fact, the ranger's report specifically states that no gun was found. (See bold text in Ranger Guild's report above.)
- The ranger's report mentions a knife sheath and specifically states that no knife was found. (See bold text in Ranger Guild's report above.)
- Chitwood's employer said that, when he left the road crew about 1 October 1920, he had about $400 with him. Unless Chitwood went down to Grand Lake and spent it all before heading into the mountains, he should have had at least some of it with him when his body was found. Neither the tourist nor the rangers mention finding any money on or near Chitwood's body.

The saga of Chitwood's death continued in the Friday, 9 September 1921 issue of the *Estes Park Trail* (Source No. 4) in an article titled "Chapter Two of Flattop Mystery Discovered by Clifford Higby." Pertinent information from this article follows:

- The September 9th article starts by summarizing the information from the 8 July 1921 article discussed immediately above.
- It then goes on to report that, on Thursday, 8 September 1921, Clifford Higby was leading a party of tourists on a hike from Bear Lake and Dream Lake to Tyndall Glacier on Flattop Mountain. At the foot of the glacier, the party found "the carcass of a horse that had evidently been used as a pack animal. The horse was lying on the ice and nearby lay a rope halter with a red bandana handkerchief tied to the under part of it, evidently to keep flies from the animal, which would indicate that the animal came to its death during fly season last year. Around the tail of the horse was tied a full length [of] halter rope, indicating another horse had been led by this one."

- Sure enough, "about fifty yards above and also on the ice was the carcass of another horse, on the head of which was found a halter from which the rope had been broken at the halter ring."
- In addition to a toothbrush, two bed blankets, and a suit of BVDs (long one-piece underwear to you young city slickers), the party found several pieces of canvas and, using field glasses, saw several pieces of what appeared to be harness on "a direct line with the bodies of the horses" and higher up on the glacier.
- Among the items that Ranger McDaniel reported when he visited the site when Chitwood's body was found in the summer of 1921 was "a cotton throw rope . . . which had evidently been used to tie packs on a horse." Thus, in September 1921, two of those horses were apparently found.
- However, the article concludes by pointing out that "it was not known that Chitwood had horses, but the theory is advanced that had the horses belonged to any living person they would have been seeking the animals and announced their escape."

The last article on Chitwood's grave that we were able to find in the *Estes Park Trail* was published on page 16 of its Friday, 13 July 1923 issue (Source No. 5). See the third quote under "Finding the Grave" above.

Another complete telling of the Chitwood tragedy can be found in "The Saga of J. P. Chitwood" on pages 23-25 of James H. Pickering's *The Way of the Mountains* (Source No. 7). Jim took us to the small grotto southwest of Estes Park in which the ashes of Julia Ann Morrissey are interred, and we showed him the location where the bones of Dr. Thornton R. Sampson are buried near the Fern Lake Trailhead (See chapters on the Julia Ann Morrissey Grave and the Reverend Thornton R. Sampson Grave and the entry for "Pickering, James H." in the "Acknowledgments" section.)

On page 25 of his chapter on Chitwood's death, discovery, burial, and reburial, Jim reports on information that he found in an article on page 43 of the 10 July 1923 issue of the *Loveland Reporter-Herald*. In that article, Roger Toll, who was by then the Superintendent of Rocky Mountain National Park, indicated that he believed that either "a rock slide had removed rocks from the [Chitwood's] grave or curious persons had uncovered the body." Then, as recorded on page 43 of the 14 July 1923 issue of the *Loveland Reporter-Herald*, Jim concludes his chapter on Chitwood by reporting that Superintendent Toll ordered Chitwood's body to be reburied in a concrete vault "in a manner becoming to a pioneer" in the hope that his body would not reappear a second time.

Obviously, Superintendent Toll either did not issue that order to rebury Chitwood's body in a concrete vault or he issued the order but it was not carried out. Since Chitwood's body has indeed reappeared a second time, perhaps the Park Service or a citizens' group will now consider reburying him in a concrete vault.

According to the records in the Library of Rocky Mountain National Park cited under "Finding the Grave" above, J. P. Chitwood became lost in a blizzard in the Park in October 1921. However, the information from the *Estes Park Trail* issues quoted above make clear that his death would have had to have occurred between 1 October and 14 October 1920.

The Park's records go on to say that Chitwood was not heard from again but that, during the spring of the next year, his body was found on Flattop Mountain and was buried where it was found. One note in the Park's record indicates that he was buried in June 1921. However, the articles in the *Estes Park Trail* indicate that his body was found first by "A Tourist"

LARIMER COUNTY CEMETERIES

sometime before 27 June 1921 and was found a second time by Rangers Guild and Wagner on 29 June 1921. Chitwood would have been buried for the first time on 6 July 1921, which is the day that the Coroner, Undersheriff, and Rangers McDaniel and Stephens went to the site where his body lay "for the purpose of holding an inquest and burying the corps [sic]."

The Park's records also state that, in 1923, his remains became disinterred and were reburied by Jack Moomaw. This would be the reburial following the discovery of Chitwood's grave on 8 July 1923 mentioned in the 13 July 1923 article in the *Estes Park Trail* quoted above. The reburial would have occurred between 9 July and 13 July 1923.

Jack Moomaw was a well-known Rocky Mountain National Park Ranger. He began working for the Park as a trail foreman in 1921, retired from active duty in 1945, and died on 10 January 1974.

On 26 March 2001, just months before her death in August 2001, Jackie Johnson called us to tell us about a transcription she had found in the Estes Park Public Library of a 1972 interview of Jack Moomaw (Source No. 6) that contained information on both the Chitwood grave and the discovery of the body of the Dr. Reverend Thorton R. Sampson, which was later buried near the Fern Lake Trail Trailhead. (As mentioned above, for information on Dr. Sampson's grave, see the applicable chapter.)

Jackie was immensely helpful to us during our search for graves and cemeteries in the Estes Park area and in Rocky Mountain Park. (For more information on Jackie, see the entry for "Jacqueline Jaye Johnson" in the chapter on Rocky Mountain National Park Scattered Cremains and the "Acknowledgments" section.)

When we found this transcription (of a 22 January 1972 interview Jack Moomaw by William "Bill" Ramaley), as Jackie had promised, we discovered on pages 14 and 15 the following intriguing statement possibly referring to Chitwood's grave which was in the middle of Jack Moomaw's answer to a question posed by Bill Ramaley:

> **Bill's Question:** "I know that some people, like Reverend Sampson, are buried. He disappeared."
>
> **Jack's Answer:** "I know. It went all these years, and then I had a crew working up there. I had surveyed through there and gone within 10 feet of where that fellow [Sampson] was, and I never did see him. I had a fellow by the name of Adams (?), one of the boys who worked on the trail. I don't know whether he went over there to take a leak or what—all the way from where he was working, which wasn't as far as from here to that door—and found Reverend Sampson over there. There was a dollar watch more or less protected by his clothing or him or something, and it still worked. (. . .Not transcribed—a few words about the man on Flattop.) I think I had a ranger one year who wanted the skull and went up there and got it. He was studying to be a doctor. I don't know why, but I just got a hunch he went up there and got it. He knew where it was because he helped bury him."

Note: We inserted the bracketed words in the above quote. The original transcriber inserted the text in parentheses.

Assuming that "the man on Flattop" was Chitwood and in the hope that the "Not transcribed" material might contain some additional clues to the location of Chitwood's grave, we asked Sybil Barnes, then the Local History Librarian at the Estes Park Public Library, if she could find the original tape from which the transcription was made. (For information on all of the help that Sybil gave us, see the entry for "Barnes, Sybil" in the "Acknowledgments" section.) Once Sybil found the tape, we transcribed the missing words, which, unfortunately, provided only the following additional question and answer:

> **Bill's Question:** I understand that there was a guy up on Flattop who was found every couple of years for a number of years and that the Park Service took him out too."
>
> **Jack's Answer:** [Jack says a few completely unintelligible words.] I guess he's still there. I don't know." [Then Jack continues with the statement above about a ranger possibly removing Chitwood's skull.]

Note: Jack Moomaw's mention of a ranger studying to be a doctor possibly removing Chitwood's skull agrees with the fact that Larry Carpenter and his team did not see a skull when they found Chitwood's body on 22 August 2009.

Unfortunately, this question and answer did not provide any additional clues as to where Chitwood was buried. Indeed, they add to the mystery surrounding Chitwood's grave:

- Was Jack Moomaw really involved with Chitwood's reburial between 9 July and 13 July 1923? He does not say either way when he was interviewed by Bill Ramaley in January 1972.

- Is Chitwood's skull really missing? *Please note that disturbing remote burials in any way is prohibited by Colorado law!*

- If Chitwood's skull is actually missing, who was the ranger who took it? Ranger Eugene R. Guild or Ranger Richard E. Wagner, who found his body on 29 June 1921? Ranger McDaniel or Ranger Stephens, both of whom participated in the Coroner's Inquest and the first burial on 6 July 1921? Or some other, unnamed ranger who was involved in Chitwood's reburial when his body reappeared in July 1923—the reburial in which Ranger Moomaw may have been involved?

- Since the Larimer County Coroner was involved with Chitwood's 6 July 1921 burial, it seems unlikely that Chitwood's skull could have been taken at that time, unless the rangers were left to bury the body after the Coroner had departed. In addition, if Chitwood's skull was missing when the Coroner examined it, the Coroner's report would surely have mentioned it. That "clears" Rangers Guild, Wagner, McDaniel, and Stephens.

- Similarly, if Chitwood's skull was missing when his body was rediscovered in 1923, it seems likely that some mention of that fact would have been made in the newspaper articles covering the event. Again, this "clears" Rangers McDaniel and Stephens.

- Consequently, IF Ranger Jack Moomaw is correct in stating that a ranger took Chitwood's skull, the "theft" probably occurred during or after Chitwood's 1923 reburial.

(For information on another case of a skull being removed from a body during reburial, see the chapter on the Alfred E. Mathews Grave, Alfred having been buried in the Big Thompson Canyon.)

CLEAVE-GRIFFITH FAMILY CEMETERY

Location: Latitude 40° 21' 37" N, Longitude 105° 33' 16" W

The Cleave-Griffith Family Cemetery is located on the property of Beaver Brook Resort in Estes Park at 1700 Colorado Highway 66, about 150 feet east of the highway. The cemetery area is surrounded by a log fence and is in the middle of a circular driveway. On the outside of the driveway are some of the units making up the Beaver Brook Resort. The cemetery is on land that is part of what was the original Albin Griffith homestead.

Description of Cemetery and Its Headstones

The cemetery proper is surrounded by a rock-cement wall. The interior "floor" of the cemetery is covered with cement, into which are imbedded the cemetery's four flat headstones.

Photo A: Cleave-Griffith Family Cemetery at the Beaver Brook Resort East of Colorado 66 in Estes Park

The inscriptions of those four headstones are as follows:

JOHN T. CLEAVE
1839 - 1925
PIONEER - 1874

MARGRET MAY CLEAVE
1845 - 1921
"WHEN AUTUMN'S SUNSET COLORS
FADE AWAY
TO REST WITH WORK WELL DONE"

**VIRGINIA CLEAVE
GRIFFITH**
1886 - 1936
BORN IN ESTES PARK

JOHN N. GRIFFITH
1884 - 1944
GONE BUT NOT FORGOTTEN

CLEAVE-GRIFFITH

For information on these individuals and how they are related, see "Biographical and Genealogical Information of the John T. Cleave Family" and "Biographical and Genealogical Information of the Albin Griffith Family" below.

Finding the Cemetery

Sybil Barnes, at the time the Local History Librarian of the Estes Park Public Library, told us about this cemetery and how to find it. We first found it following her directions during the winter of 2000. It was one of the first cemeteries that we found at the beginning of our search for graves and cemeteries in Larimer County. When we first found the cemetery, it was behind a house with a white picket fence. However, as of our visit to the cemetery on 8 December 2006, it was on the property of the newly built Beaver Brook Lodge, which was treating the old cemetery with the respect that it deserves. (For information on Sybil and all of the assistance she provided with our grave-search efforts in Rocky Mountain National Park and the Estes Park area, see "Barnes, Sybil" in the "Acknowledgments.")

Sources of Information on the Cleave and Griffith Families

1. *History of Larimer County, Colorado*, written by Ansel Watrous and published in 1911, contains two brief mentions of John T. Cleave on page 179. (See the "Bibliography" for a complete citation.)

2. *"Estes Park in the Memoirs of Lord Dunraven,"* written by Mrs. Albert Hayden, *Estes Park Trail*, 26 October 1923, pages 3, 7, and 8.

3. *Over Hill and Vale* by Harold Marion Dunning. Volume I was published in 1956, Volume II in 1962, and Volume III in 1971. (See the "Bibliography" for a complete citation.) All three volumes contain information on the Cleave and/or Griffith families.

4. *Memoirs of Eleanor E. Hondius of Elkhorn Lodge*, published in 1964. (See the "Bibliography" for a complete citation.) Chapter V, titled "Family and Friends," contains a section on "The Cleves" [*sic*].

5. Oral Interview of Dan Griffith by Ferrel Atkins conducted on 6 August 1966 as part of the Rocky Mountain National Park Oral History Project. The tape and its transcription are available in the Local History Section of the Estes Park Public Library.

6. *The Griffith Family in Estes Park; Museum Talk* presented by Don Griffith on 20 January 1977 at the Estes Park Area Historical Museum. The tape and its transcription, which were made as part of the Estes Park Oral History Project, are available in the Local History Section of the Estes Park Public Library.

    Those interested in a complete history of the Griffith family should definitely consult the transcript of this tape and *Homestead Trails and Tales* cited below.

7. *The Elkhorn Lodge; Museum Program* presented on 18 August 1977 at the Estes Park Area Historical Museum. The tape and its transcription are available in the Local History Section of the Estes Park Public Library.

8. *Homestead Trails and Tales,* written by Donald L. Griffith and published in 1992. Don wrote this Griffith family history for distribution to members of his family. However, realizing that some of its contents might be of interest to those researching the history of the Estes Park area, he generously made a copy available to the Local History Section of the Estes Park Public Library. Those interested in a detailed genealogy of the of Griffith family should consult pages 209 through 222.

9. *"This Blue Hollow,"* written by James H. Pickering and published in 1999. (See the "Bibliography" for a complete citation.) This book contains a number of references to the Cleave and Griffith families. See especially Note 29 (on page 291) for "Chapter 9. 1900-1915: The Coming of a Town and a Park."

LARIMER COUNTY CEMETERIES

10. Emails dated 14 and 16 May 2007 from Anne Griffith Toft, the great-granddaughter of both John Cleave and Albin Griffith. We met her on 20 April 2007 at the presentation we made on our Larimer County grave-search efforts at the Estes Park Area Historical Museum. We gave her our then-current version of this chapter. Her emails contained some additional Griffith-family information to include in the chapter.

11. *Social Security Death Index* as of 23 March 2009 as transcribed by Ancestry.com.

Biographical and Genealogical Information of the John T. Cleave Family

The first member of the Cleave family to come to the Estes Park area was **John T. Cleave**. According to his headstone in the Cleave-Griffith Family Cemetery, he arrived in the area in 1874. Born in Cornwall, England, in 1839, John came to Colorado from Chicago, to which he had first immigrated in response to ads for carpenters to help rebuild Chicago following the famous 1871 conflagration.

In spite of the "Pioneer - 1874" date on John's headstone, on page 291 of *"The Blue Hollow"* (Source No. 9), Jim Pickering says that John arrived in Estes Park in the spring or summer of 1875, where he worked as a foreman to help Theodore Whyte build "Lord" Dunraven's Estes Park, or English, Hotel along Fish Creek. According to page 156 of Volume II of *Over Hill and Vale* (in an article written by Clara Husted) (Source No. 3), the hotel was completed and opened for business in the summer of 1877.

According to Harold Dunning (in Volume II of *Over Hill and Vale*), John Cleave became Estes Park's postmaster in 1877, the same year that the Estes Park Hotel opened for business.

John met his **wife Margaret Cleave** ("Margret" according to her headstone in the Cleave-Griffith Family Cemetery) in May 1879 when she was working as a nurse taking care of the two daughters of Theodore Whyte and his wife Maude. Clara Husted, who was the wife of Shep Husted and the niece of Margaret May, provided the information that Margaret was born in Springfield, Ohio, and that John and Margaret were married in 1882.

Once John became a U.S. citizen, he homesteaded a parcel of land "behind the Estes Park Hotel on Fish Creek." According to page 291 of *"The Blue Hollow,"* John received his patent on this homestead on 16 November 1883. The home in which John and Margaret lived on the homestead is referred to as the "old English Ranch House" by both Clara Husted and Mrs. Gilbert, both of whom also say that John ran the Estes Park Post Office from that location as long as his family lived there. In addition, according to Clara Husted, both of John and Margaret's children were born in the "old English Ranch House" on his homesteaded land, Paul in 1884 and Virginia in 1886.

When "Lord" Dunraven wanted John and Margaret's homestead because he needed the springs on their land to provide sufficient water for his hotel, Dunraven offered John an equal-size (160-acre) homestead at the confluence of the Fall and Big Thompson Rivers in trade. John and Margaret's new property was right in the middle of what is now downtown Estes Park. As quotes from Eleanor Hondius's *Memoirs* (Source No. 4) make clear below, this land swap occurred some time after John and Margaret's daughter Virginia was born in 1886. We have not been able to find the exact date for the swap. When the Cleave family moved to "downtown" Estes Park, John continued to serve as Estes Park's postmaster, moving the post office to an 8 X 12 foot building that was next to the Cleave family's frame home (page 189 of *"The Blue Hollow"*).

The most interesting stories about the Cleave family were told by Eleanor Hondius in Chapter V of her *Memoirs* cited above. Eleanor was born Eleanor James. Her family owned the Elkhorn Lodge, which was about 3/4 of a mile west of the Cleaves' "downtown" property.

(For more information on Eleanor and the James family, see "History of the James Family and the Elkhorn Lodge" in the chapter on the Elkhorn Lodge Cemetery.)

In the story in her *Memoirs*, Eleanor agrees with Clara Husted's statement that both of the Cleave children were born in the "old English Ranch House." According to Eleanor, when John found out that his wife was expecting a second child, he decided that two children were enough and "after that, Mr. Cleve [sic] took his meals with the family but lived in the two-story building across the road which was used as a post office and store. Eventually, however, his daughter Virginia became his favorite child." It is several paragraphs after this statement that Eleanor tells us that "eventually Mr. Cleve [sic] was given land by "Lord" Dunraven where the town of Estes Park now stands. The family had its dwelling where the hotel is, and his post office and store was located on the corner now occupied by the Chez Jay building." ("Now" would be 1964, the year that Eleanor's *Memoirs* were published.)

On pages 12 and 13 of the transcription of a program on the Elkhorn Lodge presented at the Estes Park Area Historical Museum on 18 August 1977 (Source No. 7), Eleanor Hondius told several other stories about the Cleave family. One involves Eleanor making four pans of pressed chicken from about 20 hens that were killed by a coyote in the henhouse of a neighbor, Eddie Johnson. Eleanor sent half of a pan of the finished product to the Cleave family to enjoy. However, Eleanor explained:

> "It didn't take them [the Cleaves] long to decide where the chicken came from, and you would have thought I was trying to poison them. When I explained to Mrs. Cleve [sic] how sanitarily the chicken had been prepared, she exclaimed, 'But just think what violent deaths they died!' The Cleves finally forgave me. They were good neighbors."

Eleanor then explained that the two large lilac bushes outside the front of the Elkhorn Lodge dining room were given to the James family by John Cleave:

> "He dug holes and planted them, but not until he had brought some proper dirt from his meadows; he did not consider the dirt at the lodge good enough for them."

According to page 201 of *"The Blue Hollow"* (Source No. 9), in March 1905, in response to the 1903 completion of the Big Thompson Road to Estes Park, Cornelius H. Bond and three partners bought John Cleave's 160 acres at the confluence of the Big Thompson and Fall Rivers. They bought Cleave's land because it was an ideal location in which to lay out a town, was already at the intersection of several roads, and already had a schoolhouse and post office.

The same page of *"The Blue Hollow"* tells us that John Cleave was willing to sell the land because "the danged place [was being] overrun by tourists." John resigned his position as postmaster, which was then assumed by Cornelius Bond.

Note 29 on page 291 of *"The Blue Hollow"* explains what happened to John Cleave after he sold his Estes Park land to Cornelius Bond:

- In 1905 he built a house on a lot he "obtained" from George D. Reid.
- John and his wife Margaret moved to Fort Collins and then to Mancos, Colorado, before returning to Estes Park to live with their daughter Virginia Cleave Griffith.

Again, both John and Margaret are now buried in the Cleave-Griffith Family Cemetery. However, they had first been buried on the Mill Creek homestead of Albin and Mary Griffith, the parents of their daughter Virginia's husband John N. Griffith. (See Source No. 8 and the subsection titled "The Cleave and Griffith Families" in the section titled "History of Area

LARIMER COUNTY CEMETERIES

Containing the Tuxedo Park Cemetery Including Possible Occupants of Its Graves" in the chapter on the Tuxedo Park Cemetery.)

Children of John T. Cleave and Margaret May Cleave

1. **Paul Cleave**. According to page 498 of Volume III of *Over Hill and Vale* (Source No. 3), Paul Cleave was born in Estes Park on 9 April 1884. After serving in World War I, he lived on Colorado's Western Slope for a number of years before finally returning to Estes Park. He never married. He died on 31 July 1969.

2. **Virginia Cleave**. According to page 69 of Volume II of *Over Hill and Vale*, Virginia Cleave was born in Estes Park on 19 March 1886 and died on 9 February 1936, both dates agreeing with the years on her headstone in the Cleave-Griffith Family Cemetery. She married John Griffith, who is also buried in the Cleave-Griffith Family Cemetery, on 6 September 1906.

   On page 20 of his *Homestead Trails and Tales* (Source No. 8), Don Griffith says that his Aunt Virginia was the "first white girl born in the Estes Park region."

   (For information on Virginia and John Griffith's four children, see "Children of John Griffith and Virginia Cleave Griffith" below.)

Biographical and Genealogical Information of the Albin Griffith Family

According to their descendant Don Griffith in the two documents by him cited above (Source Nos. 6 and 8), his grandfather Albin Griffith, Albin's wife, and three of their children (Children Nos. 1-3 below) arrived in Loveland in 1888. (See both of these documents for very detailed and interesting information on the history and genealogy of the Albin Griffith family. When the genealogy data in these two documents disagreed, we used the data in *Homestead Trails and Tales* as it has the most current publication date.)

Albin Griffith. He was Don's grandfather. Albin and his twin, Albert, were born at Rich Hill, Illinois, on 23 February 1858. When the Reverend Albin Griffith moved to Colorado, he served as a minister of the United Brethren Church in Loveland, a position that he continued to hold until about 1900, even after he had moved to his homestead in Estes Park. He died at his home in Estes Park on 29 November 1946. See pages 13-14 of Don Griffith's *Homestead Trails and Tails* (Source No. 8) and pages 15 and 16 of *The Griffith Family in Estes Park* (Source No. 6) for Don's memories of his Grandfather Albin Griffith.

Mary Margaret Grimm, Albin's wife. (Don Griffith spells his grandmother's last name as both Grim and Grimm in different part's of his *Homestead Trails and Tails*.) Mary was Albin's wife and Don's grandmother. She was born on 27 May 1858 in Cumberland County, Illinois, close to the town of Greenup, which is close to the Wabash River. Her father was a minister. She died in Loveland at the home of her daughter Oma (Child No. 3 below) on 31 August 1917. (Don gives 31 August 1917 as the date of Mary's death on page 14 of *Homestead Trails and Tails* and gives 17 August 1917 as her death date on page 217 of the same book.) See page 19 of *Homestead Trails and Tails* and page 16 of *The Griffith Family in Estes Park* for Don's memories of his Grandmother Mary Griffith.

Albin and Mary were married 17 March 1881 in Greenup, Illinois. They are both buried in the family plot in the Loveland Burial Park.

Children of Albin and Mary Grimm Griffith

1. **Dan Braxton Griffith**. Dan was the oldest child of Albin and Mary and the father of Don.

He was born on 2 April 1882 in Hidalgo, Illinois. He died on 5 October 1969 and is buried in the Estes Valley Memorial Gardens in Estes Park.

Ellen Louise Jesser, Dan's wife. Ellen was born on 17 February 1891 in Denison, Texas. For detailed information on the lives of Ellen and her parents, especially her father, see pages 11 and 12 of *The Griffith Family in Estes Park* (Source No. 6). Dan and Ellen were married on 2 October 1913. (For information on their five children, see "Children of Dan Griffith and Ellen Louise Jesser Griffith" below.)

2. **John N. Griffith.** The second child of Albin and Mary, John was born on 24 August 1884 in Greenup, Illinois. He died on 31 October 1944. His birth and death years agree with those on his headstone in the Cleave-Griffith Family Cemetery. See pages 19-20 of Don Griffith's *Homestead Trails and Tails* for Don's memories of his Uncle John.

   Virginia Cleave, John's first wife. For genealogy data for Virginia, see No. 2 under "Children of John T. Cleave and Margaret May Cleave" above.

   John and Virginia were married on 6 September 1906. As noted above, they are both buried in the Cleave-Griffith Family Cemetery with Virginia's parents. (For information on their children, see "Children of John Griffith and Virginia Cleave Griffith" below.)

   Hildred Attberry, John's second wife. John and Hildred got married about 5 years after Virginia died in 1936. They never had any children.

3. **Oma Katherine Griffith.** The third child of Albin and Mary, Oma was born on 17 December 1886 in Mount Carmel, Illinois. She died in July 1969. See pages 13-14 of Don Griffith's *Homestead Trails and Tails* for Don's memories of his Aunt Oma.

   Robert Miller, Oma's husband. Robert was born on 24 September 1882 near Twin Mounds, Loveland, and died in Loveland on 7 April 1954.

   Oma and Robert were married on 8 February 1911. They are buried in their own plot in the Loveland Burial Park.

The remaining two of Albin and Mary Griffith's children, listed below, were born in Colorado after the above members of their family had moved to Loveland in 1888:

4. **Nellie Griffith.** The fourth child of Albin and Mary, Nellie was born on 5 July 1894 in Hygiene, Colorado. She died on 15 June 1918 and is buried in the family plot in the Loveland Burial Park. She never married. On page 22 of his *Homestead Trails and Tales*, Don Griffith says that his Aunt Nellie "was an invalid and needed rather constant care," most of it provided by his Aunt Oma.

5. **Mary Lois Griffith.** The fifth child of Albin and Mary, Mary Lois (known as "Aunt Lois" to Don Griffith) was born on 18 November 1896 in Hygiene. She died in July 1968 and is buried in the family plot in the Loveland Burial Park. She never married.

   According to Don Griffith's account of his Aunt Lois on pages 16 and 17 of *The Griffith Family in Estes Park*, Lois attended Northwestern University in Evanston, Illinois, for a year; attended the University of Colorado in Boulder; and finally graduated from the University of Northern Colorado in Greeley. She then taught music and art in Estes Park schools in the mid-1920s. She finally quit teaching to take over the bookkeeping chores of the Griffith family lumber operations.

LARIMER COUNTY CEMETERIES

As noted earlier, in 1888, Albin and Mary Griffith and their first three children (Dan, John, and Oma) left Greenup, Illinois, where Albin was an ordained United Brethren minister, for Loveland, Colorado. They left Illinois because the "low farming area" in which they lived near the Wabash River in Illinois gave them "summer fever," which was later determined to be malaria, during warm weather.

Once the Griffith family had settled in at Loveland, they joined other residents of Loveland on their "summer custom" of going to the Estes Park area to fish and relax. On page 2 of *The Griffith Family in Estes Park,* Don Griffith says that his father, Dan Griffith, thought that the family made its first trip to Estes Park in 1889. At the end of their initial journey, the family chose to camp in an area "with an Aspen grove and small running spring" (page 3 of *Homestead Trails and Tales*). This camping spot became the southeast corner of Albin Griffith's original Estes Park homestead (page 3 of *The Griffith Family in Estes Park*). According to page 3 of *Homestead Trails and Tales*, the place that they camped was "northwest of 'The Highlands,' a ranch owned by H. W. Ferguson, who had settled in that location in 1875." It was Mr. Ferguson who told Albin Griffith that the land on which he and his family were camping was government land that was available for homesteading.

After discussing a number of matters that involved such things as their ability to afford a homestead and Mary and the kids having to spend considerable time at the homestead alone, in 1890 the family decided to have papers drawn up to establish a 160-acre homestead that was in kind on "an inverted L shape." (See page 3 of *The Griffith Family in Estes Park* for a description of the land included in that "L.") The original log homestead cabin was located in the southeast corner of the homestead near the same spring by which the family had camped during their initial camping trip to the area in 1889.

Once Albin Griffith moved his family to their Estes Park homestead in 1890, he continued to "commute" between Estes Park and the churches for which he served as pastor over the years: First, as noted above, he was the pastor for the United Brethren Church in Loveland. Then, later, he was the minister for churches in Berthoud and Hygiene. His grandson Don Griffith indicates on page 3 of *The Griffith Family in Estes Park* that "there is some evidence to show that he [Albin] switched from the United Brethren Church to the Baptist Church." It is unclear to which denomination the churches in Berthoud and Hygiene belonged.

When the Griffith family moved to their homestead, they had to find ways to support themselves there. Before they started the lumbering business for which they are justly well known, they did such things as fishing, primarily for the native cutthroat trout, and then selling the fish to such establishments as the "old English Hotel" ("Lord" Dunraven's Estes Park Hotel), clearing land for hay and pastures for milk cattle and their horses, selling some of the resulting milk, and renting pasture land for horses. It was during the clearing of their own land that the family realized they could earn extra money by selling firewood. See pages 7-19 of *The Griffith Family in Estes Park* for a history of early lumbering in the Estes Park area in general and for a history of the Griffith family's involvement with lumbering and lumber in particular. A brief summary of the Griffith family's sawmill and lumbering operations in the Estes Park area follows:

- The first sawmill with which the family was involved was a dilapidated steam-powered device that was set up on their homestead by "two fellows by the name of Hallwell and Meade," with the agreement being that Hallwell and Meade would take one half of the lumber and the Griffiths would take the other half.

- This sawmill operated as a money-making venture was one they set up on the Springer property on Wind River, which was operated on the same basis: the land owner took half of the lumber, and the Griffiths took half. (For additional information on the Springer property, including the grave of Civil War veteran Harris Wellcome, which is located there, see the chapter on the Harris Wellcome Grave.)

- The Griffith family then moved the sawmill to the nearby Brinwood Hotel, where Albin and his sons John and Dan were paid for their labor, with the owner keeping all of the resulting lumber to build part of the hotel and the hotel's barn.

- During the springs and summers of 1907 and 1908, the family and a number of employees built a road from the Mill Creek Ranger Station to Bierstadt Lake and then moved their sawmill operation there. Don Griffith says that his dad estimated that the family must have cut between 600,000 and 750,00 board feet of lumber in the Bierstadt Lake area. The lumber was first taken to Estes Park Lumber on Main Street, where Dr. Homer James had a planer. Once the Griffiths' rough lumber "was surfaced" with the James planer, it was bought by F. O. Stanley for the Stanley Hotel. (For more information on the James family in general and Dr. Homer James in particular, see the chapters on the Elkhorn Lodge Cemetery and on the Mary Jane James Grave. Mary Jane was the daughter of Homer and his wife Jeannie Bachanan James.)

- In 1909, when the Griffiths completed cutting the lumber needed for the Stanley Hotel, they moved the mill "to where the Everitt Lumber Company is now," with "now" being 1977, the year that Don Griffith presented his Museum Talk on "The Griffith Family in Estes Park." At this location, they added a single-surface planer, which they bought from Shep Husted. (For information on the part that Shep Husted played in the burial of Louis Levings on Mount Ypsilon, see the chapter on the Louis Levings Grave.)

- In about 1909, in addition to selling lumber that they produced themselves, the Griffiths began also selling lumber that they bought from the U.S. West Coast.

- On 25 October 1913, the Griffith family's sawmill and nearby lumber yard was destroyed in a huge fire.

- Following the 1913 fire, Dan Griffith bought a new Curtis sawmill and a new Fisher-Davis single-surface planer and erected them at the same location where the October fire took place. The Griffiths were able to continue to use the pre-fire boiler, which had survived the fire because it was full of water (page 12 of *The Griffith Family of Estes Park*).

- Some of the first lumber produced by this new sawmill came from the Hidden Valley area and was used to build additions to the Stanley Hotel.

- When Albin Griffith died in 1946, he left the family's lumber yard to his son Dan and daughter Lois. Don Griffith reported on page 19 of *The Griffith Family in Estes Park* that his father Dan Griffith bought out his Aunt Lois's interest in the family's lumberyard "sometime in 1950-51." Then, in 1964, Dan sold his interest in the lumber yard to a man who called it "Beaver's Lumber." That man then sold the lumber company to a man named Everitt, who still owned the lumber yard when Don gave his museum talk in 1977.

In late October 2004, we asked Sybil Barnes to describe where the Griffith family's property, including their lumber yard, had been located. She provided the following information in an email dated 1 November 2004. We provided the information in brackets, some of it based on the contents of Anne Toft's emails cited above (Source No. 10):

> "The Griffith property stretched west and south from Mary's Lake Road. The lumber yard was about a half mile west of where the little cemetery [Cleave-Griffith Family Cemetery] is. When you are going toward the Y [the YMCA

of the Rockies], there's a trailer park down by the river and the RockMount Cottages and then a grassy meadow. That meadow is where the lumber yard was. The original little cabin which was at the mill site near Hollowell Park was moved down there a little further on, but it was torn down this year and now there are some kind of condos going up in the next meadow. The Griffiths owned the property on that side of the road all the way to the Glacier Lodge bridge. On the north side of the highway is the road to Valhalla cottages. I think the name of that street might be Eagle Cliff [correct]. There's a big new house on that side, which belongs to the RockMount owners [actually a relative of the former RockMount manager]. The next house is an old house, which was one of the Griffiths' [originally Albin Griffith's home across from the family's lumber yard]. Then there's a smaller log cabin, which is still in the Griffith family [belongs to Mike Walz, Anne Toft's son], and a really big new log house with a paved driveway, which belongs to the same people [belongs to Anne Toft]."

On 14 November 2004, we emailed Sybil asking if there were any remaining signs of the existence of Griffith lumber yard and its various post-Griffith iterations. In her response of 15 November, Sybil told us, "If you didn't know about the lumber yard, you would just think there had never been anything there."

In response to a 17 November 2004 email asking her when the Everitt Lumber Yard, which was the last "descendant" of the Griffith lumber yard, went out of business, Sybil replied on 18 November that it probably went out of business in the summer of 1970 when a new lumber yard opened over on Highway 7. She also added that the last time a member of the Griffith family owned the lumber yard was "sometime in the mid-1960s," which agrees with the 1964 date given by Don Griffith above.

Children of Dan Griffith and Ellen Louise Jesser Griffith

Dan is Child No. 1 above. Dan and Ellen's five children, their spouses, and children are listed below.

1.1. **Estes Braxton Griffith.** The first child of Dan and Ellen, Estes was born in 1914 in Estes Park.

   Katherine Lloyd Ellwanger, Estes's wife. Katherine was born in 1916 in Denver. She and Estes were married in 1951. They lived in Lakewood and Denver.

   Estes and Katherine had **twin girls, Debra and Sharyn**, who were born in Denver in 1953. (For more information on Estes and Katherine's children and grandchildren, see page 221 of Don Griffith's *Homestead Trails and Tails*.)

1.2. **Donald Louis Griffith.** The second child of Dan and Ellen, Don was born in 16 January 1917 in Estes Park. In addition to being a chronicler of the Griffith family, Don taught school in Estes Park. According to the *Social Security Death Index* (Source No. 11), Don died on 21 November 2008 in Tucson, Pima County, Arizona.

   Nelda Phyllis Andrews, Don's wife. Phyllis was born in 1918 in Belgrade, Nebraska. She and Don were married in 1938.

   Donald and Phyllis had **two boys**, both of whom were born in Greeley, Colorado: **Daniel Arthur**, who was born in 1940, and **Douglas Lee**, who was born in 1945. (For more information on Donald and Phyllis's children and grandchildren, see page 220 of Don Griffith's *Homestead Trails and Tails*.)

1.3. **Mary Lucille Griffith.** The third child of Dan and Ellen, Mary was born in 1918 in Estes Park.

Tom Davies, Mary's husband. Tom was born in 1916 in Rollinsville, Colorado. He and Mary were married in 1942.

Mary and Tom had **three children,** all of which were born in Denver: **Mary Louise**, who was born in 1943; **Robert Braxton**, who was born in 1945; and **Susan Bronwyn**, who was born in 1947. (For more information on Tom and Mary's children and grandchildren, see page 219 of Don Griffith's *Homestead Trails and Tails*.)

1.4. **Marjorie Louise Griffith.** The fourth child of Dan and Ellen, Marjorie was born in 1922 in Estes Park.

Robert Edward ("Ed") Gieck, Majorie's husband. Ed was born in 1920. He and Marjorie were married in 1948. They made their home in Ault, Colorado, where Ed was the Superintendent of Schools.

Marjorie and Ed had **three children**, all of whom were born in Greeley, Colorado: **Gretchen Gail**, who was born on 10 October 1952, and who died the next day; **Bryan Edgar**, who was born in 1953; and **Tom Ellwood**, who was born in 1956. (For more information on Ed and Marjorie's children and grandchildren, see page 218 of Don Griffith's *Homestead Trails and Tails*.)

1.5. **Ruth Irene Griffith.** The fifth child of Dan and Ellen, Ruth was born in 1924 in Estes Park.

Dr. William ("Billy") Wayne Mounts, Ruth's husband. Billy was born in 1923. He and Ruth were married in 1948. They made their home in Pismo Beach, California.

Ruth and William had **four children**, the first one was born in Denver and the remaining three were born in San Luis Obispo, California: **Jon Wayne**, who was born in 1950; **Dennis David** and his twin **Dean Patrick**, who were born in 1953; and **Kevin Lee**, who was born in 1955. (For more information on Billy and Ruth's children and grandchildren, see page 217 of Don Griffith's *Homestead Trails and Tails*.)

Children of John Griffith and Virginia Cleave Griffith

John is Child No. 2 above. John and Virginia's four children, their spouses, and children are listed below.

2.1. **Charles Leslie Griffith.** The first child of John and Virginia, Charles was born on 7 July 1907 in Estes Park. He died on 24 December 1973 in Marin County, California (Source No. 11).

Sarah Metta Greenacre, Charles's wife. Sarah was born on 7 November 1907 in Colorado. She and Charles were married in August 1931 in Fort Collins. She died in August 1974 in Los Angeles, California (Source No. 11).

Charles and Sarah had **three children: Georgia Anne**, who was born in Denver in 1932; **Richard Lawrence**, who was born in Fort Collins in 1933; and **Norma Kay**, who was born in Denver in 1937. (Georgia Anne is the Anne Griffith Toft whom we met at our Estes Park Museum talk on 20 April 2007. See Source No. 10 above.)

In her emails of 14 and 16 May 2007 (Source No. 10), Anne Griffith Toft provided the following information about her father and his family:

- Charles was a civil engineer and was involved with the building of Trail Ridge Road.
- The lot where the Cleave-Griffith Family Cemetery is now located belonged to Charles in the 1930s and 1940s.
- While they lived near Rocky Mountain National Park, Charles and his family lived both in Grand Lake on the west side of the Park and in a little cabin on the lot on which the cemetery is now located.
- They then moved to Denver, where Charles worked for the Denver & Rio Grande Railroad. While they lived in Denver, they spent their weekends and vacations in the Estes Park area.
- Then, in 1944, Charles and his family moved to Anchorage, Alaska, where he worked as the Assistant Superintendent of the Alaska Railroad.

2.2. **Mary Esther Griffith.** The second child of John and Virginia, Mary was born on 11 November 1909 while her family was living in Mancos, Colorado. She died on 26 October 1998 in Estes Park (Source No. 11).

Chester ("Ted") Le Roy Fenton, Mary's husband. Ted was born on 1 September 1905. He and Mary made their home in Youngstown, Ohio. He died on 15 July 1996 in Youngstown (Source No. 11).

Mary and Ted had **one child, Virginia Bell,** who was born in Youngstown in 1931.

2.3. **Dennis Michael ("Mike") Griffith.** The third child of John and Virginia, Mike was born on 2 June 1914 in Estes Park.

Florence Gorenson, Mike's wife. Florence was born on 6 September 1914 in Bynum, Montana. She and Dennis were married on 8 March 1938 in Lyons, Colorado. They made their home in Estes Park.

Mike and Florence had **three children**, all born in Longmont: **Dale Edward**, who was born in 1940; **Harvey Ernest**, who was born in 1944; and **William ("Billie") Dean**, who was born in 1956.

2.4. **John Timothy ("Tim") Griffith.** The fourth child of John and Virginia, Tim was born in 1926 in Boulder, Colorado.

Grace Nation George, Tim's wife. Grace was born in 1922. She and John were married in 1961 in Estes Park. Prior to her marriage to John, she had been married to a man with the last name of George, with whom she had had five children: Alex George, Betty Jean, Carol Dean, Mary Jane, and Michael Allen.

Tim and Grace had **one child, Orin Vaughn,** who was born in 1962 in Denver.

COMMUNITY CHURCH OF THE ROCKIES COLUMBARIUM

Location: Latitude 40° 22' 03" N, Longitude 105° 29' 37" W

The Community Church of the Rockies (Presbyterian) is at 1700 Brodie in Estes Park, CO. To reach the church and its columbarium, take Fish Creek Road 0.4 of a mile south from Colorado 36 to Brodie. Turn right or west on Brodie Avenue. The church is the first building on the south (left) side of Brodie. The columbarium is east of the church between the church and Fish Creek Road.

Description

As of our 10 October 2000 visit to the columbarium, it contained 82 cremain burials. All of the burials are in what appeared to be small bronze boxes, with two sets of cremains per box. Each box is buried in the ground and has one or two markers on top of it. The year on the oldest set of cremains was 1975; the year of the most recent was 2000. There are also several "in memory of" benches along a path east of the church that leads to and away from the columbarium.

A rock wall with a wooden cross on top of it is to the east of the oldest sections of burials. Several other, more recent sections are to the south of the older ones.

Photo A: Rock Wall With Cross in the Columbarium of the Community Church of the Rockies in Estes Park

Finding the Columbarium

We were told about this columbarium by Teddie Haines, the wife of retired Rocky Mountain National Park Ranger Bob Haines. (For more information on Teddie and Bob, see the entry for Bob's brother William Walter Haines in the chapter titled Rocky Mountain National Park Scattered Cremains and the "Acknowledgments" section.)

History of the Community Church of the Rockies

According to its website at http://www.estesparkpresbyterian.org/history.htm as of 13 February 2007, the following is the history of the Community Church of the Rockies:

> "The history of church activity in Estes Valley dates back to 1870. Services were being held in the log school house with Rev. Elkanah Lamb riding horseback from Longs Peak. Since Rev. Lamb did not believe in Sunday School, someone would watch for his arrival in order to dismiss Sunday School before he arrived. An organizational meeting was held in Estes Park on Dec. 31, 1907. The Rev. John Knox officiated and the church was chartered as "The

Presbyterian Church of Estes Park." The original charter documents seven members. The first church was built between 1908 and 1909. The church on Elkhorn, which is now "The Old Church Shops," had a bell tower that rang every Sunday morning for Sunday School at 10:00 and at 11:00 for the church service. It was the only protestant church in Estes Park for many years. There was a Catholic Church that only conducted services in the summer.

"In December of 1909, Rev. J. Mont Travis was elected pastor with a salary of $1,000 and annual vacation of four weeks. The congregation pledged $550 and asked the Presbyterian Board of Missions for $450. For the first twenty-five years a succession of pastors, sixteen in all, served the church. Relative stability came in 1928 when William Floyd Kuykendall, a recent seminary graduate, 'newly married and handsome' served until 1932.

"O. J. Bowman, a director of Christian Education in the Methodist denomination, served the Community Church of the Rockies as a summer-time volunteer adult Bible school teacher during the 1920's and 1930's. Mr. Bowman's activities in the church were not limited to the Bible studies he conducted sometimes drawing 150-200 attendees. Ably assisted by his wife at the piano, he also conducted many practices and performances of such oratorios as 'The Seven Last Words of Christ,' 'Elijah,' and the 'Messiah.' He was an accomplished fly fisherman who could be found on the stream between Olympus bridge and the village almost every morning. In the evenings he was often found dressed in his old corduroy pants and plaid shirt sitting by the miniature golf driving range on Elkhorn watching the tourists go by. He was a fisherman whom our Lord called, like the disciples of old, to be a fisher of men.

"In 1952, the church changed its name to 'The Community Church of the Rockies.'

"On July 12, 1981, ground-breaking ceremonies were held to build the church at its current location at Fish Creek Road and Brodie Avenue. A year later to the day a temporary certificate of occupancy for the new building was issued. Members started moving the office records and equipment, as well as the library books. The house where the temporary offices had been on the bank of the Fall River was badly damaged by the Lawn Lake flood. The move had been completed the day before the flood. The beautiful leaded glass windows were moved to the new church from the Elkhorn Avenue church. These windows were given in honor of early members of the church. The original bell was also moved to the existing church, only to be stored in the shed until a new bell tower was built in 1996, with memorial contributions made in honor of Mollie Holmquist, who was killed in a car crash and returned to her Lord on her 21st birthday, March 10, 1994. The bell, once again, welcomes members and visitors alike by ringing before church services."

The church's website also notes that the columbarium was established by a resolution adopted by a meeting of the congregation on 29 September 1985. Consequently, the cremains in the columbarium that predate 1985 must have been moved to the columbarium from elsewhere.

ELKHORN LODGE CEMETERY

Location: Latitude 40° 22' 42" N, Longitude 105° 32' 04" W

The Elkhorn Lodge Cemetery is between the Fall River and West Elkhorn Avenue on private property belonging to the Elkhorn Lodge & Guest Ranch in Estes Park. More specifically, the cemetery is just east of the bridge over the Fall River between West Elkhorn Avenue and Elkhorn Lodge's stables.

Description of Cemetery

The Elkhorn Lodge Cemetery contains four graves, all confirmed by our use of dowser rods. As of our 9 July 2001 visit, two of the graves were surrounded by approximately 2-foot-high walls of native stones that had been cemented into position. The east wall of the smaller, baby's or young child's grave is part of the west wall of the larger, adult's or older child's grave. The larger grave is oriented north-south.

In one corner of the baby's grave where the rock-cement wall has been broken apart (probably by the many elk that frequent the area), one can see a row of rocks that is both flush with the ground and directly under the cemented rock wall. Thus, it appears that the cemented rocks were added at a later date, probably to better mark the two graves.

Photo A: The Two Walled Graves in the Elkhorn Lodge Cemetery

As of 3 April 2001, a small pine tree was growing out of the east end of the baby's or child's grave.

About 12 feet east of the two walled graves, we found a third grave oriented east-west, which makes it parallel to the Fall River. The grave is about 5.5 feet long and is thus probably an adult grave. Before taking Photo B below, we added several pieces of wood to better outline the grave for the photo.

Photo B: Third Grave in Elkhorn Lodge Cemetery, Which Is About 12 Feet East of the Two Walled Graves

On a return visit to the site on 9 July 2001, we found a fourth grave, which was in the same orientation as the third grave (parallel to Fall River) and was about 25 to 30 feet northeast of the third grave. Grave four was outlined in small- to medium-sized native stones and was the size of an adult.

Finding the Cemetery

While walking her dog, Sybil Barnes, at the time the Local History Librarian for the Estes Park Public Library, had noticed some piled-up rocks near where we later found the four graves described above. She told us about the rock piles when we met her by chance in the parking lot of the Estes Park Public Library late in the summer of 2000. (For details on all of the help that Sybil gave us, see "Barnes, Sybil" in the "Acknowledgments" section.)

The first opportunity we had to actually look for the possible graves that Sybil had noticed was on 15 January 2001. When we arrived at the location that she had described, we immediately saw the stone structures described above, but we did not see the piled-up rocks that she had described. We then used dowser rods to confirm that the two walled-in spaces contained burials. While we were doing this, we saw Diane Gunderson, who, in 2001, was the winter caretaker and all-year wrangler for the Elkhorn Lodge, where she worked with the Lodge's horses. We asked Diane if the property on which we found the graves was public road right-of-way or belonged to Elkhorn Lodge. She confirmed that the property belonged to the Lodge.

We then showed Diane the two walled graves and asked her who owned Elkhorn Lodge and how to contact them. Diane told us that the Lodge was owned by Jerry and Carol Zahourek, and, according to the Larimer County Assessor Office's online database, as of 14 September 2013, it still was. Diane also told us about the existence of a ghost named "Eleanor" in Elkhorn Lodge's buildings.

Sybil then arrived with her dog and showed us the rock piles that she had suspected to be graves. Our use of dowser rods did not find any burials at those locations. We suspect that either the Fall River itself or children playing on the river bank may have piled up the rocks that first attracted Sybil's attention.

During our visit to the cemetery on 15 January 2001, our use of dowser rods seemed to confirm the existence of the third grave described above, but it was so cold that author Duane Kniebes could not properly handle the rods. Upon our return visit on 3 April 2001 we were able to use the dowser rods to confirm the existence of the third grave. During that visit, Diane Gunderson and two other Lodge employees told us a number of additional stories of the Lodge's ghost known as "Eleanor" and other resident apparitions. (For more information on the Lodge's ghosts, see "The Ghosts of Elkhorn Lodge" below.)

During a return visit to the site on 9 July 2001, we saw what appeared to be a fourth grave and used dowser rods to confirm the burial of an adult at that location.

We then did our first pass on history research on the Elkhorn Lodge and the James family and sent it to the Zahoureks and asked if they could provide or tell us where to find any additional information on the history of Elkhorn Lodge, especially any information about anyone who had died on the property (and thus might have been buried there as Estes Park did not have a town cemetery in those days).

From the Zahoureks' experience with buildings on the Elkhorn Lodge property for which the date of construction is known, cement was not used in construction on the property until the early 1900s. Consequently, they feel that the rock-cement walls marking two of the graves could not be from the 1880s and probably not even from the 1890s. However, as noted above, there appear to be rock outlines below the walls now marking those two graves. Thus, the graves themselves could predate the post-1900 addition of their walls.

To determine if any members of the James family might possibly be occupants of the Elkhorn Lodge Cemetery, the Zahoureks also suggested that we check the Mountain View Cemetery in Longmont, Boulder County, Colorado, for the graves of the James and Hondius families. We did. Except for Homer James, they are all there. With the help of Sybil Barnes, we were later able to ascertain that Homer James is buried in California. See details below. Other information provided by the Zahoureks is noted in the "History of the James Family and the Elkhorn Lodge" below.

The Elkhorn Lodge Graves Following the September 2013 Flood

Between 9 and 15 September 2013, Estes Park and the rest of northern Colorado experienced a historic level of flooding. That flooding included the Fall River and affected the Elkhorn Lodge property near the river, as had happened numerous times in the past. When we visited Estes Park on 21 April 2014, we could, suprisingly, still see signs of the two two walled-in graves as well as the small pine tree growing out of the smaller of the two walled-in graves.

Sources of Information on the Elkhorn Lodge and the James Family

1. The 1910 U.S. Census for Estes Park, Larimer County, Colorado, enumerated on 18 April 1910.

2. *The History of Larimer County, Colorado*, written by Ansel Watrous and published in 1911, provides a biography of William Edwin James, "one of the pioneers of Estes Park and founder and builder of Elkhorn Lodge," on page 456. (See the "Bibliography" for a complete citation.)

3. The 1920 U.S. Census for Precinct 37, Estes Park, Larimer County, Colorado, enumerated between 7 and 10 January 1920.

4. "*Estes Park in the Memoirs of Lord Dunraven*," written by Mrs. Albert Hayden, *Estes Park Trail*, 26 October 1923, page 3.

5. The 1930 U.S. Census for Precinct 37, Estes Park, Larimer County, Colorado, enumerated between 12 and 16 April 1930.

6. Obituary of Homer James, *Estes Park Trail*, 16 May 1958.

7. *Memoirs of Eleanor E. Hondius of Elkhorn Lodge*, written of Eleanor E. James Hondius and published in 1964. (See the "Bibliography" for a complete citation.) The copy we found was in the Fort Collins Public Library.

8. Volumes II and III of *Over Hill and Vale*, written by Harold Marion Dunning. Volume II was published in 1962, and Volume III was published in 1971. (See the "Bibliography" for complete citations.) Page 120 of Volume II discusses the sale of the Elkhorn Lodge to a syndicate from Lincoln, Nebraska. Page 191 of Volume III reports that William E. James and his sons W. E. James and Charlie James died of typhoid fever about 1875. Page 309 of Volume III contains information about the parents of Ella McCabe James, the wife of William E. James.

9. *The Elkhorn Lodge; Museum Program*, an indexed transcription of an audio tape made on 18 August 1977 at a historical walk of the Elkhorn Lodge conducted by Lyn Hickman. The walk, its taping, and the transcription were all done as part of the Estes Park Oral History project, which is a jointly sponsored effort of the Estes Park Area Historical Museum and the Estes Park Public Library. The tape and its indexed transcription are available in the Local History Section of that library.

10. "Magic Place in the Mountain," written by Shirley Derrick, on pages 191-192 of Volume II of *The History of Larimer County, Colorado*, edited by Arlene Ahlbrandt and Kathryn Stiebes and published in 1987. (See the "Bibliography" for a complete citation.) This chapter includes information on the James Family and Elkhorn Lodge.

11. *"This Blue Hollow,"* written by James H. Pickering and published in 1999. (See the "Bibliography" for a complete citation.) Pickering's book provides a wealth of interestingly information about Estes Park during this period, including the history of the William E. James family in Estes Park (pages 94-95 and 119-120).

12. *Larimer County, Colorado, 1885 State Census*, transcribed by the Larimer County Genealogical Society and published in book form in September 2000. Page 66 provides census information on the family of William E. James.

13. Records of the Mountain View Cemetery in Longmont, Colorado as of 16 and 18 May 2001.

14. Marginal notes to first draft of this chapter provided by Catherine Maguire in March 2006.

15. Email received from Carol Zahourek on 17 March 2006

16. Email received from Catherine Maguire on 4 April 2006.

17. *Social Security Death Index* as of 5 May 2009 as transcribed by Ancestry.com.

History of the James Family and Elkhorn Lodge

Information Provided by Catherine Maguire

In early March 2006, Carol Zahourek sent the then-current draft of our chapter on the "Elkhorn Cemetery" to Catherine Maguire of Wheat Ridge, Colorado, to review because, when Catherine was young (between 9 months old and 5 or 6 years old), her father James ("Mike") Maguire and her mother Anna had worked at the Elkhorn Lodge during the summers of 1913 through 1927. Catherine's father was the Lodge's cook, and her mother worked as a waitress and the "salad lady." During the "off season," Catherine's family returned to their home in Denver, where Mike worked as a cook for a number of hotels, including the Metropole and the Albany. Catherine returned that draft of this chapter to Carol Zahourek with marginal notes (Source No. 14) on her memories of her childhood summers at the Elkhorn Lodge, which she recalls as being "the happiest time of my childhood." Carol then sent Catherine's marked-up copy of the draft on to us. The information in Catherine's marginal notes was later supplemented by a 17 March 2006 email from Carol Zahourek (Source No. 15) and a 4 April 2006 email from Catherine herself (Source No. 16). Catherine's marginal notes and the two

ELKHORN LODGE

emails provided some very interesting details on the Elkhorn Lodge and its employees. *These "tidbits" are inserted in italics in applicable locations throughout this chapter.*

Arrival of the James Family in Estes Park

According to page 456 of Ansel Watrous's *History of Larimer County* (Source No. 2), William Edwin James arrived in Denver on 20 October 1874 and in Estes Park on 4 May 1875. In her *Memoirs* (Source No. 7), William's daughter Eleanor E. James Hondius states that her father made the trip to Estes Park from their home in Syracuse, New York, in "late 1873 or early 1874" to hunt. She then goes on to say:

> "My father was so charmed with the Estes Park area that he wrote my mother in Syracuse, N.Y., that he had found a place where he would 'file on land and make his home.'" Her mother then came to Colorado "with her three little boys: Homer, about six or seven; Charlie, about four; and Howard, the baby."

(For genealogy information on the members of the James family, see "Biographical and Genealogical Information of the James Family of Estes Park" below.)

To "synchronize" Watrous's and Eleanor's stories, it could be that William first came to Denver and then visited Estes Park on his hunting trip in October 1874 and that he and his family did not move to Estes Park until May 1875.

However, see Eleanor's comment about the "spring of 1875" under "James Family's Move to What Became the Elkhorn Lodge" below. This would make one think that maybe the 4 May 1975 date provided by Watrous is the date the family moved to the property on which the Elkhorn Lodge was eventually built. However, as discussed in the next paragraph, Jim Pickering (Source No. 11) agrees with Watrous that the family actually moved to Estes Park in May 1875.

In his discussions of the James family in "*This Blue Hollow*," Jim Pickering gives the fall of 1874 as the date of William James's first trip to Estes Park. Shortly before his trip to Estes Park, William had come to Denver from upstate New York [Syracuse, N.Y.], "where his grocery business had failed during the hard times of 1873." Pickering then goes on to report that in May 1875 William moved his wife, Ella, and the couple's three little boys (Homer, Charlie, and Howard) into a "small, one-one-room, dirt-roofed hunter's cabin near what is now known as McCreery Springs, out Dry Gulch, about three miles from the present town of Estes Park."

Concerning the family's second home in the Estes Park area, Eleanor states in her *Memoirs* that:

> "It was very difficult to determine legally what land was available since most of it was claimed by Lord Dunraven. Father took up a claim at the upper end of Black Canyon and built a cabin for his family there."

Eleanor then goes on to describe the family's first winter in the Estes Park area:

> "The first winter was a very difficult one for our family. Father and a Mr. Rowe supported their families by killing deer and elk and catching fish, which they took to Denver to sell."

However, finding food to eat wasn't William James's only problem: Eleanor describes how, because of "some legal technicalities," Mrs. Georgianna Heeney, the mother of Mrs. Clara MacGregor of the MacGregor Ranch, "jumped" William James's claim on the land in Black Canyon. Eleanor mistakenly misspells MacGregor as "McGregor," as do a number of other historians of the Estes Park area including Ansel Watrous and Harold Dunning. (For more information on the MacGregor family's ranch in the Black Canyon area, see the chapter on the MacGregor Family Cemetery.)

LARIMER COUNTY CEMETERIES

James Family's Move to What Became the Elkhorn Lodge

Because of the difficulties with their Black Canyon land and Mrs. Heeney, William James took advantage of money left to his wife when her father died in the spring of 1875 (Source No. 7) and, in November 1876, swapped his original claim along Lumpy Ridge "for a tract of land on Fall River, just west of Dunraven's property" (Source No. 11). After building a "modest frame cabin consisting of a living room, dining room, kitchen, and two bedrooms" on the land on Fall River, on 2 April 1877, William moved his family there (Source No. 11).

According to Pickering, on 5 April 1877, right after moving his family to what became the Elkhorn Lodge, "perhaps to spite his old neighbor [Georgianna Heeney], James set fire to his barn in Black Canyon." If he couldn't have his barn, well then, she couldn't either!

As is widely assumed, Elkhorn Lodge is indeed named for elk "horns," which are, of course, really antlers rather than horns. Pages 95 and 120 and the back cover of *"This Blue Hollow"* show the front of Elkhorn Lodge with its piles of elk antlers. The photos on page 95 and the back cover (which are identical) show the Lodge as it looked in the summer of 1889.

The Conversion of the James Family's Cattle Ranch Into the Elkhorn Lodge Guest Ranch

On this subject, Eleanor James Hondius (Source No. 7) has the following to say:

> "Father had no intention of having a guest ranch; he planned to go into the cattle business. But every summer people came to the ranch and begged to be allowed to stay, and each winter another cabin would be built on the ranch to house them. Father and Mother soon found there was more money in caring for summer tourists than in raising cattle."

Both Watrous (page 179 of Source No. 2) and Mrs. Albert Hayden in the 26 October 1923 issue of *Estes Park Trail* (Source No. 4) give 1877 as the year of the formal founding of the Elkhorn Lodge. Based on Eleanor's statement above and the fact that the James family moved to their Fall River ranch in April 1877, 1877 seems more likely to be the year that the family moved, not the year they actually started running a guest ranch (and hence a "lodge") rather than a cattle ranch.

Operation of the Elkhorn Lodge Under the James and Hondius Families

Until William James died in January 1895, he and his wife Ella ran Elkhorn Lodge. In addition to making a living, the James family was interested in the education of their and the other children in early Estes Park. According to Watrous (Source No. 2), "The first term of public school [in Estes Park] was held in one of the cottages at Elkhorn Lodge in the winter of 1881."

The family's interest in education went even further. According to Shirley Derrick in a chapter that she wrote on Estes Park for *The History of Larimer County, Colorado* (Source No. 10), on 17 November 1883, Charles James, Homer E. James, and Howard James were "some of the hardy homesteaders who filed a petition in the office of W. H. McCreery, Larimer County superintendent of schools, stating that the undersigned residents desired to form a new school district." The petition showed that there were 15 school-age children in the proposed new district.

Note that the 1883 date that Shirley Derrick gives as the year during which the group of homesteaders asked for the formation of an Estes Park School District is after the 1881 date provided by Watrous as the date that the first public school was held. If both dates are correct, it may mean that the public school started before an official Estes Park School District was established. The three Jameses and their fellow petitioners were successful, for Shirley Derrick tells us that "during the first three years, school was held at the Elkhorn Lodge (which still operates in 1986 as a lodge in Estes Park)."

In his discussion of the James family and Elkhorn Lodge, Watrous (Source No. 2) says that, following her husband's death in 1895, Ella James "continued to carry on Elkhorn Lodge with excellent success. This popular resort hotel has recently [1911] been greatly enlarged and has done a large business for a great many years."

Ella had some help in running Elkhorn Lodge, for according to Eleanor James Hondius (Source No. 7):

> "After my father died, Mother sent for Homer to come back and manage Elkhorn Lodge. Howard, who was several years younger than Homer, was a born hotel man, but Mother seemed to think he was too young, so Homer took over."

Before Homer returned to Estes Park to help his mother run the Elkhorn Lodge, he had become one of the first doctors to graduate from the University of Colorado, where he also played on CU's first football team. Eleanor says that his services as a doctor "were needed from time to time" after he returned to Estes Park because the only other doctor then in Estes Park "spent a good deal of time as a carpenter."

Eleanor does not explain how it came about, but, at some point, the management of Elkhorn Lodge passed from Homer to Howard, the "born hotel man." In his biography of William Edwin James (Source No. 2), Watrous tells us that Homer was "a prominent and prosperous business man in Estes Park, being a dealer in lumber and building materials, etc." Thus, Homer apparently left the hotel business, for which he was not particularly well suited, for another occupation, in which he evidently succeeded.

The transfer of the responsibility for the operation of Elkhorn Lodge must have passed from Homer to Howard by 1910 because the 1910 U.S. Census (Source No. 1) lists Howard's occupation as "proprietor of hotel" and Homer's occupation as a "retail merchant" who owned a "lumber yard."

Howard must have done a good job as the manager of the Lodge, for Eleanor says, "I've often heard Mother brag to other people about how fond the guests were of Howard. 'The women all kiss him goodbye when they leave,' she would say."

As noted above, Catherine Maguire's father and mother, Mike and Anna, worked at the Elkhorn Lodge from 1913 through 1927, all years during which Howard James was managing the Lodge. Catherine recalls that her parents thought that "Mr. James [Howard] was a wonderful boss and person." Her personal memories of Howard are also positive. For example, once they were old enough, 'Mr. James, Sr., [Howard] allowed my brother and me full use of ponies every day. It was great!!"

In spite of the Maguire family's fondness for Elkhorn Lodge in general and Howard James, Sr., in particular, Catherine told Carol Zahourek (who told us in her 17 March 2006 email to us) that "when Prohibition started, someone had a still in the barn at the Lodge and her father imbibed a little too much to suit her mother, and she put her foot down and would not let her husband go back to the Lodge [to work] again."

In her *Memoirs* (Source No. 7), Eleanor James Hondius tells us that in the spring of 1927, her husband Pieter Hondius went to the Netherlands for the summer. That fall, Eleanor; her son, young Pieter; and her room clerk, Florine Townsend met Pieter Hondius, Sr., in the Netherlands. From there they went to Italy (for 2 months), Egypt, and Honolulu. Eleanor reports that "Young Pieter celebrated his fifth birthday aboard ship in the Indian Ocean." Depending upon when the Hondiuses were in the Indian Ocean, this means that "young Pieter" was born in 1922 or 1923. [On 9 March 2002, Pieter Jr. told us that he was born in 1923 in Denver, which means that the 1930 U.S. Census (Source No. 5) was correct when it said he was 7 years old in 1930.]

When the Hondiuses returned from their extended vacation in the first part of May 1928, Eleanor tells us that they "found Howard very sick; he lived only about a month after our return." This means that Howard probably died in June 1928, when he would have been about 55. [His headstone in Longmont's Mountain View Cemetery (Source No. 16) gives his birth year as 1872 and his death year as 1928.]

Following Howard's death, Eleanor took over management of Elkhorn Lodge. (For what happened to Elkhorn Lodge after Eleanor, see "History of Elkhorn Lodge After Eleanor Hondius" below.)

Biographical and Genealogy Information on the James Family of Estes Park

Parents of William Edwin James

William James. According to the 1885 Colorado State Census for Larimer County (Source No. 12), William was born about 1807 in England, as were both of his parents; he was a widower; and his occupation was given as "butcher." The records of Longmont's Mountain View Cemetery (Source No. 13) indicate that he was born in Bath, England, and that he died on 19 November 1888 (undoubtedly in Colorado).

Interestingly, when the 1885 Colorado State Census was taken, the two boarders living with the James family were also butchers.

Ann James, William's wife. The records of Mountain View Cemetery indicate that she was born in Monmoutshire, England, on 1 August 1810 and died (undoubtedly in Colorado) on 19 December 1884.

Although we found no confirmation of this in other historical documents, apparently both of William E. James's parents accompanied William and his family when they moved from New York to Colorado.

Parents of Ella McCabe James

The only place we found a last name for Ella James's parents was on page 309 of Volume III of *Over Hill and Vale* (Source No. 8), which provides the following information:

> "Mrs. W .E. James, founder of the Elkhorn, was a McCabe. The Stanley home was built on what was the McCabe Homestead."

If this is true, one or both of Ella's parents must have also come to Estes Park, which, as noted immediately above, was also true of the parents of Ella's husband William James.

In her *Memoirs* (Source No. 7), Eleanor James Hondius does not mention her maternal grandparents as having lived in Estes Park. Her only mention of them is that, upon his death in the spring of 1875, her maternal grandfather left his daughter (Eleanor's mother) some money, which seems to have been used to help Eleanor's parents acquire the property on which the Elkhorn Lodge was eventually built.

The Larimer County Genealogical Society's transcription of the 1885 Colorado State Census for Larimer County (Source No. 12) indicates that Ella's father was born in Indiana and that her mother was born in Vermont. When we looked at the actual image of this census available on Ancestry.com, Ella's father's birth place looks more like "Ire" than "Ind," so his birth place could well be Ireland, which is the birth location Ella provided for her father in the 1910 U.S. Census. On the other hand, the abbreviation for her mother's birth place in the 1885 Colorado State Census does not look like an abbreviation for Vermont or New York, which is the birth location Ella provided for her mother in the 1910 Census. When we looked at the actual image of the 1910 Census available on Ancestry.com, Ella's mother's birth location is written out and not abbreviated and is definitely New York.

William Edwin James, His Wife Ella McCabe James, and Their Descendants

Unless otherwise noted, the genealogy information below comes from the 1910, 1920, and 1930 U.S. Censuses for Estes Park (Source Nos. 1, 3, and 5), the 1885 Colorado State Census for Larimer County (Source No. 12), and the records of Mountain View Cemetery in Longmont, Colorado (Source No. 13). We made no special effort to discover the names of William and Ella's descendants beyond their children and provide information on their grandchildren only when we learned it while doing other research.

William Edwin James, Sr. William was born on 10 December 1841 in Camden, N.Y. (Source No. 2). He married Ella McCabe on 25 December 1865 (Source No. 2). The 1885 Colorado State Census gives his occupation as "hotel proprietor." When he died in Estes Park on 15 January 1895, he had been a Master Mason for 32 years (Source No. 2). On page 191 of Volume III of *Over Hill and Vale* (Source No. 8), Harold Dunning reports that William died of typhoid fever, as did his sons Charlie James (Child No. 2 below) and William E. James, Jr. (Child No. 6 below). William E. Sr. is buried in the Mountain View Cemetery in Longmont.

Ella McCabe, William's wife. Ella was born about 1844 in Utica, New York (Source No. 2), and died in 1917. The records of Mountain View Cemetery report that she was interred on 29 January 1917. Thus, she would have died a day or two before that date.

As well as we can determine, William and Ella had the following six children, the first three of whom accompanied their parents when they moved to Colorado in 1875:

1. **Homer Edwin James**. Homer was born in 28 April 1866 in Syracuse, New York (Source No. 6). The 1885 Colorado State Census gives his occupation as "farmer." He married Jennie L. Buchanan in about 1905.

    By the time the 1910 U.S. Census was taken, his occupation is given as "retail merchant, owns a lumber yard." Recall that his sister Eleanor reports (Source No. 7) that Homer was trained as a doctor and that he helped run the Elkhorn Lodge for some time following his father's death in 1895.

    Homer's obituary in the 16 May 1958 issue of *Estes Park Trail* (Source No. 6) reports that he died in Pasadena, California, on 4 May 1958 and that he and his wife Jennie are both buried there. They do not appear in Estes Park censuses after 1910, so Homer and Jennie must have left Estes Park some time between 1910 and 1920. [For additional information on Homer James from his obituary (Source No. 6), see the chapter on the Mary Jane James Grave.]

    Jennie L. Buchanan, Homer's wife. Jennie was born about 1869 in Michigan. Her father was born in Vermont. When the 1910 U.S. Census for Estes Park was taken, Jennie's **mother Maria Chapin**, a widow, was living with Jennie and Homer in Estes Park. Maria was born in Ohio. Maria's parents were both born in New York.

    Jennie's last name "Buchanan" and the date of her marriage to Homer come from Homer's obituary (Source No. 6). Since her mother's last name in 1910 was "Chapin," either Jennie's mother had remarried following the death of Jennie's father or Jennie herself had been married to a "Mr. Buchanan" before she married Homer James.

    In the 1910 Census, Jennie reports that she was the mother of one child and that that child was no longer alive as of April 1910.

    1.1. **Mary Jane James**. Given the above information that Homer and Jennie were married about 1905 and that by 18 April 1910 Jennie had had a child who had died (Source No. 1), Mary Jane must have been born and died some time between 1905 and 1910.

Mary Jane is buried just north of Fall River Road in Estes Park. (For more information on her burial, see the chapter on the Mary Jane James Grave.)

2. **Charles ("Charlie") W. James**. Charlie was born in New York about 1872. He died of typhoid fever (Source No. 8) a few days before 21 June 1890, which was the day that he was interred in Mountain View Cemetery (Source No. 13). In the 1885 Colorado State Census, his occupation is given as "farmer."

3. **Howard Perry James, Sr.** Howard's middle name of "Perry" comes from Ansel Watrous (Source No. 2). Howard was born in 1872 in New York. The 1885 Colorado State Census gives his occupation as "farmer." By the time of the 1910 Census, his occupation was given as "proprietor of hotel" (the Elkhorn Lodge), and by the 1920 Census his occupation was "hotel owner." Sometime between 1920 and the birth of their first child in 1924, he married Edna B. Cobb Arnold Gray. (For details of Howard's death provided by his sister Eleanor James Hondius, see "Operation of the Elkhorn Lodge Under the James and Hondius Families" above.) Howard died in June 1928 and is buried in the Mountain View Cemetery in Longmont.

Edna B. Cobb Arnold Gray, Howard's wife. [For genealogical information on Edna's first two husbands "Mr. Arnold" and Walter A. Gray and the children she had with them, see "Biographical and Genealogical Information of Mr. Arnold and His Family" and "Biographical and Genealogical Information on Walter A. Gray and His Family" below. For information on Edna's husband after the death of Howard James, see "Biographical and Genealogical Information of Paul N. ('Tiny') Mills" below.]

Edna was born in 1890 in Colorado. Both of her parents were from Missouri. According to the obituary of A. L. Cobb, which was published on the first page of the 4 December 1936 issue of the *Estes Park Trail*, A. L. Cobb was Edna's father; lived in Estes Park from 1900 to 1918, where he served as the town's second mayor; died in Long Beach, California, on 25 November 1936; and was buried "near his old family home in Pueblo, Colorado."

Interestingly, when the 1930 Census was taken, Raymond R. Cobb, the single 36-year-old brother of Edna, was listed in her household and was working as a "hotel baker," undoubtedly for the Elkhorn Lodge.

Catherine Maguire recalls that Raymond Cobb's nickname was "Ty."

That same census also included Florence J. Kolbs or Kolbe (as best as we could determine from the online image of the original census at Ancestry.com), who was Edna's 27-year-old maid.

Catherine Maguire told us that Florence's actual last name was "Coughlin," not "Kolbs" or "Kolbe"; that she lived in California during the "off season"; and that Catherine's mother and Florence carried on a regular correspondence.

Edna is the "Mrs. James" to whom Eleanor James Hondius sold the Elkhorn Lodge in the late 1930s or the 1940s (Source No. 9). (See "History of the Elkhorn Lodge After Eleanor Hondius" below.)

When Edna died in 1979, she was buried under the name of "Edna B. James" in the Mountain View Cemetery in Longmont.

3.1. **Howard Perry ("Bud") James, Jr.** Bud was born in Colorado (most likely Estes Park) about 1924. As of July 2001, he was living in Steamboat Springs, Colorado. Bud took over the management of Elkhorn Lodge either immediately after Eleanor Hondius or after his mother Edna James managed it for a period. (See "History of Elkhorn Lodge After Eleanor Hondius" below.)

    3.2. **Eleanore A. James Owen.** Eleanore was born on 22 September 1925 (Source No. 17). We met Eleanore (who was then Eleanore Owen) at a program on "Guest Lodges of Rocky Mountain National Park" held in the Estes Park Municipal Building on 9 March 2002 when she was on the panel. Also on the panel was her cousin, Peter or Pieter Hondius, Jr. (Child No. 4.2 below). Sadly, Eleanore died on 9 December 2006 in Estes Park (Source No. 17).

4. **Eleanor ("Ella") Estes James.** Eleanor was born 7 January 1880 in Estes Park.

The Ella Estes James/Mrs. Hondius referred to in the histories and the censuses cited above either was actually named "Eleanor" or, once she married Pieter Hondius, she decided that "Eleanor" was a more suitable name for the wife of naturalized U.S. citizen from the Netherlands who "came from a long line of distinguished ancestors" (Source No. 7). Her name is given as "Ella E. James" in the 1885 Colorado State Census, "Eleanor Hondius" in the 1910 Census, "Ella E. Hondius" in the 1920 Census, and "Eleanor E. Hondius" in the 1930 Census. The 1910 Census does not provide an occupation for Eleanor. However, when the 1920 Census was taken, both she and her brother Howard give their occupation as "hotel owner," and in the 1930 Census her occupation is given as "hotel manager." [For details of Eleanor's life, see the *Memoirs of Eleanor E. Hondius of Elkhorn Lodge* (Source No. 7).]

In the 1910 Census, Eleanor and her husband Peter Hondius both report that they had been married for 5 years, which means that they must have gotten married about 1905.

Eleanor died on 18 November 1968 and is buried in the Mountain View Cemetery in Longmont.

Pieter ("Peter") Hondius, Sr., Eleanor's husband. "Peter" is the Americanized version of his real first name, which was "Pieter." Pieter was born on 6 December 1864 in the Netherlands. In her *Memoirs* (Source No. 7), Eleanor says that her husband came to Estes Park hoping for relief from the asthma from which he suffered in the dampness of the Netherlands. "Like all others after the season was over, he was deposited at our door," says Eleanor of how she met Pieter. He bought over 3,700 acres of land in the Estes Park area. His ranch was called "The Beaver." He eventually sold this acreage to the U.S. Government, and it became part of Rocky Mountain National Park (in 1932 or 1933).

Jerry Zahourek is the one who told us that Pieter owned approximately 3,700 acres in the what is now Rocky Mountain National Park. Zahourek knew this number because he was involved in some litigation concerning the Elkhorn Lodge's historical trail rights within Rocky Mountain National Park. How much and what land Pieter had owned in what is now the Park became significant during that litigation.

Based on information provided by Dr. D. Ferrel Atkins, a retired and now deceased Rocky Mountain National Park Ranger-Naturalist; Bob Haines, another retired and now deceased Park Ranger; and Lashelle Lyman, a Park Ranger as of 2001, part of the 3,700 acres that Pieter owned was in the Beaver Meadows area, with his old ranch house having been at the west end of Beaver Meadows (Upper Beaver Meadows) just southwest of the picnic tables. His property also included the land near the current Fall River entrance to the Park, known appropriately as "Hondius Park," and extended to almost Beaver Point, which is the land across the road from the current Park Headquarters. (For more information on Ferrel Atkins and Bob Haines, see the "Acknowledgments" section.)

LARIMER COUNTY CEMETERIES

When Jerry Zahourek described the land owned by Pieter Hondius, he said that it was in the "Horseshoe Park area." Given that Pieter owned 3,700 acres, this could certainly "spill over" into the Beaver Meadows area, which is just south of what is now identified as "West Horshoe Park" on the Park's *Rocky Mountain Official Map and Guide*, dated 1999.

Pieter purchased some of his 3,700 acres from the Hupp family in 1903 and 1904. At the time Pieter purchased the Hupp Ranch, this acreage included the graves of John T. Hupp, John's wife Eliza, and daughter Frances. (For details on the Hupp Family Cemetery, see that chapter.)

According to Eleanor's *Memoirs*, Pieter Hondius finally settled in Palm Springs, California, to avoid the pollen of the Estes Park area. He died on 17 February 1934. His and Eleanor's son Pieter, Jr., was only 11 when his father died. Pieter, Sr., is buried along with Eleanor and a very young son (Child 4.1 below) in Mountain View Cemetery in Longmont.

    4.1. **Peter Hondius**. This Peter was Eleanor and Pieter's first child. He was born on 9 April 1920 and lived only until 11 April of the same year.

    4.2. **Pieter ("Peter") Hondius, Jr.** Pieter was born in Denver in 1923. (For his mother's account of how he spent his 5th birthday, see "Operation of the Elkhorn Lodge Under the James and Hondius Families" above.)

    On 9 March 2002, we attended one of the Estes Park Area Historial Museum's program on "Guest Ranches in Rocky Mountain National Park." Pieter Hondius, Jr., was one of the panel members. He recalled some of his experiences at the Elkhorn Lodge as a child. He said that the first useful work that he did there was in the barn and that he "liked working with horses." He said he also carried firewood, which probably was not nearly as much fun as working with the horses. In describing some of cowboy and Indian programs that the Lodge enacted for the tourists, he told us that the children who could ride bareback were the Indians.

    As of March 2002, Pieter was living in Estes Park.

5. **Baby James.** The only evidence we found of this child's existence was in the records of Longmont's Mountain View Cemetery, which give the child's name only as "Baby James" and say that he/she was interred on 8 October 1885. There is no headstone for this child in the James family plot, but dowser rods confirm the existence of a baby's or child's body in an "empty" space just north of the grave of Ella James.

    The cemetery records include a "(2)" in the age portion of this baby's listing. This could mean either 2 months or 2 days. A 2-year-old (and probably even a 2-month-old) child would certainly have had a name. The cemetery's records do not include the sex of the child or the given names of his/her parents.

    One would normally assume that the baby's parents were most likely William Edwin and Ella McCabe James. However, in her entry for the 1910 U.S. Census, Ella reports that she was the mother of five children, three of whom were living. This means that two of her children had died before 1910. These two children are the Charles W. James (Child No. 2 above) and Willie James (Child No. 6 below). However, if "Baby James" lived only 2 days and was not named, Ella may not have "counted" the baby when providing information to the 1910 census taker.

6. **William ("Willie") Edwin James, Jr.** Willie's headstone at the Mountain View Cemetery says that he was 4 months, 15 days old when he died. A large root of the tree under which

he was buried covers the part of his tombstone that gives the date of his death. However, the cemetery's records say that he was interred on 21 June 1890, so he probably died a day or two before that date. That would mean that he was probably born in early February 1890.

On page 191 of Volume III of *Over Hill and Vale* (Source No. 8), Harold Dunning reports that Willie died of typhoid fever and that his full name was W. E. (William Edwin) James, Jr. Willie's father and older brother Charlie James (Child No. 2 above) also died of typhoid fever.

Biographical and Genealogical Information of Mr. Arnold and His Family
   Unknown Arnold. "Mr. Arnold" was the first husband of Edna Cobb, whose third husband was Howard Perry James, Sr. (Child No. 3 above). Mr. Arnold's last name comes from the last name of his and Edna's daughter Lois Arnold. The 1920 Census listing for Lois says that her father was born in Tennessee.
   Edna B. Cobb, Mr. Arnold's wife. [For information on Edna, see "Edna B. Cobb Arnold Gray, Howard's wife" above under "Howard Perry James, Sr." (Child No. 3 above) in the subsection "William Edwin James, His Wife Ella McCabe James, and Their Descendants" earlier in this section.]
   Since Edna and Mr. Arnold's daughter was born about 1909 (Source No. 3), Edna and Mr. Arnold must have married in 1908 or 1909. Since Edna was born in 1890, she would have been 18 or 19 when she and Mr. Arnold got married.

1. **Lois Arnold.** According for the listing for her in the household of her step-father Walter A. Gray and her mother Edna in the 1920 Census, Lois was born in Colorado about 1909. By the time that the 1930 Census was taken, Lois was not listed with her mother or with her step-father Walter Gray. However, by that date, Lois would have been about 21 and could certainly have been living on her own or have married and thus could have had a different last name.

   Catherine Maguire remembers that Lois later married a man with the last name of Sands, with whom she had two sons, and that Lois's father, "Mr. Arnold," had been a soldier, but she does not recall in which war (if any) he served.

Biographical and Genealogical Information of Walter A. Gray and His Family
   Walter A. Gray, Sr.. Walter was born in about 1885 in Massachusetts. His father was born in Vermont, and his mother was born in New Brunswick, with her native language being listed as "Irish." When the 1910 Census was taken, Walter was single, a boarder in Henry Hupp's hotel, and was a laborer who did "odd jobs."
   By the time that the 1920 Census rolled around, Walter had married Edna B. Arnold, which means either that Mr. Arnold had died between 1910 and 1920 or that Edna had divorced him. Since Walter and Edna's daughter Jeanne (Child No. 1 below) was born in August 1919, they probably had married by at least early 1919.
   Since Howard ("Bud") Perry James, Jr. (Edna's first child with her third husband Howard Perry James, Sr.) was born about 1924, Walter and Edna must have divorced by at least early 1923.
   The 1930 Census gives Walter's occupation as "house painter." In that census, his household is listed only three households below the household of his ex-wife Edna B. James.
   Catherine Maguire remembers Walter being referred to by the nickname of "Dolly."

LARIMER COUNTY CEMETERIES

Edna B. Cobb Arnold, Walter's first wife. [For information on Edna, see "Edna B. Cobb Arnold Gray, Howard's wife" above under "Howard Perry James, Sr." (Child No. 3) in the subsection "William Edwin James, His Wife Ella McCabe James, and Their Descendants" earlier in this section.]

1. **Jeanne M. Gray.** According to Jeanne's obituary in the 21 March 2001 issue of *Estes Park Trail*, she was actually born on 13 August 1919 and died on 16 March 2001. Jeanne is the Jeanne M. Seybold who told us where to find the grave of Mary Jane James in January 2000. (For more information on Jeanne, see the chapter on the Mary Jane James Grave.)

    When the 1930 Census was taken, Jeanne was listed in the household of her mother Edna B. James along with her half-siblings Howard Perry ("Bud") James, Jr., and Eleanore A. James. Recall that Edna's third husband and Jeanne's step-father Howard Perry James, Sr., had died in 1928.

    Catherine Maguire recalls playing with Jeanne when they were both children at the Elkhorn Lodge.

Marle S. Gray, Walter's second wife. It is hard to read her first name in the 1930 Census, but it looks like "Marle." Marle was born about 1893 in Kansas. The 1930 Census reports that she was first married when she was 30 years old. Assuming that Marle's first marriage was to Walter, they would have gotten married about 1923, which would agree with the earlier assumption that Edna divorced Walter Gray and married Howard James about 1923.

2. **Walter A. Gray, Jr.** Walter, Jr., was born about 1928 in Colorado (most likely Estes Park).

3. **D_ _lt E. Gray.** It is hard to read this little girl's first name. She was born about 1929 in Colorado (again, most likely in Estes Park).

Biographical and Genealogical Information of Paul N. ("Tiny") Mills

Paul N. ("Tiny") Mills. Tiny was the fourth husband of Edna B. Cobb Arnold Gray James. She would have married Tiny some time after the death of her third husband, Howard Perry James, Sr., in 1928 (Source No. 9). Since Tiny is not listed in Edna's household in the 1930 Census, they must have married some time after that census was enumerated between 12 and 16 April 1930.

According to Carl Rohrer (Source No. 9), who was the Assistant Manager of Elkhorn when it was owned and managed by Eleanor James Hondius, following Edna's marriage to Tiny, she retained the name of "Mrs. James." Indeed, when Edna died in 1979, she was buried under the name of "Edna B. James" in the James family plot in the Mountain View Cemetery in Longmont.

Catherine Maguire remembers that "Tiny" Mills either owned or worked at the livery stable "in town."

History of Elkhorn Lodge After Eleanor Hondius

Concerning what happened to Elkhorn Lodge after Eleanor James Hondius gave up managing it, in March 2001 Jerry Zahourek provided the following information: Eleanor ran the Lodge until the late 1930s or early 1940s. At that point she "passed on the possession and management to another person involved with the Hondius family." Zahourek does not remember that person's name, but he does remember that "that individual inherited a substantive amount of the Hondius estate and then invested most or all of it in the Elkhorn. The Elkhorn has a long and consistent history, starting in the 30s, of financially breaking whoever attempted to keep it going."

Zahourek went on to say that, then, "in or around 1950 Bud James. . . assumed possession and management of the Elkhorn." Zahourek felt that Bud was the only descendent of William

Edwin and Ella McCabe James "with any real skill for operating the Elkhorn." Zahourek told us that Bud operated the Elkhorn "until he was able to sell in the late 1950s to a group of investors from Nebraska. Bud's history is interesting in that I think he was involved in the creation of the Boulderado Hotel in Boulder, Colorado, and then ended his career as the president of the Sheraton International Hotel Corporation. He was the logical one in the family group to get rid of the Elkhorn."

The Elkhorn Lodge Museum Program (Source No. 9) indicates that a "Mrs. James" was the member of the James family to whom Eleanor Hondius sold the Elkhorn Lodge. We concluded above that this "Mrs. James" was Edna B. Cobb Arnold James, the wife of Howard Perry James, Sr., and the mother of Bud James, whose "real" name was Howard Perry James, Jr. (Child No. 3.1 above).

Concerning the transfer of the Elkhorn from the James/Hondius family to "a group of investors from Nebraska," page 120 of Volume II of Harold Dunninng's *Over Hill and Vale* (Source No. 8) indicates that, in November 1959, after 82 years of belonging to the James/Hondius family, the Elkhorn Lodge passed to the ownership of the Elkhorn Corporation, which was a syndicate of several Lincoln, Nebraska, businessmen. The Elkhorn Corporation was headed by Robert C. Venner, a realtor and insurance man and president of the Lincoln School Board. The vice president was Edward Stovall, and the secretary/treasurer was Edward Weaver.

Dunning goes on to say that the last members of the James family to own Elkhorn Lodge—the family members from whom the Elkhorn Corporation purchased the Lodge—were Mr. and Mrs. Howard P. James, Jr. As noted above, Howard P. James, Jr., was known as "Bud." This the Bud James that Jerry Zahourek referred to above. Bud is the grandson of William Edwin and Ella McCabe James, the founders of Elkhorn Lodge. As of July 2001, he lived in Steamboat Springs, Colorado.

As of 15 September 2013, the following website provided additional information on the history of the Elkhorn Lodge: http://historicelkhornlodge.com.

The Ghosts of Elkhorn Lodge

Earlier we referred to the ghost stories told to us by Diane Gunderson and other employees of Elkhorn Lodge in 2001. Specifically, Diane also told us about the existence of a female ghost named "Eleanor" in Elkhorn Lodge's buildings. This female ghost is surely Eleanor Estes James Hondius, who lived at the Lodge as a child and both owned and managed it as an adult. (See Child No. 4 above under "William Edwin James, His Wife Ella McCabe James, and Their Descendants.")

When we mentioned these stories to Jerry Zabourek, he provided the following very interesting commentary:

> "I am not tuned in to the spiritual world and have never really experienced seeing a ghost. However, I have no doubt but that there are lots of spirits occupying the Elkhorn. We have had dozens of reports from folks of all kinds to the extent that even I, a stanch nonbeliever, have no doubt but that spirits exist and the Elkhorn is loaded with them. The most common report is a lady in a housecoat type of attire, but we have also had reports from folks about our restaurant being full of spirits having a real party, and all kinds of reports and experiences between these two extremes. The sources of these reports come from such a wide group of people having no knowledge whatsoever of the Elkhorn history that there can be no doubting that the Elkhorn spirit world is indeed healthy or we have a measurable portion of our general population independently having essentially the same hallucinations over an extended period of years."

LARIMER COUNTY CEMETERIES

Possible Occupants of the Elkhorn Lodge Cemetery

Unless we discover historical records that provide specific information concerning who is buried in the Elkhorn Lodge Cemetery, we can only surmise who might be buried there. From our search of cemeteries in Larimer County, the Longmont Mountain View Cemetery in Boulder County, and *Estes Park Trail* obituaries, we know that the following individuals are NOT buried in the Elkhorn Lodge Cemetery because they are buried in Mountain View:

- William Edwin James, Sr.
- Ella McCabe James
- William James (William Edwin's father)
- Ann James (William Edwin's mother)
- Charles James
- William ("Willie") Edwin James, Jr.
- Unnamed baby James
- Howard P. James
- Edna B. James (Howard's wife)
- Eleanor Edna James Hondius
- Peter (Pieter) Hondius, Sr. (Eleanor's husband)
- The first Peter Hondius, Jr. (Lived only a few days in April 1920)

Recall that his obituary in *Estes Park Trail* (Source No. 6) tells us that William Edwin's and Ella McCabe's one remaining child, Homer, was buried in California. Consequently, no members of the William Edwin James family are buried in the Elkhorn Lodge Cemetery.

The names or descriptions underlined below are individuals who thus might be buried in the Elkhorn Lodge Cemetery.

- Since Eleanor's brother Homer was a doctor and since, according to Eleanor, he continued to provide some medical services to the Estes Park community even after he left official medical practice in Alma, Colorado, the burials in the Elkhorn Lodge Cemetery could be <u>patients who died while under Homer James's care.</u>
- Similarly, with all of the <u>visitors and employees that Elkhorn Lodge had over the years,</u> it would be reasonable to expect that a few of them could have died while staying or working at the Lodge. This is the possibility favored by Jerry Zahourek.
- <u>Several of the U.S. Censuses cited above list employees and guests of the Elkhorn Lodge.</u> Whether any of the Lodge's employees or guests were actually buried in the Elkhorn Lodge Cemetery is, of course, another story.
- The fact that the child's or baby's grave shares a wall with the adult's grave makes one suspect that the individuals in the two graves were related. On the other hand, the baby could have been buried next to the adult's grave just to keep from having to erect a fourth wall for the baby's grave.

Catherine Maguire does not recall any burials at the Elkhorn Lodge during her family's time there (1913-1927). However, as she was only between 9 months and 5 or 6 years old during that period, her parents might not have made her aware of any Lodge-related deaths. Catherine started her marginal notes to us by saying: "Never heard of a cemetery in Estes. 'Nobody died' was the word of the natives in the 1920s."

JOEL ESTES MEMORIAL

Location: Latitude 40° 22' 24" N, Longitude 105° 29' 30" W

The Joel Estes Memorial is located on the southeast corner of U.S. Highway 36 and Fish Creek Road and south of the eastern portion of Lake Estes in Estes Park, Colorado. As far as we could determine, it is on the public right-a-way. The memorial marker was erected on the location of the Estes family's original homestead. (See "History of Joel Estes and Estes Family" and "History of Joel Estes Memorial" below.)

Photo A: Joel Estes Memorial at Intersection of U.S. 36 and Fish Creek Road in Estes Park

Description of Memorial

The memorial is a roughly cylindrical piece of red granite. The following text appears on a bronze plaque attached to the western face of the granite:

In Memory of
Joel Estes, Discover
1859   Oct. 15   1866
Pioneers
Patsy Estes Sarah Estes Mollie Estes
Milton Estes Joel Estes F. M. Estes J. W. Estes
———
Presented by
The Chamber of Commerce
and the Grand Children
Milton Estes   Joel S. Estes   Edwin Estes
Mrs. C. H. Graham   Mrs. W. I. Myler
Mrs. C. D. Taylor   Noma Ritters

The 15 October 1859 date on the memorial marker represents the day that Joel Estes and his son Milton first saw the Estes Park valley; the 1866 date represents the year that the family left Estes Park for Iowa and New Mexico.

Finding the Memorial Marker

On our many, many trips to Estes Park while conducting our census of graves and cemeteries in Larimer County, we had repeatedly noticed what appeared to be a historical or memorial marker on the southeast corner of U.S. Highway 36 and Fish Creek Road. Finally, on 20 October 2001, we stopped and discovered that the large stone we had noticed was a memorial to Joel Estes. We then took a GPS reading, made a note of the marker's text, and took the photograph above.

LARIMER COUNTY CEMETERIES

Sources of Information on Joel Estes and the Estes Family

1. *The Golden Pioneer*, written by Colleen Estes Cassell and published in 1999. (See the "Bibliography" for a complete citation.) Written by Joel Estes's great-great-granddaughter, *The Golden Pioneer* is the most complete history of Joel Estes and the Estes family that we found.

2. "*This Blue Hollow*," written by James H. Pickering and published in 1999. (See the "Bibliography" for a complete citation.) This very readable and information-packed book contains a number of references to Joel Estes and his family. See especially "Chapter 1: Loomings."

Copious amounts of information on Joel Estes and his family also appear in every history of Larimer County, Estes Park, and even Rocky Mountain National Park that we have encountered.

History of Joel Estes and the Estes Family

Given the large amount of information available of the Estes family, repeating the complete history of Joel and his family here is not necessary. Consequently, just a summary of their history as recounted in *The Golden Pioneer* and "*This Blue Hollow*" follows.

When Joel Estes was 20, he married Martha Ann "Patsy" Stollings. Joel and Patsy moved to a farm near St. Joseph, Missouri. Between 1828 and 1849, Joel and Patsy had 13 children.

In the spring of 1833, 27-year-old Joel Estes set out for the Rocky Mountains and Sante Fe from his farm near Independence, Missouri (Source No. 1), or Liberty, Clay County, Missouri (Source No. 2). He was accompanied by his 59-year old father Peter H. Estes and a group of traders, trappers, and adventurers. Some of the group mined for awhile near Santa Fe, where they had several uncomfortable run-ins with some of the Mexican inhabitants.

In the spring of 1834, they left the Santa Fe area for the "Arapahoe Bar" on Clear Creek about 2 miles east of present-day Golden, Colorado. They mined along the creek banks in the area until the spring thaw. They then worked their way north until the winter of 1834 found them at the foot of Laramie Peak in what was then referred to as the "Black Hills." Here they had their most successful mining of the trip.

Joel, his father, and some of the others returned to Missouri, where Joel worked as a freighter between Liberty and a trading post that later became St. Joseph, Missouri. This job kept him in touch with the mountain men and others who were heading west.

When gold was discovered in California in 1849, Joel and his oldest (21) son, Hardin, decided to try their luck in the gold fields of California. At that point, Joel and his family lived in Andrew County, Missouri. Before they left, Joel and Patsy's 15-year-old daughter Martha Ann ("Patsey") married 23-year-old Joseph Hiatt. Joseph then joined Joel and Hardin on their trip west.

Supposedly, the three relatives "struck it rich" in Grass Valley, California. They then sold their claim for $30,000 and returned to Missouri in 1850.

Joseph Hiatt used his share of the selling price plus the proceeds of 9 pounds of gold dust to buy a farm north of Sidney, Iowa, for himself, "Patsey," and their eventual 17 children.

Joel and Hardin used their profits from their California gold mine to do some "wheeling and dealing" in land and various businesses. In 1851 Hardin married Miss Mahalia Ring. According to *The Golden Pioneer*, Joel bought a "fine two story home," which is still standing, in Jackson Township of Andrew County, Missouri. "*This Blue Hollow*" places this home in Holt County in northwestern Missouri and says that Joel built it. Following the establishment of the Oregon Trail, in 1855 Joel and his son Hardin got the itch to travel again and went to Baker City, Oregon, where Joel's oldest daughter had moved in 1845 immediately after her marriage. Hardin liked the area so much that, after returning to Missouri with his father, he then moved his family to Baker City.

When gold was discovered in Colorado in 1858 near Cherry Creek, Joel and his wife Patsy, both 53 years old, still had six children living at home. With the talk of Civil War, which would have meant that two sons might be called on to fight; with his previous experience traveling west and mining; and with his seemingly endless case of wanderlust, in the spring of 1859 Joel took his remaining family with five wagons and a large herd of cattle and headed west. Three weeks later on 15 June 1859, they arrived at Auraria, Colorado, on Cherry Creek.

From then until the late summer, the family camped in the foothills near what is now Golden, Colorado. Joel used the time to take a look at the placer mining in the Clear Creek area. He evidently was not very impressed because he moved his family and cattle to a ranch on the Platte River in an area called Fort Lupton Bottom, near the present town of Platteville, Colorado. There the family ranched, cut "wild hay," and built two houses and corrals.

In the middle of October 1859 (October 15th according to the bronze plaque on the Joel Estes Memorial), Joel and his son 19-year-old son Milton followed the Little Thompson River into the mountains. When they got to the top of a ridge now known as Park Hill, they looked down into what is now the valley that holds the town of Estes Park. Milton later said that he and his father at first thought that they had found North Park, the only intramountain "park" that they knew about at that point. On page 1 of "*This Blue Hollow*," Jim Pickering provides his readers with Milton's reaction to viewing Estes Park for the first time taken from page 16 of the July 1939 issue of *Colorado Magazine* in an article by Milton Estes titled "Memoirs of Estes Park":

> "We stood on the mountain looking down . . .where the Park spread out before us. No words can describe our surprise, wonder and joy at beholding such an unexpected sight. It looked like a low valley with a silver streak or thread winding its way through the tall grass, down through the valley and disappearing around a hill among the pine trees. This silver thread was Big Thompson Creek [sic]. It was a grand sight and a great surprise.
>
> "We did not know what we had found . . .We were monarchs of all we surveyed, mountain, valleys and streams. There was absolutely nothing to dispute our sway. We had a little world all to ourselves."

After exploring the area and finding no signs of current or previous habitation by white settlers, Joel and his second youngest child, Francis Marion, camped in the park during the winter of 1859-1860 in a cabin they built on the north side of the Big Thompson River about half a mile west of the end of the river's canyon. They found the winter to be surprisingly (and, as they later found, untypically) mild.

In March 1860 Joel and his 12-year-old son, Joel Estes, Jr., went back to Missouri for more supplies and cattle. They were back in Estes Park by summer. Because of the mildness of the preceding winter, Joel figured he could stay there over the winter, making a living by raising cattle, hunting, and fishing. He and one or more sons built two log houses and some corrals on what is now lower Fish Creek. (The Joel Estes Memorial marks this location.) According to page 10 of "*This Blue Hollow*," Joel and son(s) then "brought in whatever household goods [that] could be packed on animals, and then drove up cattle from their claim on the Platte, fencing the trail at the entrance to the park to prevent the animals from returning to the valley."

LARIMER COUNTY CEMETERIES

With the Civil War looming, Joel returned to Missouri in 1861 to settle his affairs there. During the winter of 1861-1862, he was again in the park minding his cattle. By 1863, he was convinced that he could really make a go of raising cattle in the park, so he moved his family from the family's ranch in Fort Lupton Bottom to his Estes Park ranch. Again, according to page 10 of "*This Blue Hollow*," the Estes family members who moved to Estes Park in 1863 included: Joel; his wife, Patsy; Wesley Jasper, 26; Milton, 23; Francis Marion, 17; Joel Jr., 15; Sarah, 21; Milton's wife, Mary Louise; and Milton and Mary's two sons Newton and George. Later, on 19 February 1865, Milton and Mary's third son, Charles F. Estes, was born, making him the first white child born in Estes Park.

The family had Estes Park to themselves for 3 years. They found the hunting of deer, elk, and mountain sheep excellent and were able to sell in Denver the skins and hindquarters of many of the animals they shot in Estes Park. Fish were also plentiful. To get their cattle and game products to market, the family built and then maintained a cart road, which was an extension of a "wood road" built by early settlers of the foothills and plains to harvest the wood they needed for builds, fence posts, and firewood.

According to page 11 of "*This Blue Hollow*," the "Estes road," which was never much more than a trail for pack animals, "entered the mountains about halfway between the St. Vrain and Little Thompson and followed the Little Thompson up through the foothills, staying whenever possible close to the mountainsides." Then, once it reached what is now Pinewood Springs, the road/trail "passed down a steep draw to the Little Thompson and then up and over a ridge to Muggins Gulch."

Joel hired help when he needed it, and visitors in search of game, gold, or "just" scenery showed up from time to time. So the Estes family was not alone in Estes Park. One of those whom Joel hired was Dunham Wright, who spent the winters of 1860-61 and 1861-1862 with the family. In a letter dated 2 September 1920 and quoted on page 12 of "*This Blue Hollow*," Dunham provides the following description of Joel Estes: "Mr. Estes was a typical frontiersman of the Daniel Boone style. A generous, kindhearted, good natured man. To know him was to admire him. . . ."

The land on which the Estes family settled in Estes Park had never been surveyed, so they had little more than squatter's rights to it. On 15 April 1866, the family left the area, never to return. Wesley Jasper, Francis Marion, and Sarah went east to Iowa. Already 60 years old, Joel and Patsy, Joel Jr., and Milton and his family moved to New Mexico. (For details on what happened to the family after that, see Note 32 on page 247 of "*This Blue Hollow*.")

According to Note 32, Joel died 31 December 1875 at the age of 69 while he and Patsy were staying with their by-then-married son Joel Jr. in Farmington, New Mexico. Patsy then went to live with her daughter Sarah in Sidney, Iowa, where she died on 6 August 1882 at the age of 76. Joel's burial place is unknown. Patsy is buried in the town cemetery of Sidney, Iowa.

As Jim Pickering points out on page 15 of "*This Blue Hollow*," the Estes family established a pattern—making a living from ranching, hunting, and providing hospitality to tourists—that was followed by many other of the pioneer families in the Estes Park area. Just three examples include the William E. James family, who founded Elkhorn Lodge; the John Hupp family; and the Alexander Q. MacGregor family. (For information on these families, see the chapters on the Elkhorn Lodge Cemetery, Hupp Family Cemetery, and MacGregor Family Cemetery.)

History of the Joel Estes Memorial

A complete history of the Joel Estes Memorial and the 1927 Estes Family Reunion during which the memorial marker was dedicated can be found in "Chapter 7: Remembering Joel; The Monument, The 1927 Reunion" in *The Golden Pioneer* (Source No. 1). A photo of the family members present at the reunion gathered around the memorial can be found on page 101 of Chapter 7.

The unveiling of the Joel Estes Memorial was evidently the highlight of Estes Park's 1927 Fourth of July celebration, which was labeled "Estes Park Pioneer Day." The memorial's unveiling and dedication occurred following the obligatory Fourth of July parade, which ended at the site of the Estes family's original Estes Park homestead, "where a program of music and speeches were [sic] given."

Two of the speakers were descendants of Joel and Patsy Estes: Judge Joel E. Estes, who was Chief Justice of the Oklahoma Supreme Court, and Harry Ruffner of Denver. Judge Estes was the son of Francis Marion, one of Joel and Patsy's sons who accompanied them during their sojourn in Estes Park. Harry was the "son of Mary Jane." We assume that she was one of Joel and Patsy's 13 children.

As the photo on page 101 of Chapter 7 of *The Golden Pioneer* makes clear, a significant number of the descendants of Joel and Patsy Estes were present for the memorial's dedication on 4 July 1927. Remarkably, when the Estes family held its second reunion 54 years later in 1981, 177 of their descendants attended!

ESTES VALLEY MEMORIAL GARDENS

Location: Latitude 40° 23′ 53″ N, Longitude 105° 34′ 50″ W

The Estes Valley Memorial Gardens is at 1672 Fish Hatchery Road in Estes Park. To reach Fish Hatchery Road, take U.S. Highway 34 about 3 miles west of Estes Park and look for the green road sign at the Fish Hatchery Road exit directing you to a "Cemetery." The cemetery is on the south side of Fish Hatchery Road.

Description

The Estes Valley Memorial Gardens is a "typical" cemetery with the exception that a higher than usual percentage of its graves contain burials of cremains under the headstones rather than the more typical burials of bodies in front of the headstones.

Finding the Cemetery

The list of cemeteries and graves in Larimer County in the 1985 edition of the Colorado Council of Genealogical Societies' *Colorado Cemetery Directory* does NOT include any mention of the Estes Valley Memorial Gardens, and none of our Estes Park acquaintances told us about it. We found it just by chance when we noticed the sign on U.S. Highway 34 pointing toward a "Cemetery" if we took the Fish Hatchery Road exit.

Since the 1985 edition of the *Colorado Cemetery Directory* does not mention the Estes Valley Memorial Gardens, we assume that it came into existence after 1985.

Photo A: Estes Valley Memorial Gardens West of Estes Park Off U.S. Highway 34

F.H.R. CEMETERY

Location: Latitude 40° 21' 19" N, Longitude 105° 30' 25" W

The F.H.R. Cemetery is on private property behind and just west of the detached garage/workshop of the home belonging to Scott and Keelee Doan at 1555 South St. Vrain Avenue (Colorado Highway 7 or Peak-to-Peak Highway) near the southern edge of Estes Park. The Doans' home and the cemetery are behind (north) of the church belonging to the Mountain View Bible Fellowship. Indeed, the only way to reach the Doans' home is to drive through the parking lot of the Mountain View Bible Fellowship.

Description of Graves in the F.H.R. Cemetery

The F.H.R. Cemetery contains two graves. Our use of dowser rods indicated that both graves contain burials of babies or young children.

The grave shown in Photo A is covered by a 51 inch by 51 inch cement slab with a cross in the center of the slab and the initials "F.H.R." below the cross. The cross appears to have been made by pressing an actual cross, probably made of iron or some other metal, into the wet cement. The person who took us to this grave, Truman Nicholas, was told by Glen Manske, the person who told him about the grave, that when he first saw the grave, the "notches" in each corner of the slab held posts that supported a small a chain, thus creating a sort of fence around the grave. (For more about Truman and Glen, see "Finding the Cemetery" below.)

Photo A: F.H.R Grave Behind the Mountain View Bible Fellowship in South Estes Park

The grave shown in Photo B is about 9 feet southeast of the F.H.R. grave. This child-size grave is covered by an oval pile of local stones. Notice the F.H.R. grave in the background.

Photo B: Oval, Stone-Covered Grave 9 Feet Southeast of F.H.R. Grave

LARIMER COUNTY CEMETERIES

Finding the Cemetery

We were told about the F.H.R grave by Truman L. Nicholas, whom we first met in on 1 August 2001 when we made a presentation on our grave-search efforts in Larimer County to the Estes Park Genealogical Society, of which Truman is a member. (For more information on all of the help that Truman provided to our grave-search efforts, see the "Acknowledgments" section.) As noted above, Truman learned about the F.H.R. grave from Glen Manske, who used to do excavation work in the Estes Park area and who noticed the F.H.R. grave when he was excavating nearby.

Truman first visited the F.H.R. grave with his wife Beverly in early October 2004 right before they left for their winter home in Arizona. After several unsuccessful efforts to get together once the Nicholases returned to Estes Park for the summer of 2005, on 14 July 2005, Truman and Beverly took us to see the F.H.R. grave. We arrived there right behind the owner Keelee Doan, who had just come home for lunch from her job as the Restaurant and Group Sales Manager at the historic Crags Lodge.

Accompanied by Keelee and several of her children, who were also home for lunch, we went to visit the F.H.R. grave (Photo A above). Because of our, by then, 6 years of experience finding remote graves in Larimer County, we immediately realized that the "pile of rocks" just 9 feet southeast of the F.H.R. grave was probably another grave, which, as noted above, our use of dowser rods indicated it indeed was. See Photo B above. We decided to name the small cemetery the "F.H.R. Cemetery" for the only identification on either of its two graves.

History of Property Containing the F.H.R. Cemetery

In an email dated 9 October 2004, Truman Nicholas told us that earlier that month he had contacted a past pastor of the Mountain View Bible Fellowship, Mr. Tom Weitzel, and the church's historian, Mrs. Joyce Bennett, to see if either of them knew anything about the two graves in the F.H.R. Cemetery and if the church had ever owned the property on which the cemetery is located. Neither of these two individuals knew anything about the two graves or about the church's ever having owned the land on which the graves are located.

The Doans told us that we and the Nicholases were not the first people to have asked for permission to visit the F.H.R. grave. They recall that someone who used to live in the area told them that the F.H.R. grave was the cremation burial of "an older preacher" from the church. Surely, if this were true, one would think that Tom Weitzel and/or Joyce Bennett would have known about it.

As we have noted in situations when urns of ashes are buried in regular cemeteries (the Estes Valley Memorial Gardens, for example) or in columbariums (the Poudre Canyon Chapel Columbarium, for example), dowser rods can detect such ash burials if they are directly over the buried ashes. However, the rods indicate that the ash burial sites are considerable smaller than the burial sites of even a baby. As noted above, our use of dowser rods on the two graves in the F.H.R. Cemetery indicated that the burial sites are large enough to be babies or younger children and are, thus, probably not cremain burials.

Immediately after our visit to what we named the "F.H.R. Cemetery," we contacted Sybil Barnes, then the Local History Librarian of the Estes Park Public Library, to see if she could help us answer several questions that might lead to the names of the children buried in the F.H.R. Cemetery or, at least, to the name(s) of their possible parents. (For information on all of the help that Sybil provided to our grave-search efforts, see the "Acknowledgments" section.) Our questions to Sybil and the answers Sybil kindly provided follow:

- When was the church of the Mountain View Bible Fellowship built? Sybil believes that it was built in the in the late 1970s or early 1980s.

- When was cement first used in Estes Park? About 1905.

   Thus, at least the marking of the F.H.R. grave with a cement slab and probably also the burial itself would have taken place on or after 1905.

- Any ideas about when the house at 1555 South St. Vrain Avenue was built? Sybil thinks that it was probably the only building in the area from about 1911 through 1950s. At one time, much of the surrounding area belonged to the old Venner Ranch.

During the last week of February 2006, we spent several hours going through microfilm of the 1910 and 1920 U.S. Censuses for Estes Park looking for families whose last name started with *R* who might have lived in the general vicinity of the Doans' home at 1555 South St. Vrain Avenue and who thus might have been the parents of the child buried in the F.H.R. grave (and possibly of the child buried in the second grave as well). We picked the 1910 and 1920 Censuses because they were the first two censuses after 1905, the date at which cement began to be used in the Estes Park area. The only people who appeared to live the closest to what is now South St. Vrain Avenue were single men. We have kept the information we gathered on the "R" families and individuals in case we later learn that one of them actually was associated in some way with the F.H.R. child.

In an email dated 1 March 2006, Keelee Doan agreed to try to find the title search that was done when they bought their home in 1988. Since the title search should show the owners of her property from the first homesteader on, our and her hope was that the title search might give us a clue as to the name(s) of the parents of the children buried in the F.H.R. Cemetery.

In emails from Keelee dated 3 March, 4 March, and 7 March 2006, she told us that they actually moved into their house in January 1989 and that the house had been empty for 3 years before they bought it.

In those same emails, Keelee also told us that the church was there when they moved in in January 1989 but that it had a different name. However, the church there in 1989 and the church there now (the Mountain View Bible Fellowship) are both of the Baptist denomination. In 1989, the Doans did not share a driveway with the church but instead drove straight in from South St. Vrain Avenue. When the church paved its parking lot, it gave the Doans a new easement, their current one, which gives them access to their property through the church's parking lot.

In her 3 March 2006 email, Keelee said that it was her understanding "that at one point the person who owned that house [the house the Doans currently live in] owned all the land where the church sits, maybe even more."

In the end, she was unable to find the title search done on their property.

On 8 May 2006, we did an online search (www.glorecords.blm.gov) of the Bureau of Land Management's General Land Office Records to see if we could find anyone with a last name starting with *R* who had received a land patent on land in the vicinity of the Doan's home and the F.H.R. Cemetery. The search provided a number of names, but, unfortunately, none of them started with an *R*! On 8 December 2006, we visited the Local History Section of the Estes Park Public Library and went through their card file index of last names and other subjects mentioned in Estes Park newspapers and in the Library's lateral files containing pamphlets, transcriptions of interviews, etc., to see if we could find any information on anyone with the initials of "F. R." or "F.H.R." who might be the F.H.R. buried on the Doans' property on the west side of South St. Vrain Avenue. We did not find anyone.

Thus, we have not been able to determine the names of the babies or young children buried in the F.H.R. Cemetery.

LARIMER COUNTY CEMETERIES

CARRIE CASSEDY FULLER GRAVE

Locations: Ashes Burial: Latitude 40° 19' 42" N, Longitude 105° 41' 11" W
Memorial Plaque: Latitude 40° 21' 52" N, Longitude 105° 29' 33" W

The ashes of Carrie Cassedy Fuller were buried on or to the rear of a large boulder at the head of the small meadow at the southwesterly end of Odessa Lake in Rocky Mountain National Park. The boulder is about 300 feet from the lake. Originally, the gray-granite plaque shown in Photo F below was attached to the boulder. The plaque is no longer there; instead it is on private property east of Fish Creek Road that, as of September 2009, belonged to the Saurino family. See "Finding Carrie Cassedy Fuller's Plaque" below.

Records in the Library of the Rocky Mountain National Park contain copies of photographs taken of Carrie Fuller's ash burial by Chief Ranger J. Barton Herschler between 30 July and 1 August 1944 of:

1. The boulder with the plaque still attached to it.

2. The west end of Odessa Lake with an arrow pointing to the plaque and a dashed line showing the foot trail at that end of the lake.

3. The top of the boulder on which the plaque was located. The top arrow on the photo points to the location of the plaque on the opposite side of the boulder, and a side arrow points to the place on the boulder where the earth had recently been disturbed at the time the photo was taken and where Ranger Herschler surmised that the burial of Carrie Fuller's ashes may have taken place.

4. Odessa Lake taken from the top of the boulder looking in a northeasterly direction across the meadow and toward the far end of Odessa Lake.

5. The southwest end of Odessa Lake taken from near the northeast corner of the lake with an arrow pointing to the rock on which the plaque was attached.

We have xerographic copies of these photographs, but they are not suitable for inclusion in this book. However, as pointed out above, the Park's Library contains the "original" copies of these photos. Our copies and all of our background information on this grave can be found in the Local History Archive of the Fort Collins Museum of Discovery, to which we have donated all of our research materials for this project.

Finding the Location Where Carrie Cassedy Fuller's Ashes Were Buried

Fortunately for this record, on 1 July 2001, we visited the Aspenglen Campground in Rocky Mountain National Park to look for the grave of a 3-year-old child with the initials "F.A.J." who may have been buried there in 1886. (For information on the graves that we found in the campground, see the chapter on the "Aspenglen Campground Cemetery.") While we were there, we met Ira Goldfarb, then a first-year Ranger working at Aspenglen Campground. Ira became interested in our efforts to document the graves, cemeteries, and memorials in the Park. Later that summer, he and his then fiancée and now his wife, Joan Feder, took our copies of Ranger Herschler's photos and his written report with them and hiked to Odessa Lake to try to find the exact location where Carrie Cassedy Fuller's ashes were buried. As the following photos show, they succeeded. Photos A through E below were taken by Ira and Joan during their summer 2001 visit to the location where Carrie's ashes had been buried in 1944.

Photo A below shows approximately the same location as Ranger Hershler's Photo 1 above, except the photo taken by Ira and Joan shows the bolt holes in the rock where the plaque had been before it was removed. (See "History of Carrie Fuller, Her Death, Burial, and Memorial Plaque" below for an explanation of why the plaque was removed.) The arrows in the photo point to the bolt holes.

Photo A: Holes in Boulder Showing the Original Location of the Plaque Marking the Location Where Carrie Cassedy Fuller's Ashes Had Been Buried. Arrows Show the Bolt Holes.

Ira and Joan took Photo B below, a "duplicate" of Ranger Herschler's Photo 2, while looking southwest from the south end of Odessa Lake. It shows the general vicinity of the area containing the boulder on which Carrie's ashes were buried. An arrow points to the exact boulder containing the bolt holes, the same boulder on which Ranger Herschler surmised Carrie's ashes had been buried.

Photo B: View From South End of Odessa Lake Looking Southwest Toward Boulder on Which Carrie Cassedy Fuller's Ashes Had Been Buried

Photo C, a "duplicate of Ranger Herschler's Photo 3, shows the location where Ranger Herschler surmised that Carrie's ashes had been buried because "the earth had been recently disturbed."

Photo C: Top of Boulder Showing Location Where Ranger Herschler Surmised That Carrie Cassedy Fuller's Ashes Had Been Buried

Photo D is a "duplicate" of Ranger Herschler's Photo 4. Ira and Joan took it while standing on the boulder with the bolt holes and looking in a northeasterly direction across the meadow and toward the far end of Odessa Lake.

Photo D: Looking Northeast From Boulder With Bolt Holes Toward the Far End of Odessa Lake

Photo E is a "duplicate" of Ranger Herschler's Photo 5. Ira and Joan took is from the northeast corner of Odessa Lake looking southwest toward the end of the lake where the boulder with the bolt holes is located.

Photo E: Looking From Northeast Corner of Odessa Lake Southwest Toward Boulder With Bolt Holes

(For information on the other graves in the Park with which Ira and Joan provided assistance, see "Goldfarb, Ira and Joan Feder" in the "Acknowledgments" section.)

Finding Carrie Cassedy Fuller's Plaque

As per Ranger Herschler's report on finding the site where Carrie's ashes were buried, the plaque found near the burial site read:

Carrie Cassedy Fuller
1881-1943
Her sweet spirit rests in
these her native peaks.

Ranger Herschler also reported that the gray-granite plaque containing the above inscription was about 10.25 inches wide, 18 inches long, and 1.75 inches thick.

The "History of of Carrie Fuller, Her Death, Burial, and Memorial Plaque" below for an explanation of why the plaque was removed from the site where Carrie's ashes were buried. Since the plaque was no longer at the burial site, that left us with the desire to locate Carrie's plaque.

During our research, we came across page 317 of Volume III of *Over Hill and Vale; History of Northern Colorado* written by Harold Marion Dunning and published in 1971, which reported that Carrie's gray-granite plaque "now rests high up on a big section of rocks to the north and east of the Dunraven home on Fish Creek." After quoting the inscription on Carrie's plaque, Dunning goes on to say that "there is a ponderosa pine similar to the one that used to be on the High Drive Road over the plaque. Who knows this history of this lady?"

When we gave a presentation on our Larimer County grave search to the Estes Park Genealogical Society on 8 August 2001, we passed out a list of questions that we had concerning Estes Park area graves and their history. One of our questions was if anyone knew the current location of Carrie's plaque. Larry Carpenter, then the Secretary of the Estes Park Genealogical Society, took up the challenge and contacted a friend who was a long-time resident of the Fish Creek area of Estes Park and who, as a young girl, had ridden horse back all over the area. Fortunately, she had encountered the plaque on one of her childhood rides and remembered where it was. She returned to the site to confirm that the plaque was still there and then reported to Larry that the plaque was on property belonging to Judy Saurino at 890 Fish Creek Road. Larry contacted us with his good news.

(For information on other assistance that Larry gave to our grave-search efforts, see "Carpenter, Larry E." in the "Acknowledgments" section.)

We immediately contacted Judy. She said that her children had found the plaque on the Saurinos' property years before and had always wondered who Carrie Cassedy Fuller was and if her ashes had been scattered or buried near the plaque. Judy kindly agreed to show us the plaque. So, on Saturday morning 6 October 2001, we met Judy at her home, and she took us on a brief hike and short climb to view the plaque.

The plaque is located on the top of a boulder outcrop about 100 feet north of Judy's home and a little north and west of a children's playhouse behind the main house. Our dowser rods confirmed that there were not any ashes buried at the site, which agrees with the history information provided below.

The photograph below shows Carrie's plaque in its final resting place on the Saurinos' property.

Note that the inscription on the plaque exactly matches the inscription reported by Ranger Herschler when he saw the plaque in its original location.

Photo F: The Final Resting Place of Carrie's Plaque

History of Carrie Fuller, Her Death, Burial, and Memorial Plaque

The 17 December 1943 issue of *Estes Park Trail* contained the following obituary for Carrie Fuller:

> "Carrie C. Fuller died suddenly in Pittsburg on Monday, November 6. Born in Canon City, married Samuel Leslie Fuller. Surviving children: Mrs. Will H. Shove, Miss Caroline S. Fuller, Mr. Sam Fuller, Jr."

According to a summary (in RMNP File No. 608, "Memorials") of the Park's information concerning the burial of Carrie Fuller's ashes and the disposition of the plaque that originally marked the site:

> "On the afternoon of July 30, 1944, J. Barton Herschler, Chief Ranger, Rocky Mountain National Park, received a report that the remains of a person had been buried near Odessa Lake and that the personnel of Stead's Ranch had been involved. Mr. Herschler called on Mr. Will Lewis, proprietor, of Stead's

Ranch and Mr. Phil Jenkins, the wrangler, but both denied any knowledge of the incident.

"Having heard that the family of the deceased had spent several summers at Fall River Lodge, Mr. Herschler interviewed Mr. and Mrs. McKelvey. They told him that Mr. and Mrs. S. L. Fuller of Pittsburg, Pennsylvania, had indeed spent a number of summers with them—during which time they had become quite friendly with Phil Jenkins, formerly the wrangler at the Fall River Lodge. Mr. Fuller had made reservations for himself and two daughters at the Lodge for June 12 [1944], but had without explanation canceled their reservations and went instead to Stead's Ranch."

Ranger Herschler then visited the site where Carrie Fuller's ashes were buried, took the photos described above below the "Locations" heading, and provided the location information also noted above.

The summary then goes on to state:

"The National Park Service was obviously reluctant to enter into this delicate matter and nothing was done immediately. U.S. Commissioner Wayne Hackett was apparently asked to search for regulations relating to this sort of thing and, judging from the tenuous connection of the quoted regulations to a human burial, found the regulations embarrassingly vague on this subject.

"On August 23 [1944], Ranger Allan Hartong went to Odessa Lake to clean up the area and, having heard the story of the burial, searched for the site. He found the boulder, but the plaque had been removed by persons unknown. Herschler guessed that Phil Jenkins had removed it and perhaps installed it in a less conspicuous location.

"When Regional Director Merriam, Supt. Dorr, and two other members of the staff inspected the site on October 18 [1944], Dorr found the plaque, which had been tossed into the shallow water near the Odessa Lake inlet. Supt. Dorr wrote to Mr. Fuller on October 25 mentioning 'regulations concerning the erection of monuments in National Park Service areas' but emphasizing the vandalizing of the plaque and its recovery by the Service."

Sometime in 1999 or 2000, Dr. D. Ferrel Atkins, a volunteer ranger and unofficial Park historian, met with John Drake, a former wrangler at Stead's Ranch. Recall that, back in 1944, Chief Ranger Herschler had guessed that Phil Jenkins, another wrangler at Stead's Ranch, might have been the one that removed Carrie's plaque from the boulder and placed it in Odessa Lake. When Ferrel talked to John, John said that he had indeed removed the plaque from the boulder, but that he buried it in the sand on the shore of Odessa Lake. He does not know how it ended up in the shallow water near the Odessa Lake inlet.

(For more information on Ferrel Atkins and the considerable assistance he provided to our grave-search efforts in Rocky Mountain National Park, see "Atkins, D. Ferrel" in the "Acknowledgments" section.)

LARIMER COUNTY CEMETERIES

GASKILL CEMETERY

Locations: Graves 1-4: Latitude 40° 19' 46" N, Longitude 105° 51' 59' W
　　　　　　 Grave 5: Latitude 40° 19' 49" N, Longitude 105° 52' 00" W

　　The Gaskill Cemetery is in the ghost town of Gaskill, which is located on the west side of Rocky Mountain National Park in Grand County. (See "History of Town of Gaskill" below.) Gaskill is on the west side of Trail Ridge Road about 8 miles northwest of Grand Lake, just south/southwest of Gaskill Creek, and at the mouth of Bowen Gulch. It is accessible via a private, locked road or by hiking on the Bowen Gulch Trail through Park property.

　　The map of "The Town of Gaskill" on the next page was created by John Gubbins in July 1986 as part of his research on old mining towns and mines in Grand County. John reported that following his retirement at the end of September 2013, he was going to concentrate on getting the book encompassing his research published. The map is used with John's permission. When John created this map, the only graves that he knew about in the area encompassed by the map were the graves Thomas Booth and Jack Williams. At John's suggestion, in April 2005 we added to his original map the two children's graves, even though they were not discovered until September 2001, and the "Indian grave," which was also discovered after July 1986.

　　For an explanation of the lettered items in John's "The Town of Gaskill" map, which are building sites, see the Appendix to this chapter. (For more information on John Gubbins, see "Gubbins, John" in the "Acknowledgments" section.)

　　Since the cemetery itself is in Rocky Mountain National Park, you can hike to it if you avoid private property. However, to access it via road, you would need the permission of the Park in-holders who own the private road.

Cemetery Description

　　As indicated by the two GPS readings given under "Locations" above, the Gaskill Cemetery is more of a collection of graves than a typical cemetery. It certainly was never a "formal" cemetery like the nearby Grand Lake Cemetery. The Gaskill Cemetery includes the following five graves:

　　Graves 1 and 2: Local history indicates that these are the graves of Thomas Booth and Jack Williams (Photo A), killed in the snowslide at the Toponis Mine in February 1883. These two graves are the east-most graves (farthest east of Site D) on John Gubbins's map on the next page. (For information on the deaths and burial of these two men, see "Toponis Mine Snowslide" in the chapter on the Grand Lake Cemetery.) When John took us to the Gaskill Cemetery, he told us a story that was passed on to him by Patience Kemp, the daughter of Mary Lyons Cairns, the author of *Grand Lake in the Olden Days* (more about which below under "Sources of Information on the Town of Gaskill").

　　According to Patience, when her mother was collecting information for her book, she received a visit from the son of Joseph Rogerson. (Joseph was the owner of The Rogerson House, a well-known Gaskill hotel.) Joseph's son told Mary that, when he was about 10 years old, Gaskill was visited by either a doctor or a medical student. (Patience could not recall which.) That individual told the boy that he would pay him $10 if he would dig up the grave of one of the Toponis miners, remove the body, and strip the flesh from the bones to yield a medical skeleton, which the boy (as a adult) claimed that he did. Patience said that her mother was so upset by the story that she asked the by-then elderly gentleman to leave immediately and did not include the story in *Grand Lake in the Olden Days*. John pointed out that one of the two graves of the Toponis miners does look like it was indeed disturbed.

Suffice it to say, Subsection (b) of Section 18-9-113 of the Colorado Criminal Code states that "a person commits a class 1 misdemeanor if he knowingly desecrates any place or worship or burial of human remains." Consequently, damaging a headstone, removing a headstone, and, most certainly, removing human remains from a cemetery or a single burial are all definitely illegal, not to mention unethical!

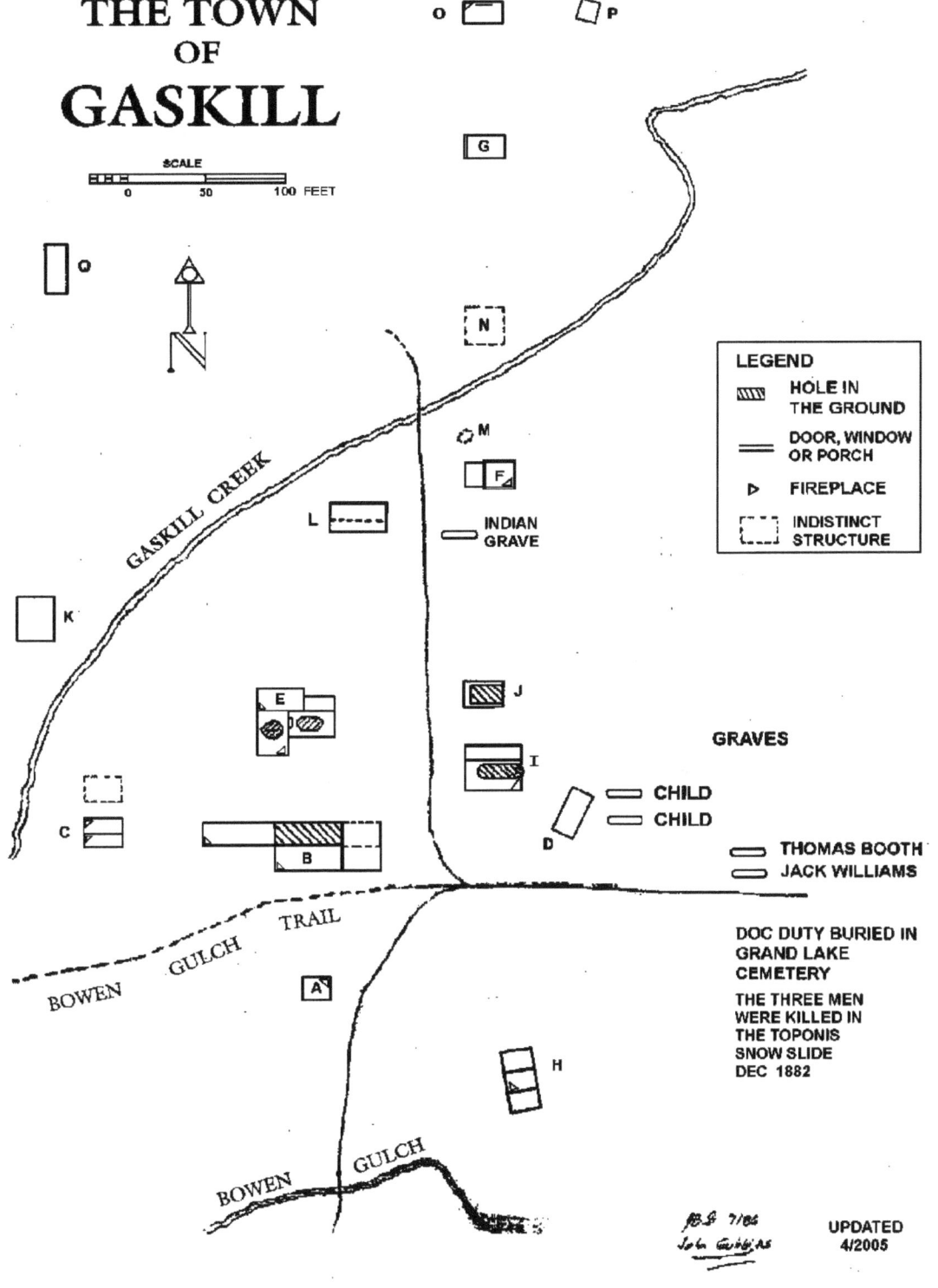

Photo A: Graves 1 and 2 in the Gaskill Cemetery, the Graves of Thomas Booth and Jack Williams

Graves 3 and 4: As the map on the preceding page shows, these two graves are just east of Site **D**, which puts them a little to the north and west of the graves of Thomas Booth and Jack Williams. Dowser rods indicated that children are buried in Graves 3 and 4 (Photo B).

Photo B: Graves 3 and 4 in the Gaskill Cemetery, the Graves of Two Children

Grave 5: This grave (Photo C) is by itself in the forest about 200-300 feet north of the other four graves and just southwest of Site **F** on John's map. John told us he was the one who first concluded that mound of rocks at the site must be a grave. John then showed the site to Bill Butler, a Rocky Mountain National Park archaeologist, who identified the collection of rocks as a grave of a Native American. Indeed, the grave is covered with a mound of rocks and is in an east-west orientation as are a number of graves in contiguous Larimer County that are also probable Native American graves.

Photo C: Native American Grave in Gaskill

Finding the Cemetery

John Gubbins took us to the Gaskill Cemetery on 14 September 2001. He knew about the cemetery, the old ghost town of Gaskill, and their history because Gaskill is near John's family's summer home on the west side of Rocky Mountain National Park. (For information on the other graves and cemeteries that John helped us find in Grand County, see "Gubbins, John" in the "Acknowledgments" section.)

Sources of Information on the Town of Gaskill

1. Information on Joseph Rogerson, *The Prospector*, 14 February 1884.
2. Information on the Grand Lake Mining and Smelting Company, *The Georgetwon Miner*, 27 March 1884.
3. Information on Colorado's oldest billard table, *The Prospector*, 14 February 1885.
4. *Grand Lake in the Olden Days*, written by Mary Lyons Cairns and published in 1971. (See the "Bibliography" for a complete citation.) Pages 149-152 provide a brief history of the town of Gaskill.
5. Information on Gaskill from www.geocities.com/Heartland/Ranch/7638/gtowns.htm as of 1 April 2005.

History of the Town of Gaskill

On page 149 of Source No. 4, Mary Cairns says that "nothing remains of Gaskill today"; however, when John Gubbins took us there on 14 September 2001, he showed us one old log building that was still standing. He also showed us the remains of the wine cellar that Mary Cairns describes on page 151 of Source No. 4 as being the wine cellar of one of the town's saloons. John had been told that the old wine cellar had belonged to a Gaskill hotel, most likely The Rogerson House (more about which below), and that it once held the largest collection of wine west of the Mississippi. (See Site **B** on John Gubbins' map above for the probable location of The Rogerson House and "Site B" in the Appendix to this chapter for information about the ruins of what may have been this hotel.)

Mary Cairns reported that the *Colorado Business Directory of 1884* provided the following information on Gaskill:

> "Gaskill. Also known as Auburn, a village on the North Fork of the Grand River [the original name of the Colorado River], 112 miles northwest of Denver, 8 miles northwest of Grand Lake, the County Seat, and 65 miles northwest of Georgetown, the nearest railroad station and banking point. Settled in 1880. The shipments comprise gold, silver, and lead ore. Stages to Georgetown and Hot Sulphur Springs."

The *Directory* went on to list the facilities of Gaskill, which included a store, a hotel, a restaurant, a mining and smelting company, a mining expert, and a mine superintendent.

The town was named for Captain L.D.C. Gaskill, who was the manager of the Wolverine Mine at the time the mining town came into being.

The Rogerson House mentioned above was owned by Joseph Rogerson of Greeley, Colorado. An item in the 14 February 1884 issue of *The Prospector* (Source No. 1), Grand Lake's newspaper, indicated that Joseph was coming to Gaskill to build his hotel, so the hotel came into existence about 4 years after the town was "founded."

The Wolverine Mine was owned by the Grand Lake Mining and Milling Company Another mining company in the area was the Pioneers' Mining Company.

The 27 March 1884 issue of *The Georgetown Miner* (Source No. 2) provided the following information on the Grand Lake Mining and Milling Company:

> "We learn, from reliable authority, that the Grand Lake Mining and Milling Company of Chicago and Quincy, Illinois, has bought a large mill, to be put in at Gaskill. This company owns the Wolverine, one of the best developed mines in the state, and also one of the most valuable. There is now something over two thousand tons of ore on the dump that will millrun about 100 ounces to the ton. No stoping has yet been done, and in one place in the mine, where the main shaft was sunk to connect the lower and upper levels, a body of ore 30 feet in width was cut. The advent of this mill will insure the working of a great many mines now lying idle for want of a mill on the ground to treat their ores."

John Gubbins told us that the mines in the Gaskill area were economically productive longer than the mines in the area of Lulu City, so the town itself also lasted longer, with Gaskill lasting from 1880 to 1886 and Lulu City being a viable town from only 1879 to 1883. (For information on Lulu City, see the chapter on the Lulu City Graves.)

Gaskill must have been in its death throes, at least as a town, by 14 February 1885, when the following item appeared in an issue of *The Prospector* (Source No. 3):

> "The State Historical Society should purchase the billiard table, now the property of Mowry Bros. of Gaskill. It was the first billiard table ever brought to Colorado. It was first the property of Central City parties, and was then moved to Georgetown. In 1881 J. F. Buxton purchased it from Thomas Barnes and brought it to Grand Lake where it remained until last summer, when it was taken to Gaskill, having been purchased by Mowry Bros."

We checked the Internet for "Gaskill Ghost Town" to try and find more information on the "end date" for Gaskill. On 1 April 2005, in the entry for Gaskill at www.geocities.com/Heartland/Ranch/7638/gtowns.htm (Source No. 5), we learned that "by 1885 the town was already dying. It had a post office from 1880 to 1886."

Appendix: Explanation of Lettered Building Sites in John Gubbins's Map of the "Town of Gaskill"

This Appendix contains John Gubbins's explanations of the lettered building sites on the map of "The Town of Gaskill," which he created in July 1986 and which we updated in April 2005 with John's permission. See the second page of this chapter for a copy of this map. The site explanations below are preceded by John's general discussion of Gaskill.

"The site of Gaskill is at the mouth of Bowen Gulch. Upon first glance, especially to the uninitiated, Gaskill is nothing but holes in a grassy glen. Perhaps the casual visitor will find a bottle shard or a rusty can. If he looks closer, a shrunken leather shoe sole may be seen.

"Actually, there is quite a lot to be seen in Gaskill. With the aid of the map and this guide, the visitor will be able to find the better building sites, and perhaps find others that are not included here. The historical record of the actual layout of Gaskill other than the platting is extremely sparse. Lulu City had photographs and drawings made of it, but none were made of Gaskill. Below are brief descriptions of the sites and what they may have been."

Site A: "A is a square of raised ground. It sits in a bunch of trees. There is a depression in the center that is full of trash thrown in there for years by the Bowker Club."

In an email that we received from John on 26 March 2005, he told us that there is a "road" running between Sites A and B. In a second email John sent us on 27 March 2005, he explained that the Bowker Club was an about 160-acre fishing club that had been owned by several families.

Site B: "B is a multi-room house that may have been The Rogerson House. The western portion is fairly well defined by the rocks that made up the foundation and the fireplace. A large hole is in what was probably the main room. I would guess these cellars to be storage or, perhaps in the case of cabins, a sunken floor. In this case, it was probably a storage cellar. The hole is roughly rectangular, with the dimensions 45x15 feet and currently [1986] about 60 inches deep. Further east, the remains become unclear. But I would guess that the 'shadows' on the ground to be another room or two.

"The main room was large, with a large fireplace. Judging by the size of the rubble heap, it must have been a colossal fireplace. Under this room, an oval hole lurked. Probably it was stocked with many of the bottles that the miners drained as they discussed their mineral futures. To the east of this common room was the kitchen. It had a stove on a mantel between the two rooms. It was a wood-burning stove of the conventional iron type so common in this area. Under the kitchen was another hole where the food was stored. To the west of the common room and the kitchen was the bunk room. Long and narrow, with a fireplace at the west end, this room probably saw many hours of exhausted sleep. The little room at the northeast corner is . . . who knows?"

In a fax that we received from John on 3 April 2005, he said that another resident of the Gaskill area, Judy Capra, felt that Site B was a saloon, but that he still feels that Site B was The Rogerson House, which could certainly have contained a bar, just as many modern hotels do.

Site C: "This is a double cabin that seemed to be a near clone of itself twice. There is no evidence of a door between the two cabins so I surmise that the common wall was just used for efficiency. I bet there was a door between them, however. Who would want to go outside in a raging Kawuneeche winter storm just to visit people who were only 6 inches away? There is another structure just north of Site C."

Site D: "This is a possible structure. There is no firm evidence that anything stood here except that there appears to be a foundation. It is of the correct size and in the correct location, so maybe something did stand here once."

LARIMER COUNTY CEMETERIES

In an email that we received from John on 26 March 2005, he pointed out that the two children's graves identified as Graves 3 and 4 under "Cemetery Description" above appear to be associated with this site. We have found that children's graves tend to be much nearer their parents' home than is typically the case with adult graves. (See the information on Grave 2C, another child's grave, in the "Description of Graves" section of the chapter on the Lulu City Graves for an example of another child's grave being near its parents' home.)

Site E: "This is the most complex of all the ruins. I would bet that it was the P. J. Wade General Store. It was large and had fireplaces in every room. The eastern room had a stove. Some of its ruins may still be seen."

In an email that we received from John on 28 March 2005, he indicated that Site E might instead be a possible second Gaskill hotel, this one owned by Snell and Larosh. These two gentlemen had first had a hotel at Lulu City and may have established a hotel at Gaskill "after Lulu died." (See the chapter on the Lulu City. Graves)

Site F: "There is little of Gaskill in this particular place, just one old cabin site. This site has a rectangular rip rap foundation and shows the feature I call a 'porch cabin.' This means that there is a porch-like structure away from the foundation. I discovered later that this is not a porch but rather the mark the wall made when it fell. The wall fell out like a domino and as it rotted away it left a mark in the earth. This feature is very common in the Kawuneeche."

Site G: "Appears separate from group. Site is sunken with ill-defined boundaries."

Site H: "The northern appearing room has been excavated. Can't tell if it is indeed separate. Many bottle shards in the area. Most appear to have been shot, as if set up on a bench and shot one, two . . . three! There are also remains of a stove at this site. It is obvious that the site has been dug in."

In an email that we received from John on 28 March 2005, he added the following information about Site H: "It appears to have three rooms, one kind of sunken and dug up. Twenty years ago it had a shelf with bottles that were all shot up. Of course, it was flat on the ground. Bowen Creek flooded over and exposed it. Now it is possibly still there but would take more excavation to find it."

Site I: "Two-room structures with hole. Lots of cans in hole. Hole 43 inches deep. Second room is likely a 'porch.'"

Site J: "Surviving log foundation. Very deep hole, 70 inches deep. Cabins, I, J, and K were probably living quarters and the west end was probably a porch or door. Rotten log and rock basal foundation, rises in mounds, 18 inches high."

Site K: "A very well preserved 2-room rock foundation cabin site. Very well preserved, but no wood left. This site still stood with a roof into the 1970s. Part of a wall still stands. One room had horizontal log construction, the other vertical. Thelma Losasso always claimed this was the assay office, but there is no evidence either pro or con for this opinion."

In an email that we received from John on 28 March 2005, he provided some additional information on Thelma Losasso: She was married to Charley Losasso, who was a printer in Denver and "was a character" who "never remembered anyone's name." He sold his place to Rocky Mountain National Park in the 1970s and but continued to vacation there until sometime in the early 1990s. Following Charley's death, the Park tore down the place he and his family had owned.

Site L: "Possible structure of uncertain dimensions. If it was a cabin, it was burned! The logs which outline it are charred. The foundation is about half there. The ridgepole fell allowing one to infer the dimensions. There are nails sticking up so watch out walking around this site!"

Site M: "Another possible cabin but most likely wasn't one. Dimensions are too small. It is a strange little square rock-lined hole. Privy?"

Site N: "This is another uncertain cabin, but it is just where one may expect one. There is a rubble-type fireplace pile."

Site O: "The only remaining log structure. Logs uniform in diameter, about 5-6 inches. In places milled boards covered the inside walls. A fireplace of beaten cans nailed in the northwest corner served rather than rubble. It apparently had a sod roof. The remains are about 28 inches high. Rock foundation, saddle construction. Best cabin in Gaskill. There are excavations just to the south of this site."

Site P: "May or may not be a structure. Dimensions are good, but it is 25 degrees off north, which is unusual. It is delineated by raised ground, few rocks, and lots of artifacts."

Site Q: "This is where a sawmill was. There is a 'T' shaped rock foundation that the sawmill sat on and lots of sawdust around. The 'T' shaped footprint is very typical of sawmills."

LARIMER COUNTY CEMETERIES

BRUCE WILLIAM GERLING MEMORIAL

Location: The memorial to Bruce William Gerling is located on Flattop Mountain in Rocky Mountain National Park. As discussed below, the exact location of this memorial is unknown.

Description of Memorial
The memorial to Bruce William Gerling reads as follows:

> **Bruce Gerling**
> **Age 21 Lost 10-49**

Effort to Locate the Memorial
We began looking for information on this memorial because it was on a list of "historic structures" in Rocky Mountain National Park provided to us by Dr. D. Ferrel Atkins. (For additional information about Ferrel see the "Acknowledgements" section.)

We did not attempt to make the climb to personally visit this site. Rocky Mountain National Park Rangers Ira Goldfarb and Joan Feder, who were engaged to be married when we met them in July 2001 and who later married, climbed Flattop to make an effort to find this high Rocky Mountain National Park memorial, as they did for us for a number of other Park graves and cemeteries. However, time and weather constraints kept them from finding the memorial. (For additional information on Ira and Joan, see the "Acknwledgements" section.)

Rocky Mountain National Park's Records on the "Bruce William Gerling Incident"
Records in the Library of the Rocky Mountain National Park contain copies of photographs of the boulder on which the memorial to Bruce William Gerling was carved.

- One photo shows the inscription itself.
- The other photo shows the boulder containing the inscription in the right foreground among other boulders on the top of Flattop Mountain.

The photos are attached to a 15 May 1959 memo from Park Superintendent James V. Lloyd to "The Director." The subject of the memo is "Bruce William Gerling Incident."

We have xerographic copies of these photographs, but they are not suitable for inclusion in this book. However, as pointed out above, the Park's Library contains the "original" copies of these photos. Our copies of these photograhs and all of our background information on this memorial can be found in the Local History Archive of the Fort Collins Museum of Discovery, to which we have donated all of our research materials for this book.

The Disappearance of Bruce William Gerling and His Father's Creation of His Memorial
Some time in October 1949 before October 21st, Bruce William Gerling and another young man were hiking in Rocky Mountain National Park. They became lost and were never heard from again. The 15 May 1959 memo from Superintendent Lloyd on the "Bruce Gerling Incident" referred to above begins by stating that "the original detailed report of the tragedy was submitted to the Regional Director on October 21, 1949."

Superintendent Lloyd's memo goes on to say that "on the afternoon of September 1, 1958, the Park Ranger on patrol on the Flattop trail received a report from a horse party that an elderly gentleman had been observed chiseling an inscription on a boulder on the top of Flattop Mountain. Shortly afterward he encountered a gentleman on horseback coming down the trail." This gentleman was William J. Gerling of Phoenix, Arizona, the father of Bruce William Gerling, one of the two missing young men. Superintendent Lloyd's memo goes on to state that "Mr. Gerling readily admitted chiseling an inscription on a boulder as a memorial to his son, Bruce."

On 2 September 1958, Mr. Gerling met with the Chief Ranger, who explained to him the policy against the erection of memorials, monuments, tablets, or plaques in National Parks. But Mr. Gerling could see nothing wrong with his having chiseled a memorial to his son.

After 2-day search, the Park Rangers found the memorial boulder and took the photographs described above. The Park decided to leave the memorial as Mr. Gerling had left it because:

- It was inconspicuous.
- Of the tragic circumstances surrounding the Gerlings' loss of their only son.
- Mr. Gerling had completed the memorial before he knew there was a policy against it.

Evidently, Superintendent Lloyd's 15 May 1959 memo was occasioned by an inquiry from Senator Barry Goldwater in response to a letter he had received from Mrs. Gerling. Superintendent Lloyd attached extra copies of the above photographs to his memo to "The Director" in case Senator Goldwater wanted to send them to Mrs. Gerling.

Superintendent Lloyd's memo ends by saying that he recommended that "no further action be taken, either to destroy or improve upon the inscription carved by Mr. Gerling."

LARIMER COUNTY CEMETERIES

GRAND LAKE CEMETERY

Location: Latitude 40° 15' 37" N, Longitude 105° 55' 17" W

The Grand Lake Cemetery is located on the west side of Rocky Mountain National Park in Grand County. It is on the west side of Trail Ridge Road just south of the western entrance to the Park but is within the Park's boundaries. Even though Grand Lake Cemetery is in the Park, the cemetery is maintained by the City of Grand Lake, Colorado, which also keeps the cemetery's records.

Cemetery Description

The Grand Lake Cemetery is in a pine forest (Photo A). Unlike the grave markers found in more "formal" cemeteries such as Grandview Cemetery in Fort Collins, some of the markers in the Grand Lake Cemetery are quite creative, including a large wooden replica of pipe wrench placed on the grave of a plumber (Photo B) and a crossed pair of skis on another grave.

Photo A: Overview of Grand Lake Cemetery

Photo B: Grave in Grand Lake Cemetery Decorated With a Large Red Pipe Wrench

GRAND LAKE

A number of graves were marked by weathered tree roots that are similar to those that mark a grave in the Black Mountain Ranch Cemetery and a memorial for Second Lieutenant Robert Thomas Moore in the Mosier Ranch Cemetery. (See the chapters for those two cemeteries.)

The following are the inscriptions on the three oldest headstones that we found in the Grand Lake Cemetery.

Minerva Simmonds
Sep. 10, 1879
Aged 75 Years 4 Months

DOC DUTY
Killed in Snowslide
at Toponis Mine
Feb. 1883

Thomas Booth and Jack Williams, who were also killed in the snowslide at the Toponis Mine, were buried in the Gaskill Cemetery. (For information on that cemetery, see that chapter. For details on the snowslide, see "Toponis Mine Snowslide" below.)

Alfonzo R. Warner
1848-1889

The listing for Grand Lake Cemetery in the 1985 edition of the Colorado Council of Genealogical Societies' *Colorado Cemetery Directory* says that the oldest marked grave is dated 1877, but we did not find it.

According to John Gubbins (more about whom below) and John G. Holzwarth III, the grave on John G. Holzwarth II ("Johnnie") in the Grand Lake Cemetery is actually a cenotaph, for John III scattered all of the ashes of his father Johnnie Holzwarth on the Holzwarth family's Never Summer Ranch on the west side of Rocky Mountain National Park following his death on 1 April 1983. (The ranch became part of the Park in 1972.) (See the entry for "John G. Holzwarth II" in the chapter on Rocky Mountain National Park Scattered Cremains.)

As of 29 June 2010, an online transcription of the headstones in the Grand Lake Cemetery can be found at http://files.usgwarchives.org/co/grand/cemeteries/grandlake.txt.

Finding the Cemetery

Since Grand Lake Cemetery is a public cemetery that is still in use, it was not hard to find. However, we had a local guide, John Gubbins, whose family is an in-holder of a summer home on the west side of Rocky Mountain National Park near the old ghost town of Gaskill. Former Park Ranger Bob Haines gave us contact information for John in the hope that John would help us find the Grand Lake and Gaskill Cemeteries and the graves at Lulu City, which John most kindly did. (For more information on those two sites, see the applicable chapters. For more information on John Gubbins and Bob Haines, see the "Acknowledgments" section.)

We met John at the Visitors' Center for the Park's west entrance on the morning of 14 September 2001. Before the day was over, he had taken us to the Grand Lake and Gaskill Cemeteries and to the location where the ashes of George Frederick Dick III were scattered on what was then the in-holding of Fred's family at Trail River Ranch on the west side of Rocky Mountain National Park. (See the section on "George Frederick Dick III and Betty Dick" in the chapter on Rocky Mountain National Park Scattered Cremains.)

LARIMER COUNTY CEMETERIES

Grand Lake's First Burial Ground

According to page 185 of *Grand Lake in the Olden Days; A Compilation of Grand Lake, The Pioneers and The Olden Days* by Mary Lyons Cairns, published in 1971, the first cemetery in Grand Lake was a "little burying ground [that] lay in a forest of pine trees that bordered the west side of the Sagebrush Flat." The bodies of all of the individuals buried in the "Sagebrush Flat Cemetery" were moved to Grand Lake Cemetery in 1945 because the area of Sagebrush Flat was going to be inundated by the construction of Shadow Mountain Reservoir.

Below is a list of the first eight individuals buried in the Sagebrush Flat Cemetery. Note that a number of them met violent ends, with the causes being either nature (snowslide and lightening) or bullets.

1. Minerva Simmonds. The inscription on her grave marker in Grand Lake Cemetery is cited above. She died on 10 September 1879.

2. Robert Plummer, who was "shot and killed by Wilson Waldron" (also spelled Waldern) on 31 December 1882.

3. Edward R. ("Doc") Duty. The inscription of his grave marker in Grand Lake Cemetery is cited above. He was killed in February 1883 in the snowslide at the Toponis Mine. (See "Toponis Mine Snowslide" below.)

4. Andy Meyers, who was killed by lightning in the summer of 1883 while he was "digging a well east of the Grand Lake courthouse."

5. Commissioner John G. Mills, who was "killed in a shooting affray" on 4 July 1883.

6. Winslow Nickerson. He died in December 1883.

7. Lillian Nickerson, the wife of Winslow Nickerson. She died in early July 1884. The graves of Lillian and her husband were enclosed in a fence that "was made entirely of wood, even to the pegs that held the boards to the posts."

8. A baby of Mr. and Mrs. Willard Miner.

Toponis Mine Snowslide

On pages 183 and 184 of *Grand Lake in the Olden Days*, cited above, Mary Cairns tells about the snowslide at the Toponis Mine, which occurred 2 weeks after 25 January 1883: She first quotes the 25 January 1883 issue of the *Prospector*, then at least one of Grand Lake's newspapers, as saying that "Tom Booth and Mike Flynn left on Monday for the Toponis mine, where they will stay for the balance of the winter." Then she says that 2 weeks later the same paper provided details of the deadly snowslide at the Toponis Mine.

The story of the slide can be told in some detail since two of the miners spending the winter at the mine, C. W. Royer and a Mr. Stokes, survived the slide because they "hastily climbed behind a large tree." They saw the lower part of the slide stop before it hit the miners' cabin, but, unfortunately, the upper part of the slide continued on, "carrying with it the roof of the cabin." The upper part of the slide deposited the roof of the cabin "a few rods away." In addition, it partially covered Royer and Stokes. As soon as the two miners dug themselves out, they hightailed it to the nearby Wolverine Mine for assistance.

With that assistance in hand (which evidently took some time given the information below), they returned to dig through the miners' cabin in the hope of finding the remaining winter miners alive. About 10 a.m. they found Mike Flynn, who was still alive after having spent about 13 hours trapped under a log before losing consciousness. Mike reported that he could hear Doc Duty, who was found at Mike's feet, groaning for 3 or 4 hours. Enough of the snow around Doc's body was melted by his body's warmth that the local investigators concluded that he must have lived about 10 hours before he died. They also found no sign that Doc had tried to dig himself out, which led them to further conclude that he had either been fatally hurt or had lost consciousness at the time the slide hit.

Near Doc, they found Thomas Booth, who must have been killed instantly. His back was broken and his face was badly smashed. Jack Williams was found "a little distance from the rest." He evidently had also been killed instantly, by a severe blow to his forehead.

The rescuers took the bodies of the three victims—Doc Duty, Thomas Booth, and Jack Williams—to the town of Gaskill on trail sleds. Booth and Williams were buried in the Gaskill Cemetery. "A delegation of the citizens of Grand Lake took possession of the body of E. R. Duty" and took it to Grand Lake, where a funeral was conducted at the residence of W. H. Throckmorton by Sylvester Butler. Then Doc's body was buried "in the Grand Lake Cemetery," which, at that time, was the cemetery at Sagebrush Flat, not the current Grand Lake Cemetery. However, as noted above, Doc's body was moved to the current Grand Lake Cemetery in 1945 just before Shadow Mountain Reservoir filled with water and covered Sagebrush Flat.

(For information on the location of the graves of Thomas Booth and Jack Williams in the Gaskill Cemetery, see the subsection on "Graves 1 and 2" under "Cemetery Description" in the chapter on the Gaskill Cemetery.)

LARIMER COUNTY CEMETERIES

LILLIAN GEORGINA FEARNLY HAINES CREMAINS

Location: Latitude 40° 20' 51" N, Longitude 105° 31' 11" W

Following her death in September 1985, the ashes of Lillian Haines were scattered on private property about 70 yards northwest of the home of her son and daughter-in-law Robert and Theodora ("Teddie") A. Haines at 2037 South Saint Vrain Avenue in Estes Park. (Lillian was known as "Hainsey" to her friends.) Bob, a retired Rocky Mountain National Park Ranger, scattered his mother's ashes between a very large boulder on the west and a smaller boulder on the east. In the accompanying photo, the smaller bolder is partially obscured by the left-most branches of the small pine tree on the right side of the photo.

Photo A: Location Northwest of 2037 South Saint Vrain Avenue in Estes Park Where the Ashes of Lillian Georgina Fearnley Haines Were Scattered

Description of Grave

As of February 2001, the site where Hainsey's ashes were scattered did not have a marker. The site can be located by its GPS reading and the above location information.

Brief Biography of Lillian Georgina Fearnly Haines

This brief biography is based on information provided by Hainsey's son Bob Haines and his wife Teddie in 2000 and 2001.

Hainsey was born Lillian Georgina Fearnly on 28 September 1892 in London, England. Her father was George Fearnly. Her mother's maiden name may have been Annie Ryder.

Hainsey said that her birth mother deserted her and that her father, left with a young daughter to raise, "sold" her into servitude as a maid in the household of a wealthy Member of Parliament. She told of being forced to carry hot dishes in her bare hands.

She had very little time off from her duties as a servant, probably as little as half of an afternoon a week. She told her daughter-in-law Teddie Haines that she rode her bicycle on her day off and that her uniform and room and board were furnished in partial recompense for her serving duties.

She married Walter Hunt Haines on 19 May 1918, in All Saint's Church, St. John's Wood, South Marylebone Parish, London, England. Walter Haines was a member of the WWI American Expeditionary Forces. Hainsey and Walter's son William Walter Haines was born in Liverpool on 16 April 1919. Two years later in 1921, when she was pregnant with the couple's second son Robert John Haines, she and William emigrated to the United States on the White Star Liner, passing through Ellis Island on their way to Omaha, Nebraska. Hainsey came to Omaha to be with some of her husband Walter's distant relatives. Walter was still stationed in England at the time.

Hainsey and Walter's son Robert ("Bob") John Haines was born in 1921 in Omaha, Nebraska. Unfortunately, Bob died in Estes Park on 12 May 2008. (For additional information on William Walter Haines, Bob Haines, and Bob's wife Teddie and her parents Harry Mereness and Mary Shreve Mereness, see the entry for "William Walter Haines" in the chapter on Rocky Mountain National Park Scattered Cremains and the entry for "Haines, Robert" in the "Acknowledgments" section.)

Hainsey worked as a babysitter while living in Omaha. Hainsey and Walter were separated in 1949. They never divorced.

While living in Omaha with Hainsey, Bob made over 24 vacation trips from Omaha to Estes Park, with his mother accompanying him on one of the trips. Finally, in 1956, Bob and Hainsey moved to Estes Park.

Although Hainsey was illiterate, she could play the piano by ear, being able to repeat on the piano melodies that she had just heard.

HORSESHOE PARK GRAVES

Locations

We have found what appear to be two individual graves and one cemetery in Horseshoe Park in Rocky Mountain National Park: the Unknown Child No. 4 Grave, the Unknown Child No. 5 Grave, and the Horseshoe Park Cemetery. Both the two graves and the cemetery may have been associated in some way with the former Horseshoe Inn or at least with the lodges and/or early homes in that area.

Grave of Unknown Child No. 4

Location: Latitude 40° 24' 15" N, Longitude 105° 37' 27" W

The grave of this child is at the west end of Horseshoe Park in Rocky Mountain National Park but on the east side of U.S. Highway 34. (See "Child No. 4" on Map 1.) The grave is on a small hill about 200 feet directly east of the bridge over the Fall River on U.S. Highway 34. We found the grave during our early search for the grave of the Ashton child associated with Horseshoe Inn—before we knew that the old Horseshoe Inn had actually been located on the *west* side of U.S. 34. Our use of dowser rods confirmed a burial and indicated that the remains are small enough to be those of a child.

Unknown Child No. 5 Grave

Location: Latitude 40° 24' 11" N, Longitude 105° 38' 03" W

The second child's grave that may have been associated with Horseshoe Inn, one of its neighbors, or one of the early homesteads in the area is on a game trail that went up a hill behind the Inn. (See "Child No. 5" on Map 1 and "Grave of Little Girl" on Map 2.) This grave is in a small clearing on a flat area between two rises, is about 2,000 feet southwest of the parking lot on the east side of U.S. 34 where the interpretive sign for Horseshoe Inn is located, and is about 184 feet higher than that lot. The flat area on which this grave is located would have been behind (south of) and to the west of Horseshoe Inn. You will probably need the GPS reading above to find the grave. Our use of dowser rods confirmed that the burial of a child is located at the site. As noted below under "Finding the Graves in Horseshoe Park," local lore indicates that this is the grave of a 5-year-old girl. As will be significant later, the area where this grave is located could have been treeless when Horseshoe Inn existed. However, the evergreen trees in this area are currently larger than those near the Horseshoe Park Cemetery. Consequently, younger and smaller versions of the current trees could have been growing in the vicinity of this grave during the heyday of the Inn, but they would have been larger than those between the Horseshoe Park Cemetery and the Inn.

Horseshoe Park Cemetery

Location: Latitude 40° 24' 01" N, Longitude 105° 37' 40" W

This is at least a seven-grave cemetery, which was probably also associated with Horseshoe Inn and/or its neighbors, is located on a ridge about 500 feet southwest of the above-mentioned parking lot and about 400 feet directly west of U.S. 34 itself. (See "Horseshoe Park Cem" on Map 1 and "Old Burial Ground" south of "H.S. Inn" on Map 2.) The ridge on which this cemetery is located would have been behind (south of) and to the east of the old Horseshoe Inn. You will probably need the GPS reading to find the cemetery.

HORSESHHOE PARK

Our use of dowser rods confirmed the presence of the graves of at least seven children. No graves of adults appear to be there. (There may be more graves in the area, but seven were all that we could confirm.)

As will be significant later, this cemetery would have had an excellent view of Horseshoe Inn before the evergreens and aspen trees north of it grew up. In old photos of Horseshoe Inn, these trees are much smaller than they are now. To get the lumber to build the numerous buildings in the area and to supply the inns and early homes in the area with firewood, much of the old-growth timber in the area would have been cut down in the late 1800s and early 1900s. For one view of how large the surrounding trees would have been at that time, see Photo E below, which is a photo of Horseshoe Inn and the vicinity taken some time between 1917 and 1931, probably closer to 1917 than 1931.

Map 1: Horseshoe Park Graves and Land Parcels in the Horseshoe Park Area Homesteaded or Purchased From the U.S. Government Between 1880 and 1922

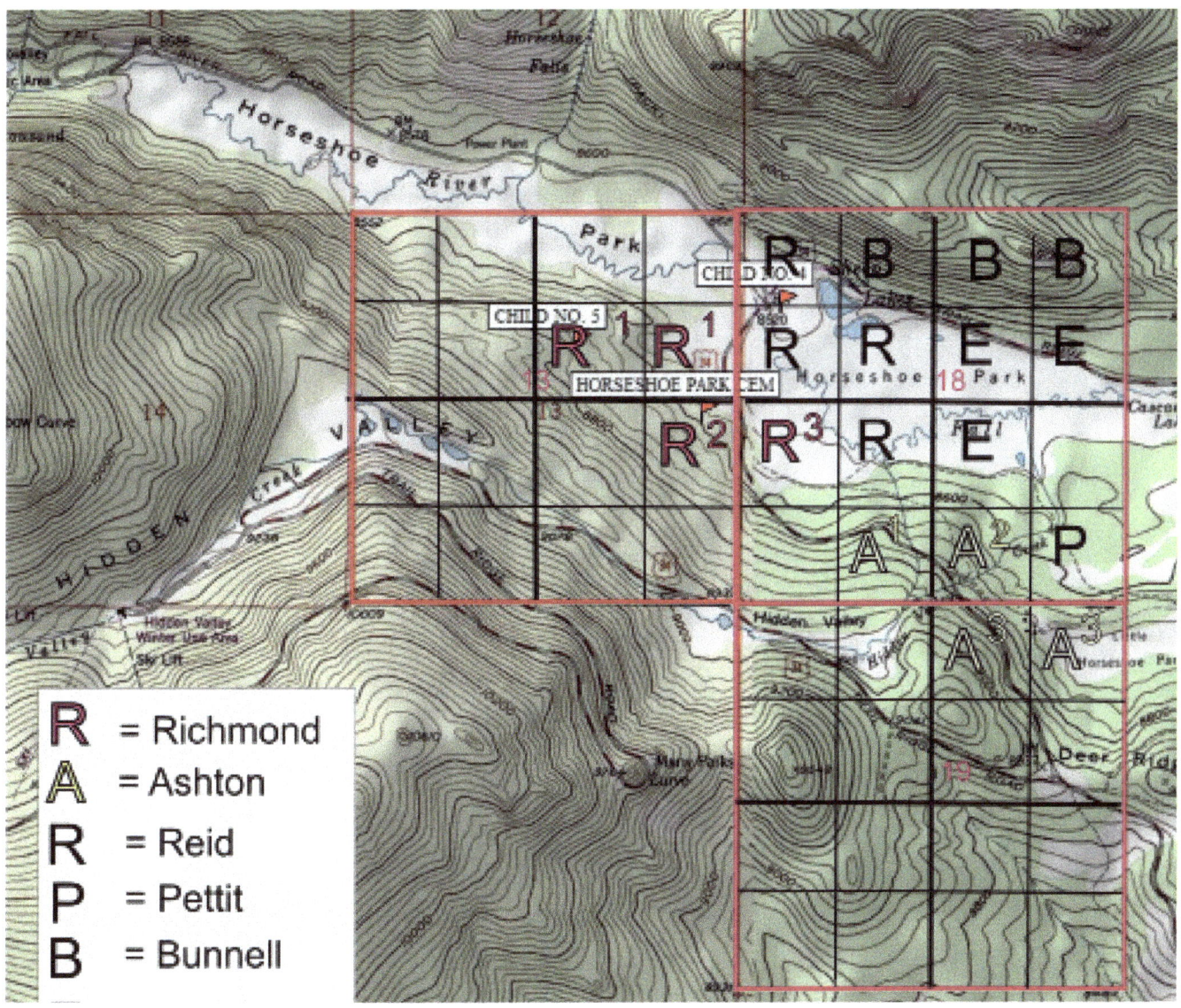

Map Legend: Richmond, Ashton, Reid, Pettit, Bunnell, and Ewart are the individuals who homesteaded or purchased the indicated land parcels. The heavy red lines mark the boundaries of Sections (640 acres/section). The heavy black lines mark the boundaries of Quarter Sections (160 acres/quarter section). The thin black lines mark the boundaries of Sixteenth Sections (40 acres/sixteenth section).

LARIMER COUNTY CEMETERIES

Map 2: Horseshoe Park About 1915, with Some Modern Rocky Mountain National Park Sites Also Included*

*This map was created by Sharon Olson Babbitt and her husband Dell Babbitt based on their research and their many hikes exploring the Horseshoe Park area. It is used with their kind permission. Note: The map is not to scale. (For more information on the Babbitts and their research on the family of Willard Ashton and on Horseshoe Park, see "Finding the Graves in Horseshoe Park" and Source No. 21 in "Sources of Information on the Horseshoe Inn and the Willard Ashton Family" below.)

HORSESHHOE PARK

Descriptions of Horseshoe Park Graves and Cemetery

Unknown Child No. 4 Grave

When we found this grave, it was marked by three 8-10 inch diameter stones placed in the shape of a triangle. We added a fourth stone to better mark the grave. This grave is in a grassy area, and the stones appear not to be a natural part of it. From the grave there are beautiful views of both Hidden Valley to the southwest and the western section of Horseshoe Park on the west. Photo A below shows the view looking west from just east of the grave itself. The grave is in the lower left of the photo.

Photo A: Unknown Child No. 4 Grave in Horseshoe Park on the East Side on U.S. 34, Looking West Toward Where the Horseshoe Inn Was Once Located

Unknown Child No. 5 Grave

This grave is marked by an oval of stones about 8-10 inches in diameter. It has an east-west orientation. (See Photo B below.) Our use of dowser rods confirmed the burial of a child at the site and indicate that the child in this grave is too long to have been an infant. The black wire trellis, found nearby and held by the ladies in Photo B, originally stood over the grave, which is supposed to be the burial location of a 5-year-old girl. (See "Finding the Horseshoe Park Graves" below.)

Photo B: Unknown Child No. 5 Grave, Possibly Associated With Horseshoe Inn and Southwest of Where the Inn Used to Be Located

LARIMER COUNTY CEMETERIES

Horseshoe Park Cemetery

The at least seven graves in this cemetery are marked by local rocks, varying in number and in size from fist-size to about 8 inches in diameter. (See Photos C and D below.) These graves appear to almost be arranged in a circle. For reasons discussed below under "Possible Occupants of the Graves Near the Former Horseshoe Inn," we are assuming that the grave of Willard and Cora Ashton's young son is Grave No. 1 at the base of the boulder in Photo C.

As will be significant later, anyone sitting on the boulder above Grave No. 1 in Photo C and looking north, east, and west in the early 1900s should have had a good view of Horseshoe Inn and Horseshoe Park below.

Nearby we found several piles of "logs" of a size that could have originally been used to make a fence around the cemetery. Since it has been the policy of the National Park Service to remove virtually all evidence of previous human habitation in Rocky Mountain National Park, if there originally was a log fence around the cemetery, the Park Service would have removed it, most likely because they were not aware that it was erected to protect graves.

Photo C: Boulder at the North End of the Horseshoe Park Cemetery Overlooking the Site of the Horseshoe Inn With the Orange Cone Marking the Grave on the Boulder's South Side

Photo D: Horseshoe Park Cemetery With Orange Cones Marking the Seven Graves

Finding the Graves in Horseshoe Park

According to records in the Park's Library and Dr. Ferrel Atkins (see "Acknowledgments"), the grave of an "Ashton child" is associated with the old Horseshoe Inn. Ferrel's original typewritten notes indicate that "this child, according to Ruth Ashton Nelson, was buried on the Ashton Ranch in Little Horseshoe Park. The exact site is unknown." Ferrel later told us that Ruth Ashton Nelson was a sister of the deceased child. (See Child No. 1 under "Wives and Children of Willard H. Ashton" below.)

Ferrel's typewritten notes in the records in the Park's Library are followed by a handwritten note made by Dwight L. Hamilton in 1973 when Dwight was the Chief Park Naturalist. (Dwight retired in 1980 and died at his home in Hawaii in 2003.) Dwight's handwritten notes indicate that Ruth Ashton Nelson confirmed that the grave was not in Little Horseshoe Park (near east-most yellow A3 on Map 1) but was instead behind the old Horseshoe Inn. (Following his death, Dwight's ashes as well as those of a number of other members of his family were scattered on Sundance Mountain in Rocky Mountain National Park. See the entry for "Dwight Linton Hamilton" in the chapter on Rocky Mountain National Park Scattered Cremains.)

Armed with this information and with the mistaken impression that the old Horseshoe Inn used to be on the east side of U.S. 34 in Horseshoe Park, on 28 September 2000, we went to that area looking for a child's grave and found one in Horseshoe Park on the east side of U.S. 34. However, when we later learned that the Horseshoe Inn was on the west side of what is now U.S. 34, we realized that this child's grave (Unknown Child No. 4 Grave) was most likely not the grave of the "Ashton child" referred to in Ferrel Atkins's and Dwight Hamilton's notes.

Retired Rocky Mountain National Park Ranger Bob Haines (see "Acknowledgments") and his wife Teddie told us that, before the Park tore it down, the Horseshoe Inn used to be on the west side of U.S. 34. (Bob also retired in 1980.) They also told us about Bill Robinson, who used to be a wrangler in the area and thus might know about the "Ashton child" grave.

By the time we talked to Bill, the winter of 2000-2001 had set in. He was pretty sure that either he or his niece Trudy Yeros could take us to a child's grave that could be associated with the old Horseshoe Inn. He asked that we contact him again during the spring of 2001. Bill had once owned the livery at Fall River Lodge, which had been just north of the old Horseshoe Inn. When he and his employees took tourists on horseback rides, they often went through the parts of the Park that had once belonged to Horseshoe Inn.

When we talked to Bill again in May 2001, he said that he was on supplemental oxygen and was having too much trouble breathing to make the trip to try to find the child's grave himself. He suggested that we contact his niece Trudy Yeros, who, as of November 2001, lived in Aurora, Colorado

When we talked to Trudy, she was pretty sure that she would be able to find the grave again, although she had not seen it since the summer of 1959 when she was a 9-year-old girl. She told us that when she was young, she spent a number of summers working with Bill, who was her mother's fraternal twin brother. Trudy told us that after the Fall River Lodge was closed at the end of the 1959 season, Bill had owned and operated, first, the Stead's Ranch livery and, then, the YMCA livery until he retired.

Because of Trudy's schedule, she was not able to show us the child's grave that might be associated with the old Horseshoe Inn until 6 October 2001. Thus, on 16 August 2001, armed with general location information from Bill Robinson and Trudy and with a photograph of the old Horseshoe Inn from page 496 of Volume III of Harold Dunning's *Over Hill and Vale; History of Larimer County* (published in 1971), we made a second stab at finding the grave ourselves. This time we found the first grave in what turned out to be Horseshoe Park Cemetery discussed under "Locations" and "Descriptions of Horseshoe Park Graves and Cemetery" above.

Between August 16 and October 6, 2001, Sybil Barnes, then the Local History Librarian at the Estes Park Public Library, informed us that Sharon Olson Babbitt and her husband Dell Babbitt of Estes Park had been trying to find the Ashton child's grave for about 10 years. The Babbitts, who are of the Baha'i Faith, were writing the history of the child and its parents because the child was the first person of the Baha'i Faith to die in Colorado (Source 21g below). (For more information on Sybil, see the "Acknowledgments" section.)

Consequently, when Trudy was able to come to the Park to try to find the child's grave on 6 October 2001, we invited both the Babbitts and Sybil Barnes to accompany us. Trudy's memory of the grave was that it was on a game trail behind (south) and west of where the Horseshoe Inn had been, that it was marked by a ring of rocks and a black wire trellis on which wild roses grew, and that it was the grave of a 5-year-old girl that had died in some type of horseback riding accident.

As the whole group of us, including Trudy's teenage daughter Alex and Alex's boyfriend Josh, hiked to where Trudy thought the grave might be, we passed evidence of the old foundations of Horseshoe Inn and areas that must have been the trash heaps for the Inn because broken pottery and glass were scattered all around. Then, about 75 to 100 feet below the flat area that ended up containing the Unknown Child No. 5 Grave discussed under "Locations" and "Descriptions of Horseshoe Park Graves and Cemetery" above, Dell Babbitt found a black wire trellis laying on the ground. Recall that Trudy remembered that a black wire trellis had marked the little girl's grave when she last saw it. Author Duane Kniebes's use of dowser rods at several locations in the area of the trellis that looked like they could be graves indicated that there were no burials in those locations.

When we reached the flat area containing a ring of rocks like the one that Trudy remembered, sure enough the game trail that Trudy also remembered ran almost right over the grave. Not far below the grave was a second flat area that Dell, a long-time hunter, said elk obviously frequently used for sleeping.

Duane used the dowser rods to confirm the burial of a child within the ring of rocks. Then nearly every other member of the party used the rods to confirm the burial, and everyone who tried the rods got the same result that Duane did: A child was buried there.

We put the black wire trellis around a tree behind the grave. We did not try to place the trellis over the grave as it would have been a hazard to the elk in the area. We surmised that it was probably elk that, over the years, had moved the trellis from the grave site to the location where we found it.

Over the next few years, we made several return trips to the Horseshoe Park Cemetery with the Babbitts and, in June 2005, with Duane's daughter Carrie Kniebes Miller and her family. Our final trip to the Horseshoe Park Cemetery on 19 September 2009 was with the Babbitts and a number of their friends of the Baha'i Faith. During that visit, we again used dowser rods over the entire area of the Horseshoe Park Cemetery and came to the conclusion that at least seven and possibly more children are buried there.

Sources of Information on the Horseshoe Inn and the Willard Ashton Family

1. The 1860 U.S. Census for Des Moines, Lee County, Iowa, enumerated on 27 July 1860, which contains information on the Even/Evan/Aven Nelson (later the husband of Ruth Elizabeth Ashton), his parents, and siblings.

2. The 1880 U.S. Census for Rockford, Winnebago County, Illinois, enumerated on 9 June 1880, which contains information on Willard H. Ashton, his parents, and siblings.

HORSESHHOE PARK

3. The 1900 U.S. Census for Tisbury, Dukes County, Massachusetts, enumerated on 5 June 1990, which contains information on Willard H. Ashton (apparently while he was on a business trip).

4. The 1910 U.S. Census for Ward 3 of Rockford, Winnebago County, Illinois, enumerated on 25 April 1910, which contains information on Willard H. Ashton, his father, widowed sister-in-law, and niece.

5. The 1910 U.S. Census for Laramie, Albany County, Wyoming, enumerated on 27 April 1910, which contains information on Aven/Even/Evan Nelson (later husband of Ruth Elizabeth Ashton), Aven's first wife Celia A. Nelson, and their daughter Helen Nelson.

6. "Social and Personal" column containing information on Willard H. Ashton recently arriving in Estes Park for the season and planning to soon "open Horseshoe Inn to tourists," *Estes Park Trail*, 6 July 1912, page 18 as found at http://coloradohistoricnewspapers.org.

7. "Social and Personal" column containing information on Mr. Ashton expecting to "have his Lawn lake cabin ready for guests next week," *Estes Park Trail*, 20 July 1912, page 16 as found at http://coloradohistoricnewspapers.org.

8. "Social and Personal" column containing information on Mrs. Cooper, the "sister of Mr. Ashton, owner of Horse Shoe ranch," arriving in Estes Park with her two children and her sister, *Estes Park Trail*, 27 July 1912, page 15 as found at http://coloradohistoricnewspapers.org.

9. "Social and Personal" column containing information on Mrs. Willard Ashton having "left on Monday for her home in the east," *Estes Park Trail*, 28 September 1912, page 19 as found at http://coloradohistoricnewspapers.org.

10. Passport Application for Willard H. Ashton signed 22 January 1912 for passport issued on 25 January 1912, *U.S. Passport Applications, 1795-1925* as transcribed by Ancestry.com. Willard gives his birth date as 2 March 1869; birth location as Durand, Illinois; his wife as Cora B. Ashton (who was accompanying him); and his current residence as Rockford, Illinois.

11. Entry for Grace Ashton's 5 May 1913 arrival in New York City from Naples, Italy, aboard the *Carpathia, New York Passenger Lists, 1826-1957* as transcribed by Ancestry.com. She was accompanied by her son John D. Andrew.

12. Ad for the "Horse Shoe Inn" listing W. L. Melis as the Inn's manager, *Estes Park Trail*, 24 July 1914, page 38 as found at http://coloradohistoricnewspapers.org.

13. Article on the "Horse Shoe Inn" noting that Mr. W. K. Melis began as the Inn's manager for the 1914 summer season, *Estes Park Trail*, 5 September 1914, page 27 as found at http://coloradohistoricnewspapers.org. (Note that Source Nos. 12 and 13 disagree on Mr. Melis's middle initial.)

14. Entry for Cora Ashton's 5 April 1920 arrival in San Francisco from Honolulu aboard the *Ventura, Califonria Passenger and Crew Lists, 1893-1957* as transcribed by Ancestry.com.

15. Mention of Mr. H. C. Bradley coming up from Fort Collins to spend July 4th with Mrs. Bradley at the Horseshoe Inn and Mr. C. C. Patrick returning to Fort Collins with Mr. Bradley after the Fourth, *Estes Park Trail*, 9 July 1920, page 16 as found at http://coloradohistoricnewspapers.org.

16. The 1920 U.S. Census for Ward 3 of Rockford, Winnebago County, Illinois, enumerated on 14 January 1920, which contains information on Willard H. Ashton, his wife Cora/Cara B. Ashton, his foster son Alfred Ashton, and his niece Mary A. Cooper.

17. Passport Application for Willard H. Ashton signed 12 January 1921 for passport issued on 13 January 1921, *U.S. Passport Applications, 1795-1925* as transcribed by Ancestry.com. Willard provides the same information concerning himself given in Source No. 10 above. Application also reports that his father's name was Andrew Ashton, that Andrew was born in New York State, that his father was deceased, and that Willard was departing from New York on the *Saronia* on 22 January 1921.

LARIMER COUNTY CEMETERIES

18. The 1930 U.S. Census for Boston, Suffolk County, Massachusetts, enumerated on 6 June 1930, which contains information on a Cora Ashton who was a boarder at the "Home of the Healing Light."

19. *Those Castles of Wood: The Story of the Early Lodges of Rocky Mountain National Park and Pioneer Days of Estes Park, Colorado,* written by Henry F. Pedersen, Jr., and self-published in 1993.

20. *California Death Index, 1940-1997* as transcribed by Ancestry.com, which contains entries for the Los Angeles deaths of Grace Eure Jones Ashton (died 1943), Willard Herbert Ashton (died 1947), and Cora B. Ashton (died 1948).

21. *The Ashton Family and Horseshoe Inn at Rocky Mountain National Park,* two notebooks self-published by Sharon Olson Babbitt in September 2009 based on research she conducted between 1980 and 2009.

    Sharon's two "notebooks" (as she refers to them) are available in their entirety in the Local History Section of the Estes Park Library and in the Library of Rocky Mountain National Park. Sharon's research for these two notebooks included information from the following sources, listed from general to specific, with the specific sources listed in ascending date order:

    a. Genealogy research on the Ashton family using U.S. Census records and other genealogical research sources.

    b. Information provided by the Archives Department of the National Baha'i Center, Wilmette, Illinois. This information includes a letter written by Willard Ashton in which he has the following to say about the burial of his and Cora Ashton's young child: "We buried our baby in a circle of stones."

    c. Information provided by the Metro Denver Baha'i Center (at the corner of South Grant and Bayaud in Denver).

    d. A "moving description" of the funeral of Willard and Cora Ashton's child published in the *Star of the West,* an early magazine of the Baha'i Faith.

    e. "Beautiful New Hotel for Horseshoe Park," found in *The Mountaineer,* Vol. I, No. I, 4 June 1908. The original article was evidently published in an issue of *The Loveland Herald.*

    f. Passenger list for the *S.S. Cedric,* which arrived at New York City from Naples, Italy, on 11 April 1912, included information on Abdu'l-Baha Abbas (the son of the Baha'i founder), his personal attendant, and other companions, including Mr. and Mrs. Willard H. Ashton of Denver.

    g. *A Brief History of the Colorado Baha'i Community, 1900-1921.* Researched and compiled by Jeanette Brayton, Marie Griffith, and Richard Dodge.

    h. A brief mention of "Mrs. W. H. Ashton" from column 4 of page 4 of the 21 May 1921 issue of *Estes Park Trail.*

    i. Listings in the *Estes Park Business and Cottage Directory,* 1930, for W. H. Ashton's Aspen Glen Art Studio at Hidden Valley Ranch, Grace Ashton's Dance Studio (assumed by the Babbitts to be located in Estes Park), Ruth Ashton's Sky Land Ranch (located "5 miles north on Devil's Gulch Road"), and Horseshoe Inn, the listing for which says "W. H. Ashton–Horseshoe Inn" and "C. C. Patrick, Proprietor."

    j. Letter written in about 1930 and transcribed by Sharon Jo Babbitt from a copy of the original handwritten letter in the Colorado History Files of the Estes Park Public Library. The letter appears to have been written by Cora Ashton (or some other Mrs. W. H. Ashton) to friends who were planning on visiting Estes Park and Rocky Mountain National Park.

k. Lecture on the Ashtons that included information on the death and burial of the son of Willard and Cora Ashton in Horseshoe Park, given by Marie Griffith "around 1980" at a Baha'i commemoration at Glenwood Springs, Colorado.

l. Notes concerning the ownership of Horseshoe Inn made by Sharon Olson Babbitt during her 12 September 2009 interview of Nancy Judith Patrick Artman, the granddaughter of Mr. C C Patrick, who was one of the owners of Horseshoe Inn.

22. Our notes from the presentation made by Nancy Judith Patrick Artman at a picnic "meeting" on the Ashtons and Horseshoe Inn arranged by Sharon Olson Babbitt and held at the End Valley Picnic Grounds in Rocky Mountain Park on 19 September 2009.

23. Email received from Nancy Judith Patrick Artman on 29 October 2009 in which she reports that her father (son of C C Patrick) showed her and her brother the grave site of the Ashtons' girl "north of the Inn and west of the lake."

24. Online homestead property records of the Bureau of Land Management at www.glorecords.blm.gov as of 1 November 2009. These records contain details on the following land parcels in the Horseshoe Park area that were either homesteaded or were purchased from the U.S. Government between 1880 and 1922:

    a. On 1 October 1880, George W. Pettit purchased 160 acres. (See black P on Map 1 for a fourth of Pettit's purchase.)

    b. On 1 October 1880, William Dana Ewart purchased 160 acres. (See black E's on Map 1 for three-fourths of Ewart's purchase.)

    c. On 15 December 1882, John G. Reid purchased 161.09 acres using some type of script. (See black R's on Map 1.) **The Unknown Child No. 4 Grave is on this parcel**. (See the northwest-most black R on Map 1.)

    d. On 25 March 1902, Edmond E. Richmond received a homestead patent on 160.77 acres. **The site of the old Horseshoe Inn** (east-most red R1 on Map 1), the **Unknown Child No. 5 Grave** (west-most red R1 on Map 1), and the **Horseshoe Park Cemetery** (red R2 on Map 1) are all of this parcel.

    e. On 29 November 1909, Willard H. Ashton purchased 160 acres. (See yellow A's on Map 1.)

    f. On 12 September 1922, Fred E. Bunnell received a homestead patent on 120 acres. (See black B's on Map 1.)

25. Entry for Aven Nelson in the *Biography & Genealogy Master Index* as available on Ancestry.com on 19 December 2009. The Index reports that Aven was born in 1859 and died in 1952.

26. Runnells Family Tree as available on Ancestry.com on 19 December 2009. It includes genealogy information on Willard Herbert Ashton; his first wife, Grace Eure Jones; and three of their children.

27. Email received from Nancy Judith Patrick Artman on 29 January 2010 in which she provided answers to our questions accompanying the 23 January 2010 draft of this chapter.

28. Email received from Sharon Olson Babbitt on 9 February 2010 in which she provided answers to our questions accompanying the 23 January 2010 draft of this chapter.

Reports of the Burial of a Child of Willard Ashton in Horseshoe Park

Recall that earlier under "Finding the Graves in Horseshoe Park" we quoted the records of Rocky Mountain National Park as saying that, according to Ruth Ashton Nelson (a daughter of Willard Ashton and his first wife Grace Eure Jones Ashton), the grave of an Ashton child was "behind the old Horseshoe Inn." (For more information on Willard Ashton and his somewhat complicated family, see "Biographical and Genealogical Information of Willard H. Ashton Family" below.)

LARIMER COUNTY CEMETERIES

On 2 November 2000, Lashell Lyman, a Rocky Mountain National Park Ranger, provided us with the following quote concerning the Horseshoe Inn and the death of the Ashtons' child from page 89 of *Those Castles of Wood* by Henry F. Pedersen (Source No. 19):

> "But sadness was to seek out the Ashtons when Willard and his second wife Cora buried their small child behind the lodge [Horseshoe Inn], the result of an accident on a horse."

Details concerning the cause of death of Willard and Cora Ashton's child, which also identify that child as a son, can be found in the two "notebooks" by Sharon Olson Babbitt titled *The Ashton Family and Horseshoe Inn at Rocky Mountain National Park* (Source Nos. 21b, d, g, and k). Page 11 of the Sharon's Notebook One provides most of these details:

> "One day, between 1912-1915, the Ashtons took invited guests [at the Horseshoe Inn], who were also members of the Baha'i Faith, for a drive in a horse-drawn buggy. The Ashtons' guests, Mrs. Ella Nash and her daughter, were both prominent Denver residents. . . . The horse pulling the buggy was 'spooked' by a chugging early-model automobile, which could have been speeding and might have honked. The horse lurched, the buggy overturned on uneven terrain, and all passengers were thrown to the ground. Mrs. Nash sustained a broken collar bone, and the Ashtons' young son, whom Mrs. Nash was holding on her lap, was killed."

Willard sent a moving description of their child's funeral to the *Star of the West*, which was an early magazine of the Bahai'i Faith (Source No. 21d). That description contains the following information about the child's grave:

> "Our baby's body was laid to rest in a circle of stones, near some large boulders, above the Horseshoe Inn on a beautiful hilltop overlooking the valley."

On page 13 of her Notebook One (Source No. 21k), Sharon Olson Babbitt provides the following additional information about the death of the Ashtons' son:

> "Sometime around 1980, we [Sharon and her husband Dell Babbitt] were attending a Baha'i commemoration at Glenwood Springs [Colorado] when I heard my friend, Marie Griffith, lecture about the Ashtons, owners of the old Horseshoe Inn, and a tragedy when their young son died in an accident and he was buried on the rise above Horseshoe Inn. There, Mrs. Ashton sat on a boulder, beside his grave, to pray and look over the valley to the east of the Inn."

Note that all four of the above quotes concerning the death and burial of the child of Willard Ashton and his second wife Cora Ashton identify the child as either just a child or as a son and place the location of the child's burial as "above" or "behind" the Horseshoe Inn (most likely the hill on the left or south side of Photo E below).

However, in an email that we received from Nancy Judith Patrick Artman (a granddaughter of C C Patrick) on 29 October 2009 (Source No. 23), she told us that she and her brother had been shown the grave site of an Ashton child by their father, who told them that the child was a girl (not a son) and that the grave was located north of the Horseshoe Inn and west of the lake associated with the Inn. Judy does not recall having been told the age of the Ashtons' girl when she died. She also wondered if Cora Ashton might have had the girl's body moved to the Rockford, Illinois, area when Cora returned there. (For more information on C C Patrick, an owner of Horseshoe Inn, see "History and Ownership of the Horseshoe Inn" below.)

Note that north of the Inn and west of the lake would place the grave somewhere behind the lake in the middle of Photo E below.

To determine if any the remains of any Ashton children had been buried in Rockford, Illinois, in the early 1900s, Judy Artman contacted the same cemetery in Rockford where Willard Ashton's father Andrew was buried and asked them that question. The answer was negative (Source No. 27).

For our thoughts concerning the occupants of the two single graves (the graves of Unknown Child No. 4 and Unknown Child No. 5) and of the Horseshoe Park Cemetery possibly associated with Horseshoe Inn, see "Possible Occupants of the Graves Near the Former Horseshoe Inn" below.

History and Ownership of the Horseshoe Inn

Photo E below is a photograph of the Horseshoe Inn and its vicinity taken by C C Patrick, the grandfather of Nancy Judith Patrick Artman, some time between 1917 and 1931. (As discussed later in this section, the photograph was most likely taken earlier in this period than later.) It was Judy who kindly provided us with a copy of the photo and gave us permission to use it in this book. As will be discussed below, Judy's grandfather was one-half of a two-man partnership who owned the Horseshoe Inn between 1915 and 1932. [Note that the only published mention that we found to Mr. Patrick at http://coloradohistoricnewspapers.org (Source No. 15) followed the usual convention of inserting periods at the end of his initials (C. C. Patrick), but he and his family wrote his initials without periods (C C Patrick).]

As of October 2001, the parking lot on the east side of U.S. 34, and thus across the road from where the old Horseshoe Inn was located, contained the following interpretative sign provided by Rocky Mountain National Park:

> "A summer resort called Horseshoe Inn once stood across this road. Established by Willard H. Ashton in 1907, Horseshoe Inn was one of several resorts that dotted this area before Rocky Mountain National Park was established in 1915. Though rustic by modern standards, these retreats offered islands of comfort within this wilderness.
>
> "The National Park Service bought this property in 1931, after tourist services were established outside of the park boundary. The resort structures were removed, allowing nature to gradually reclaim this meadow—now habitat for coyote, deer, and elk."

The ownership of the Horseshoe Inn during its approximately 15 years of existence is quite complex, with difference sources providing somewhat contradictory information. As best we can determine, the following is the history of ownership of the Horseshoe Inn, the land on which it was located, and related parcels of land in its vicinity:

1902: On 25 March 1902, Edmond E. Richmond received a homestead patent on the following 160.77 acres in the Horseshoe Park area (Source No. 24d):

1. South Half of the Northeast Quarter of Section 13, Township 5 North, Range 74 West, 6th P.M. (See red R1's on Map 1.) **The Unknown Child No. 5 Grave is in the west half of this parcel. The Horseshoe Inn was most likely on the east half of this parcel.**

2. Northeast Quarter of the Southeast Quarter of Section 13, Township 5 North, Range 74 West, 6th P.M. (See red R2 on Map 1.) **The Horseshoe Park Cemetery is in the north half of this parcel.**

3. Northwest Quarter of the Southwest Quarter of Section 18 (which is immediately east of Section 13), Township 5 North, Range 73 West, 6th P.M. (See red R3 on Map 1.)

1905: This year, Edmond Richmond and his wife Emma sold the above 160.77 acres to Willard H. Ashton for $3,000. Some buildings were already on this land when Willard Ashton bought it (Source Nos. 22 and 27).

This same year, Willard Ashton bought 140 acres west of Horseshoe Park in the Hidden Valley area. He later sold 120 acres but kept 20, which became the Ashton family's "Hidden Valley Ranch" (page 19 of Notebook Two of Source No. 21). Note that, according to the Bureau of Land Management's online records reported under "1909" below, that year Willard bought 160 acres in a second "Hidden Valley" southeast of Horseshoe Park. Did he own land in both Hidden Valleys: the one west of Horseshoe Park and the one southeast of Horseshoe Park?

1907: According to the Park's interpretive sign quoted above, this is the year that Willard Ashton established the Horseshoe Inn.

1908: At this point, the Horseshoe Inn is described (page 24 of Notebook One of Source No. 21) as being able to accommodate 50 guests and including 12 small log cabins and some "tent-cabins" that were northeast of the Inn. The Inn itself had a long covered porch that faced the trout pond, which was "below the trail that approached the Inn from the southeast" (page 19 of Notebook Two, Source No. 2l1).

1909: On 29 November 1909, Willard H. Ashton purchased from the U.S. Government the following 160 acres just south of Horseshoe Park area (Source No. 24e):

1. Southeast Quarter of the Southwest Quarter of Section 18, Township 5 North, Range 73 West, 6th P.M. (See yellow A1 on Map 1.) **Hidden Valley Creek runs through the southeast corner of this parcel.**

2. Southwest Quarter of the Southeast Quarter of Section 18, Township 5 North, Range 73 West, 6th P.M. (See yellow A2 on Map 1.) **Hidden Valley Creek runs through the middle of this parcel.**

3. North Half of the Northeast Quarter of Section 19 (which is immediately south of Section 18), Township 5 North, Range 73 West, 6th P.M. (See two yellow A3's on Map 1.) **The east half of this parcel includes the west half of "Little Horseshoe Park."**

As discussed above under "1905," the U.S. Geological Survey's Quad Maps label two areas as "Hidden Valley": On one hand, the Trail Ridge Quad Map labels the valley west of Horseshoe Park as "Hidden Valley." This is probably the "Hidden Valley" referred to at the beginning of the second paragraph under "1905" above and is the "Hidden Valley" that once incorporated a ski hill within the Park. On the other hand, the Estes Park Quad Map also refers to the valley through which Hidden Valley Creek runs in Parcels 1909.1 and 2 above as "Hidden Valley." This makes one wonder if some confusion might have arisen concerning the Hidden Valley in which the Ashton family owned property.

Similarly, the west portion of Little Horseshoe Park included in Parcel 1909.3 above is surely the Little Horseshoe Park referred to in Ferrel Atkins's notes concerning the grave of an Ashton child in Little Horseshoe Park cited in the first paragraph of "Finding the Graves in Horseshoe Park" above. (Recall that the second paragraph of that same section reports that a 1973 interview with Ruth Ashton Nelson, the deceased child's sister, states that the Ashton child was buried "behind the Old Horseshoe Inn" rather than in Little Horseshoe Park.)

In a letter probably written by Willard's second wife Cora about 1930, she states that "Willard, my husband, in his early manhood, homesteaded 150 acres about 7 miles from the village [Estes Park], at an altitude of 9000 ft, at the foot of Deer Mountain" (Source No. 21j). The writer of the letter is probably referring to Parcels 1909.1-3 above (yellow A's on Map 1), even though Willard bought them from the U.S. Government rather than homesteaded them.

The above quote from *Those Castles of Wood* concerning the death of the Ashton child comes at the end of a discussion of the physical structure of Horseshoe Inn, its gardens, and the activities that it provided its guests after "the first guests arrived in the summer of 1909" (Source No. 19).

1911: On 11 May 1911, while in Illinois Willard transferred to his wife Cora via a quit claim deed that land that he originally purchased in Horseshoe Park from Edmond Richmond (Source Nos. 22 and 27): Parcels 1902.1-3 above (red R's on Map 1). Thus, 10 May 1911 was the last day that Willard personally owned any of the property associated with the Horseshoe Inn.

1912: This year the *Estes Park Trail* makes three references connecting the Ashtons with the then-current version of the Horseshoe Inn:

1. On 6 July 1912: "Willard H. Ashton returned on Monday and will soon open Horseshoe Inn to tourists" (Source No. 6).

2. On 20 July 1912: "Mr. Ashton expects to have his Lawn lake cabin ready for guests next week" (Source No. 7). (Lawn Lake is a little more than 2 miles north of Horseshoe Inn just southwest of Mummy Mountain.)

3. On 27 July 1912: "Mrs. Cooper, sister of Mr. Ashton, owner of Horse Shoe ranch, with her two children and sister left Rockford, Illinois, arrived in an auto on Monday morning. They arrived in Fort Collins, last Friday, making the trip of 1,160 miles in five days" (Source No. 8).

1914: This year an ad and an article in the *Estes Park Trail* indicate that the "Horse Shoe Inn" was under new management:

> **Ad**: The ad lists W. L. Melis as the manager, says that the Inn was at the junction of "new Ward Lake road and High Drive," and touts the Inn's nearness to "fine trout streams," its "splendid cuisine," and its "complete livery in connection" (Source No. 12).

> **Article**: The article mentions the cabin that the Inn maintained at Lawn Lake "for the benefit of fishermen and the climbers on their way to Hallet glacier"; describes the Inn's "great granite fireplace"; says that the main lodge has 14 rooms, "some of which have private baths, and all have hot and cold water"; adds that the Inn also has "four log cabins and twelve tent cottages"; and has the following to say about the Inn's new management: "The hotel is under the efficient management of Mr. W. K. Melis, who has had charge only during this season, but has conducted it with a master-hand and has succeeded well where other have failed" (Source No. 13).

1915: This was the year that Rocky Mountain National Park was established. That same year, C C Patrick (the grandfather of Nancy Judith Patrick Artman) and his partner H. C. Bradley bought the Horseshoe Inn and some of the contiguous land from Willard Ashton. The "purchase price" included paying off the loans that Willard had incurred when he originally bought the property (Source No. 22). Willard kept 40 acres. (Exactly which land parcels mentioned above were involved in this sale and which 40 acres Willard kept are not known).

Recall that, as discussed above, in 1911 Willard transferred ownership of the Horseshoe Inn property to his second wife Cora. Thus, technically, Patrick and Bradley bought the Horseshoe Inn property from Cora, not Willard.

This land included the house that Edmond and Emma Richmond had built in Horseshoe Park (most likely in parcel 1902.1 above or east-most R1 on Map 1). Based on old family photos, Judith Artman describes this house as having two stories, small dormers on its upstairs windows, and a long porch on its east side (page 2 of Notebook Two of Source No. 21l).

1917: C C Patrick and his wife Esta Snedaker Patrick had Esta's brother James Snedaker, who was also a contractor, make two-story additions with large dormers on the north and south ends of the original Richmond home. With these two additions, which provided guest quarters for vacationers, the Patricks created a Horseshoe Inn separate from the Patrick family's home (Source Nos. 22 and 27 and page 2 of Notebook Two of Source No. 21l).

1920: This year *Estes Park Trail* provides two mentions of Horseshoe Inn on page 16 of its 9 July 1920 issue (Source No. 15):

1. "Mr. H. C. Bradley came up from Fort Collins to spend the Fourth with Mrs. Bradley at Horseshoe Inn. Mr. C. C. Patrick returned with him to Fort Collins."

2. The very next paragraph lists six families from Indianapolis, Chicago, Winnipeg, Denver, and Missouri who were spending the month of July at the Horseshoe Inn.

1926: An article on page 4 of the 21 May 1921 issue of *Estes Park Trail* (Source No. 21h) mentions the ownership of Horseshoe Inn: "Mrs. W. H. Ashton, the original owner of Horseshoe Inn, who owns a homestead on the north side of Deer Mountain and is the wife of one of the proprietors on the Ashton Dry Goods Store of Rockford, Ill., arrived at the Park this week for the summer." We are assuming that the article is referring to Mr. W. H. Ashton as the "original owner," not Mrs. Ashton. We also assume that the "homestead" in question is the land that Willard Ashton purchased from the U.S. Government in 1909, which is certainly on the "north side of Deer Mountain."

1930: The entry for Horseshoe Inn in the 1930 *Estes Park Business and Cottage Directory* (Source No. 21i) reads as follows:

> "Horseshoe Inn
> W. H. Ashton—Horseshoe Inn   C. C. Patrick, Proprietor
>
> "Horseshoe Inn is a home-like place located inside Rocky Mountain National Park, at Fall River Road and High Drive, at the starting point of most of the best trails in Rocky Mountain National Park and one of the best scenic points."

Either the *Directory* is completely in error, or Willard Ashton still had some association with the Horseshoe Inn in 1930.

Some point between 1917 and 1932: See Photo E below, which shows this stage of Horseshoe Inn. "The Patricks erected a much larger two-story inn, south of the original inn [and, as Photo E shows, attached to the original inn]." During its heyday, the Inn offered "rodeos, dances, a tea room, tennis courts and a casino" (page 2 of Notebook Two of Source 21l). In her 29 January 2010 email to us (Source No. 27), Judy Artman told us that while Photo E was taken some time between 1917 and 1932, she believes that it was taken "earlier rather than later" during that period.

HORSESHHOE PARK

Photo E: Horseshoe Inn, Its Outbuildings, Pond, and Surroundings
(Photo Taken by C C Patrick Some Time Between 1917 and 1931 and Used With the Permission of His Granddaughter Nancy Judith Patrick Artman)

1932: On 2 February 1932, the U.S. Government purchased Horseshoe Inn and its contiguous land from H. C. Bradley and C C Patrick for $32,450 (Source No. 22). As noted on the Park's interpretive sign in the parking lot across from the former site of the Horseshoe Inn: Following the Park's purchase, "the resort structures were removed, allowing nature to gradually reclaim this meadow—now habitat for coyote, deer, and elk."

Biographical and Genealogical Information of Willard H. Ashton Family

Parents of Willard H. Ashton

Father: Andrew Ashton. Andrew was born about 1832 in New York State, which is where his parents were also born (Source Nos. 2 and 3). On page 3 of Notebook One of Source No. 21, Sharon Olson Babbitt reports that Andrew was born in Argyle, New York. Both the 1880 and 1910 Censuses (Source Nos. 2 and 4) report that he was the merchant of a dry good store in Rockford, Illinois, which the Ashton family evidently owned because it was called the "Ashton Dry Goods Store" (Source No. 21h).

The Runnels Family Tree (Source No. 26) gives Andrew's death date as 1910. Andrew was still alive when his family's entries for the 1910 U.S. Census (Source No. 4) were taken on 25 April 1910. Thus, the 18 August 1910 death date for Andrew that Sharon Olson Babbitt reports on page 3 of Notebook One of Source No. 21 certainly makes sense.

Mother: Mary Johnson, Andrew's wife. Mary was born in New York State about 1833 (Source Nos. 2 and 3). On page 3 of her Notebook One (Source No. 21), Sharon Olson Babbitt reports that Mary's **parents** were **Richard and Helen Johnson** and that Mary was born on 21

LARIMER COUNTY CEMETERIES

June 1833 in New York. The Runnels Family Tree (Source No. 26) gives Mary's death year as 1901.

Children of Andrew and Mary Ashton

Andrew and Mary had the following four children:

1. **Carrie M. Ashton.** Carrie was born about 1863 in Rockford, Illinois (Source No. 2 and page 3 of Notebook One of Source No. 21).

2. **Frank J. Ashton.** Frank was born about 1868 in Rockford, Illinois (Source No. 2 and page 3 of Notebook One of Source No. 21).

3. **Willard Herbert Ashton.** Willard was born on 2 March 1869 (Source Nos. 10, 17, and 20) in the Village of Durand, Winnebago County, Illinois (Source Nos. 10 and 17). His middle name comes from his entry in the *California Death Index, 1940-1997* (Source No. 20) and from the Runnells Family Tree (Source No. 26).

   His entry in the 1900 U.S. Census for Tisbury, Massachusetts (Source No. 3), where he was staying in a boarding house (evidently while traveling on business), gives his occupation as photographer and reports that he was married. His entry in the 1910 U.S. Census for Rockford, Illinois (Source No. 4) gives his occupation as "works in a dry goods store." His U.S. Passport Applications signed on 22 January 1912 (Source No. 10) and 12 January 1921 (Source No. 17) give his occupation as "retail merchant."

   It is seems clear that some time between the dates the 1900 and 1910 U.S. Censuses were taken Willard and his first wife Grace were living in Massachusetts because at least the first three of their children (Children Nos. 1-3 under "Wives and Children of Willard H. Ashton" below) were born in Massachusetts, with their son Willard Andrew actually being born in Tisbury, Massachusetts, the very town in which Willard H. was boarding in 1900.

   The information provided above under "History and Ownership of the Horseshoe Inn" makes it clear that Willard was somehow associated with the Horseshoe Inn between 1905/07 and 1930, with his exact association with the Inn changing over time.

   As the two mentions of U.S. Passport Applications above (Source Nos. 10 and 17) indicate, Willard had the wherewithal to travel oversees several times during his life:

   - In 1912, he and his second wife Cora B. Ashton (more about whom below) traveled overseas and first traveled from Italy to Egypt and then from Naples, Italy, to New York City aboard the *S. S. Cedric* with Abdu'l-Baha Abbas, the son of Baha'u'llah (the prophet-founder of the Baha'i World Faith), and five other members of his entourage (Source No. 10 and pages 16-21 of Notebook One of Source Nos. 21f and 21g). Interestingly, on the ship manifest for the *S. S. Cedric*, Willard and Cora Ashton list their "Last Residence" as Colorado rather than Illinois.

   - On 21 January 1921, Willard completed an application (Source No. 17) that indicated that his current residence was Winnebago County, Illinois; that he planned on departing New York on the *Saronia* on 22 January 1921 for Beruit, Lebanon; and that he planned on traveling to Romania, Greece, Italy, Poland, Bulgaria, Belgium, Holland, and Spain while he was overseas. There is no mention on this application of anyone accompanying Willard on this trip.

   (For information on Willard's wives and children, see "Wives and Children of Willard H. Ashton" below.)

HORSESHHOE PARK

Willard died on 27 November 1947 in Los Angeles, California (Source No. 20). Interestingly, as noted below, Willard's first and second wives also died in Los Angeles. This makes one wonder if the Baha'i Faith might have maintained a retirement home of some type there.

4. **Bertha S. Ashton.** Bertha was born about 1873 in Rockford, Illinois (Source No. 2 and page 3 of Notebook One of Source No. 21).

Wives and Children of Willard H. Ashton
Grace Maggie Eure Jones, Willard H. Ashton's first wife. Grace's first middle name of "Maggie" comes from page 4 of Notebook One of Source No. 21. According to the Runnells Family Tree (Source No. 26), Grace was born 5 August 1867 in Des Moines, Polk County, Iowa. However, for the passenger list for her 5 May 1913 arrival in New York City from Naples, Italy, on the *Carpathia* (Source No. 11), Grace gives her birth location as Palymore, Iowa, but she does indeed report 1867 as her birth year. Her entry in the *California Death Index, 1940-1997* (Source No. 20) agrees that she was born on 5 August 1867.

Her parents were **John W. Jones**, who was born in Indiana in 1816 and died in Iowa before 1876, and **Amelia Wright**, who was born in 1846 in Indiana and who married a second husband with the last name of Thompson some time between 1870 and 1876 (Source No. 26)

Grace and Willard were married on 10 October 1895 in Dansville, New York (Source No. 26). They were divorced some time in 1908 (page 3 of Notebook One of Source No. 21).

As the above reference to her 1913 trip to Italy indicates, Grace obviously had sufficient finances to pay for such an expensive trip following her divorce from Willard.

In 1930, a Grace Ashton has a dance studio in Estes Park (Source No. 21i). This could have been this Grace Ashton, but was more likely her and Willard's daughter Grace (Child No. 2 below).

Grace Eure Jones Ashton died in Los Angeles on 17 November 1943 (Source No. 20).

Grace and Willard had the following four children:

1. **Ruth Elizabeth Ashton.** Ruth was born in 1896 in Massachusetts (Source No. 26). According to pages 10 and 11 of Notebook Two of Source No. 21, Ruth came with her parents to the Estes Park area about 1905. After graduating from Mt. Holyoke College in Massachusetts about 1915, Ruth returned to Colorado's Rocky Mountains to locate and identify fauna. In 1930, she owned the Sky Land Ranch 5 miles north of Estes Park just off Devil's Gulch Road (Source No. 21i). In 1931, Ruth married Aven/Evan/Even Nelson, who was 37 years her senior. Ruth and Aven never had any children.

   Ruth is the one who reported to Rocky Mountain National Park (first two paragraphs under "Finding the Graves in Horseshoe Park" above) that one of her siblings was buried behind Horseshoe Inn.

   Ruth died in 1987 (page 22 of Notebook One of Source No. 21).

   Aven/Evan/Even Nelson, Ruth's husband. According to the 1860 U.S. Census of Des Moines, Lee County, Iowa (Source No. 1), Aven was born as Evan Nelson in 1859 in Iowa (probably Des Moines) to **Christian Nelson** and his wife **Ann Nelson**, both of whom were born in Norway. **Aven's two older siblings (Martha and Bertha)** were also born in Iowa. On page 10 of Notebook Two of Source No. 21, Sharon Olson Babbitt reports that Aven's first name was changed from Evan to Aven when he entered primary school. She also provides information on Aven's life up to his marriage to Ruth, which includes his being hired as one of the first five faculty members at Wyoming University in Laramie, Wyoming Territory.

   Aven died in on 31 March 1952 in Colorado Springs (page 22 of Notebook One of Source No. 21).

Ceclia Alice Calhoun, Aven's first wife. According to the 1910 U.S. Census for Laramie, Wyoming (Source No. 5), in about 1886, Even married Ceclia, who was born about 1861 in Missouri. At the time the 1910 Census was taken on 27 April 1910, the only **child** living with them was **Helen Nelson**, who was born in Massachusetts about 1892. In that same census, Ceclia reports that she was the mother of two children both of whom were still living, and Aven reports that he was a university teacher. Ceclia's middle and maiden name come from page 10 of Notebook Two of Source No. 21.

2. **Grace Ashton**. According to the Runnells Family Tree (Source No. 26), Grace was born on 18 November 1898 in Massachusetts, **married** a **Russell Pendalton Carter** with whom she had one child (name not reported because was still living in December 2009), and died on 8 January 1980 in Eugene, Lane County, Oregon. It was most likely her rather than her mother who was the Grace Ashton who operated a dance studio in Estes Park in 1930 (Source No. 21i).

3. **Willard Andrew Ashton**. According to the Runnells Family Tree (Source No. 26), Willard Andrew was born in 1902 in Tisbury, Massachusetts; **married Catherine Colby** in 1925 in San Diego, California; and died on 21 December 1985 in Seattle, Washington (was living in Edmonds at the time of his death). No children are reported for Willard Andrew and Catherine. On page 7 of Notebook One of Source No. 21, Sharon Olson Babbitt reports that Willard Andrew was born in Tisbury, Massachusetts, on 14 March 1902.

4. **Annette Ashton**. Evidence of Annette's existence was found only in the Ashton Family Trees on pages 4 and 5 of Sharon Olson Babbitt's Notebook One and on page 18 of her Notebook Two of Source No. 21. [In her 9 February 2010 email to us (Source No. 28), Sharon told us that her information on Annette Ashton came from data that she obtained from the National Baha'i Archives in Wilmette, Illinois.] On these pages, Sharon lists Annette as the last natural-born child of Willard and Grace Ashton and reports that she was born in 1904. Annette is not included as a child of Willard and Grace in the Runnells Family Tree (Source No. 26), leading one to conclude that she may have died young or at least did not live into adulthood.

In an email we received from Sharon on 29 June 2013, she provided additional information that she had found in her Ashton research files: that research indicated that Annette was buried on a hillside west of Horseshoe Inn overlooking the Inn. Thus, Annette *might* be the little girl buried in the Unknown Child No. 5 Grave.

Following her divorce from Willard in 1908, Grace evidently adopted a young boy because on the passenger list for her 5 May 1913 arrival in New York City from Naples, Italy (Source No. 11), she is accompanied by a "son" named **John D. Andrew**, who was born on 14 March 1902 in Vineyardhaven, Iowa, which Grace also lists as the home to which she and John were returning following their overseas trip.

Cora E. Bush, Willard H. Ashton's second wife. On page 3 of Notebook One of Source No. 21, Sharon Olson Babbitt reports that Willard and Cora were married on 10 April 1909 at Grass Lake, Jackson County, Michigan. Sharon notes that she found a second record of Willard and Cora's marriage that says that they were married on 15 September 1900; however, that would have been before Willard and Grace's son Willard Andrew and daughter Annette (Children Nos. 3 and 4 above) were born and before Willard and Grace's 1908 divorce.

On page 3 of her Notebook One (Source No 21), Sharon reports that Cora was **born** in Jackson County, Michigan, **to Henry Bush** and that her **mother's maiden name** was **Boland**. In the 1920 U.S. Census for Rockford, Illinois (Source No. 16), and the 1930 U.S. Census for

Boston, Massachusetts (Source No. 18), Cora reports that she and both of her parents were all born in Michigan.

Note that in its transcription of the entry for Cora B. Ashton in the 1920 U.S. Census, Ancestry.com transcribes her first name and middle initial as "Cara B." However, if one looks at Ancestry.com's electronic version of the actual handwritten record, the first vowel in her name could be either an *a* or an *o*. Consequently, we are confident that the Cora Bush whom Willard married in 1909 and the lady to whom he was still married on 14 January 1920 were the same person.

The data that Cora provides in different records yield different birth dates:

- When Cora provided information for her arrival in California on 5 April 1920 from Honolulu aboard the *Ventura* (Source No. 14), she reports that she was born on 1 January 1869 in Jackson County, Michigan, and that her home at the time was Rockford, Illinois. We list this birth date first because it is probably the most accurate since it results in her being older than she reports elsewhere.

- Interestingly, earlier that same year on 14 January 1920 when the 1920 U.S. Census for Rockford, Illinois (Source No. 16), was taken, Cora reports that she was born in Michigan and that she was 48 years old, which would yield a birth year of about 1872 instead of 1869.

- When the 1930 U.S. Census was taken (Source No. 18), Cora was a boarder at the "Home of the Healing Light" in Boston, Massachusetts, which was operated by Anna C. MacPherson. (One can't help but wonder if this might have been some type of medical or rehabilitation facility associated with the Baha'i Faith.) In that census, Cora reports that she was 55 years old, which would yield a birth year of about 1875, which makes her younger yet.

Interestingly (and perplexingly), for her 1930 Census entry, Cora also gives her marital status as "widowed," which was not true if the Cora Ashton in the 1930 Census is the same Cora Ashton once married to Willard H. Ashton. Many of the other female boarders at the "Home of the Healing Light" also report that they were widows. If Cora had "passed herself off" to her fellow boarders as a widow rather than as a divorcée, perhaps when the census taker arrived, she had to stick to her original story.

In that same census, Cora also reports that she was 19 when she was first married. Depending upon which of Cora's possible birth years listed above is true, she would thus have been married in 1888, 1891, or 1894. Perhaps she was married to someone else before she married Willard Ashton? Or perhaps she didn't want to admit to her fellow boarders that she was actually somewhere between 34 and 40 when she married Willard, depending upon the year she was actually born.

Cora died on 8 April 1948 in Los Angeles (Source No. 20).

According to the records available to us, Cora and Willard had one natural child and one foster child:

5. **Son who died at Horseshoe Inn**. The research done by Sharon Olson Babbitt for her Ashton/Horseshoe Inn history (Source No. 21) and based primarily on a lecture given by Baha'i member Marie Griffith "around 1980" (Source 21k) indicates that this boy was born some time between 1909 and 1910 and died some time between 1912 and 1915. This means that the little boy would have been between 3 and 6 when he died. (For more information on this young boy and his death, see Source No. 21 and "Reports of the Burial of a Child of Willard Ashton in Horseshoe Park" above.)

LARIMER COUNTY CEMETERIES

6. **Alfred Ashton.** According to the 1920 U.S. Census for Rockford, Illinois (Source No. 16), Alfred was born about 1911 in Illinois but both of his parents were born in Lithuania. In the 1920 Census records, he is listed as Willard's "foster son." Note that Alfred was born after Willard and Cora married in 1909.

Sharon Olson Babbitt found evidence that Cora and Willard divorced at some point and that Willard either remarried following their divorce or was married to more than one woman at the same time (pages 3 and 4 of Notebook One and pages 8 and 18 of Notebook Two of Source No. 21). Possibly the confusion results from there being more than one Willard Ashton in history and genealogy records?

If Willard and Cora did divorce, it must have been after 14 January 1920 because Cora, Willard, and their foster son Alfred all appear together in the same household in Rockford, Illinois, when the 1920 U.S. Census was taken on that date. In addition, Cora is listed as Willard's wife in that census. Even later that year on 4 April 1920, Cora lists Rockford as her home when she returns to California from a sea cruise to Hawaii aboard the *Ventura* (Source No. 14). Of course, it is possible that Willard and Cora divorced between January and April 1920 and that their divorce was the reason for Cora's going on the cruise.

Additional evidence that Willard and Cora may have divorced some time in 1920 comes from the fact that Willard traveled oversees to eight countries without Cora in early 1921 (Source No. 17).

Possible Occupants of the Graves Near the Former Horseshoe Inn

While we have no way of knowing for sure who is buried in the at least 10 graves near the location of the former Horseshoe Inn, below we have evaluated the information provided above concerning the history of the Inn and of those living near the Inn, including the family of Willard H. Ashton, and have provided our thoughts as to possible occupants of those graves. As a reminder, those 10 graves are:

1. Unknown Child No. 4 Grave
2. Unknown Child No. 5 Grave
3-9. Horseshoe Park Cemetery and its seven (at least) graves
10. The Ashton girl's grave north of Horseshoe Inn and west of the Inn's lake shown to Nancy Judith Patrick Artman by her father.

Grave of the Willard and Cora Ashton's Infant Child/Son

It seems fairly clear to us that the occupant of one of the graves behind the old Horseshoe Inn is the infant child (son?) of Willard and Cora Ashton who died in a buggy accident near Horseshoe Inn some time between 1912 and 1915.

On one hand, since the Unknown Child No. 5 Grave (the one on the game trail that we found with the help of Trudy Yeros) was the best marked, that grave at first seems to be the most likely candidate for the burial location of the Ashtons' child/son. That grave and the seven graves in Horseshoe Park Cemetery are all "above" and "behind" Horseshoe Inn, all had the good views of the Horseshoe Park valley at the time that the Horseshoe Inn was active, and all have nearby boulders to sit on while taking in those views. (See the first four quotes in "Reports of the Burial of a Child of Willard Ashton in Horseshoe Park" for historical references to the location of the Ashton child's grave, the view from the grave, and the association of a boulder with the grave.)

On the other hand, as noted in the subsections on the "Horseshoe Park Cemetery" in the "Locations" and "Descriptions of Horseshoe Park Graves and Cemetery" sections above:

- The Horseshoe Park Cemetery would have had an excellent view of the Horseshoe Inn and the valley around it before the evergreen and aspen trees north of the Inn grew to their current size.
- Anyone sitting on the boulder on the north side of the cemetery (shown in Photo C above) would have had an especially good view of Horseshoe Inn and its valley.

In addition:

- Grave No. 1 in Photo C is immediately to the south of a large boulder on the north (valley) side of Horseshoe Park Cemetery.
- While both our use of dowser rods and the size of the circle of stones marking Grave No. 1 in the Horseshoe Park Cemetery indicate that a young child or infant is buried in that grave, both the dowser rods and the size of the circle of stones in the grave of Unknown Child No. 5 indicate that the child buried in that grave was larger and hence older than the 3- to 6-year-old little Ashton boy.

Thus, we conclude that Grave No. 1 in the Horseshoe Park Cemetery is the most likely burial location for the child (son or otherwise) of Willard and Cora Ashton who died in the buggy accident.

Grave of Ashton Girl Buried Near Horseshoe Inn

Recall that in the 11th paragraph of the section above titled "Reports of the Burial of a Child of Willard Ashton in Horseshoe Park," Nancy Judith Patrick Artman reports (Source No. 23) that her father had shown her and her brother the grave of an Ashton girl north of the Horseshoe Inn and west of the Inn's lake. We have not attempted to find this grave. At first we thought this might be the Unknown Child No. 4 Grave that we found in Horseshoe Park on the east side of U.S. Highway 34. However, that grave would be too far east to be on the west side of the lake shown in Photo E.

Then we wondered if it might be located in the east-most red R^1 on Map 1. However, recall that in June 2010, Sharon Babbitt reported to us that she had found information in her Ashton research files indicating that Annette Ashton (Child No. 4 above under "Wives and Children of Willard H. Ashton) was buried on a hillside *west* of Horseshoe Inn. Thus, if the little girl buried in "the grave of an Ashton girl" that Judy Artman's father showed her and her brother is Annette Ashton, then Annette Ashton *might* be buried in Unknown Child No. 5 Grave, a child that local lore indicates was a little girl.

Graves of Unknown Children Nos. 4 and 5 and Grave Nos. 2-7 in the Horseshoe Park Cemetery

The graves that do not contain the remains of the Ashtons' infant son and/or daughter may well contain the remains of other children who died at the Horseshoe Inn or Ranch, possibly the children of employees or even visitors. On the other hand, some or all of the children buried in these grave could have died in the area before the Ashtons' 1905 purchase of the existing building that became the Horseshoe Inn and the surrounding land.

Recall that both the Unknown Child No. 5 Grave and the Horseshoe Park Cemetery are on land for which Edmond E. Richmond received a homestead patent in 1902 (Source No. 24d)—land that was later purchased by the Ashtons in 1905 and then by C C Patrick and H. C. Bradley in 1915 (Source No. 22). We tried unsuccessfully to find census or other records for an Edmond E. Richmond with a wife named Emma in the Estes Park area during the applicable period. However, since they were a married couple and since they lived in the area for at least 8 years (5 years to homestead the land plus the 3 years between 1902 and 1905), they could well have had one or more children who died young and were buried in either the Unknown Child

No. 5 Grave or in Grave Nos. 2-7 of the Horseshoe Park Cemetery. Also recall that our use of dowser rods at the Horseshoe Park Cemetery indicated that children are buried in all of its at least seven graves.

Any of the other early residents in the Horseshoe Park area (including at least the individuals listed in Source Nos. 24a, b, c, and f) could also have buried children in the Horseshoe Park Cemetery once it was an "established" burial ground. (See the parcels labeled with black letters on Map 1.)

So what about the Unknown Child No. 4 Grave east of both the Horseshoe Inn site and U.S. Highway 34? The records of the Bureau of Land Management (Source No. 24c) indicate that the 161.09-acre parcel that includes this grave was purchased by John G. Reid using some sort of script on 15 December 1880. (See the southwest-most black R on Map 1.) Again, we were unable to find any census or other records for him in this area during the applicable period. However, if he was married, he and his wife could have lost a child who was then buried in that grave.

HUPP FAMILY CEMETERY

Location: Latitude 40° 22' 19" N, Longitude 105° 35' 41" W

The Hupp Family Cemetery is in Upper Beaver Meadows in Rocky Mountain National Park. It is north of Upper Beaver Meadows Road about 0.2 of a mile from the beginning of the intersection of Upper Beaver Meadows Road (a dirt road) and the paved road leading to the Beaver Meadows Entrance Station.

Description of Cemetery

The cemetery is marked by the single, red-granite headstone shown below. The headstone's inscription is on the right below:

HUPP FAMILY
John Hupp
Sept. 24, 1820 • Dec. 29, 1877

Eliza E. Hupp
Oct. 2, 1830 • Sept. 17, 1900

Francis A. Hupp
Sept. 24, 1853 • Jan. 11, 1901

Photo A: Hupp Family Cemetery in Rocky Mountain National Park, Looking Southwest

The headstone faces east, so it is perpendicular to Upper Beaver Meadows Road. In addition, as of February 2001, there is a small pine tree between the headstone and the road. Consequently, the headstone cannot be seen from the road. You will probably need the above GPS reading to find it.

Note that although the headstone at the Hupp Family Cemetery spells Fannie's name as "Francis," all of the other references to her spell her name as "Frances."

When we originally visited the Hupp Family Cemetery on 2 October 2000, we did not use dowser rods to confirm the burials because they were marked with a headstone. However, during our communications with several descendants of the Hupp family (discussed below), one of them, William ("Bill") Ervin Hupp, reported that he remembered being told that Fannie might not be buried there after all. Thus, in February 2001, we returned to the Hupp Family Cemetery and used dowser rods to confirm that three individuals are indeed buried in the cemetery. However, the south-most burial is actually outside of the four metal stakes that mark the cemetery site: It is under the small pine tree that is south of the area marked by the stakes. (For information on how these stakes came to be, see the third paragraph of "History of Hupp Family Cemetery and Headstone" below.)

After our February 2001 visit to the Hupp Family Cemetery, Bill Hupp contacted us again with the following information:

> "Some time prior to the grave marker being installed, Walter Jones took Bill Armstead [William Ervin Armstead] to Upper Beaver Meadows to see where the Hupp homestead was located and where the graves of John, Eliza, and Frances were. Walter informed Bill at that time that two graves were within the area marked by the metal stakes and that one grave was beneath the pine tree outside of the markers. Bill cannot remember what Walter told him about the grave beneath the pine tree. It seems logical to Bill Armstead, Ray Davis, and me that John and Eliza would have been buried side by side and that Frances, who died last, would be the person buried beneath the pine tree."

(For more about Bill Hupp, see Child No. 3.1; for about Bill Armstead, see Child No. 2.2; and for more about Ray Davis, see Child No. 4.4 under "Descendants of William Horace Hupp and Grace Hunter Hupp" below.)

Finding the Cemetery

We originally went in search of the Hupp Family Cemetery because it was included on a list of graves in Rocky Mountain National Park provided to us by Dr. D. Ferrel Atkins. (For more information on Ferrel, see the "Acknowledgments" section.) The typewritten information on Ferrel's list concerning the Hupp Family Cemetery follows:

> "John Hupp, Eliza Hupp (his wife), and Fannie Hupp (their daughter) are buried in Beaver Meadows. They are relatives of Mr. Allyn Hanks, and Mr. Hanks intended to put up a marker about 4 years ago, but the writer does not know whether this was done."

Following up on Ferrel's notes, on 2 October 2000, we went to the Park's Beaver Meadows Entrance Station and asked if anyone knew where the three Hupps were buried. An Estes Park resident working in the gift shop told us where to find the burials and told us that they had a marker. After we spent some time searching, we finally found the cemetery.

Sources of Information on the Hupp Family Cemetery and the Hupp Family

Except as specifically indicated, the information about the John T. Hupp family below comes from *John T. Hupp, The Unfinished Saga of John T. Hupp of Virginia*, compiled by John T. Hupp's great-grandson Raymond Merritt Davis of Tucson, Arizona; a printout of genealogy records titled "Descendants of John T. Hupp, Sr." provided by Coral Ervin Davis (Ray's brother) of Charlo, Montana; letters from and phone and personal conversations with William Ervin Hupp of Boulder; and emails from Raymond Davis, especially one dated 10 August 2006. William Hupp is the first cousin of Ray and Ervin Davis.

Copies of *John T. Hupp, The Unfinished Saga of John T. Hupp of Virginia* and "Descendants of John T. Hupp, Sr." are available in the Estes Park Library, Estes Park Museum, and the Rocky Mountain National Park Library.

Those two documents and all of our background research on the Hupp Family Cemetery are available in the Local History Archive of the Fort Collins Museum of Discovery, which has received all of our background research for this project.

History of Hupp Family Cemetery and Headstone

As noted above, John and Eliza Hupp were husband and wife, and Frances ("Fannie") was their daughter. They were early homesteaders in what is now Rocky Mountain National Park. (For more information on the Hupp family, see "Biographical and Genealogical Information of the John T. Hupp Family" below.)

The Hupp family were friends of Ransom Kendall, who is buried 0.4 of a mile west of the Hupp Family Cemetery on the southwest side of Upper Beaver Meadows Road. (See the chapter on the Ransom S. Kendall Grave.)

Accordingly to information provided by Ferrel Atkins in December 2000, the location of the Hupp Family Cemetery was saved by Chief Ranger J. Barton Herschler, who told Ferrel that he took some discarded car axles and drove them into the corners on the grave site. Those car axles can still be seen. (See the fourth and fifth paragraphs under "Description of Cemetery" above.)

Ferrel also told us that it was Rocky Mountain National Park Superintendent Allyn Frank Hanks who, during a visit to the grave site with Ferrel and fellow Ranger Roger Contor, decided that a marker could be erected for the Hupp Family Cemetery as long as that marker was not visible from the Upper Beaver Meadows Road. Hanks' wife, Hazel Williams Hanks, was a distant relative of the Hupps. Her ashes (along with those of her husband) were scattered about a mile from the Cub Lake Trailhead. (For more information on Allyn Frank Hanks and Hazel Williams Hanks, see their entries in the chapter titled Rocky Mountain National Park Scattered Cremains.)

In January 2001, the Hanks' son, Allyn Williams ("Bill") Hanks, who lived in Estes Park, told us that the headstone at the Hupp Family Cemetery was paid for and erected by descendants of the Hupps. Page 6 of *John T. Hupp, The Unfinished Saga of John T. Hupp of Virginia* provides additional information on the headstone at the Hupp Family Cemetery:

- It was in June 1963 that Park Superintendent Allyn Hanks and Rangers Ferrel Atkins and Roger Contor made the visit to the Hupp Family Cemetery that resulted in Superintendent Hanks granting permission for the erection of a headstone.

- The "descendants of the Hupps" who bought the headstone were John Ervin Hupp and Pearl Etha Williams.

John Ervin was one of the sons of William Horace Hupp, who was one of the sons of the John and Eliza Hupp buried in the Hupp Family Cemetery. (For more information on William Horace Hupp, see Child No. 8 under "Biographical and Genealogical Information of the John T. Hupp Family" below. For more information on John Ervin Hupp, see Child No. 3 under "Descendants of William Horace Hupp and Grace Hunter Hupp" below.)

Pearl's brother was Frank Williams. Frank's daughter, and thus Pearl's niece, was Hazel Williams, the wife of Allyn Frank Hanks, the Park Superintendent who gave permission for a headstone to be erected at the Hupp Family Cemetery.

- John Ervin's and Pearl Etha's children are thus the only descendants of John T. Hupp who are related by blood to the children of Allyn Frank Hanks and Hazel Williams Hanks. This means that two of the individuals who helped us with our research on the Hupp and Hanks families are second cousins: William ("Bill") Ervin Hupp is the son of John Ervin and Pearl Etha; Allyn Williams ("Bill") Hanks is Pearl's great-nephew. Thus, William Ervin Hupp and Allyn Williams Hanks are second cousins. (For more information on William Ervin Hupp, see Child No. 3.1 under "Descendants of William Horace Hupp and Grace Hunter Hupp" below.)

When we visited with William ("Bill") Hupp and his wife Betty Lou in late March 2001, Bill told us that his mother really did not like her middle name "Etha" and, once she was married, always signed her name as "Pearl Williams Hupp."

- The Boulder Marble & Granite Works made the headstone for the Hupp Family Cemetery.

- Rocky Mountain National Park personnel erected the headstone in July 1964. (The date that the headstone was erected comes from a note in the Hupp folder in the Estes Park Library. The note says that the date came from research done in the Rocky Mountain National Park's library, probably by Librarian Sybil Barnes, who at one time worked in both libraries.)

Biographical and Genealogical Information of the John T. Hupp Family

John T. Hupp, Jr., and **his younger brother Aaron** were the **sons of John Hupp, Sr., and Catherine Stoutemeye**r, who were married in 1803 in Rockingham County, Virginia, where all of their children were born. In the early 1820s, they relocated from Virginia to Newark, Licking County, Ohio.

Even though his headstone at the Hupp Family Cemetery indicates that John T. Hupp, Jr., was born on 24 September 1820, Ray Davis told us in his 8 August 2006 email that his more recent research indicated that John could have been born as early as 1814 and as late as the date on his tombstone. Even though Ray had originally thought that Aaron was older than John, Jr., by 2006 he had concluded that John was most likely the older brother.

By the 1850 U.S. Census, John and Aaron, both still single, were farming on property (two large parcels joined at one corner) in Morgan County, Missouri, which records show they held in joint tenancy.

On 3 April 1851, **John married Eliza A. Grant**, the 20-year-old **daughter of George Grant and Nancy Brannin Grant**, who farmed nearby. According to the Hupp family's genealogy records, Eliza was born on 3 October 1830 in Otterville, Missouri. However, the headstone at the Hupp Family Cemetery says that she was born on 2 October 1830 and that her middle initial was "E" rather than "A" as shown by the Hupp family records.

On 7 October 1852, **Aaron Hupp married Mary Homan**, a young lady who lived across the county line in Cooper County, Missouri. In August 1855, Aaron and Mary sold John and Eliza the Morgan County property plus two smaller parcels nearby.

John T. and Eliza A. Hupp had nine children, all of whom were born in the Otterville, Missouri area:

1. **George Tipton Hupp.** George was born on 27 January 1852 and died on 10 February 10 1863 in Otterville, Missouri. His place of burial is unknown but most likely is on the family's farm 2 miles south of Otterville.

2. **Frances Ann Hupp.** Frances was born on 24 September 1853. She made the trip to Colorado with her parents. She died on 11 January 1901 in Longmont, Colorado, and

was buried in Hupp Family Cemetery in Rocky Mountain National Park. (For more information on Frances, see "The Hupp Family Ranch" below.)

The headstone at the Hupp Family Cemetery spells her first name as "Francis," but all other records spell it as "Frances," which is the usual feminine spelling of the name.

3. **Mary Elizabeth ("Mollie") Hupp.** Mollie was born on 10 September 1856 and made the trip to Colorado with her parents. Mollie died on 15 June 1917 in Estes Park and is buried in Lakeside Cemetery in Loveland.

   John J. Jones, Mollie's husband. Mollie married John in 1882 in Estes Park. John was born in March 1845 in Iowa. He died on 16 November 1907.

   Mary and John homesteaded in the Estes Valley around 1885 near Mary's Lake and operated the Jones Inn there. They had six children. (See *John T. Hupp, The Unfinished Saga of John T. Hupp of Virginia* and "Descendants of John T. Hupp, Sr." for details on Mollie and John's children.)

4. **Ellen Truitt Hupp.** Ellen was born on 20 September 1858 and made the trip to Colorado with her parents. She died on 7 January 1916 in Loveland and is buried in Loveland's Lakeside Cemetery. Ellen never married. She helped her sister-in-law Josephine Hupp with the hotel business in Estes Park, where she worked as a cook in the hotels' restaurants. (For information on Josephine's hotel operations, see "Hupp Hotels in Estes Park" below.)

5. **John T. ("Wallace") Hupp.** Wallace was born on 13 September 1860 and died on 10 February 1863 in Otterville, Missouri. His place of burial unknown but most likely is on the family's farm 2 miles south of Otterville.

6. **Henry Aaron Hupp.** He was born on 29 August 1862 and made the trip to Colorado with his parents. On 29 December 1893, he married Josephine Blinn. Henry was a butcher, such a good one in fact that Charles Edwin Hewes wrote a poem titled *Hank Hupp— Our Butcher* about him. [For a copy of this poem see page 150 of Volume II of Harold Dunning's *Over Hill and Vale*. (See the "Bibliography" for a complete citation.)] Henry died on 10 May 1931 in Loveland.

   Josephine Leach Blinn, Henry's wife. Josephine had been born Josephine Leach in Rockford, Michigan in July 1857. Her **first husband** was **Augustus Blinn**, with whom she had a **son** named **Harry Elmer Blinn**, who was born in 1878. (He is reportedly the first child born in Loveland, Colorado.) After Augustus's death, Josephine married Henry Hupp. They did not have any children. Josie (as she was affectionately called) died on 12 November 1932 in Loveland. (For information on Josephine's hotel operations in Estes Park, see "Hupp Hotels in Estes Park" below.)

7. **Nancy ("Nan") Maria Hupp.** Nan was born on 16 June 1864 and made the trip to Colorado with her parents. She married Harold Mortimer ("Mort") Ely on 1 November 1882. Nan died on 28 November 1944 in Jackson, Wyoming.

   Harold Mortimer ("Mort") Ely, Nan's husband. Mort had been born on 8 July 1855 in Lake Ariel, Pennsylvania. He died on 1 May 1932, also in Jackson, Wyoming. Both Nan and Mort are buried in the Jackson Cemetery.

   At first Nan and Mort homesteaded near the Hupp Family Ranch, but in 1895 they moved to Jackson, Wyoming, where they homesteaded and farmed and where they remained for the rest of their lives. Mort was also a game warden and, for a time, served as the Jackson Town Marshal.

Nan and Mort had three children. (See *John T. Hupp, The Unfinished Saga of John T. Hupp of Virginia* and "Descendants of John T. Hupp, Sr." for details on Nan and Mort's children.)

8. **William ("Bill") Horace Hupp.** Bill was born on 16 November 1867 and made the trip to Colorado with his parents. He was married twice. He married his first wife Grace Hunter on 18 January 1895 in Fort Collins. He married his second wife Mary Heck on 29 March 1905 in Boulder. Bill died on 2 October 1912 in Boulder.

Grace Elizabeth Hunter, Bill's first wife. Grace was born on 21 November 1873 in Greenville, Illinois. She died in May 1901 in Guthrie, Oklahoma, where she had gone with her youngest daughter, Inez, to visit relatives. She is buried in the Summit View Cemetery there.

William and Grace had four children. All of the Hupp relatives still living in the Boulder area and others with whom we corresponded during our research on the John T. Hupp family are descendants of William and Grace's four children. Information on these children and their descendants is provided below under "Descendants of William Horace Hupp and Grace Hunter Hupp."

At the time of Grace's death, William was living in Estes Park, where he was carrying mail for the U.S. Post Office.

Myral ("Mary") Heck, Bill's second wife. Mary was born in Ft. Wayne, Indiana. She and William had four children. The first two children were twins, who died shortly after they were born. (See *John T. Hupp, The Unfinished Saga of John T. Hupp of Virginia* and "Descendants of John T. Hupp, Sr." for details.)

At least part of the time they lived in Boulder, William and Mary operated a grocery store there. William then sold the grocery store and moved to Estes Park, where he became Postmaster, a post that he still held at the time of his death in 1912.

Bill's death caused the same Charles Edwin Hewes who wrote the poem about Henry Hupp referred to above to pen the following remembrance of Charles, which is quoted from page 151 of Volume II of Harold Dunning's *Over Hill and Vale*:

> "Bill Hupp's gone, passed away, you say!
>
> "Gosh! It's tough to hit us hard that way.
>
> "We loved Bill Hupp. He was a mighty good man. He handled the mail fine for Uncle Sam. He loved to accommodate everyone, and he never bothered much with red tape and he never hemmed and hawed. He would hurry to get your mail so you could hit the trail for home. He loved his work, his friends and the town. He loved the old hills and always had a cheer-up word for rich or poor. If the weather was cutting with blizzard and storm, Bill's smile would make you warm and comfortable.
>
> "Hang me! This here poor little life of ours is filled with much sorrow and it is just such things as Bill's taking away that makes me feel that there is a Judgement Day when men like Bill Hupp, so full of kindness and love, will stand with the sheep at the Golden Gate and watch them old he-goats go bellering past."

9. **Charles Richard Hupp.** Charles was born on 24 January 1872 and made the trip to Colorado with his parents. He died at the Horseshoe Inn in what is now Rocky Mountain National Park on Sunday, 4 April 1926. His burial place is unknown.

Not much is known about Charles except that he never married, ran the Hupp Livery in Estes Park, and did odd jobs around Estes Park. His last known job was as the caretaker for the Horseshoe Inn. For more information on his death, see "Jack Moomaw's Discovery of Charles Hupp's Body" below.

The Hupp Family Ranch

In 1875, the John T. Hupp, his wife Eliza, and seven of their children joined a group migrating from Missouri to the Loveland/Estes Park areas. The first piece of land that they chose to homestead was in Beaver Flats (Lower Beaver Meadows). However, the Englishman "Lord" Dunraven wanted to control the whole valley containing the parcel that the Hupps had chosen.

As Ray Davis explains on page 5 of *John T. Hupp, The Unfinished Saga of John T. Hupp of Virginia*, "Lord" Dunraven's "methods for acquiring land were a bit unscrupulous. In order to homestead land one had to live on the property for a certain length of time and make certain improvements upon it. When all of the government requirements had been met, a Patent to the land was issued and the homesteader became sole owner of the property."

Ray goes on to explain that "Lord Dunraven sort of skirted some of the requirements by hiring people off the streets to put in homestead claims which he planned to later take off their hands for paltry sums. He had tied up large amounts of land using this questionable approach. One of the parcels in dispute was the land in Beaver Flats which John Hupp had settled on. Rather than fight, John left the Beaver Flats property and moved further north to a place called Beaver Meadows. It turned out to be a very good move as there was a spring which provided plenty of quality water for all of the family's and farm's needs plus the setting was beautiful." (Both Beaver Flats and Beaver Meadows are now in Rocky Mountain National Park.)

Unfortunately, John T. Hupp died in December 1877, prior to the amount of time required to get a land patent. However, the Hupp children helped their mother carry out the necessary homesteading activities to establish a family farm in Upper Beaver Meadows. (John's date of death on his headstone is 29 December 1877. However, other records show his date of death as 29 December 1878 and 29 October 1877.) He was the first member of the Hupp family to be buried in the Hupp Family Cemetery.

In a letter that we received from him on 24 January 2001 and in subsequent information we received from him in March and June 2001, William Ervin Hupp of Boulder provided us with the following legal descriptions (which report research originally done by retired Rocky Mountain National Park Ranger and Naturalist Ferrel Atkins in May 1993) for the land that Eliza Hupp and her children homesteaded in the Upper Beaver Meadows, land that became the Hupp Family Ranch:

1. Eliza Hupp, Southeast Quarter of Section 29, Township 5 North, Range 73 West, 160 acres, Patent granted 5 June 1890. (Source: Larimer County, County Clerk, Book 113, page 246.)

2. Fannie Hupp, North Half of the Southwest Quarter plus South Half of the Northwest Quarter of Section 29, Township 5 North, Range 73 West, 160 acres, Patent granted 19 May 1892. (Source: Larimer County, County Clerk, Book 113, page 245.)

3. Charles Hupp, South Half of the Northeast Quarter plus the Northwest Quarter of Section 9 and the Southwest Quarter of the Southeast Quarter of Section 20, Township 5 North, Range 73 West, 160 acres, Patent granted 30 June 1906. (Source: Larimer County, County Clerk, Book 238, page 21.)

or, from research done by Ray Davis:

Charles Hupp, South Half of the Northeast Quarter **(contains the Hupp Family Cemetery)** plus the Northwest Quarter of Section 29 and the Southwest Quarter of the Southeast Quarter of Section 20, Township 5 North, Range 73 West, 160 acres, Patent granted 20 February 1905. (Source: Larimer County, County Clerk, Book 85, page 337.)

In addition, William Horace Hupp homesteaded additional land that was not part of the Hupp Family Ranch: Lots 1, 2, and 3 of Section 6, Township 4 North, Range 73 West, 135.62 acres, Patent granted 7 September 1900. (Source: Larimer County, County Clerk, Book 113, page 261.)

Before John died, he and his boys were able to build the ranch's hewn-log house, which was added on to later, and to start several outbuildings. The house and a number of Hupp family members are shown on the cover of *John T. Hupp, The Unfinished Saga of John T. Hupp of Virginia* and on page 103 of *"This Blue Hollow": Estes Park, the Early Years, 1859-1915* by James H. Pickering. (See the "Bibliography" for a complete citation.)

Eventually, the Hupp Family Ranch included an enlarged ranch house, fencing, corrals, a fruit cellar, chicken house, and stables. The family raised various grain crops and a garden and managed a small herd of cattle. According to an article by Carmen Johnson titled "The Hupps in Estes Park: Part One, 1875-1900" in the Summer 2003 issue of *Rocky Mountain Nature Association Quarterly*, while the Hupp family sometimes allowed paying visitors to stay in spare rooms, they "were one of the few early Estes Park families who did not end up making their living from the growing business of tourism."

Frances ("Fannie") Hupp never married and stayed on the ranch, which she helped her mother manage. Eliza died on 16 September 1900 after a long illness, and Fannie died about 4 months later on 11 January 1901 of "neuralgia of the heart." Note that the headstone at the Hupp Family Cemetery says that Eliza died on 17 September 1900, but her obituary says that she died on 16 September 1900 and that she was buried on 19 September 1900 with Elder Elkanah J. Lamb officiating.

In 1904 and 1905, the Hupp Family Ranch (the three patented parcels belonging to Eliza, Fannie, and Charles Hupp mentioned above) was sold to Pieter Hondius, Sr.

Pieter Hondius, Sr., was married to Eleanor Estes James, the daughter of William Edwin James, the founder of the Elkhorn Lodge. The land that Pieter purchased from the Hupps was part of the about 3,700 acres he owned in the Estes Park area, which eventually became part of Rocky Mountain National Park. When the Park purchased what had been the Hupp Family Ranch, it tore down the buildings on that property "to return the park to its natural state."

(For more information on Pieter Hondius, Sr., see the chapter on the Elkhorn Lodge Cemetery.)

Hupp Hotels in Estes Park

As mentioned above, Mary Elizabeth ("Mollie") Hupp and her husband John Jones operated the Jones Inn near Mary's Lake. However, the Hupp family member with biggest stake in hotel operations in the Estes Park area was Josephine ("Josie") Hupp, the wife of Henry Aaron Hupp.

The earliest of her land transactions relating to hotel property was the acquisition of property on the southwest corner of Elkhorn and Moraine Avenues in downtown Estes Park from Jane L. James in 1906. Josie built the Hupp Hotel on this property, which she operated jointly with her sister-in-law Ellen Truitt Hupp.

Josie and Ellen next purchased the Manford Hotel diagonally across from the Hupp Hotel on the northeast corner of Elkhorn and Moraine Avenues. This acquisition was made from John J. Manford in 1908. They renamed the establishment the Hupp Annex.

When the two sisters-in-law later sold the Hupp Hotel to Nina Higby, who renamed it the Park Hotel, they then changed the name of the Hupp Annex to the Hupp Hotel.

In 1916, Josie acquired the property across the street from the Hupp Hotel and had a two-story hotel built there, a hotel which she named The Josephine. In 1920, she sold The Josephine to Lewiston Hotels Co. In 1926, she bought The Josephine back, only to again sell it, this time to Ted Jelsema, who renamed it the Riverside Hotel. When the top floor of the Riverside Hotel later burned, it was never rebuilt. However, the ground floor continues to house businesses, including the Wheel Bar.

In 1926, Josie bought the Sherwood Hotel from Magers and Dawson. But, since this meant that she was simultaneously operating three hotels and a couple of restaurants, she sold the Sherwood to interests in Canyon City, Colorado, the same year that she bought it. She finally also sold the Hupp Hotel, originally the Hupp Annex, to William F. and Anna May Derby, who were already managing it for her.

Then, on 5 July 1913, Josie purchased the Boyd Market, which was just west of the Hupp Annex/Hupp Hotel. Her husband Henry operated it for several years. (Remember that Henry was a butcher.)

Jack Moomaw's Discovery of Charles Hupp's Body

Jack Moomaw was a well-known Rocky Mountain National Park Ranger. He began working for the Park as a trail foreman in 1921, retired from active duty in 1945, and died on 10 January 1974.

In 1963, Jack self-published his memories of his days as a ranger in *Recollections of a Rocky Mountain Ranger*. The self-published version of Jack's memoirs was printed by Times-Call Publishing Company, Longmont. The book was then reissued in 1994 by the YMCA of the Rockies with a biography of Jack Moomaw and editing provided by Jack R. Melton and Lulabeth Melton. This second version was printed by Johnson Publishing Company, Boulder. In 2001 Jack Melton and the YMCA of the Rockies issued on an "updated" version of the 1994 edition.

In one chapter of that book, titled "So Long, Old Timer" (pages 90-91 in the self-published 1963 edition and pages 96-98 of the Meltons' 1994 edition), Jack recounts both the times he spent visiting with Charles Hupp and his discovery of Charlie's body after he died.

At the time of his death, Charlie was working as the winter caretaker of the Horseshoe Inn, which was then only half a mile from the Ranger Station where Jack worked. The Inn was demolished after the Park purchased the property on which it is located. Before its destruction, it was at the west end of Horshoe Park, west of the current Highway 34, and south of the Old Fall River Road. Jack had been worried about Charlie because "his heart had been bothering him and he had not been any too well all winter." (For more information on the Horseshoe Inn and its history, see the chapter on the Horseshoe Park Graves. Although all of these graves appear to be graves of children, since the location of Charlie Hupp's burial is unknown, he might be buried in one of the graves in or near the Horseshoe Park Cemetery.)

When Jack stopped by the Inn during a day in late March 1926 for one of his regular "bull sessions" with Charlie, he was pleased to find Charlie "in fine spirits" and had an enjoyable visit with him. Then Jack got busy with his ranger duties and did not have time to return until Sunday, 4 April 1926, when he found Charlie dead:

> "The room was cold, but freshly clean and tidied up, dishes washed, and everything set to rights. I walked over to the bed and slowly pulled the covers back a little. Charlie was stiff and cold, his eyes closed and mouth slightly open. He might well have been asleep, except that his head was thrown back a little farther than natural. He had shaved and apparently taken a bath, and his clothes were neatly folded on a chair."

> "I cannot say that I felt any horror or sorrow, but a great loneliness came over me as I went to the telephone. . . . . Back on a little hill near the Ranger Station, as I watched the bus [that came in response to Jack's call to pick up Charlie's body] picking its way around the snowbanks in the twilit valley below, I murmured, 'So long, old timer.'"

Descendants of William Horace Hupp and Grace Hunter Hupp

Bill (Child No. 8 above under "Biographical and Genealogical Information of the John T. Hupp Family) and Grace had four children:

1. **Doris Sidney Hupp.** Doris was born on 10 December 1895, in Estes Park. According to information provided by William Ervin Hupp in late March 2001, following her father's death in 1912, Doris lived in Estes Park until her marriage, probably living with her Uncle Henry and Aunt Josephine and Aunt Ellen. During this time, Doris ran the Estes Park Post Office. On 3 December 1914, Doris married James Sidney Williams, Sr., of Estes Park. Doris died in April 1963 in Boulder.

   James Sidney ("Sid") Williams, Sr., Dori's husband. Sid was born on 10 October 1888 in Brownwood, Texas. In 1928, Doris and Sid moved from Estes Park to Fairplay, Colorado, where Sid worked for the Park County Highway Department. Sid died on 12 September 1957 in Fairplay.

   Doris and Sid had four children:

   1.1. **Martha Elizabeth Williams.** Martha was born 21 February 1916 in Fairplay, Colorado. She was married three times: 1. Manford Hickel, 2. Jess Fitzsimmons, and 3. Leroy Hessenflow. (For information on the two children that she had with Manford Hickel, see the "Descendants of John T. Hupp, Sr." document.) Martha died of emphysema on 9 July 1987 in Sun City, Arizona.

   1.2. **James Sidney Williams, Jr.** James was born 14 July 1917 in Estes Park. He died in June 1950 in Fairplay.

   1.3. **Mary Jane Williams.** Mary was born 5 October 1918 in the original town of Dillon, Colorado, which is now under Lake Dillon. She married Harry A. Tuell on 3 April 1954. She graduated from the University of Colorado with a law degree in 1942, being the only woman to graduate from the law school that year. Mary Jane died on 1 December 1994 in Boulder.

   Harry A. Tuell, Mary's husband.

   (For information on the Mary and Harry's daughter, see the "Descendants of John T. Hupp, Sr." document.)

   1.4. **Thomas Ervin Williams.** Thomas was born 3 September 1920, also in Dillon, Colorado. Thomas died on 28 December 1948 in Denver. He married Aileen Ann

Popst on 21 February 1940.

Aileen Ann Popst, Thomas's wife.

(For information on Thomas and Aileen's four children, see the "Descendants of John T. Hupp, Sr." document.)

2. **Wilberta Ellen Hupp.** Wilberta was born 17 April 1897 in Estes Park. Following her father William's death in 1912, Wilberta was raised in and around the various Hupp hotel properties in Estes Park by her Uncle Henry and Aunt Josephine and Aunt Ellen. On 10 November 1917, she married Seth Abraham Armstead, Sr., in Denver.

   Seth Abraham Armstead, Sr., Wilberta's husband. Seth was born on 27 May 1892 in Byron, Nebraska. He owned a scenic tour guide company, which operated mainly between Boulder, Denver, and Estes Park. In the winters, he went to California to work.

   After Wilberta died in September 1949 in Boulder, Seth married Leah Jane Lee. Seth died on 18 April 1970 in Boulder. Leah survived Seth; however, in an email dated 10 August 2006, Ray Davis told us that she had died sometime between June 2001 and 2006. Neither he nor we could find her obituary in *The Daily Camera*, Boulder's daily paper.

   Wilberta and Seth had two children:

   2.1. **Seth Abraham Armstead, Jr.** Seth, Jr., was born 27 September 1918 in Boulder. Seth grew up in Boulder, where he graduated from Boulder High School and the University of Colorado. He was in the U.S. Air Force for 30 years, serving in World War II, Korea, and Vietnam. In World War II, he flew 43 bombing missions over Germany. Following his military career, he was the city manager of Grand Terrace, California, from 1976 to 1986. He married Virginia June McCaffrey on 2 January 1943 in Douglas, Arizona. After his retirement, he raised cattle in Banning, California, where he died on 26 February 1996.

   Virginia June McCaffrey, Seth, Jr.'s wife.

   (For information on Seth, Jr. and Virginia's four children that he had with Virginia, see the "Descendants of John T. Hupp, Sr." document.)

   2.2. **William ("Bill") Ervin Armstead.** Bill was born 22 January 1920 in Boulder, Colorado. Bill was a Master Sargent in the Army Air Forces during World War II and served in the European theater. He married Dorothy Eileen Hall on 29 October 1949 in Boulder. At the time he retired, Bill was the Fire Chief at Rocky Mountain Arsenal south of Boulder. Bill died in Boulder on 5 May 2004. He is buried in the Mountain View Memorial Park in Boulder.

   Dorothy Eileen Hall, Bill's wife.

3. **John Ervin Hupp.** Ervin, as he was known, was born on 22 October 1898 in Estes Park. When his father William died in 1912, Ervin went to Jackson, Wyoming, to live with his Aunt Nan and Uncle Mort. He returned to Estes Park to attend Estes Park High School. It was while he was in Jackson that he met Pearl Etha Williams, the young lady whom he would later marry.

   After serving in the U.S. Army during World War I, Ervin graduated from the University of Colorado with a degree in petroleum geology. He married Pearl Etha Williams (about whom more below) on 2 June 1927 in Laramie, Wyoming. In 1931, the couple moved to Cut Bank, Montana. Ervin became a well-renowned geologist in Wyoming, Montana, and Canada. At the time of his retirement in November 1963, he was the chief geologist for the Montana Power Company. Ervin died of a heart attack on 7 May 1964 in Cut Bank and was buried there 4 days later.

Pearl Etha Williams, Ervin's wife. Pearl was the **daughter of Otho Eli Williams and Josephine Sullivan**. She was born on 24 October 1897 in Loveland, Colorado. In 1920, she was elected the first woman marshal in Jackson, Wyoming, by the all-woman town council. As Pearl's obituary put it (from a clipping in an unidentified paper in the Estes Park Library from an Associate Press wire story), "the 22-year-old Hupp was appointed marshal by the five-woman town council swept into office after years of inefficient administration from men in Jackson."

Pearl's obituary goes on to say that "national newspaper writers portrayed the then-Pearl Williams as a tough, no-nonsense, gun-toting law-woman. She has said she encouraged the image by lying to one reporter that local lawbreakers gave her no trouble after she shot three dead and buried them herself."

In reality, "the lady marshal actually spent most [of] her time locking up drunks and chasing cows from downtown. She would deputize her older brothers when she needed help."

After serving about a year as marshal, Pearl resigned to attend the University of Wyoming. After graduation, she taught school at Wilson and Jenny Lake, Wyoming.

Pearl died on 23 May 1994 in Cut Bank, where she is buried.

Ervin and Pearl Hupp were instrumental in getting the headstone placed on the Hupp Family Cemetery in Rocky Mountain National Park. (See "History of the Hupp Family Cemetery and Headstone" above.)

Ervin and Pearl had two children:

3.1. **William ("Bill") Ervin Hupp.** Bill was born in 1929, in Jackson, Wyoming. He married Betty Lou King in 1952 in Cut Bank, Montana.

Bill graduated from Cut Bank High School in 1947 and from Montana State University in Bozeman in 1952 with a degree in Business Administration. Then, like his father before him, Bill attended and graduated from the University of Colorado with a degree in petroleum geology.

Betty Lou King, Bill's wife.

As of June 2001, Bill was retired, and he and Betty Lou lived in Boulder. One of his sons, Michael Ervin Hupp, and Michael's family live nearby in Longmont. However, in October 2003, William's cousin Ray Davis told us that Bill and Betty had moved to Bozeman, Montana.

Bill is one of the John T. Hupp descendants who helped us gather the information that we used to provide this history of the John T. Hupp family.

(For information on Bill and Betty's six children, see "Descendants of John T. Hupp, Sr." document.)

3.2. **Betty Jo Hupp.** Betty was born in 1932 in Great Falls, Montana. In 1955, she married Gerald Gregg Whitney in Cut Bank. As of June 2001, Betty Jo resided in Orangevale, California.

Gerald Gregg Whitney, Betty's husband.

(For information on Betty and Gerald's three children, see "Descendants of John T. Hupp, Sr.")

4. **Inez Ethel Hupp.** Inez was born on 3 October 1900 in Estes Park. Following her father William's death in 1912, Inez was raised in and around the various Hupp hotel properties in Estes Park by her Uncle Henry and Aunt Josephine and Aunt Ellen.

   Inez attended college for a short time, after which she became a school teacher in the Johnstown-Milliken, Colorado, schools and then became the Postmistress of Milliken (around 1923-1924) until she married Earl Kenneth Davis on 6 May 1924 in Greeley, Colorado.

   Earl Kenneth Davis, Inez's husband. Earl was born on 15 December 1898 in Pendleton, Indiana. He was involved in a number of occupations but was best known for his work in the oil fields in and around Cut Bank, Montana. When Earl became 49, he turned from oil field work to the real estate business, in which he was involved until he retired and he and Inez moved to Tucson, Arizona.

   While Inez and Earl lived in Cut Bank, Inez worked as a postal clerk between 1941 and 1946.

   Inez died on 7 July 1973 in Tucson, Arizona. Earl died on 1 August 1980, also in Tucson. Their cremains are interred at the South Lawn Cemetery in Tucson.

   Inez and Earl had the following four children:

   4.1. **Thomas Earl Davis.** Thomas was born in 1925 in Kerville, Texas. He married Carmela Catherine Vaticano in 1946 in Perth Amboy, New Jersey. Tom is a retired Army Colonel and dentist.

   Carmela Catherine Vaticano, Thomas's wife.

   After Tom's retirement, he and Carmela lived for a time in Las Vegas, Nevada, but they then moved back to New Jersey to be closer to their daughter (Patricia Ann Davis born in 1947) and grandchildren.

   4.2. **Coral Ervin Davis.** Ervin was born in 1926 in Jenks, Oklahoma. Ervin married Irene Elizabeth Koebel in 1949 in Grand Junction, Colorado.

   Ervin was raised in Cut Bank, Montana. After spending some time as a radio operator in the U.S. Navy, Ervin became a school teacher in Charlo, Montana, an occupation from which he retired in 1983. In 1989, Ervin was elected to the Montana State House of Representatives, a position to which he was re-elected in both 1991 and 1993. As of June 2001, Ervin still resided in Charlo.

   Ervin is one of the John T. Hupp descendants who helped us gather the information that we used to provide this history of the John T. Hupp family.

   Elizabeth Koebel, Coral Ervin's wife. Elizabeth died on 18 March 1995 in Ronan, Montana.

   (For information on Ervin and Elizabeth's three children, see the "Descendants of John T. Hupp, Sr." document.)

4.3. **Telpha LaVonne Davis.** Telpha was born on 27 July 1927 in Jenks, Oklahoma. She married Richard Earl Foxhoven in 1948 in Grand Junction, Colorado. Telpha is a retired executive secretary for a large soils engineering firm in Houston, Texas. As of June 2001, she lived in Denton, Texas. However, according to the *Social Security Death Index* on 27 September 2013, Telpha died on 4 October 2010, with her last address given as Webster, Harris County, Texas.

Richard Earl Foxhoven, Telpha's husband.

(For information on Telpha and Richard's four children, see the "Descendants of John T. Hupp, Sr." document.)

4.4. **Raymond ("Ray") Merritt Davis.** Ray was born in 1928 in Jenks, Oklahoma. He married Wanda Elizabeth Dunning in 1948 in San Antonio, Texas. Ray was in the U.S. Air Force at the time. Later, he was stationed at Warren Air Force Base in Cheyenne, Wyoming, where his and Wanda's two sons were born. After Ray finished his stint in the Air Force, he attended and graduated from the University of Northern Colorado in Greeley. While he was there, his and Wanda's daughter was born.

Wanda Elizabeth Dunning, Ray's wife.

After Ray graduated from college, he and his family moved to Tucson, Arizona, where he and Wanda have lived ever since. Before Ray retired, he was a professional educator from the Tucson public high school system.

Ray is one of the John T. Hupp descendants who helped us gather the information that we used to provide this history of the John T. Hupp family.

(For information on Ray and Wanda's three children, see the "Descendants of John T. Hupp, Sr." document.)

MARY JANE JAMES GRAVE

Location: Latitude 40° 22' 57" N, Longitude 105° 33' 10" W

The grave of Mary Jane James is in the public right-away between the western city limits of Estes Park and the Fall River entrance to Rocky Mountain National Park. The grave is just off the north side of Fall River Road between a pine tree and a two-wire fence. Just north of the grave and north of the fence is a large granite outcrop. To the immediate east of the grave are two medium-sized weathered boulders, both of which are primarily buried in the ground.

As of August 2001, about 25 feet west of the grave was the end of a wooden privacy fence belonging to Sunnyside Knoll. Directly across the road from the grave, there were no buildings because the Fall River is very close to the road at that point. However, on the south side of Fall River Road and to the west of the grave was The Inn on the Fall River and to the south and east was the Pine Haven Resort.

Description of Grave

When we found Mary Jane's grave, it was marked with a small granite boulder that served as its uninscribed "headstone." See "Finding the Grave" below for an explanation of how we were able to finally locate the grave. Once we found the grave and used dowser rods to confirm an infant burial, we returned and enhanced the marking of the grave by adding small stones to outline it, including a piece of Lyons sandstone from Boulder County to make it clear to those looking for the grave in the future that the rocks marking the grave were not a natural occurrence.

Photo A: Grave of Mary Jane James, West of Estes Park on North Side of Fall River Road (The Black Arrow Points to Her Grave.)

Finding the Grave

We knew approximately where to look for this grave from the entry provided for it in the 1985 edition of the Colorado Council of Genealogical Societies' *Colorado Cemetery Directory*. The entry for this grave provided the following information:

- "Cemetery" Name: Grave of Mary Jane James
- Location: Near Fall River, northwestern part of Estes Park (SW 1/4 of Sec. 23, T5N, R73W, 6th P.M.)

Armed with this information, in January 2000 we stopped at Nicky's Restaurant on the south side of Fall River Road and asked if they knew anything about the grave of Mary Jane

James. The owners of Nicky's knew the Seybold family and recalled that they were somehow associated with the James family. They got us in touch with a member of the Seybold family, who knew nothing about the grave. After talking to several different members of the Seybold family, we ended up talking to Dianne Seybold, who talked to her mother-in-law, Jeanne M. Seybold. Jeanne was rather ill, but, through Dianne, provided us with the following information:

- The grave was "in front of a big rock on the north side of the road [Fall River Road] up [west] from Nicky's Restaurant."
- The grave had originally been marked with steel posts connected by a chain, but tourists camping in the area thought that the chained-in area was a fire pit and built fires in it. So the family removed the posts and chain.
- Mary Jane James was an infant about 1 or 2 months old when she died and was buried in 1910.
- Her parents were Homer and Jennie James. They later moved to California, where they adopted a girl and gave her the same name. They had no other children.

Dianne told us that in a day or two she would be taking Jeanne to the doctor and would have Jeanne direct her to the exact location of the grave north of Fall River Road and would then show us exactly where it was.

While we were waiting for Dianne to get back to us, using just the location information provided above, we tried to find Mary Jane's grave on our own. Although we found several likely looking locations, our use of dowser rods did not indicate that any of them marked burials.

A few days later Dianne showed author Duane Kniebes where the grave was. (Remember that Dianne was shown the location of the grave by Jeanne.) This time Duane's use of dowser rods confirmed the burial of an infant at the location Dianne indicated.

Dianne told Duane that, until our call to the Seybold family, no one in the family knew about the existence of Mary Jane James or her grave.

Unfortunately, Jeanne Seybold passed away on 16 March 2001 (Source No. 6 below). Had this project not sent us looking for Mary Jane's grave when we did, the exact location of her grave might have been lost forever.

Sources of Information on Mary Jane James and the James and Seybold Families

1. The 1910 U.S. Census for Estes Park, Larimer County, Colorado, enumerated on 18 April 1910.
2. The 1920 U.S. Census for Precinct 37, Estes Park, Larimer County, Colorado, enumerated between 7 and 10 January 1920.
3. The 1930 U.S. Census for precinct 37, Estes Park, Larimer County, Colorado, enumerated between 12 and 16 April 1930.
4. "Old Park Resident Buried in Pueblo," *Estes Park Trail*, 4 December 1936, page 1. This article contains the obituary of A. L. Cobb, the grandfather of Jeanne Gray Seybold.
5. "Dr. H. E. James, Pioneer Villager, Dies After an Extended Illness," *Estes Park Trail*, 16 May 1958.
6. "Service set for today for local resident," *Estes Park Trail*, 21 March 2001. This article contains the obituary of Jeanne M. Gray Seybold.

Source Nos. 4-6 were found for us by Sybil Barnes, then the Local History Librarian of the Estes Park Public Library. (For additional information on Sybil, see the "Acknowledgments" section.)

Date of Mary Jane James's Death

The 1910 U.S. Census for Estes Park (Source No. 1) tells us that Homer James and his wife Jennie were married for 5 years in 1910 and that Jennie's only child, who we know was Mary Jane James, was dead as of 18 April 1910 (the day Homer, Jennie, and Jennie's mother were enumerated for the 1910 U.S. Census). Consequently, Mary Jane would have died between approximately 1905 and 18 April 1910. (For details, see the Child No. 1.1 in the section titled "Biographical and Genealogical Information of the James Family of Estes Park" in the chapter on the Elkhorn Lodge Cemetery.)

Recall that Jeanne Seybold told us, through her daughter-in-law Dianne Seybold, that Mary Jane died in 1910. Thus, the above census data and Jeanne Seybold agree.

Relation of Mary Jane James and Jeanne Seybold to the James Family

The James family of which Mary Jane was a part and to which Jeanne Seybold was related by marriage is the William Edwin James family, who were the founders of Elkhorn Lodge. (For detailed information on the William Edwin James family, see the chapter on the Elkhorn Lodge Cemetery, especially the section titled "Biographical and Genealogical Information of the James Family of Estes Park.")

The Homer James who was Mary Jane's father was the oldest son of William Edwin James. He was trained as a medical doctor but also managed the Elkhorn Lodge for a time following his father's death.

Homer was 19 when the 1885 Colorado State Census was taken, so he would have been born in 1865 or 1866. However, more exact information is found in his obituary in the 16 May 1958 issue of *Estes Park Trail* (Source No. 5), which provides the following information about Homer and his wife:

- Homer was a resident of Glendale, California, when he died on Sunday morning, 4 May 1958 at the age of 92. His remains were interred in a cemetery in Pasadena, California.

- For the 3 years before his death, he was living in the Mission Sanitorium.

- He was born on 28 April 1866 in Syracuse, New York.

- He graduated from the Medical School of the University of Colorado and was a member of the University's first football team.

- He attended a post-graduate course at the New York Polyclinic for a year and then practiced medicine in Alma, Colorado, for 2 years.

- Following the death of his father in January 1895, he helped his mother run the Elkhorn Lodge.

    (For information on Homer's medical and hotel management careers from the perspective of his sister Eleanor Estes James Hondius , see the section titled "Operation of the Elkhorn Lodge Under the James and Hondius Families" in the chapter on the Elkhorn Lodge Cemetery.)

- He married Miss Jennie Buchanan. (It is hard to read her last name, but it appears to be "Buchanan.") [For additional information on Jennie, see "Jennie L. Buchanan" under the entry for her husband Homer Edwin James (Child No. 1) in the section titled "Biographical and Genealogical Information of the James Family of Estes Park" in the chapter on the Elkhorn Lodge Cemetery.]

- He started the Estes Park Lumber Yard.
- He moved to Watsonville, California, where he owned a fruit ranch for 3 or 4 years.
- After Watsonville, he returned to Estes Park, where he opened a real estate business.
- He organized the Estes Park Country Club and managed it for 2 years.
- Some time after that, he and his wife Jennie must have returned to California because he and, we assume, also Jennie are buried in California, Jennie dying "a few years" before he did.
- At his death, he was survived by:
  - An adopted daughter, Mary Peterson. (Remember that Jeanne Seybold told us that Homer and Jennie had given their adopted daughter the name "Mary Jane," the same name they gave their biological daughter buried on Fall River Road.)
  - Two grandchildren.
  - One sister, Mrs. Pieter Hondius, Sr., (Eleanor Estes James Hondius).

Jeanne Seybold's relationship to the William Edwin James family is through her mother's third husband, Howard James, Sr., who was a younger brother of Homer James. Jeanne's mother was born Edna B. Cobb. The obituary of Edna's father, A. L. Cobb, published on the first page of the 4 December 1936 issue of the *Estes Park Trail* (Source No. 4), tells us that he was Edna's father.

Jeanne M. Seybold's obituary published in the 21 March 2001 issue of the *Estes Park Trail* (Source No. 6) listed Jeanne's parents as "Walter and Edna (Cobb) Gray." From the 1920 and 1930 U.S. Censuses of Estes Park (Source Nos. 2 and 3), we were able to determine that Jeanne's mother had been married to Walter Gray at the time of Jeanne's birth and had divorced Walter and married Howard James sometime in about 1923.

As far as we can determine, Edna Cobb Gray James and Howard James had two children together: Howard ("Bud") James, Jr., who was living in Steamboat Springs, Colorado, as of July 2001, and Eleanore A. James Owen, who was living in Estes Park as of March 2002 but who, sadly, died in Estes Park on 9 December 2006. Bud and Eleanore are thus the half-siblings of Jeanne Seybold.

For additional information on Howard James, Edna B. James, Howard ("Bud") James, and Eleanore A. James Owen, see the sections titled "History of the James Family and Elkhorn Lodge" and "Biographical and Genealogical Information of the James Family in Estes Park" in the chapter on the Elkhorn Lodge Cemetery. For more information on Bud James, see the "History of Elkhorn Lodge After Eleanor Hondius" section in the same chapter.

For additional information on Jeanne M. Gray Seybold and her family, especially the husbands of her mother Edna B. Cobb Arnold Gray James Mills, see the sections titled "Biographical and Genealogical Information on Walter A. Gray and His Family" and "Biographical and Genealogical Information of Paul N. ('Tiny') Mills" in the same chapter. Jeanne herself is included as Jeanne M. Gray (Child No. 1) in the "Biographical and Genealogical Information on Walter A. Gray and His Family" section of the same chapter.

RANSOM S. KENDALL GRAVE

Location: Latitude 40° 22' 24" N, Longitude 105° 36' 04" W

Ransom S. Kendall's grave is in Beaver Meadows in Rocky Mountain National Park. It is southwest of Upper Beaver Meadows Road and about 0.6 of a mile from the beginning of the intersection of Upper Beaver Meadows Road (a dirt road) and the paved road leading to the Beaver Meadows Entrance Station.

As noted below, Kendall was a friend of the Hupp family, three members of which are buried in the Hupp Family Cemetery, which is 0.4 of a mile east of Kendall's grave on the north side of Upper Beaver Meadows Road. (See the chapter on the Hupp Family Cemetery.)

Description of Grave

The grave has an east-west orientation. It is covered with a variety on native rocks, none of which is inscribed. What looks like a small squaw bush is growing on the grave. It does not appear to have been purposely planted. Our use of dowser rods confirms an adult burial at this location.

Photo A: Grave of Ransom S. Kendall in Beaver Meadows in Rocky Mountain National Park

Finding the Grave

Jackie Johnson of Estes Park told us about Ransom S. Kendall's grave and took us to see it on 17 September 2000.

Biographical Information on Ransom F. Kendall

Jackie Johnson also provided the following historical information from the pages of Volume II of *Historic Structures in Rocky Mountain National Park* that talked about Ransom Kendall's cabin and burial:

> "A 'house' is shown in Section 6, T4N, R73W in the survey of 1892 (made, incidentally, by Abner Sprague), and ownership is attributed to R. S. Kendall [RMNP maps, unpaged]. According to the record of the Bureau of Land Management, Ransom S. Kendall homesteaded this location in 1892 and canceled in 1894."

> [Kniebes note: Kendall's homestead being canceled in 1894 may mean that he died that year. The three individuals buried in the Hupp Family Cemetery died between 1877 and 1901.]

"It is awkward to describe the location [of Kendall's house and homestead] since Section 6 is 1-1/4 miles long in a north-south direction. Of the four 40-acre tracts lying along the north side of Section 6, the house lies near the center of the NW quarter of the third forty from the east side. In terms of topographical features, we can say that the house lay in the extreme southwest corner of Moraine Park, slightly north of the point where today's Cub Lake Trail swings to the west up Cub Creek."

[Kniebes note: This location coincides with the place where the Hanks family scattered the ashes of Allyn Frank Hanks, a Superintendent of the Park in the 1960s, and his wife Hazel Williams Hanks. See the sections on Allyn and Hazel Hanks in the chapter on Rocky Mountain National Park Scattered Cremains.]

"Little is found of Kendall: We know he was buried with the Hupp family in Beaver Meadows (J. E. Hupp letter); according to Mrs. Walter Jones (Interview, June 27, 1963), he was a friend of the family; Stopher said (Interview, Aug. 23, 1962) that he remembered the cabin, adding 'Abner gave Kendall permission to build a cabin there.' This seems unlikely, in view of the B.L.M. record."

[Kniebes note: J. E. Hupp is probably John Ervin Hupp. Abner is probably Abner E. Sprague. The reference to J. E. Hupp's letter could be interpreted to mean that Kendall was buried in the Hupp Family Cemetery. As the "Location" information above makes clear, this is not the case. Instead, while the three Hupp graves and Kendall's burial site are all in Beaver Meadows, they are in *different* locations.]

"Mr. and Mrs. Julian Hayden (Interview, July 19, 1962) remembered a cabin on that site–'above and across the river from the Brinwood'–which was, in the early days of the century occupied by Tom Bass, a remittance man. Bass has often cooked on the survey parties. About 1915 there was some sort of wrangle at Steads over a poker game, and Bass was killed by a Hallowell. After the shooting, it was learned that [his] last name was really Bassford."

Jackie Johnson also provided us with the following information from the Bureau of Land Management Tract Books, which show that Ransom S. Kendall filed for a homestead for Lots 1, 2, and 3 at the north end of Section 6. Jackie's research indicates that Abner E. Sprague's 1892 survey shows that Lots 1, 2, and 3 were located as shown in the diagram below. Her research also indicates that the map of 1892 shows a house located in the northwest corner of Lot 3 (house graphic in diagram below).

North end of Section 6.

Lot 4	Lot 3 ⌂	Lot 2	Lot 1

[For more information on Jackie Johnson, who was extremely helpful to us in our grave-search efforts in the Rocky Mountain Nation Park and Estes Park areas and who died in August 2001, see "Johnson, Jacqueline ("Jackie") Jaye" in the "Ackowledgments" section.]

On 6 August 1966, Dr. D. Ferrel Atkins conducted an interview of Dan Griffith in which he asked Dan about Ransom Kendall. (At the time Ferrel was helping us, he was a retired Rocky Mountain National Park Ranger-Naturalist. For more information about Ferrel, who died on 16 September 2011, see "Atkins, D. Ferrel" in the "Acknowledgments" section. For more information on Dan Griffith, see the chapter on the Cleave-Griffith Family Cemetery.)

A transcription of the pertinent parts from page 16 of the interview, which is available in its entirety in both audio tape and transcribed formats in the Local History Section of the Estes Park Public Library, follows:

> Ferrel: "Incidentally, we've got some record of a fellow by the name of Kendall over in that corner of Moraine Park. Now, do you know Kendall? He would have lived over there in the southwest corner of Moraine Park, if we've got it straight—Ranson Kendall."
>
> Dan: "Well, there was somebody had a homestead over there. It was just below that Cub Lake."
>
> Ferrel: "Yes, yes."
>
> Dan: "It was in the Moraine Park plat, but I thought that was somebody that was related to the Hupps. I'm not sure of it."
>
> Ferrel: "Oh, well, that might be the fellow because it seems to be that I have heard some stories that relate this fellow Kendall to the Hupps, but you don't remember ever having seem him or anything?"
>
> Dan: "No."
>
> Ferrel: "Obviously, he didn't stay around there very long then."
>
> Dan: "Well, I was a pretty young fellow then, and I couldn't say."

After having found the above interview, in July 2002 we contacted the Hupp family's genealogist, Ray Davis of Tucson, and ask him if he had ever heard that Ransom Kendall was actually related to the Hupps. His reply to us, in an email dated 19 July 2002, follows:

> "I am sure that Ransom Kendall was just a family friend. Remember that there were two unmarried Hupp girls in the family and that may have been one reasons he hung around their house."

Then, in another email, this one dated 20 July 2002, Ray provided the following additional information:

> "Of course, I don't know anything about Ransom Kendall for sure, but I do know that I read somewhere he was a frequent visitor over at the Hupp spread. He may have been a good friend of one of the boys, but the fact that Frances (Fannie) and Ellen were single and living there is a more interesting theory, don't you think? Frances also had a homestead adjacent to her mother's and helped her mother with her farm chores. Ellen, on the other hand, was a working partner with Aunt Josie in the hotel businesses in town [Estes Park]. All we can do is speculate on any of those matters as there is no living person nor any written record I have found to tell me any different. Both girls died relatively young. [Frances died at 48 in 1901, and Ellen died at 58 in 1916.] Hard to tell if they would have ever gotten married if they had lived longer. My mother knew them well and tried to tell me things as I was growing up, but I just wasn't interested at the time, I'm sorry to say."

LARIMER COUNTY CEMETERIES

(For more information on the Hupp family and Ray Davis, see the chapter on the Hupp Family Cemetery. For information on Ray, see specifically the information Raymond Merritt Davis under the subheading titled "Descendants of William Horace Hupp and Grace Hunt Hupp" in the that chapter.)

In January 2004, we checked the 1870 through 1900 Censuses in an effort to learn more about Kendall's point of origin, date of birth, etc. Unfortunately, no Ransom Kendalls show up in any of the censuses for anywhere in Colorado. The only two possible Ransom Kendalls were found in the 1870 Census:

- One Ransom Kendall was a 33-year-old white male who was living in Brimfield, Hampden County, Massachusetts, at the time of the 1870 Census and who was born in Massachusetts. If he was 33 in 1870, he would have been born in about 1837. IF this Ramson Kendall and Larimer County's Ransom Kendall are the same person, he would thus have been about 57 in 1894 when the Moraine Park homestead of Larimer County's Ransom Kendall was canceled; he would have been about 16 years older than Frances Hupp, who was born in 1853; and he would have been about 21 years older than Ellen Hupp, who was born in 1858.

- The other Ransom Kendall was a 54-year old white male who was living in Union Township in Ritchie County, West Virginia, at the time of the 1970 Census and who was born in Virginia. This Ransom Kendall seems a little old to have left West Virginia and started homesteading in Colorado in 1892, when he would have been 76!

Other Kendalls or Kendals in the Larimer County area between 1870 and 1885 are listed below:

- The 1870 Colorado Census (M593, Roll 95, Page 387) shows a 38-year-old John Kendall being in the Cache la Poudre District of Larimer County. This John Kendall, who was a white male, was born in Vermont.

- The 1880 Colorado Census shows a 28-year-old John Kendall in Big Thompson, Larimer County, who had been born in Ohio.

- The 1885 Larimer County Census shows a 55-year-old William Kendal (with a wife named Pauline and seven children) and a 39-year-old John Kendall (with a wife named Mary). Both of these families are enumerated next to each other somewhere in the Loveland-Estes Park area, which might lead one to conclude that they were related. However, William Kendal was born in North Carolina, as were both of his parents, and John Kendall was born in Iowa and his parents were both born in Tennessee. So, while these two gentlemen might have been related, they were not brothers.

One or more of these Colorado Kendal(l)s may have been related to Ransom Kendall.

LEO J. KERSTIEN GRAVE

Location: Latitude 40° 22' 53" N, Longitude 105° 30' 30" W

Leo J. Kerstien's grave is located in Estes Park southwest of the main entrance to Our Lady of the Mountains Catholic Church on the north side of the cement path connecting the Stations of the Cross and between that path and a pine tree. Leo's grave is between the following two Stations of the Cross: "Jesus is condemned" and "Jesus takes up the cross."

Our Lady of the Mountains is at 920 Big Thompson Avenue (Colorado Highway 34) overlooking Estes Park.

Description

Leo J. Kerstien's horizontal grave marker reads as follows:

Leo J. Kerstien
Sept. 14, 1918
Jan. 3, 1983
Beloved husband & father

Because our use of dowser rods at the grave inconsistently indicated a burial and because of the small space between the pine tree behind Leo's grave marker and the cement path in front of it, we assume that Leo's ashes are probably buried below his grave marker. The photo below shows Leo's grave.

Photo A: Grave of Leo J. Kerstien on the Grounds of Our Lady of the Mountains Catholic Church in Estes Park

Finding the Grave

We were told about Leo Kerstien's grave by an Estes Park resident. Unfortunately, we do not recall whom among the numerous Estes Park residents who helped us with our grave-search efforts provided this information.

On 18 May 2000 we visited the grounds of Our Lady of the Mountains and located, photographed, and obtained a GPS reading for Leo's grave.

In January 2011 we contact the Reverend Joseph Hartmann, the pastor of Our Lady of the Mountains since June 2009, to see if he could provide any additional information about Leo and if there had been any additional ash burials on the grounds of Our Lady of the Mountains

LARIMER COUNTY CEMETERIES

since our May 2000 visit. Father Hartmann was not aware of Leo's ash burial until we told him about it. He also told us that he knew of no additional burials on the church's grounds.

Indeed, when we visited the church's office prior to finding Leo's grave on 18 May 2000, we were told that Our Lady of the Mountains Catholic Church did not consider its grounds as an appropriate place for burials, even ash burials. (For more information on this church, see "History of Our Lady of the Mountains Catholic Church" below.)

Sources of Information on Leo J. Kerstien and Our Lady of the Mountains Catholic Church

1. The 1930 U.S. Census for Chicago, Cook County, Illinois, enumerated between 10 and 11 April 1930, which contains information on 11-year-old Leo Kerstien, his parents, and four of his siblings.

2. *U.S. World War II Army Enlistment Records, 1938-1946* as transcribed by Ancestry.com.

3. *U.S. Public Records Index, Volume 2, 1950-1993* as transcribed by Ancestry.com.

4. Our Lady of the Mountains Catholic Church website as found at http://www.olmestes.org on 13 January 2011.

5. *Social Security Death Index* as of 6 September 2011 as transcribed by Ancestry.com.

Genealogy of Leo J. Kerstien

Except as noted, the information below comes from the 1930 U.S. Census for Chicago, Illinois (Source No. 1).

Parents of Leo J. Kerstien

Frank Kerstien, Leo's father. Frank was born in Illinois about 1896. Both of his parents were born in Poland. At the time that the 1930 Census was taken in April 1930, Frank was working as a machinist for an electric company and he and his family were living at 2723 S. Keeler in Chicago.

Julia Kerstien, Leo's mother. Julia was born in Illinois about 1898. Both of her parents were also born in Poland.

Leo Kerstien and His Siblings

As of April 1938, Frank and Julia Kerstien had the following five children, all of whom were born in Illinois:

1. **Bernice Kerstien**. Bernice was born about 1917.

2. **Leo Kerstien**. According to his grave marker, Leo was born on 14 September 1918 and died on 3 January 1983. The *Social Security Death Index* (Source No. 5) reports that Leo was living in Estes Park when he died, was born on 14 September 1918, and died in January 1983.

   Leo enlisted in the U.S. Army in Chicago on 11 April 1941 (Source No. 2). The same enlistment record reports that, as of that date, Leo had attended 4 years of high school and was single with no dependents. The *U.S. Public Records Index* (Source No. 3) reports that Leo and/or his family were living in Estes Park between 1935 and 1993, the last year covered by the cited *Index*.

3. **Lawrence Kerstien**. Lawrence was born about 1923.

4. **Loretta Kerstien**. Loretta was born about 1928.

5. **Theresa Kerstien**. Theresa was born about 1929.

History of Our Lady of the Mountains Catholic Church

According to the church's website (Source No. 4), before the church was established members of the Roman Catholic faith in the Estes Park area attended masses held in the homes of the faithful. Then, about 1915, with the help of Reverend William Howlett of Loveland, the little St. Walter's Catholic Church was built on the hill above the Stanley Hotel at the intersection of Highways 36 and 34.

Attendance at St. Walter's was so significant in the summers that some of those attending masses had to stand outside. And, then, since the church had no heat or insulation, in 1944 winter masses began to be held in the auditorium of the Estes Park High School.

In 1946, ground was broken for the construction of the current Our Lady of the Mountains parish church. Then, in 1947, using native timber and stone from the McGraw Ranch, construction of the church actually began. On 9 June 1947, the 300-seat church was completed.

As the winter and summer populations of the Estes Park Valley grew, the church had to add both offices and what the website describes as "expandable worship space."

LOUIS R. LEVINGS GRAVE

Location: Latitude 40° 27′ 17″ N, Longitude 105° 40′ 25″ W

The grave of Louis Raymond Levings is on a flat shelf behind an upright boulder about 700 feet above the west-most of the two Spectacle Lakes on the southeast face of Ypsilon Mountain/Mount Ypsilon in Rocky Mountain National Park. A photograph pinpointing the site of Louis's grave follows. It was taken by Ted Ronald Matthews in 1950 and is used with his permission.

Photo A: Arrow Points to the Location of the Grave of Louis Levings on Ypsilon Mountain Between Two Snow Fields Above the West-Most Spectacle Lake (Courtesy Ted Matthews)

Description of Grave Marker

The text of Louis's bronze marker reads as follows:

HERE LIES
LOUIS RAYMOND LEVINGS
BORN OCTOBER 26th 1884
FELL FROM MOUNT YPSILON
AUGUST 2nd 1905

ΔΤΔ Γβ   A.I.T.

The photograph of this marker below was taken by Bob Haines in 1959 and is used with his permission.

Photo B: Louis Levings's Bronze Grave Marker (Courtesy Bob Haines)

The Delta Tau Delta (ΔTΔ) in the lower left corner of the marker is a college social fraternity. Gamma Beta (Γβ) is the Illinois Institute of Technology (IIT) Chapter of that fraternity. We checked with the Delta Tau Delta office in Carmel, Indiana. They said that Louis was indeed a member of the Gamma Beta Chapter of Delta Tau Delta and that he was scheduled to graduate in 1906. Thus, he would have died during the summer between his junior and senior years.

Kenneth A. File, the President of the Delta Tau Delta Educational Foundation in 2001, also explained the meaning of the "A.I.T." in the lower right corner of Louis's marker to us: When Louis was attending IIT, which is on the south side of Chicago, it was known as the Armour Institute of Technology ("A.I.T"). It was not until 1940 that the Armour Institute of Technology and the Lewis Institute merged to form the Illinois Institute of Technology. (Coincidentally, Duane Kniebes, one of the author's of this document, worked at the Institute of Gas Technology on the IIT campus for 35 years and his wife Susan Briles Kniebes, the other author, worked there for 18 years.)

Kenneth File also told us that Louis's first cousin Dean Babcock, who figures prominently in the section below on "Louis Levings's Death, Burial, and Reburial, Including Biographical Information on Ted Matthews, " was a member of the Alpha Chapter of Delta Tau Delta at Allegheny College in Meadville, PA. (Dean's mother, Josephine McCall Babcock, was the sister of Agnes McCall Levings, Louis Levings's mother.) For additional information on Dean Babcock, see "Biographical Information on Dean Babcock" below.

On 16 January 2001, Kenneth File also provided the following photograph of Louis Levings from an article about his death in the November 1905 (Volume 29, No. 1, pages 156-158) issue of the fraternity's quarterly magazine, *The Rainbow*:

LARIMER COUNTY CEMETERIES

Photo C: Louis Raymond Levings (Courtesy the Delta Tau Delta Educational Foundation)

Finding the Grave

We knew the approximately location of Louis Levings's grave because of the entry provided for it in the 1985 edition of the Colorado Council of Genealogical Societies' *Colorado Cemetery Directory*. That entry told us the Louis's grave was located at base of east face of Mt. Ypsilon (Sec. 27, T6N, R74W, 6th P.M.), that it was a single grave, and that Louis died in 1905.

Early on in our search for graves in Rocky Mountain National Park, we were referred to Dr. D. Ferrel Atkins because, as part of his interest in the history of the Park, he compiled information about "historical structures" in the Park, including graves. (For more information on Ferrel, who sadly died on 16 September 2011, see the "Acknowledgments" section.)

Ferrel referred us to Robert Haines, a former Rocky Mountain National Park Ranger, because Ferrel recalled that Bob knew about the "grave on Ypsilon Mountain." When we visited Bob and his wife Teddie on 6 October 2000, Bob showed us photographs of Louis's grave that he had taken when he visited the site in 1959. Bob was also able to show us the exact location of the grave on the U.S. Geological Survey's Trail Ridge Quad Map.

Bob also provided us with a great deal of information on the grave of Rev. Thornton R. Sampson, also in the Park. (For more information on Rev. Sampson's grave, see the chapter on the Reverend Thornton R. Sampson Grave. For more information on Bob Haines, who sadly died on 12 May 2008, see the "Acknowledgments" section.)

Bob referred us to Ted R. Matthews, then the last surviving member of the team involved with the reburial of Louis's body on 29 August 1929. (For more information about Louis's reburial, see "Louis Levings's Death, Burial, and Reburial, Including Biographical Information on Ted Matthews" below.)

When we visited with Ted Matthews in Loveland on 22 October 2000, we showed him the Trail Ridge Quad Map with the flag marking Louis's grave. Ted agreed with Bob Haines's memory of the location of the grave. Ted had last visited Levings's grave about 1950 when he and Ted Scott had gone up to the Spectacle Lakes to fish. The fish weren't biting, so Ted Matthews hiked up to and photographed the grave. (See Photo A above.) (For more information on Ted Matthews, who sadly died on 18 September 2001 and is buried in Loveland Burial Park, see the section below titled "Louis Levings's Death, Burial, and Reburial, Including Biographical Information on Ted Matthews.")

On 1 July 2001, we visited to the Aspenglen Campground in Rocky Mountain National Park to look for the grave of a 3-year-old child with the initials "F.A.J." who may have been buried there in 1886. (For information on the graves that we found in the campground, see the chapter on the Aspenglen Campground Cemetery.) While we were there, we met Ira Goldfarb, then a first-year Ranger working at Aspenglen Campground. Ira became interested in our efforts to document the graves, cemeteries, and memorials in the Park. Later that same week, he and his then fiancée and now wife, Joan Feder, climbed Ypsilon Mountain and visited Louis Levings's grave.

When we again met with Ira on July 9th, he confirmed that the grave and the marker are both still there in the exact location described by Bob Haines and Ted Matthews. The GPS reading that Ira and Joan took at the grave site matched exactly the GPS reading of the grave site identified by Bob Haines when we visited him on 6 October 2000. (For more information on Ira Goldfarb and his wife Joan Feder Goldfarb and the help the gave us in our search for graves in Rocky Mountain National Park, see the "Acknowledgments" section.)

Sources of Information Concerning Louis Levings and Ted Matthews

1. Obituary of Louis Raymond Levings, *The Rainbow* (Delta Tau Delta's quarterly magazine), Volume 29, Issue 1, November 1905, pages 156-158.

2. Pages 530-534 of Volume I of *Over Hill and Vale*, written by Harold Marion Dunning, published in 1956. (See the "Bibliography" for a complete citation.)

3. Pages 113-116 of Volume III of *Over Hill &Vale*, written by Harold Marion Dunning and published in 1971. (See the "Bibliography" for a complete citation.)

4. "Ypsilon grave is climber's final legacy," Letter to the Editor by Ted Matthews, *Estes Park Trail*, 23 September 1994. A copy of this letter and Ted's accompanying corrections are part of our research files for this chapter. (All of our research files have been donated to the Local History Archive of the Fort Collins Museum of Discovery.)

5. Obituary of Ted Ronald Matthews, *Estes Park Trail-Gazette*, 21 September 2001.

6. Note 28 on pages 119-120, *In the Vale of Elkanah*, written by James H. Pickering, and published in 2003. (See the "Bibliography" for a complete citation.)

Louis Levings's Death, Burial, and Reburial, Including Biographical Information on Ted Matthews

As noted above, when we visited Bob Haines on 6 October 2000, he told us that we should arrange to visit with Ted Matthews if we wanted to get details concerning the Louis Levings's reburial from someone who was personally involved. Also as noted above, we visited with Ted on October 22nd. When we visited with Ted for a second time on 1 December 2000, he loaned us some slides. (A copy of one of those slides is Photo A above.) He also provided us with a corrected copy of his letter to the editor of the *Estes Park Trail* that was published on 23 September 1994 (Source No. 4). Except as noted, the remainder of this section is based on information that Ted either provided in his letter to the editor (Source No. 4) or told us during our two visits with him.

LARIMER COUNTY CEMETERIES

Ted Ronald Matthews, who was born on 24 May 1905 in Lyons Colorado (Source No. 5), is the half brother to Harold Marion Dunning, the author of *Over Hill and Vale* who reports on Louis's death, burial, and subsequent reburial in Volumes I and III of that three-volume series (Source Nos. 2 and 3). (Ted and Harold had the same mother but different fathers. Harold was the older of the two brothers.) Ted's parents were Arthur C. Matthews and Ella M. Wright (Source No. 5).

Ted worked for Harold for about 15 years in Harold's shoe store and shoe repair shop in Loveland. Ted married Lois E. Bates in Fort Collins on 7 June 1942. From June 1942 through June 1945, he served in the U.S. Army, reaching the rank of sergeant. Then, in 1945, Ted opened a shoe repair shop of his own in Estes Park. Later he and his wife Lois ran a gift shop in Estes Park for a number of years. Ted also worked for Rocky Mountain National Park for five winters as a member of the ski patrol at the Hidden Valley Ski Resort. Ted and his wife were avid climbers and hikers and professional wildlife photographers. Ted climbed Longs Peak at least 46 times, including at least once each month of the year. Once he climbed it three times in 8 days.

In 1990, Ted was a guest of honor at the 75th anniversary of the dedication of Rocky Mountain National Park because he was the only known survivor of the original dedication of the Park in 1915 (Source No. 5).

Because of their enthusiasm for climbing, during the summer of 1928, Ted Matthews and Harold Dunning decided to see if they could locate Louis Levings's grave. As per Ted, to reach the grave one would turn right at the second stream above Ypsilon Lake and then follow the gully to the lower of the two Spectacle Lakes. Next one would cross between the two lakes to the foot of the "Y," with the grave being about 700 feet above that. (See the "Location" information above.)

Ted said that Louis, Louis's cousin Dean Babcock, and George Black began their fateful climb of Ypsilon Mountain on 2 August 1905, after having camped the previous night at Lawn Lake east of Fairchild Mountain. On August 2nd, they first climbed from Lawn Lake up Fairchild Mountain and then, from Fairchild, they went over to Ypsilon Mountain. (At 13,502 feet and 13,514 feet, Fairchild and Ypsilon are about the same height.) The two mountains are connected by a ridge running from northeast to southwest. The ridge reaches Ypsilon at the top of one of the arms of the "Y." The morning of August 2nd Dean Babcock returned to Lawn Lake, but Louis and George decided to descend the east face of Ypsilon Mountain by climbing down that arm of the "Y." It was at that point that Louis fell 150 feet to his death.

According to Jim Pickering (Source No. 6), Louis's fall occurred in the effort to obtain a photograph:

> "To obtain the desired photograph, Levings and [George] Black worked themselves down to a spot 600 feet to the left branch of the 'Y,' only to discover that retreat was impossible. Their only choice was to continue the descent. Levings had lowered himself from a rock to a foothold below when the rock he was holding broke off. He fell about 50 feet, then rolled and fell between one and two hundred feet more, after which he did not move. Black was more fortunate, managing to get down to safety, though at one point he fell and hurt his hip."

Ted Matthews recalls that George Black went for help, and someone was sent to Lawn Lake to tell Dean Babcock.

Shep Husted, Johnny Adams, and George Black were in the group that climbed Ypsilon Mountain to bring Louis's body down. They managed to lower Louis's body using ropes to the scree slope at the foot of the "Y." Ted also recalls that Shep Husted was the one who decided that it was appropriate to bury Louis's body on the mountain below where he died. They carried up cement on their backs, and then used sand that they obtained from the scree slope and water from the melting snow to make concrete. Louis's body was buried against a large boulder, and rocks were added to the cement that held his body in place.

Because of the difficulty of bringing Louis's body down the mountain, his parents agreed to leave him buried on Ypsilon Mountain.

Both Bob Haines and Ted Matthews said that they had heard that Louis's parents had climbed the mountain to visit Louis's grave after he was buried and were satisfied with the site as being an appropriate one for their son's interment.

Jim Pickering (Source No. 6) adds Dean Babcock and Enos Mills to the group who retrieved and then buried Louis's body and leaves out George Black:

> "The rescue party, which included Dean Babcock, Shep Husted, Enos Mills, and Johnny Adams, originally intended to bring out the remains by horseback. But it was nearly dark when the body was finally lowered down the western arm of the 'Y' to a ledge, and it was decided to bury it at the foot of a large boulder several feet above timberline below Spectacle Lake. [Louis's grave is actually above the west-most of the two Spectacle Lakes. See "Location" above.] The next month another party, accompanied by Estes Park mason Carl Piltz, packed cement on horseback to within a fourth mile of Ypsilon Lake and the next morning carried it up a trail covered by several inches of new snow to the gravesite. Then, using sand from the scree slope and melting water, Piltz constructed a crude monument, with a simple plaque." [See "Description of Grave Marker" above for the wording of this plaque.]

When Ted Matthews and a group of climbers that included Ted's full brother Bryan Matthews and Ted's half brother Harold Dunning reached Louis's grave on Ypsilon Mountain the summer in 1928, they discovered that the grave was in poor repair and that "varmits" had been disturbing the grave site. Following their descent from the mountain, Harold contacted Louis's father, who was going to have a galvanized iron container made for the remains.

When nothing had been done by the summer of 1929, Harold Dunning arranged to have a galvanized steel box made in pieces (by the McGeorge Tin Shop in Loveland) that could be "easily" carried up to Louis's grave and then reassembled there, which is indeed what happened on 15 August 1929. Ted was not a member of the group who made the return trip to rebury Louis's body because "someone had to stay in Loveland to run the shoe shop."

On pages 530-534 of Volume I of *Over Hill and Vale* (Source No. 2), Harold Dunning recounts pretty much the same story, but adds:

- Part of a poem titled "Songs of the Rockies" written by Charles Edwin Hewes in memory of Louis.

- Quotes from a letter written to Harold Dunning by Louis's father Charles Levings on 10 October 1928 in response to a letter that Charles had received from Harold describing the condition of Louis's grave. In the letter, Charles says that he had directed his nephew Dean Babcock to visit the grave.

- Information from another letter written by Charles to Harold on 16 October 1928 in which Charles states that Dean had visited the grave and found it just as Harold had described. In this letter, Charles outlines plans for reburial in a galvanized iron container. Harold goes on to explain that Charles was 80 years old when he wrote these two letters and that weather conditions that fall meant that they had to wait until the following summer to carry out the reburial.

- Quotes from a third letter written to Harold Dunning from Charles Levings following Louis's 1929 reburial, in which Charles thanks Harold for the part he played in carrying out that reburial.

On pages 113-116 of Volume III of *Over Hill and Vale* (Source No. 3), Harold Dunning provides four photos taken during the reburial of Louis R. Levings on 15 August 1929. (Note that *Over Hill and Vale* says that Levings's first name was "Lewis," but his memorial marker and all other sources, including Delta Tau Delta's records, say that it was "Louis." We have thus used "Louis" throughout this chapter.)

- Photo 1 (page 113) shows Louis's burial place from a distance and is captioned: "Our loved one slumbers on: As the ages chant their measures, On the slopes of Ypsilon." The source of this quote is the poem referred to earlier that Charles Edwin Hewes wrote in the memory of Louis Levings.

- Photo 2 (page 114) was taken at Louis's burial site. It shows the following individuals: Rocky Mountain National Park Ranger Walter Finn, Minister Cy Albertson, Louis's cousin Dean Babcock, and Harold M. Dunning. Recall that Dean Babcock had been one of Louis's climbing partners on the day he fell to his death.

- Photo 3 (page 115) is taken immediately across the west-most Spectacle Lake looking toward the "Y" on Ypsilon Mountain. The caption says: "At the foot of the 'Y' in Ypsilon the ice fans out in a great glacier of ice that empties into the upper lake or Leving's [sic] Lake. [He surely meant "Levings's Lake."] The grave is about 700 feet above the lake." Ted Matthews pointed out that, when he last visited Louis's grave in 1950, the glacier had melted and was just "a shadow of its former self."

- Photo 4 (page 116) appears to have been taken from Louis's grave looking downhill toward the Spectacle Lakes. In his caption, Dunning first indicates that the pair of lakes were referred to as the "Spectacle Lakes." But he then goes on to say that "We call the upper one [the west-most on a map] Leving's [sic] Lake. The lower lake we call Chapin Lake because Mrs. Frederick H. Chapin named Mount Ypsilon [Ypsilon Mountain on the Trail Ridge Quad Map] while she and her husband were in the Park before 1890." The Trail Ridge Quad Map does not provide separate names for these lakes. Instead, it simply names the pair the "Spectacle Lakes."

When we corresponded with Kenneth A. File, President of Delta Tau Delta Educational Foundation, in addition to providing us with the name of the university (Illinois Institute of Technology) represented by the Gamma Beta Chapter of Delta Tau Delta, he provided us with the photograph of Louis Levings that appears earlier in this chapter and with Louis's obituary (Source No. 1) from Delta Tau Delta's quarterly magazine. This obituary provided the following additional information about Louis's death not found in any of our other sources:

> "Levings had been tramping through the mountains of Colorado with two of his cousins, Dean Babcock, A-'05, and John Black, and was at the time, Wednesday, August 2nd, attempting the ascent of Mount Upsilon [Ypsilon Mountain] with Black in order to photograph the almost perfect Upsilon formed by a glacier which gives the mountain its name. He turned aside to do a little investigating and started down a steep declivity, followed by his cousin. Coming to a place where it was necessary to hang full length and drop a few feet from one ledge to another, he swung over, when, without warning, the rock from which he hung gave way and he was carried down with it to his death."

[Note that Ted Matthews, Harold Dunning, and James Pickering all give Black's first name as "George" rather than "John." (See above.)]

"By his ever cheerful disposition, friendliness and acknowledged abilities he made his friends. There was so much to admire and so little to criticize in his character that all who knew him grieve his loss."

Both records in the Rocky Mountain National Park Library and information provided by Bob Haines indicate that the ashes of Louis Levings's parents, Charles and Agnes, were scattered on Twin Sisters Peaks (mountains east and south of Ypsilon Mountain) "in line of sight" of Ypsilon Mountain. (For more information on Charles and Agnes Levings, see the section on them in the chapter on Rocky Mountain National Park Scattered Cremains.)

Biographical Information on Dean Babcock

Interestingly enough, the wonderful etchings in all three volumes of Harold Dunning's *Over Hill and Vale* were created by Louis Levings's cousin Dean Babcock. In the preface pages of Volume III (Source No. 3 above), Harold acknowledges Dean's contribution to his books and notes that Dean died on Christmas Day 1969 in Kirkland, Washington. Pages 588-590 of Volume I of *Over Hill and Vale* (Source No. 2 above) contain a biography of Dean Babcock in the form of a letter from Dean to Harold in response to Harold's request that Dean provide biographical information for *Over Hill and Vale*.

Some of the information from Dean's autobiography pertinent here follows:

Dean was born 14 January 1888 in Canton, Illinois. He first came to Estes Park in 1903. While there, he stayed at Longs Peak Inn, climbed Longs Peak with Enos Mills, and climbed many peaks by himself. In 1904, he returned to Colorado with his cousin Louis Levings. During this trip Dean and Louis walked from Boulder through Rocky Mountain National Park to Middle Park and back to Boulder. In 1905, he and Louis returned to continue their hiking/climbing adventures. It was during this trip that Louis was killed on Ypsilon Mountain.

In 1908 Dean worked with Prof. Edward Orton on a geological survey party that was making glacial records of the Longs Peak region. He also worked with William S. Cooper on the "first authentic map" of the Longs Peak-Wild Basin region.

In 1914 Dean married Adele Ramsey. He and his wife had two daughters: Evelyn (Mrs. Edward J. Harn), who was born in Greeley in July 1916, and Sylvia (Mrs. Harold L. Tacker), who was born in Denver in July 1919.

From 1918 through 1921, Dean worked for the National Park Service (probably at Rocky Mountain National Park) as a Ranger Naturalist, Surveyor, and, for a time, as Assistant to the Superintendent in charge of construction.

Page 47 of the "New Neighbors" chapter and Note 26 (page 118) in James H. Pickering's *In the Vale of Elkanah* (Source No. 6 above) provides some additional information on Dean Babcock and his parents:

Dean's mother Josephine McCall married his father William Babcock, Jr., on 14 September 1876. Recall that Josephine was the sister of Louis Levings's mother, Agnes McCall Levings. Josephine died in 1931. William was born in 1853 and died in 1914.

During the fall of 1908, Josephine acquired an 80-acre "Timber and Stone" claim half a mile north of Charles Hewes's Bleak House. On the lower slopes of the Estes Cone, Josephine's claim was in an area of "red granite terraces and ledges." 1903 was the year that Dean first came to the Estes Park area. Once the Babcocks built their summer home, "The Ledges," 2 years later, Dean spent at least the "summer" season there for the next 60 years.

September 1922 Ascent of Ypsilon Mountain

The 22 September 1922, issue of *Estes Park Trail* (the same issue that announces the death of Enos Mills on September 21st) contains a front-page article titled "Descent of East Face of Ypsilon Made First Time in Seventeen Years." This article recounts how, on 14 September 1922, Superintendent of Rocky Mountain National Park Roger W. Toll, Chief Ranger T. J. Allen, and Clifford Higby, guide, "made the descent of the east face of the peak, coming down the west fork of the Y, a feat which has not been attempted in the past 17 years, due to the hazards encountered in so doing."

The article goes on to say that "the descent through the Y to Spectacle Lakes at the base was made in two hours and thirty minutes and at considerable peril, due to the crumbly condition of the entire eastern face, and without mishap. A repetition of the feat is not to be recommended because of the treacherous formation."

The article concludes with the following remembrance of Louis Levings's death:

> "It will be remembered that seventeen years ago on August 2, 1905, Louis Raymond Levings lost his life on the face of the peak and that his body is buried there and a bronze tablet erected, where the body lies, to his memory. So far as is known no one has since attempted to ascend or descend this portion of the peak and the accomplishment of these three will ever remain an outstanding feature of the history of the mountain."

Ypsilon Mountain Claims Another Life

Sometime between 29 July and 8 August 2005, Jeff Christensen, a 31-year-old Rocky Mountain National Park Ranger, fell to his death near Ypsilon Mountain, almost 100 years to the day after the 2 August 1905 death of Louis Levings during a fall on the same mountain. According to an article by Steve Lipsher titled "Body of missing ranger is found" on pages 1A and 14A of *The Sunday Denver Post*, Jeff had left for his first back-country foot patrol of the Mummy Range on July 29.

When Jeff didn't return as scheduled, more than 200 searchers, including "dog crews and helicopters," began looking for him. Finally, a hiker found Jeff's body "near the Spectacle Lakes, two alpine tarns just below the sheer east face of Mount Ypsilon."

Park authorities concluded that Jeff had fallen to his death but would not say how they reached that conclusion. They also indicated that they would reconsider their policy of sending rangers on foot patrols alone.

Jeff Christensen was the first Ranger to have died on duty since Rocky Mountain National Park was founded in 1915.

LULU CITY GRAVES

Location

The remains of the ghost town of Lulu City are located on the west side of Rocky Mountain National Park in Grand County. Today Lulu City can be reached by hiking the 7.2-mile (round trip) Lulu City-Colorado River Trail, which leaves the west side of Trail Ridge Road about 9.5 miles north of Grand Lake. The few GPS readings available for the graves associated with Lulu City are given under "Description of Graves" below.

Description of Graves

In an email that he sent us on 7 October 2001, John Gubbins reported that, as of his visit to Lulu City on 2 October 2001, there were six "for sure" graves and one "possible" grave in the Lulu City area. By June 2005, he and we had concluded that there were eight fairly certain graves and one possible grave at Lulu City.

The numbers we use for these graves below are the same numbers that John used on the proprietary map of Lulu City that he produced in December 1988 as part of his research on old mining towns and mines in Grand County. John reported that, following his retirement at the end of September 2013, he was going to concentrate on getting the book encompassing his research published in 2014 or 2015. The portion of that map that shows the Lulu City graves is duplicated on the next page and is used with John's permission.

We showed John how to use dowser rods on 14 September 2001 when he took us to the Grand Lake Cemetery and the Gaskill Cemetery in the western portion of Rocky Mountain National Park. (For information on these two cemeteries, see the applicable chapters. For more information on John Gubbins, see the "Acknowledgments" section.) John went to Lulu City on his own on 2 October 2001 to check previously suspected graves with the dowser rods to see if the graves actually contained bodies. Unless otherwise noted, he provided the information on the Lulu City graves given below.

Grave 1 (1st Lulu City Grave): This grave (1 on the Lulu City map on the next page) is marked by a rectangular outline of rocks and has a non-inscribed "headstone" at one end. Dowser rods confirm an adult burial.

Graves 2a, 2b, and 2c (2nd, 3rd, and 4th Lulu City Graves): These three graves are in the general location of 2 on John's map and are at Latitude 40° 26' 45" N and Longitude 105° 50' 52" W. The GPS reading for these graves was provided by both John Gubbins and by Rocky Mountain National Park Rangers Ira Goldfarb and his then fiancée Joan Feder, who visited Lulu City shortly before John's visit on 2 October 2001. (For information on the assistance that Ira and Joan provided in helping us locate the graves in Lulu City, see "Finding the Graves" below. For information on the help they provided with other graves in the Park, see the "Acknowlegements" section.)

In his 7 October 2001 email, John said that, on his 2 October visit to Lulu City, he found two graves (2b and 2c) that he had not previously noticed. John describes Grave 2c as being "up on the hill just west of the cabin ruin and stump and just south of the other two" (2a and 2b). He went on to say that this particular grave is "actually fairly well marked and had a strong signal [from the dowser rods]."

Ira and Joan determined that Grave 2c was the grave of a child. We had found previously that children's graves are often placed much nearer the parents' home than are graves of adults. This grave agrees with that trend. (For examples of other graves in which children's graves are near their parents' homes, see the chapters for the following graves: Cook Child Grave, Christopher Charles Cradock, Guy Place Child's Grave, Kitty Lyon Grave, and Usher Child Grave.)

LARIMER COUNTY CEMETERIES

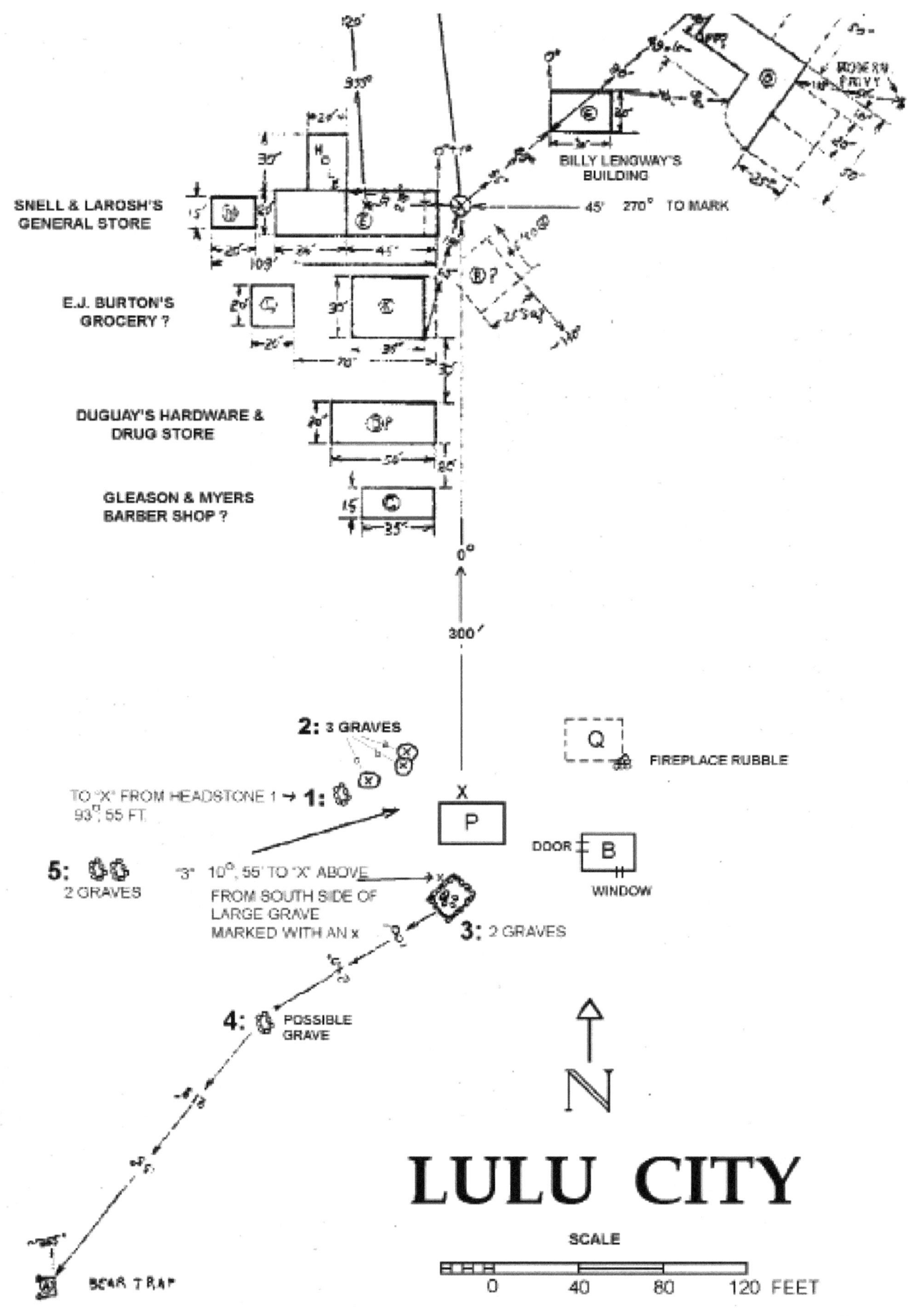

According to John's map, Graves 2a, 2b, and 2c are about 30 feet northeast of Grave 1. John says that two of the graves (2a and 2b) are depressions in a hillside and yielded strong dowser rod reactions that indicated that the graves contain two adults. Ira and Joan provided us with several photographs of these two graves, which indicate that the graves are also covered by rocks. Photo A is one of these photos.

Photo A: Adult Graves 2a and 2b in Lulu City (Courtesy Ira Goldfarb and Joan Feder Goldfarb)

Photo B is a close-up of the rocks that mark Grave 2c. Photo C shows Grave 2c in relation to the corner of the nearby cabin. In that photo, the gray arrow is pointing to the grave, which is covered by the evergreen tree to the right of the arrow.

Photo B: Close-up of Rocks Marking Child Grave 2c in Lulu City (Courtesy Ira Goldfarb and Joan Feder Goldfarb)

Photo C: Child Grave 2c in Relation to Nearby Cabin. The Arrow points to the Grave. (Courtesy Ira Goldfarb and Joan Feder Goldfarb)

Graves 3a and 3b (5th and 6th Lulu City Graves): These "twin graves" are at location 3 on John's map, which is about 55 feet south of Grave 2c above. There is a rock rectangle around the two graves. When John used dowser rods on these two graves, he found that they were both adult graves. Prior to his 2 October 2001 visit to Lulu City, John had thought that the east-most of the two graves was of a child because it was "mostly obscured visually" and thus appeared to be smaller than the west-most grave. However, in handwritten comments he made on a draft of this chapter that he returned to us in late June 2005, John felt that Graves 3a and 3b might be those of a mother and her child because "one is larger than the other."

Grave 4: Possible Grave: In the comments that John made on that draft of this chapter that he returned to us in late June 2005, he said that this was either "a grave or a natural rock mound" and that its proportions were right for it to be a grave. Since this grave was not checked with dowser rods, we are not counting it as a Lulu City grave. It is at location 4 on John's map.

Graves 5a and 5b (7th and 8th Lulu City Graves): John did not discover these possible graves until he visited Lulu City on 2 October 2001. (See location 5 on John's map.) John reports that the these two graves are at Latitude 40° 26' 45" N and Longitude 105° 50' 53" W, that the graves are marked by two mounds of rocks with a north-south alignment, and that they "crossed the [dowser] rods just fine." However, John goes on to note that the mounds of rocks are "in a drainage," which is unusual for graves, and could very well be natural. Unfortunately, as noted below, we did not succeed in our effort to hike to Lulu City, so we could not verify John's experience with his dowser rods at these possible graves.

Child's Grave at Shipler's Cabin: A well-known set of ruins in the Lulu City area is the cabin of Joe Shipler, which is about a mile south of Lulu City and about 2.5 miles north of the trailhead for Lulu City-Colorado River Trail. (For more information on Joe, see "Joe Shipler, First and Last Miner in the Lulu City Area" below.) In his 7 October 2001 email, John told us that a child had once been buried near Shipler's Cabin but that the child's body had since been removed.

In late June 2005, John said that he did not know whose child this was but that speculation among the "Grand Lake old timers" was that it was the child of Marcus Coon, an early partner of Joe Shipler's, and that Marcus left the area a long time before Shipler did. (Perhaps the death of their child made Marcus and his wife lose their interest in mining in such a remote location?)

Finding the Cemetery

On 14 September 2001, John Gubbins told us about the graves at Lulu City when he took us to the Grand Lake Cemetery, the Gaskill Cemetery, and the location where the ashes of George Frederick Dick III were scattered—all on the west side of Rocky Mountain National Park.

Shortly after 14 September 2001, John sent us a copy of his December 1988 map of Lulu City, which showed, among other things, what he had assumed were graves when he created the map. We gave a copy of that map to Rocky Mountain National Park Rangers Ira Golbfarb and Joan Feder, who hiked to Lulu City in late September 2001, where they found, photographed, and GPS-pinpointed Graves 2a, 2b, and 2c above.

Park Rangers Ira Goldfarb and Joan Feder, who were engaged to be married when we met them in July 2001, climbed and hiked to a number of graves in Rocky Mountain National Park that we were not physically capable of reaching. (For information on the Park burial sites that Ira or Ira and Joan helped us locate, see the "Acknowledgments" section.)

Then, on 2 October 2001, John Gubbins hiked to Shipler's Cabin and Lulu City himself. On 7 October 2001, he emailed us the information provided under "Description of Graves" above.

Finally, later in October 2001, we tried to hike to Lulu City ourselves, but were not able to go the distance in the time that we had.

History of the Town of Lulu City

Sources of Information on Lulu City

1. Volume II of *Over Hill and Vale*, written by Harold Marion Dunning and published in 1971. (See "Bibliography for complete citation.") Pages 52-55 of Volume II quote a letter sent to the author by Frank Jones Burnett in 1959.

   Frank was the son of Captain Benjamin Franklin Burnett and the grandson of William N. Burnett. Captain Benjamin Burnett and William B. Baker were charter members of the mining company that established and promoted Lulu City. (See "Founding of Lulu City" below.) In his letter to Harold Dunning, Frank Burnett provides information about both Lulu City and the mining town of Manhattan, where his family moved after the demise of Lulu City. (For information on the mining town of Manhattan and the Manhattan Cemetery, see the chapter on the Manhattan Cemetery.)

2. *Grand Lake in the Olden Days; A Compilation of Grand Lake, The Pioneers and The Olden Days*, written by Mary Lyons Cairns and published in 1971. (See the "Bibliography" for a complete citation.") Pages 143-149 provide a brief history of the town of Lulu City.

3. *Rocky Mountain National Park; A History*, written by C. W. Buchholtz and published in 1983. (See the "Bibliography" for a complete citation.) We don't have access to this book, which Stanley Case recommended for a "detailed account of the history of Lulu City."

4. *The Poudre*, written by Stanley R. Case and published in 1995. (See the "Bibliography" for a complete citation.) See especially pages 28-29, 30, and 122-123 for information on Lulu City; pages

LARIMER COUNTY CEMETERIES

24-27 and 120 for information on Stewart's Toll Road, which connected Lulu City with Fort Collins; and page 37 for a photo and brief biographical information on Benjamin Franklin Burnett. See also the entries for "Lulu City" and "Stewart Toll Road" in the book's Index.

5. Information on Lulu City available on the http://hometown.aol.com website as of 10 March 2005.

The information that follows comes from these five sources.

Joe Shipler, First and Last Miner in the Lulu City Area

Joe Shipler was one of the miners who came to Colorado during the gold rush of 1859. After first visiting many of the active Colorado mining districts and staking a number of claims west of the Never Summer Mountains, in June 1879, Joe and three other miners gathered the equipment and supplies that they needed in Fort Collins and went to the headwaters of what is now the Colorado River and was then called the Grand River. According to the http://hometown.aol.com website information on Lulu City (Source No. 5), the three men "staked two promising silver claims on the slope of Shipler Mountain," which is southeast of what became Lulu City. When the word of these strikes spread, the rush to the area began.

Joe Shipler himself settled along the Grand River near his claims, where he built several sod-roofed log cabins, one of which is the cabin mentioned above next to which a child was once buried.

Joe stuck it out in the Lulu City area much longer than the other miners, but, by 1914, he finally left the area. Joe's departure was most likely encouraged by both his rheumatism and the fact that his silver strikes never brought him the wealth he dreamed about. When Joe abandoned his mine, he had dug only about 100 yards into Shipler Mountain.

Stewart's Toll Road

According to references to Stewart's Toll Road in Stan Case's *The Poudre* (Source No. 4), as the tie-cutting industry was beginning its demise, businessmen in Fort Collins started lobbying for the creation of a road between Fort Collins and the North Park area, which was then still part of Larimer County. Three different proposals were submitted. The winning proposal was submitted by the Cache la Poudre and North Park Toll Road Company, which was incorporated in the spring of 1879.

A. H. Patterson, S. B. Stewart, and L. R. Rhodes were on the company's Board of Directors, with Stewart lending his name to what became popularly known as "Stewart's Toll Road" or "Stewart's Road to the Mines." This wagon road began at the foot of Pingree Hill, where it connected on the east with an already existing road to Fort Collins. From there it went "south from Cameron Pass, followed the Michigan River watershed up to its source and over the Continental Divide at what was called Lulu Pass [while Lulu City was active] (now Thunder Pass). It went down the other side into the bottom of the Grand River [now Colorado River] Valley."

Over Stewart's Toll Road, mail, miners, supply wagons, and stages moved between Lulu City and Fort Collins. Beginning in the summer of 1880, one stage line, owned by Luke Voorhees of Cheyenne, Wyoming, ran three stages per week between Fort Collins and Lulu City over Stewart's Toll Road. Later an additional stage ran two times a week between Grand Lake and Lulu City.

The charges for the use of Stewart's Toll Road were $2/horse, ox, or mule; $3/"single span" of horses plus $1/each additional horse; $0.40/cow; and $0.20/sheep. During the first few years of its existence, the toll road made money for its owners. But, in 1902, the road became free to the public.

See pages 24-27, 28, and 361 of *The Poudre* (Source No. 4) for photographs of various parts of Stewart's Toll Road.

LULU CITY

Founding of Lulu City

When the excitement caused by the silver strikes of Joe Shipler and his fellow miners was at its height, Fort Collins residents William B. Baker and Benjamin Franklin Burnett visited the area over Stewart's Toll Road. Seeing a potential there, they joined with a few others to form the Middle Park and Grand River Mining and Land Improvement Company, which established and promoted the 9,400-foot-high town of Lulu City. By June 1880, the town had been platted into 100 blocks, with 16 lots per block. According to page 144 of *Grand Lake in the Olden Days* (Source No. 2), Lulu City's streets were numbered between First and Nineteenth with the cross streets named Mountain, Trout, Riverside, and Ward.

The entry for Lulu City at the http://hometown.aol.com website disagrees as to the street names and instead says that the east-west streets were numbered between First and Ninth (rather than Nineteenth) and the north-south streets were named Lead, Mountain, Trout, Riverside, and Howard.

Lulu City's Namesake

On page 29 of his *The Poudre* (Source No. 4), Stan Case says that *High Country Names, Rocky Mountain National Park* (by Louise Ward Arps, Elinor Eppich Kingery, and Hugh E. Kingery) lists two possible young girls for whom Lulu City could have been named. One of those possibilities is Lulu May Burnett, the daughter of Benjamin F. Burnett, one of the founders of Lulu City. Most of the other references that we found to Lulu City's namesake agree that Lulu May Burnett deserves the honor.

However, *High Country Names* indicates that H. N. Wheeler (the first superintendent of the Colorado National Forest) and other pioneers in the Poudre Canyon area believed that the city was, instead, named for Lulu Stewart, the daughter of S. B. Stewart, a member of the board of directors of the company that built Stewart's Toll Road. (See "Stewart's Toll Road" above.)

In late June 2005, John Gubbins told us that "most think Lulu Burnett is the correct one."

The city was first named just plain "Lulu," with the word "City" added later to give the mining town a more important-sounding name.

Lulu City as a Going Concern

The lots in Lulu City sold for between $20 and $50 each as rumors of gold strikes spread. During the winter of 1880, an old prospector named Ben Dunshee actually did strike gold, which encouraged both more miners to make their way to the Lulu City area and more businessmen to set up establishments to provide services to those miners. According to John Gubbins's map on the second page of this chapter and the http://hometown.aol.com website, some of Lulu City's businesses were Parker and Godsmark's or the Godsmark Brothers' Park Hotel, Snell and Larosh's General Store, E.J. Burton's Grocery (and several other grocery stores), Duguay's Hardware and Drug Store, Gleason and Myer's Barber Shop, Burnett's clothing store, an assay office, a liquor store, two sawmills, and, of course, a whore house, which was in the "redlight district north of town."

Twenty dairy cows were even driven up from Denver to provide milk for Lulu City residents.

As an example of how encouraged folks were about the mining possibilities around Lulu City, the Parker and Godsmark's Hotel mentioned above was built in 1881. It provided the miners and others who could afford it meals served on fine linen, silverware, and crystal.

According to page 148 of *Grand Lake in the Olden Days* (Source No. 2), the best-known mines in the Lulu City area were the Silver Heels, Ptarmigan, Georgianna, Garden City,

LARIMER COUNTY CEMETERIES

Carbonate, and Eureka. In late June 2005, John Gubbins told us that there were over 400 mine claims in the Lulu City area and gave us the names of two of the better know ones:
- The North Star: This was Joe Shipler's mine. It is on the Lulu City-Colorado Trail that leads to Lulu City from the west side of Trail Ridge Road.
- The Southern Cross: This was the old gold mine in the area and had a 300-foot shaft.

Lulu City's Demise

The boom in the Lulu City area continued into 1882, but the silver ore found in abundance near Lulu City was of such low grade that it simply did not pay to ship the unrefined ore to a smelter without a railroad to carry it. The plan of the Wolverine Mine near Gaskill to build a smelter in the area never came to fruition, and a rail line was never built.

Thus, by the summer of 1883, miners and businessmen alike were leaving Lulu City. According to pages 122-123 of *The Poudre* (Source No. 4), postal service to Lulu City ceased on 24 November 1883. Then, according to page 149 of *Grand Lake in the Olden Days* (Source No. 2), the 3 July 1884 issue of *The Prospector*, a Grand Lake newspaper, reported the following:

> "John R. Brennan and Jack Henry, two of Lulu's old timers, arrived there [Lulu City] a few days ago and have been down to pay Grand Lake a visit. They say that Lulu is in a very dilapidated condition with the exception of the mines, and they look as bright as ever. They have contacts on the Ptarmagin and several other lodes."

Hard-rock miners seem to have been a most hopeful and positive lot!

LUMPY RIDGE SKELETON

Location
On 13 September 1964, this skeleton was found west of Gem Lake on Lumpy Ridge in Rocky Mountain National Park. Its current location is not known.

Finding the Skeleton
As discussed under "History of Lumpy Ridge Skeleton" below, it was Jean Weaver of the Estes Park Thursday Hiking Club who first told us about the "Lumpy Ridge Skeleton" on 15 January 2001. She did not know what became of the skeleton after the Park's legal investigation was over. We then asked Park Ranger Lashelle Lyman to try to find out for us. On 13 February 2001, Lashelle informed us that the "Park has no record of the skeleton." Evidently, the Park's Law Enforcement and Dispatcher records do not go back that far.

On 9 March 2001, Jackie Johnson told us that she had conducted her own research on the "Lumpy Ridge Skeleton." By talking to various retired Park Rangers, Jackie had found out that the FBI had returned the bones of skeleton to the Park in a wooden box and that, as of 1972, they were still somewhere in the Park's offices. (For more information on Jackie Johnson, see the "Acknowledgments" section.)

Sources of Information on the Lumpy Ridge Skeleton

1. "Human Skeleton Found Tuesday Near Gem Lake," *Estes Park Trail*, Friday, 18 September 1964.

2. "Found Skeleton Mystery Deepens After Report From FBI Laboratory," *Estes Park Trail*, Friday, 6 November 1964.

History of Lumpy Ridge Skeleton
The story of the Lumpy Ridge skeleton recounted below comes from information provided by Jean Weaver on 15 January 2001, from the two articles in the *Estes Park Trail* cited above (Source Nos. 1 and 2), and from Jackie Johnson on 9 March 2001. Along with Pat Rogers and Ky Bissell, the two women who found the skeleton, Jean is a long-time member of the informal Estes Park Thursday Hiking Club, so named because they seldom hike on Thursdays.

On Tuesday, 13 September 1964, Pat Rogers and Ky Bissell were hiking the Gem Lake Trail when they climbed up on Lumpy Ridge west of Gem Lake to get their bearings. At that point the two women encountered a skeleton. At first they thought it was the skeleton of an animal, as finding skeletons of deer or elk is not unusual in the Park. However, they soon realized that they had found a human skeleton accompanied by only two articles of clothing, a belt and a pair of boots.

After marking the trail to the site, Pat and Ky reported their find to the Park Service. Several Park Service employees and the two women then returned to the site on Wednesday, 14 September. They thoroughly searched the area and removed the skeleton. Source No. 1 cites Roger Contor, a management assistant at the Park, as saying that "the skeleton was quite old and that of a person teen-age or older, probably an adult. A 1945 half-dollar was found at the site indicating that death could have occurred as long as 19 years ago."

Source No. 1 then goes on to say that the damage to the skeleton's skull indicated that a fall could have caused the individual's death. However, due to the age of the skeleton, the cause of the person's death was not easy to determine.

The Park Service then sent the skeleton to the FBI Forensic Laboratory in Washington, D.C., to see if they could shed any light on the cause of the individual's death and/or identity. The FBI's report (Source No. 2) provided the following information:

- There was a "neatly drilled hole in the skull . . . and an exit opening."
- The face bones "were damaged from a fall soon after death or from a very severe blow."
- The skeleton was that of a man about 66-68 inches tall of average build, and the individual had had dental care within a few years of his death.

The article quoted Park Superintendent Granville B. Liles as saying that their only hope of determining the identity of the "male between 40 and 60" was "information from people who might remember someone missing from 1947 on." Superintendent Liles also said that "the revolver found in rubble near the body is being examined and traced."

We were unable to find any other articles in *Estes Park Trail* about the skeleton. However, Jean Weaver was able to provide the following additional information:

- The gun, a Harrington & Richardson 22 caliber pistol, was traced to a pawn shop in Denver, but this information did not help identify the skeleton.
- One missing person who might possibly be the skeleton was a truck driver who was going to the Western Slope from Denver to pick up a load of potatoes. He had been given cash to pay for the potatoes when he picked them up. He also was having marital difficulties and thus may have been depressed. His truck was found in Glenwood Canyon, but he was never located.

As noted above, Jackie Johnson of Estes Park heard about our efforts to find the current location of the skeleton. (If it was buried, we'd have a grave to report.) After contacting a number of "old time" Park Rangers, on 9 March 2001 Jackie told us that her research had provided the following additional information:

- After completing its investigations, the FBI had returned the skeleton to the Park in a wooden box.
- As of 1972, the Park still had the skeleton. However, as of March 2001, its location was not known.

MACGREGOR FAMILY CEMETERY

Location: Latitude 40° 23′ 43″ N, Longitude 105° 31′ 18″ W

The MacGregor Family Cemetery is north of Estes Park and east of a private road on the MacGregor Ranch, which is operated as part of the Muriel L. MacGregor Charitable Trust. The private road takes off to the north from Devil's Gulch Road at the point where that road changes from going north to going east.

Description of Cemetery and Its Inscriptions

The cemetery is actually a rectangular mausoleum made of local boulders and concrete.

Photo A: MacGregor Family Cemetery on the MacGregor Ranch

The following inscriptions are found on a bronze plaque toward the bottom of the south side of the mausoleum:

MACGREGOR RANCH

DEDICATED TO EDUCATION BY MURIEL L. MACGREGOR 1970
HOMESTEADED BY A. Q. AND CLARA MACGREGOR 1873
OPERATED AND ENLARGED BY DONALD AND MAUDE MACGREGOR 1902-1950
PRESERVED AND CONSOLIDATED BY MURIEL L. MACGREGOR 1950-1970

INTERRED HERE

DONALD MACGREGOR 1878-1950
MAUDE MACGREGOR 1878-1950
MURIEL L. MACGREGOR 1904-1970

(For information on these individuals and on how they are related, see "History of the MacGregor Family and the MacGregor Ranch" below.)

LARIMER COUNTY CEMETERIES

Finding the Cemetery

We were told about the MacGregor Family Cemetery in the fall of 1999 by Eva Carran when she went with us when we found the grave of Charlie Stevens. Charlie was Eva's maternal great-uncle, who died at the age of 11 in 1881 and is buried on what was his family's ranch at the south end of Chimney Hollow, which is southwest of Carter Lake. (For information on the Stevens family, see the chapter on the Charlie Stevens Grave. For information on Eva's paternal Boothroyd relatives, see the chapters on the Boothroyd Baby Girl Grave and the Boothroyd-Hutchinson Cemetery.)

When Eva told us about the MacGregor Family Cemetery, she said that she had learned of its existence when she lived in Estes Park as a child. Eva said that she and her friends would ride their bicycles out to the MacGregor Ranch to visit the family mausoleum and "scare themselves." The visit "scared" them because the two coffins in the mausoleum at the time (those containing the remains of Donald and Maude MacGregor) had glass tops through which visitors could see the bodies interred inside. Following the death of Donald and Maude's daughter Muriel in 1970, the entrance to the mausoleum was rocked in, decreasing the appeal of the mausoleum to the Estes Park's youngsters.

History of the MacGregor Family and the MacGregor Ranch

Sources of Information on the MacGregor Family and the MacGregor Ranch

1. 1900, 1910, and 1920 U.S. Censuses, Indexes and Digitized Images online at <u>heritagequestonline.com</u>, available to holders of library cards at the Fort Collins Public Library.

2. *History of Larimer County, Colorado,* written by Ansel Watrous and published in 1911. (See the "Bibliography" for a complete citation.) Page 179 contains several brief mentions of Alexander ("Alex") Quiner MacGregor, the first member of the MacGregor family to settle in the Estes Park area. However, Watrous mistakenly gives Alex's name of " R. Q. McGregor." (Handwritten capiltal *A* and *R* can look quite similar.)

3. Volumes I and II of *Over Hill and Vale,* written by Harold Marion Dunning. Volume I was published in 1956, and Volume II in 1962. (See the "Bibliography" for a complete citation.) Page 124 of Volume I provides the same basic information that Watrous did with the same misnaming of Alex MacGregor as "R. Q. McGregor." Pages 224 and 225 of Volume II provide information on the MacGregor Ranch; Alex MacGregor; Alex's son, Donald MacGregor; and Donald's daughter, Muriel MacGregor.

4. *Memoirs of Eleanor E. Hondius of Elkhorn Lodge,* written by Eleanor E. Hondius and published in 1964. (See the "Bibliography" for a complete citation.) In Chapter II, titled "Early Days at Elkhorn Lodge," Eleanor talks about Mrs. Georgianna Heeney, the mother of Alex MacGregor's wife, "jumping" the Black Canyon homestead claim of Eleanor's father William James "because of some legal technicality." This caused the James family to move from Black Canyon to the banks of Fall River, where they built the very successful Elkhorn Lodge. The James family must have at least partially blamed Alex for the loss of their Black Canyon homestead, for Eleanor says, "My mother called Mr. McGregor [sic] a 'pettifogging' lawyer. I never knew what a 'pettifogging' lawyer was, except that Mother said that Mr. McGregor was one."

    As the "*sic*" above points out, like Ansel Watrous and Harold Dunning in Volume I of *Over Hill and Vale,* Eleanor misspells the MacGregor's last name as McGregor. (For more information on the James family, see our chapters on the Elkhorn Lodge Cemetery and the Mary Jane James Grave.)

5. *The MacGregor Ranch Story,* a Library Talk presented by Harriett Burgess on 16 July 1981 at the Estes Park Public Library. The tape and its transcription, which were made as part of the Estes Park oral history project, are available in the Local History Section of the Estes Park Public

Library. The Estes Park oral history project is a joint effort of the Estes Park Area Historical Museum and the Estes Park Public Library.

Those interested in a complete history of the MacGregor family in the Estes Park area should definitely consult this document. At the time Harriett Burgess gave this presentation, she was the coordinator of volunteers at the MacGregor Ranch Museum.

6. Volume II of *The History of Larimer County, Colorado*, edited by Arlene Ahlbrandt and Kathryn Stiebes and published in 1987. (See the "Bibliography" for a complete citation.) Pages 195 and 196 contains an article titled "Ranching the Old Fashioned Way" by Andrea Koutonen Galliher. In her article, Andrea refers to Alex MacGregor and his wife Marie Clara Heeney MacGregor as "Grandfather MacGregor" and "Grandmother MacGregor." However, neither our genealogy research on the MacGregor family nor the research conducted by the MacGregor Ranch Museum (Source No. 12 below) found any evidence that Andrea Galliher was Alex and Clara's granddaughter.

7. "This Blue Hollow," written by James H. Pickering and published in 1999. (See the "Bibliography" for a complete citation.) The book contains a number of references to the MacGregor family: For photographs of Alex MacGregor and his wife Clara, see page 82. For photographs of the toll road that Alex and his partners built between Glen Evans (west of the present town of Lyons) and Estes Park, see pages 84 and 85. For an early photograph of the MacGregor Ranch, see page 87. For a photograph of the MacGregor's "second ranch house" (built in 1882), see page 129.

8. The MacGregor Ranch website, www.macgregorranch.org, as of 23 January 2005.

9. *The MacGregors of Black Canyon, An American Story*, written by James H. Pickering and published in 2008 in limited edition by the Muriel L. MacGregor Charitable Trust, Estes Park, Colorado.

10. Greive Haslach Famly Tree that includes information on the MacGregor family of Estes Park as available on Ancestry.com on 28 February 2011. This family tree includes at least one and sometimes multiple primary source citations for most of its genealogical facts.

11. *Social Security Death Index* as of 1 March 2011 as transcribed by Ancesty.com.

12. Letter dated 14 March 2011 from Rita Schageman, then the Volunteer Coordinator of the MacGregor Ranch Museum, providing corrections to the second draft of this chapter and additional information found in Source No. 9 above and in other sources available to the museum.

The Ancestors of Alexander Quiner MacGregor

According to the MacGregor Ranch website (Source No. 8), Alex MacGregor's known ancestors, starting with his great-grandfather, were:

Duncan McGregor, Sr., Alex's great-grandfather. Duncan was born in 1755 in Scotland. In return for his services as a British soldier in the American Revolution, Canada gave Duncan 500 acres of land. However, when the U.S.-Canadian border was settled following the war, Duncan found that his land was actually in the United States near Alburg, Vermont.

Note that at this point, the family's last name was spelled "McGregor."

Duncan McGregor, Jr., Alex's grandfather. Duncan, Jr., was born in Montreal, Canada, in 1781 and moved to Alburg, Vermont, with his parents when he was 1 year old. He **married Elanor Burget** (or Burghardt), with whom he had 11 or 12 children. The seventh of these children was Alexander McGregor, the father of Alexander Quiner MacGregor.

Alexander McGregor, Alex's father. Alexander was born in Alburg, Vermont. He **married Margaret Goodwin Quiner** on 16 May 1844. On 2 November 1845, he drowned on the schooner *Ocean* on Lake Michigan.

Alexander and Margaret had **two children: Duncan**, who died at birth, was born in March 1845, **and Alexander Quiner**, who was born on 4 March 1846.

LARIMER COUNTY CEMETERIES

Alexander Quiner MacGregor and Maria Clara Heeney MacGregor

On pages 1 and 2 of her 1982 presentation (Source No. 5), Harriet Burgess says that Alexander ("Alex") Quiner MacGregor was born in March 1846 in Alburg, Vermont, and that he never knew his father, "who had been drowned on a schooner in Lake Michigan the November before he was born." The information from the MacGregor Ranch website cited above gives us the exact dates for both the death of Alex's father and the birth of Alex.

Page 82 of *"This Blue Hollow"* (Source No. 7) says that Alex was raised in Milwaukee, Wisconsin, by his widowed mother, from whom he "developed a strong work ethic at an early age." Starting as a newsboy at Milwaukee's *Daily Evening Wisconsin* at the age of 8, by the time he was 14 he was working in the office, where he eventually "learned the trade of job printer." *"This Blue Hollow"* says that Alex founded *La Belle Mirror* in Oconomowoc, Wisconsin in 1867 and that he continued to publish that paper until August 1870. It also says that he arrived in Denver in late 1870 or early 1871. Rita Schageman (Source No. 12) agrees, telling us that MacGregor Ranch Museum's sources (including page 53 of Source No. 9) also have Alex leaving Oconomowoc in August 1870 and entering the "Denver picture" on 9 February 1871.

Once Alex arrived in Denver, he became an attorney by reading law with Judge Henry P.H. Bromwell and was subsequently admitted to the Colorado Bar on 4 December 1873 (Source Nos. 12 and pages 62-64 of Source No. 9). According to a brief biography of Alex published in the 27 October 1883 issue of the *Fort Collins Daily Express* when he was running for Larimer County Judge on the Republican ticket and quoted on page 82 of *"This Blue Hollow,"* in 1873, Alex "formed a legal partnership with Judge Westbrook S. Decker, which lasted until the MacGregors moved to Estes Park."

The MacGregor Ranch website (Source No. 8) says that, in the early 1870s, Alex changed his last name from "McGregor" to "MacGregor," which may explain some of the discrepancies in the reporting of his last name that occur in Source Nos. 2, 3, and 4 cited above.

Harriet Burgess and *"This Blue Hollow"* agree that, like many other of Estes Park's early residents, Alex's introduction to the incipient Estes Park was on a camping trip, in his case in the summer of 1872. At the same time, his soon-to-be wife Maria Clara Henney of Madison, Wisconsin, had come to Colorado on a sketching trip with Henry Crawford Ford, founder of the Chicago Academy of Design, which later became the Art Institute of Chicago. (Clara was born on 9 May 1852.) She and the other young ladies on the trip were chaperoned by Clara's mother, Georgianna Heeney. The trip started around Colorado Springs and moved north to the Estes Park area, where Clara evidently encountered Alex.

When Clara and her mother returned home, Alex and Clara corresponded. Harriet Burgess says that they were married in Black Earth, Wisconsin, on Christmas Day of 1872. However, page 81 of *"This Blue Hollow"* and the MacGregor Ranch website say that they were married on Christmas Day in 1873.

According to Clara's biography on the MacGregor Ranch website, she was a very well-educated young women for her time, having attended both a "normal preparatory college," which was really a high school of sorts at the University of Wisconsin in Madison, and the Milwaukee Female College before she entered the Chicago Academy of Design when she was 19.

MacGregor Homestead in Black Canyon

Given that Alex was in a legal partnership in Denver in 1873, when the MacGregors began their homestead in the Black Canyon area north of Estes Park, they must have divided their time, as they did later, between Denver and their homestead. Andrea Koutonen Galliher (Source No. 6) and the MacGregor Ranch website (Source No. 8) both agree that Alex and

Clara began their Black Canyon homestead in 1873. Their selection of this parcel must thus have pre-dated (page 83 of *"This Blue Hollow,"* Source No. 7) the Oaks and Kellogg survey, which was necessary to open the land for homesteading under the Homestead Act—for the contracts for this survey were signed on 12 January and 4 February 1874 and the survey was not complete until May 1874 (page 37 of *"This Blue Hollow"*).

Alex and Clara acquired land under both the Homestead Act and later under the Pre-emption Act. (See "Unoccupied Land Acquisition Acts" in the "Introduction.") According to Harriet Burgess (Source No. 5), their original parcels were "along what is now Devil's Gulch Road northward past the Twin Owls on the west."

Clara's mother, Georgianna Heeney, liked the area that her daughter and son-in-law had selected so much that she sold her large farm in Wisconsin and took up her own homestead. Again according to Harriett Burgess, this homestead was "eastward of Black Canyon, south to where the present Stanley Hotel is." *"This Blue Hollow"* gives the date for Georgianna's claim as 5 October 1875 and says that she built her homestead cabin on "a wooded section east of the creek" (Black Canyon Creek). This is probably the land over which Georgianna and the James family had the disagreement described above in the discussion of what Eleanor James Hondius had to say about the MacGregors in the *Memoirs of Eleanor E. Hondius of Elkhorn Lodge* (Source No. 4).

To unify the MacGregor claims, in 1876 Georgianna traded the southern part of her original claim to "Lord" Dunraven for a section along Black Canyon Creek. (Although he was known locally as "Lord Dunraven," he was actually Windham Thomas Wyndham-Quin, the Earl of Dunraven, who already owned 40,000 acres in Ireland and Wales. See pages 33-34 of *"This Blue Hollow."*)

By the 1970 death of Muriel MacGregor, Alex and Clara's granddaughter, the MacGregor holdings had grown to 2,931 acres with value of $4.25 million (as per page 83 of *"This Blue Hollow"*). Note 5 on page 263 of *"This Blue Hollow"* points out that a great deal of the land that Alex acquired came from paying the back taxes on individual parcels of land and that "only two of the approximately twenty pieces of land that he acquired between February 5, 1878, and his death on June 17, 1896, were acquired from the U.S. government."

Alex MacGregor vs. "Lord" Dunraven

For a very complete discussion of "Land Grabbing in Estes Park" and "Lord" Dunraven's involvement therein, see Chapter 3 of *"This Blue Hollow"* (Source No. 7).

One of the most interesting stories of Estes Park's early days involves the attempt of Dunraven to acquire as much of the Estes Park valley as possible as his private hunting reserve. Since one had to be or become an American citizen to obtain land via the Homestead Act or the Preemption Act, Dunraven could not legally acquire land by either method. In addition, no American citizen could acquire more than two quarter sections or 320 acres by these methods. However, it was permissible for foreigners or others to buy land that had been legally homesteaded by others.

Consequently, to "collect" the land he desired, Dunraven sought the services of Theodore George William Whyte, an Irish-Canadian mining engineer. Whyte would buy land that was supposedly legally homesteaded by a questionable collection of Americans. Alex MacGregor did not take kindly to Dunraven and Whyte's efforts. Consequently, according to page 2 of Harriet Burgess's 1981 presentation (Source No. 5), following some detective work, on 23 July 1881, Alex sent a handwritten letter to the Federal Court in Laramie, Wyoming, in which he provided evidence of 30 cases of fraud perpetrated by Dunraven and Whyte. The Grand Jury that investigated Alex's evidence found it to be substantially correct. Consequently, as Harriet points out, "AQ was very instrumental in ending Lord Dunraven's domain in the Estes Park valley."

(For other information on Dunraven's dealings in the Estes Park area, including his hotel operations, see "History of Cleave and Griffith Families" in the chapter on the Cleave-Griffith Family Cemetery.)

MacGregor Toll Road

Realizing that the beauty of the Estes Park valley would attract both settlers and tourists and finding that existing roads from "civilization" to the valley were woefully inadequate, on 11 September 1874, Alex, his mother-in-law Georgianna Heeney, and Marshall Bradford filed papers to incorporate the Park Road Company. The toll road ran from Glen Evans just west of the present town of Lyons on the northwest bank of the St. Vrain River to, of course, the MacGregor Ranch.

The road was completed on 28 July 1875. Since the road wasn't the financial success that Alex had hoped, in 1882, he sold it to a group of men from Longmont. The road was closed in 1885.

MacGregor Sawmill

Realizing that both he and his neighbors needed lumber and shingles to build their cabins and ranch buildings, in 1876, Alex built a sawmill. According to both page 3 of Harriet Burgess's presentation (Source No. 5) and page 84 of *"This Blue Hollow"* (Source No. 7), to get power for the sawmill, Alex collected water from Black Canyon Creek into a penstock. The water from the penstock was then allowed to fall 30 feet to a Leffel wheel, which produced 18 horsepower for the sawmill.

(For information on the extensive sawmill and lumber yard operations of the Griffith family in the Estes Park area, see "History of the Griffith Family" in the chapter on the Cleave-Griffith Family Cemetery.)

MacGregor Post Office and Store

According to page 3 of Harriet Burgess's presentation (Source No. 5) and page 86 of *"This Blue Hollow"* (Source No. 7), in 1876, Alex's wife Clara began a dual enterprise of her own: On 2 June 1876 the first post office in the Estes Park area was established on the MacGregor Ranch with Clara as post mistress. The post office, which was in a small cabin on the hillside north of Black Canyon Creek, also served as a store, in which Clara sold "flour, corn meal, sugar, salt, butter, baking powder, soda, potatoes, bacon, fat pork, tea, coffee, candles, and kerosene, all brought in over the MacGregor Toll Road from Longmont, and butter and potatoes produced locally" (page 86 of *"This Blue Hollow"*).

Clara remained post mistress until 21 March 1877, when Mrs. Griff Evans took over the job.

At that point, Clara returned to the not-inconsiderable job in those days of housewife. However, according to Harriet Burgess, Clara "spent a lot of her time painting since she was an accomplished artist." Recall that Clara and Alex met when she was on a sketching trip to the Rockies.

MacGregor Ranch as Operated by the MacGregor Family

Over the years that they lived there, Alex and Clara built three different houses on their ranch, not counting their original homestead cabins:

1. The first ranch house was built in 1875, part of which became the combination post office and store discussed above.

2. The second ranch house was built in 1882 and incorporated one of the MacGregors' original homestead cabins. For a photo of this home, see Figure 6.6 on page 129 of "*This Blue Hollow*" (Source No. 7). On page 3 of her 1981 presentation (Source No. 5), Harriet Burgess says that "this house is just north of Devil's Gulch Road. You can see it from the road as you're driving toward Glen Haven. . . . it is now part of the educational facility providing housing for the students [of the current not-for-profit Muriel L. MacGregor Charitable Trust]."

3. The third ranch house was started in 1896 following the birth of Alex and Clara's three sons. (See "Alex and Clara MacGregor's Descendants" below for information on these boys.) According to Harriet Burgess on page 4 of her presentation, "Having lived in [the] second ranch house for a period of years, they decided they wanted a really up-town house with two stories. So, in 1896 they decided to build the third ranch house, which is the site of the present [MacGregor Ranch] museum."

On their ranch, the MacGregors raised cattle and grew hay, wheat, barley, oats, and vegetables. They also "harvested" ice in the winter. As noted above, they also produced lumber and shingles.

According to page 4 of the 9 October 1884 issue of the *Fort Collins Daily Express* quoted on page 128 of "*This Blue Hollow*," Alex had "over a hundred head of fine Shorthorn cattle [branded **XIX**], which he is now [1884] crossing with thoroughbred Hereford stock."

In its biography of Alex, the MacGregor Ranch website (Source No. 8) notes that his ranch hands referred to him as "Mac."

Like a number of the early settlers in the Estes Park area (the James family and their Elkhorn Lodge being probably the prime example), the MacGregors realized that catering to tourists was an obvious way to increase the income they derived from their ranch. Harriet Burgess (page 3 of her presentation) places this realization at about the time they built their second ranch house in 1882.

In response to this realization, page 86 of "*This Blue Hollow*" reports that "they constructed a series of log cabins of varying sizes and a dining hall among the trees on the hillside to the north of the creek. New cabins were being added as late as 1895." The MacGregors also allowed tourists to "pitch their tents in a grove of trees across from the MacGregor house."

In addition, Harriet tells us (pages 3 and 4) that "AQ gave long-term leases on parcels of land along Lumpy Ridge for building houses. Quite a few houses were built up there." Some of the families Harriet lists as having built on these leases or later bought houses built on the original leases were the Lights, Colliers, Grogans, Emily Quiner (a Chicago cousin of Alex, who was given her land), Reverend Walker, the Freemans, and John Ramey.

Several quotes from 1876 and 1877 issues of the *Boulder County News* that appear on page 87 of "*This Blue Hollow*" make it clear that the tourist accommodations on the MacGregor Ranch were quite a success, with the visitors being pleasantly surprised by the "obvious culture and refinement that Clara brought to her rustic environment" via her sewing, piano-playing, and painting talents.

Alex's Jobs

According to page 128 of "*This Blue Hollow*" (Source No. 7), during the early part of the 1880s, the family lived during all but the summer months on College Avenue in Fort Collins. From May 1882 through January 1885, Alex served as County Judge of Larimer County in Fort Collins. When that term was up, he entered legal practice in, first, Fort Collins, and, then, in 1886, he moved his law practice and his family to Denver.

Alex's various legal-related jobs kept the family away from the ranch except during the summers until the fall of 1894, when, according to page 129 of *"This Blue Hollow,"* the family permanently left Denver for the MacGregor Ranch in Estes Park.

On page 4 of her presentation (Source No. 5), Harriet Burgess says that the MacGregor Ranch was "leased to a Mr. McCabe" during the time the family was "absentee landlords." In her letter to us, Rita Schageman (Source No. 12) provides Mr. McCabe's full name: James J. McCabe.

Deaths of Alex and Clara MacGregor

Alex died on 17 June 1896. According to Andrea Galliher on page 195 of her article on the MacGregor Ranch (Source No. 6), Alex and his son George were prospecting for gold on Fall River Pass when Alex was struck by lightening and killed.

Page 129 of *"This Blue Hollow"* (Source No. 7) provides additional information:

> "Alexander MacGregor was killed by a bolt of lightning while doing assessment work on a mining claim near the Poudre Lakes at the edge of a cliff at the head of Forest Canyon."

The third ranch house, which was unfinished at the time of Alex's death, was finished by his family. Andrea Galliher tells us that:

> "Grandmother MacGregor [Clara], along with her three sons—George, Donald and Halbert, were left to run the ranch. Clara MacGregor did offer the ranch for sale once, but declined just prior to a bid. She decided the family should never give up their land."

Clara died in January 1901 in Denver, where she had returned after completing the third ranch house.

Alex and Clara MacGregor's Descendants

Alex and Clara MacGregor had three sons, all of whom were born in Denver according to the MacGregor Ranch website (Source No. 8):

1. **George Heeney MacGregor.** According to his biography on the MacGregor Ranch website (Source No. 8) and Source No. 12, George was born in Colorado on 22 January 1875. He graduated from the Colorado School of Mines in Golden in 1897. Following his graduation, he served as a mining engineer in various mining towns in Colorado, including Central City. At the time that the 1910 U.S. Census was taken in May 1910 (Source No. 1), George, his first wife, and their two oldest children were living in Drake, Colorado, where George's occupation was listed as "civil engineer."

    By 1917 when he married his second wife, he had moved to Deschutes County, Oregon (Source No. 12), where he continued to work as a mining engineer (Source No. 8). The MacGregor Ranch website says that "George's last known whereabouts was Terrebonne, Oregon." Indeed, when the 1930 U.S. Census was taken, George was living in Terrebonne, Deschutes, Oregon (Source No. 12). George was still living in Oregon when he died on 20 May 1959 (Source No. 12).

    Zada Alderdyce, George's first wife. Zada was from Drake, Colorado, where her father Frank owned the Forks Hotel. The 1910 U.S. Census (Source No. 1) gives Zada's age as 24, which means that she was born about 1886.

    The 1910 U.S. Census also indicates that George and Zada were married 6 years in 1910, which means that they were married about 1904.

George and Zada had three sons, all of whom stayed with George after the couple divorced in 1915 (Source Nos. 8 and 12).

- 1.1. **Bruce A. MacGregor.** The 1910 Census says that Bruce was born in Colorado and that he was 6 years old in May 1910, yielding a birth year of about 1904. The Greive Haslach Family Tree (Source No. 12) agrees that Bruce was born in Colorado and gives 3 March 1904 as his exact birth date. Also according to the Greive Haslach Family Tree's sources, in 1920 Bruce was in Bend, Deschutes County, Oregon, with his father, but, by 1930, he had moved to Portland, Oregon. Then on 31 October 1940, he departed San Pedro, California, for Honolulu, Hawaii, where he died on 27 April 1992 (Source No. 12).

- 1.2. **Cecil Malcolm MacGregor.** Cecil was born on 10 February 1908 in Gilpin County, Colorado (Source Nos. 10 and 11). Once Cecil moved to Oregon with his father, he stayed there the remainder of his life, dying in Corvallis, Benton County, Oregon, on 27 May 2003 (Source No. 12).

- 1.3. **Ronald MacGregor.** Ronald was born in Colorado on 8 July 1910 (Source Nos. 10 and 12). Like his brother Cecil, once Ronald moved to Oregon with his father, he remained there the remainder of his life, dying in Portland, Multnomah County, Oregon, on 1 January 1997 (Source No. 11).

Alice C. Detzman, George's second wife. According to the Oregon Marriage Index cited in Source No. 10, George married Alice on 22 November 1917. The two either divorced or Alice died before George's third marriage in 1928. Alice was born in 1871.

Inez C. Tuckfield, George's third wife. According to Source No. 10, George married Inez on 9 February 1928. She was born in 1876.

2. **Donald MacGregor.** Donald, who was the only one of the three sons of Alex and Clara MacGregor to stay on the ranch, was born on 11 February 1880 according to his biography on the MacGregor Ranch website (Source No. 8). However, the plaque on the family mausoleum gives his birth year as 1878. (For more information on Donald, including additional confusion as to his birth date, see "Donald MacGregor and Minnie Maude Koontz MacGregor" below.)

Donald died in March 1950 of pneumonia complicated by asthma according to page 5 of Harriet Burgess's presentation (Source No. 5). Donald's biography on the MacGregor Ranch website gives the exact date of his death as 13 March 1950, which is the same death date provided on page 224 of Volume II of *Over Hill and Vale* (Source No. 3).

Minnie Maude Koontz, Donald's wife. Rita Schageman (Source No. 12) provided Maude's correct first name of "Minnie." Some of the sources we had consulted incorrectly listed her first name as "Muriel." According to page 4 of Harriet Burgess's presentation and Maude's biography on the MacGregor Ranch website, Donald and Maude were married on 17 January 1903. (For details on the considerable confusion concerning Maude's birth date and additional information on Maude, see "Donald MacGregor and Minnie Maude Koontz MacGregor" below.)

About Maude's death date there is no disagreement: Harriet Burgess (Source No. 5) and Andrea Galliher (Source No. 6) both say that Maude died in December 1950. Her biography on the MacGregor Ranch website gives her exact date of death as 18 December 1950, which agrees with the death date provided by Harold Dunning (Source No. 3). Harriet adds that Maude had been "mentally and physically ill for about 2 years" at the time of her death. The website says that "she became mentally helpless in the 1940s." Although it is certainly not possible to post-diagnose Maude's illness as Alzheimer's, it does sounds like that might be the condition with which she was afflicted.

All of these sources agree that Maude died in 1950, the death year on the bronze plaque on the mausoleum.

George and Maude had only one child:

2.1. **Muriel Lurilla MacGregor.** Muriel was born on 2 April 1904 in Denver and died, also in Denver, on 22 October 1970 (Source No. 5). Both her birth and death years agree with the inscription on the bronze plaque on the mausoleum. On page 225 of Volume II of *Over Hill and Vale* (Source No. 3), Harold Dunning tells us that Muriel's "middle name seems to be from her great-grandmother Georgianna Lurilla Heeney." However, Rita Schageman (Source No. 12) disagrees, telling us that her middle name came from the first name of her "maternal grandmother (Maude's mom) whose name was Lurilla Veysey Hall Koontz." Rita adds that Georgianna's middle name was actually Needham.

(For considerable additional information on Muriel, see "Muriel Lurilla MacGregor" below.)

3. **Halbert MacGregor**: According to his biography on the MacGregor Ranch website (Source No. 8), Halbert was born on 6 November 1886. However, the Greive Haslach Family Tree, the *Social Security Death Index,* and Rita Schageman (Source Nos. 10-12) all report that he was born on 6 November 1887. Source No. 10 gives his birth location as Estes Park; however, the MacGregor Ranch website and Rita Schageman (Source No.12) both report that all three of Alex and Clara's sons were born in Denver. The website also reports that Halbert graduated from University of Illinois with a degree in chemical engineering in 1912. His job required him to live in a number of locations including California, Illinois, Ohio, and Missouri.

Once he became an adult, Halbert visited the ranch several times, the last time being several months after his second wife Florence died in the fall of 1963 (Source No. 8).

The MacGregor Ranch website reports that Halbert died in a nursing home in St. Louis on 21 February 1972. The Greive Haslach Family Tree and the *Social Security Death Index* agree that he died in St. Louis in February 1972.

Ethel Michael, Hal's first wife. Both the MacGregor Ranch website and the Greive Haslach Family Tree agree that Hal and Ethel married about 1914. They had one child.

3.1. **Beatrice Jean MacGregor.** The MacGregor Ranch website provides her name and gives 1919 as her birth year.

Florence Unknown, Hal's second wife. Her last name is unknown. The Greive Haslach Family Tree reports that Hal and Florence married some time after 1921.

As noted above, the MacGregor Ranch website reports that Florence died in 1963.

Donald MacGregor and Minnie Maude Koontz MacGregor

Following the death of his father in 1896, Donald took over running the MacGregor Ranch between 1897 and 1902 and then leased it to Charles and Edward Johnson to operate for a number of years (page 129 of *"This Blue Hollow,"* Source No. 7). When Donald turned over the operation of the ranch, he returned to Denver, where he worked as a pricing agent for Hendrie & Bolthoff, which was a Denver hardware and machinery company.

According to Rita Schageman's research (Source No. 12 and pages 170-174 of Source No. 9), a letter written to George from his mother Clara in the winter of 1897 or 1898 suggests that George was "on the ranch then and occasionally in 1899." Donald himself recorded financial transactions between January 1899 and December 1901 which indicate that he was running the ranch during that period. Then, in early 1902, he leased the ranch to Charles and Edward Johnson.

While he was in Denver, Donald met Minnie Maude Koontz, who was evidently a lot like his mother, for Maude was also petite, an artist, and came from Wisconsin. The entry for Maude in the 27 April 1910 Census for Estes Park Precinct 20 (Source No. 1) tells us that she was 36 and was born in Wisconsin, that her father was born in Ohio, and that her mother was born in Michigan. That same census gives Donald's age as 31, which means that Maude would have been 5 years older than Donald. However, if Donald was 31 in April 1910, he would have been born in 1879 rather than the 1880 reported on the MacGregor Ranch website (Source No. 8) or the 1878 recorded on the plaque on the family mausoleum.

Note that we looked at the digital image of the handwritten 1910 Census, not at some transcription of it. There is no question but that the census shows Maude's age as 36 and Donald's as 31.

The 1920 Census for Precinct 37 in Estes Park (Source No. 1), taken between 14 and 16 January 1920, unfortunately also provides conflicting data:

- It gives Donald's age as 40, which would mean that he was born in 1880, which does agree with his birth year reported on the MacGregor Ranch website.
- It gives Maude's age as 42. Given that the MacGregor Ranch website (Source No. 8) says that Maude was born on 9 June and that the 1920 Census for Precinct 37 was taken in January, if Maude was really 42 in 1920, she was born in 1877 rather than the 1880 reported on the MacGregor Ranch website or the 1878 recorded on the family mausoleum.

Again, we looked at the digital image of the handwritten 1920 Census, not at a transcription of it. There is no question but that the census shows Donald's age as 40 and Maude's as 42.

To add to the confusion, on page 224 of Volume II of *Over Hill and Vale* (Source No. 3), Harold Dunning says that Donald was born on 11 February 1880 in Denver and that he attended schools in Denver including North Denver High School, which is exactly the same information with almost identical wording that appears in Donald's biography on the MacGregor Ranch website. Note that while the day and month of Donald's birth provided by Harold Dunning and by the website agree with those provided by Harriet Burgess (Source No. 5), the 1880 birth year provided by Dunning and the website and the 1880 birth year that can be ascertained from the 1920 Census do not agree with the 1878 birth year on the bronze plaque on the mausoleum, the 1878 birth year provided by Harriet Burgess, or the 1878 birth year that can be ascertained from the 1910 Census.

Similarly, on the same page Harold Dunning gives the following birth date and place for Minnie Maude Koonts [sic]: born 9 June 1880 in Waupaca, Wisconsin. Again, this information is repeated almost word for word in Maude's biography on the MacGregor Ranch website. This disagrees with the 1878 birth year on the bronze plaque on the mausoleum and, probably more significantly, with the 1873 birth year that can be ascertained from the 1910 Census and the 1877 birth year yielded by the 1920 Census.

We'll let Rita Schageman, the Volunteer Coordinator of the MacGregor Museum in 2011, have the final say on this subject (Source No. 12): She reports that page 183 of Source No. 9 gives Maude's birth date as 9 June 1880 and that MacGregor Ranch "estate" files give Donald's birth date as 11 February 1880.

On page 4 of her presentation (Source No. 5), Harriet Burgess says that Donald and his family returned to the MacGregor Ranch full time in 1907 after having bought out his two brothers' shares. Rita Schageman's research (Source No. 12) agrees with the 1907 date. Page 129 of "This Blue Hollow" (Source No. 7) says that Donald bought out George's and Halbert's shares in 1909 and 1910, which means that Donald bought out his brothers' shares after he had decided to make running the ranch his full-time occupation.

By the time Donald and family returned to the MacGregor Ranch, the tourist business had pretty much died out. Instead, for 40 years, Donald ran the ranch as an agricultural business. Harriet says that he increased the size of the ranch to 3,000 acres. Rita Schageman (Source No. 12) tells us that page 225 of Source No. 9 indicates that the ranch contained 2,500 acres in 1940. On page 195 of her article (Source No. 6), Andrea Galliher says that the size of the ranch at Donald's death in 1950 was 2,000 acres.

Donald changed the ranch's cattle to Black Aberdeen Angus, with a herd size of about 200. He also increased the size of the hay crop and raised oats and wheat and had a big vegetable garden.

Harriet Burgess (on page 4) says that Donald had time for civic activities, serving on the Estes Park School Board beginning in 1917 and as School Board President until May 1921. He also was on the board of the Estes Park Bank for a short time. Harriet says that he found his position on the bank's board to be too time consuming and resigned after serving only briefly.

Donald left half of his estate to his wife and half to his daughter. According to page 195 of Andrea Galliher's article, "the estate consisted of the ranch home, four summer cottages, and several outbuildings, valued at $84,872." Donald's biography on the MacGregor Ranch website says that the value of his estate was $86,222, that the ranch consisted "about 4,000 acres," and that it was appraised at $66,000.

Andrea tells us that when Maude died in 1950, she left her half of Donald's estate to her daughter, which means that by the end of 1950, the entire MacGregor Ranch belonged to Muriel MacGregor.

On page 225 of Volume II of *Over Hill and Vale*, Dunning tells us that:

> "The bodies of both Donald and Maude were kept by Kibbey in Loveland until a mausoleum of stone was built near the home place on the ranch and they have been interred there since."

Muriel Lurilla MacGregor

As noted above, Muriel was born on 2 April 1904 in Denver.

Muriel was well educated by any standards, but especially by the standards of her day. Harriet Burgess (page 5 of Source No. 5) provides the following information on Muriel's education and law practice.

She attended grade school in Estes Park. Her father built a shed on the back of the school for Muriel's black pony Zephyr, which she rode to and from school each day.

She graduated from high school after only 3 years in 1921. According to her and her father's biographies on the MacGregor Ranch website (Source No. 8), in 1921 following Muriel's graduation from high school, her parents took her on a trip (must have been a cruise) to Panama, New Orleans, Guatemala, and Cuba. At the time of the family's trip, the Panama Canal had been open for only 7 years.

According to her website biography (Source No. 8), from high school, Muriel immediately went to Colorado College, from which she graduated in 1925 with Bachelor of Arts degree in math. Then, in 1931, she received a Master of Arts degree in history from the University of Colorado. Finally, in 1934, she received a Bachelor of Law degree from the University of Denver. In 1936, she was "one of the first two women admitted to practice before the Supreme Court of Colorado."

However, her law practice was rather limited, including, interestingly, handling several legal matters for Esther A. Burnell Mills, who was the wife of Enos Mills, and making a will for the daughter of Robert Frost. Before her father died, Muriel also acted as his attorney in cases involving land and water disputes. (For more information on Esther Mills, see the chapter on the Mills and Kiley Grave and Scattered Cremains. For more information on Enos Mills, see the section on him in the chapter on Rocky Mountain National Park Scattered Cremains.)

According to Harriet Burgess (page 5), until Muriel's parents died in 1950, she had had a "pretty leisurely life on the ranch" and "really hadn't been involved in ranch life." However, following her parents' deaths, "here she was, all by herself, with this enormous ranch to try to manage."

Probably because she didn't fit the traditionally accepted definition of a "ranch wife," Muriel was never accepted by her Estes Park neighbors. According to Harriet, "The townspeople taunted her, the children jeered her, stories and rumors were rampant."

Even though she was "land rich," she was definitely "cash poor," which increased the difficulties she had in running the ranch. But, remaining true to the desires of her grandmother Clara MacGregor, Muriel never considered selling the ranch.

As the end of her life neared, things became even more difficult for Muriel (pages 5 and 6 of Harriet Burgess's presentation): On 4 July 1969, her barn was burned down, and she received a post card saying that her house would be next. She was so frightened that she spent several nights sleeping in her car before finally returning to her home. According to her biography on the MacGregor Ranch website, "Federal authorities were unable to find the party responsible."

Then on 27 May 1970 when she was 66 years old, she had a stroke when she was alone in her home and wasn't found until 24 hours had past. Following the stroke, Muriel was moved to a rental house across the creek from her home because her home was dirty. She remained there for 5 weeks. At that point, someone broke into Muriel's home and left a light on. Muriel became so upset that she suffered a massive coronary. The folks taking care of Muriel figured that, for her physical and mental well being, she would be better off in her own home. So a group of friends cleaned up her home, and she was returned there.

In July 1970 Muriel spent several days in the Greeley hospital recovering from surgery. Her biography on the website indicated that she had cancer. In October 1970, the doctors determined that she again needed surgery. (Both the July and October surgeries were probably attempts to remove the cancer mentioned in her biography.) She was taken to the Beth Israel Hospital in Denver for the October surgery.

Following the October operation, Muriel died of peritonitis and secondary heart complications on 22 October 1970. She was then interred in the same mausoleum as her parents, and the mausoleum was sealed.

LARIMER COUNTY CEMETERIES

Upon her death, Muriel left 2,931 acres of land, 200 head of cattle, and debts of $13, 263. However, because of the value of the land, her estate was valued at a quarter of a million dollars, which was a lot more money in 1970 than it is now.

Muriel MacGregor's Will and the Muriel L. MacGregor Charitable Trust

According to pages 6 and 7 of Harriet Burgess's presentation (Source No. 5) and page 195 of Andrea Galliher's article (Source No. 6), before Muriel entered Beth Israel Hospital, she wrote a three-page will. In it she put "everything in a trust to be operated as a working ranch for educational and charitable purposes": the Muriel L. MacGregor Charitable Trust. Her will appointed three trustees to oversee the operation of the ranch: Albion Carlson of Greeley, her lawyer at the time of her death; Jane Carlson, Albion's wife; and Victoria Gross, Muriel's long-time friend. Another close friend, Mrs. Orpha Kendall, volunteered to see the plans through.

Following the filing of Muriel's will, the IRS at first said that her estate owed $1.7 million in estate taxes. Before the estate was finally settled, this had grown to $3 million with accrued interest. Finally, in October 1978, the IRS agreed that the MacGregor Ranch established by Muriel's will and trust was indeed an educational operation and was thus tax exempt, so no taxes were owed.

However, about this time 31 cousins "came out of the woodwork" and wanted their shares of the estate. According to page 12 of Harriet Burgess's presentation, these cousins were the children of the brothers of Muriel's father Donald MacGregor: George and Halbert. Recall, however, that Donald had bought his brothers' shares of the MacGregor Ranch in 1909 and 1910. Consequently, one would think that these particular cousins of Muriel's would have had no reasonable claims upon her estate. The other cousins who wanted their shares were on the Koontz side of the family: the children of the sisters and half-sisters of Muriel's mother, Minnie Maude Koontz MacGregor. Recall that Maude had left her half of her husband Donald's estate to their daughter Muriel, so again one can't help but wonder how these cousins could have any legitimate claims on Muriel's estate.

Nonetheless, according to page 6 of Harriet Burgess's presentation, an out-of-court settlement awarded 16 of these 31 cousins with 343 acres along Fish Creek and 56 acres of what was in 1981 (when Harriet gave her presentation) Black Canyon Hills.

The MacGregor Ranch property was further depleted by the sale of 400 acres along the ranch's west side to the National Park Service for inclusion in Rocky Mountain National Park. This sale was necessary to get money to pay outstanding bills.

At the date of Harriet's 1981 presentation, this left the MacGregor Ranch with 2,131 acres, of which only 231 have been deeded to the trust, with the remaining 1900 assigned to the unsettled estate and not able to be transferred to the trust until all the legal fees of the numerous attorneys involved with the estate had been settled. Harriet says on page 6 of her presentation that both the Colorado Attorney-General and a lawsuit filed by the University of Northern Colorado declared the attorneys' fees to be exorbitant.

Harriet referred the members of her audience who wanted more information on the legal battles involving Muriel MacGregor's will, estate, and trust to several article on that subject printed in spring 1981 issues of the *Estes Park Trail-Gazette*. We do the same.

Finally, according to the last paragraph of Muriel's biography on the MacGregor Ranch website (Source No. 8):

> "After a long process, the [National] Park Service and the Ranch Trustees came to a final agreement on September 30, 1983; $4,000,000 for the purchase of a conservation easement on the main ranch—1200 acres. Formal closing ceremonies were held on October 13, 1983. The Park [Rocky Mountain

National Park] holds the easement on the Ranch but does not own or operate the Ranch. The Ranch continues today, aiming to carry on the MacGregor legacy following the wishes of Muriel."

MacGregor Ranch as Operated by the Muriel L. MacGregor Charitable Trust

Again according to the MacGregor Ranch website (Source No. 8), the "Mission Statement" of the Muriel L. MacGregor Charitable Trust is:

> "To continue operation of the MacGregor Ranch as a high mountain historic working cattle ranch and to support youth education. This mission will be carried out by maintaining the presence of a cattle and horse herd, preservation and interpretation of historic buildings and educational tours. The focus of the Ranch will be on quality experiences through respect for the land, the ranch and its history—For the future generations of tomorrow's leaders."

This Trust, which is a private, non-profit operating foundation, provides the funds for and manages all of the activities of the MacGregor Ranch, its museum, and all of its education programs. Also according to the website, "The MacGregor Trust relies heavily on donations, grants and investments to operate the historic Ranch."

The ranch includes the MacGregor Ranch Historic District, which includes 43 buildings, 28 of which are listed on The National Register of Historic Places. In addition to the main ranch house (built in 1896 as the "third ranch house" of Alex and Clara MacGregor), which is also the MacGregor Ranch Museum, the buildings on the ranch include a milk house, blacksmith shop, root cellar, smokehouse, and Alex and Clara's "second ranch house" (built in 1882).

The ranch is the last remaining working cattle ranch in the Estes Park area. In fact, the ranch isn't just an ordinary working ranch; as Andrea Galliher put it on page 195 of her 1987 article on the ranch titled "Ranching the Old Fashioned Way" (Source No. 6), "the ranch freezes a frame in history from appearance to function."

For example, all the ranch work, from herding cows to pulling the hay-making equipment, is done with horses. Horses are also used for branding the cows, which is done "by the rope and throw method, not with the chute." In addition, "lumber repairs are done with rough sawn wood that's often hand hewn into the proper shape and form." And, finally, the ranch's cows "are serviced naturally by three [in 1987] bulls, not artificially inseminated." However, so as to not put the lives of the ranch's animals in jeopardy, the animals all receive modern vaccinations, and veterinarians are called whenever they are needed.

To make the ranch's lessons available to the public, especially to young people, the MacGregor Ranch provides a variety of docent-guided and self-guided tours. Each summer the MacGregor Ranch Museum sponsors a history-based day camp for children who have just completed the 3rd and 4th grades.

Finally, the MacGregor Ranch Museum, which is located in what was the MacGregors' six-room "third ranch house," preserves and displays the original furniture, wall coverings, clothing, utensils, and personal memorabilia (diaries, books, early historic photographs, original oil paintings, and rock and mineral collections) of the three generations of the MacGregors who lived on the ranch. Each year nearly 5,000 school children and 3,000 summer tourists and local residents visit the museum.

CHARLES D. MILLER GRAVE

Location: Latitude 40° 22' 57" N, Longitude 105° 33' 10" W

The grave of Charles D. Miller is located in the front yard of a private home 5.2 miles from Drake, Colorado, at 43 Streamside Drive near Devils Gulch Road. The headstone is in the front yard (pie-shaped with the point next to the road) of a house on the north side of the road. As of 22 February 2012, this house belonged to Michael and Lola Markovich. A side road goes north along the side of the lot. The headstone inscription is facing away from the road. As of 18 January 2000, the date of author Duane Kniebes's visit to the grave, there were two large blue spruce trees behind the grave.

Photo A: The Grave of Charles D. Miller in Front Yard of Private Home Near Drake

Photo B: Headstone of Charles D. Miller (Courtesy of Bill Meirath)

Headstone Inscription

CHARLES MILLER
SHOT
ACCIDENTLY
MAY 17, 1871
BY
CHARLES
W.
DENNISON

Finding the Grave

We knew the approximately location of Charles Miller's grave because of the entry provided for it in the 1985 edition of the Colorado Council of Genealogical Societies' *Colorado Cemetery Directory*. That entry provided the following information for Charles's grave:

- Location: Near junction of Miller's Fork & North Fork of the Big Thompson River (Sec. 25, T6N, R72W, 6th P.M.)
- Type: Single Grave
- History: Killed 1871

Using this information and more specific directions provided by Duke Sumonia of Glen Haven, Duane found Charles Miller's grave on 18 January 2000, got permission from the property owners to enter the property, obtained the grave's GPS reading, and took the above photograph. (Before Duke Sumonia retired, he was a cartographer for the Defense Mapping Agency. It was as a result of his hobby of visiting the locations of remote plane crashes in Colorado that Duke learned the location of Charles Miller's grave.)

History of Charles Miller's Death and Grave

The information below on Charles Miller's death, burial, and grave marker is from pages 40-41 and 48-50 of Volume I (published in 1956) and page 193 of Volume III (published in 1971) of Harold Marion Dunning's *Over Hill and Vale*. (See the "Bibliography" for complete citations.)

Harold Dunning first heard about Charles Miller's death when he read Elkanah J. Lamb's *Miscellaneous Meditations*. From Lamb's text Harold learned that on 17 May 1871 Charles D. Miller and his good friend Charles W. Dennison were stalking a deer through the underbrush close to the junction of the North Fork of the Big Thompson River and the Big Thompson River itself. Dennison's gun accidentally discharged, with the bullet, unfortunately, hitting and killing Miller. Dunning tells us that Miller was the father of several children and lived on the St. Vrain River west of Longmont.

Dunning provides the following quote from Lamb's book to explain why Miller was buried near where he fell rather being taken back to "civilization" for burial:

> "As there were only pony trails in these wild glens at the time, it was impractical—almost impossible to get the body out, and it was consigned to its last resting place close to the tragic spot where he fell by a lovely stream whose purling, pure waters murmured his last requiem, and which has been named Miller's Fork ever since."

An article on Miller's death on the first page of the 24 May 1871 issue of the *Rocky Mountain News* reports that Miller died on 18 May 1871 and provides other details of his death.

On 10 October 1929, Harold Dunning received a letter from Charles Miller's daughter Cora Miller Hardin, who lived in Saratoga, Wyoming, at the time. What was in Cora's letter, Dunning doesn't say. However, shortly thereafter, he and his friend Lucas Brandt had a sandstone headstone created for Miller's grave and made the trip to Miller's grave where they "set a suitable stone in cement, marking the sacred spot permanently."

On 11 November 1963, Cora's daughter and her husband R. D. Martin came to Loveland to see Harold Dunning and asked Dunning if he could take them to visit the grave of Mrs. Martin's grandfather. So Dunning took them "to the location where he had died in that long ago."

When Dunning published Volume I of *Over Hill and Vale* in 1956, the property on which Miller's grave was located belonged to Roy Bryant. By the time he published Volume III in 1971, Miller's grave was on property belonging to Walter Beavis. When Duane visited the grave on 18 January 2000, the property belonged to Dave and Pat McCormick. As noted above, as of 22 February 2012, the property containing Miller's grave belonged to Michael and Lola Markovich.

LARIMER COUNTY CEMETERIES

MILLS AND KILEY GRAVE AND SCATTERED CREMAINS

Location: Latitude 40° 16′ 56″ N, Longitude 105° 32′ 26″ W

The Mills-Kiley Grave and Scattered Cremains are on private property owned by members of the Mills and Kiley families near the old homestead cabin of Enos Mills, which is 8 miles south of Estes Park on the east side of the Peak to Peak Highway (Colorado Highway 7) across from the current incarnation of the Longs Peak Inn. The family is keeping the exact locations of the graves private; thus, the latitude and longitude information above is only for the parking lot used by those who wish to visit the Enos Mills Cabin and Gallery (Address: 6760 Highway 7, Estes Park, CO 80517).

(For biographical information on Enos Mills and his brother Joe Mills, see the applicable subsections of the chapter on Rocky Mountain National Park Scattered Cremains.)

On 3 July 1973, the Enos Mills Cabin was placed on the National Register of Historic Places.

This grave and scattered cremains are on private property and their location is private. Do not request permission to visit.

Sources of Information on the Mills and Kiley Family Members Associated With the Mills and Kiley Grave and Scattered Cremains

1. The 1870 U.S. Census for Sheridan, Linn County, Kansas, date of enumeration illegible. This census record contains information on the parents and siblings of Enos A. Mills.

2. Obituary of Enos Mills, *Estes Park Trail*, 22 September 1922, page 1.

3. "Home Ties" chapter of *Enos A. Mills of the Rockies*, written by Hildegarde Hawthorne and Esther Burnell Mills and originally published in 1935. (See the "Bibliography" for a complete citation.) This chapter discusses Enos and Esther's courtship and marriage and the birth of their daughter Enda.

4. Obituary of Joe Mills, *Estes Park Trail,* 4 October 1935, page 1.

5. Volume II of *Over Hill and Vale,* written by Harold Marion Dunning and published in 1962. (See the "Bibliography" for a complete citation.) Page 220 provides a biography of Enoch "Joe" Mills.

6. "Granddaughter of Enos Mills dies in Nevada," *Estes Park Trail-Gazette*, Wednesday, 24 April 1991. This is the obituary of Kathleen Patricia Kiley.

7. "A long life rooted in the Rockies: Enos Mills' daughter gets new home near beloved national park," written by Deborah Frazier, *Rocky Mountain News*, Saturday, 27 March 2004, page 26A.

8. Obituary of Enda Kiley, *Estes Park Trail-Gazette,* 16 January 2009. This obituary is also available at http://www.enosmills.com/emkobit.html.

9. Obituary of Patrick Vincent Kiley, *Estes Park Trail-Gazette,* 16 August 2010 as found online on Ancestry.com.

10. *Social Security Death Index* as of 14 January and 15 February 2011 as transcribed by Ancestry.com.

11. Susan Cain-Hipple Family Tree, which includes information on the parents and siblings of Esther A. Burnell Mills as available on Ancestory.com on 14 January 2011. This family tree is particularly well documented as it includes numerous source citations to support its data.

12. Online homestead property records of the Bureau of Land Management at www.glorecords.blm.gov as of 15 January 2010.

13. *U.S. Veterans Gravesites* as of 16 January 2011 as transcribed by Ancestry.com.

14. Email from direct descendants of Enos Mills, received on 13 February and 21 July 2011 containing corrections to the first and second drafts of this chapter.

15. The "Enos A. Mills Genealogy" section of the Enos Mills Cabin and Gallery website at http://www.enosmills.com/genes.html as of 13 February 2011.

16. Emails from Pat Washburn, a granddaughter of Joe Mills, received on 14 and 15 February 2011 answering our questions about Joe, his wife, and his children.

List of Individuals Whose Remains Are Interred or Ashes Are Scattered on the Mills Property South of Estes Park

When we visited with Enda Kiley, the only child of Enos Mills and his wife Esther Burnell Mills, at her father's famous cabin on 16 August 2001, Enda told us that the remains of three members of the Mills and Kiley families were scattered or buried on the Mills property as of that date:

- Esther A. Burnell Mills, the wife of Enos Mills and the mother of Enda Kiley. Enda told us that Esther's ashes were scattered on the property.

- Elizabeth Burnell Smith, Enda's aunt and the older sister of Enda's mother Esther A. Burnell Mills. Enda told us that Elizabeth's ashes were scattered on the property.

- Kathleen Patricia Kiley, Enda's oldest child, is buried on the property in a pine box. Her grave has a sandstone marker (Source No. 14).

(For genealogy information on these individuals, see "Biographical and Genealogical Information of the Mills and Kiley Families" below.)

Biographical and Genealogical Information of the Mills and Kiley Families

At the request of the Mills and Kiley families, no living individuals are listed.

Parents and Siblings of Enos A. Mills

Enos Mills, Sr., father of Enos A. Mills. Enos Mills, Sr., was born on 26 December 1834 near Richmond, Wayne County, Indiana, and died on 17 February 1910 in Pleasanton, Linn County, Kansas (Source Nos. 1 and 15). His **parents were Abijah Mills and Sarah Moon** (Source No. 15).

Enos Sr. married Ann Lamb in Dallas County, Iowa, on 28 August 1855 (Source No. 15).

Ann Lamb, mother of Enos A. Mills. Ann Lamb was born on 8 November 1837 in Grand County, Indiana, and died on 4 March 1923 in Linn County, Kansas (Source No. 15). Her **parents were Josiah Lamb and Ruth Lamb** (Source No. 15). Ruth's maiden name was also "Lamb."

For genealogical information on the ancestors of Enos Mills, Sr., and Ann Lamb Mills, see Source No. 15.

Children of Enos Mills, Sr., and Ann Lamb Mills

Enos Mills, Sr., and Ann Lamb Mills had the following 11 children:

1. **Augustus E. Mills.** Augusta was born 22 May 1856 in Iowa City, Wright County, Iowa, and died in 22 October 1859 in Pleasanton, Linn County, Kansas (Source No. 15).

2. **Elkanah F. Mills.** He was born on 27 July 1857 in Iowa City, Wright County, Iowa, and died on 2 November 1859 in Pleasanton, Linn County, Kansas (Source No. 15).

3. **Mary E. Mills.** Mary was born on 22 December 1858 in Kansas City, Jackson County, Missouri, and died 16 February 1860 (Source No. 15).

LARIMER COUNTY CEMETERIES

4. **Naomi Victoria Mills**. Naomi was born on 2 April 1861 in Pleasanton, Linn County, Kansas (Source Nos. 1, 14, and 15), and died on 16 February 1891 in Los Angeles, California, where she is buried there (Source Nos. 14 and 15). Her obituary cited in Source No. 15 mentions that she was a mother, so she and Moie must have had children.

   Moie D. Dodsworth, Namoi's husband. (Source No. 15)

5. **Ruth Mills**. Ruth was born and died on 2 March 1862 in Pleasanton, Linn County, Kansas (Source No. 15).

6. **Sarah A. Mills**. Sarah was born in 1863 in Kansas City, Jackson County, Missouri (Source Nos. 1, 14, and 15), and died in 1922 (Source No. 15).

   Charles T. Winslow, Sarah's husband. (Source No. 15)

7. **Ellen ("Ella") Mills**. Ella was born about 1865 in Pleasanton, Linn County, Kansas (Source Nos. 1 and 15). Her death date could not be determined. The 1870 U.S. Census for Sheridan, Linn County, Kansas (Source No. 1), lists her as Rhoda E. Mills in the family of Enos Mills and Ann Mills, with Enos Mills as one of her siblings.

   Ella's husbands. She married a **Mr. Zybach** in Grandview, Missouri, in 1910 and was married to a **Mr. Hart** by 1923 (Source No. 15).

8. **Sabina Isabella ("Belle") Mills**. Belle was born about 1868 in Kansas (Source Nos. 1 and 15). Her death date could not be determined.

   Belle's husbands. Belle married a **Mr. Wasson** in Oregon in 1910 and a **Mr. Carse** by 1923 (Source No. 15).

9. **Enos Abijah Mills** . Enos A. Mills, the naturalist who encouraged the creation of Rocky Mountain National Park, was born on 22 April 1870 in Pleasanton, Linn County, Kansas (Source No. 15 and his daughter Enda Kiley), and died on 21 September 1922 in Estes Park (Source Nos. 2 and 15 and his daughter Enda Kiley). His middle name of "Abijah" comes from Source No. 15 and was the first name of Enos's paternal grandfather. (For more information on Enos, see the "Enos A. Mills" section of the chapter on Rocky Mountain National Park Scattered Cremains.) Enos married Esther A. Burnell on 12 August 1918 at Enos's homestead cabin with Esther's sister Elizabeth and "a few associates" in attendance (page 159 of Source No. 3).

   Esther A. Burnell, Enos's wife. Esther was born on 3 August 1889 in Kansas (Source Nos. 10 and 11). She received the land patent for her homestead of 120 acres near what is now Fall River Road in Rocky Mountain National Park on 20 September 1920 (Source No. 12), about 2 years after her marriage to Enos and about 17 months before the birth of her and Enos's daughter Enda. Following Esther's death in April 1964 (Source No. 10), her cremains were scattered on the Mills property south of Estes Park. The *Social Security Death Index* (Source No. 10) indicates that Esther's legal address at the time of her death was Englewood, Arapahoe County, Colorado.

   (For information on Esther's parents and siblings, see "Parents and Siblings of Esther A. Burnell Mills" below. For information on Enos and Esther's daughter and her descendants, see "Descendants of Enos A. Mills and Esther A. Burnell Mills" below.)

10. **Horace Greeley Mills**. Horace was born about 1875 in Kansas City, Missouri (Source No. 15). His death date could not be determined.

11. **Enoch Josiah ("Joe") Mills.** Joe was born on 23 July 1880 in Pleasanton, Linn County, Kansas, and died on 3 October 1935 in Denver, Adams County, Colorado (Source Nos. 4 and 5). (For more information on Joe Mills, see the "Joe Mills" section of the chapter on Rocky Mountain National Park Scattered Cremains.) His middle name was provided by his granddaughter Pat Washburn (Source No. 16).

Joe married Ethel M. Steere (Source Nos. 5, 15, and 16) on 18 May 1908 (Source Nos. 5 and 16) or in May 1910 (Source No. 15). Joe's obituary (Source No. 4) gives his wife's last name as "Speere," but all other sources, including his granddaughter Pat Washburn (Source No. 16), agree that her maiden name was "Steere." Pat also told us that Jim Pickering's introduction to Joe's autobiography *A Mountain Boyhood* reports that her grandparents were married in Fort Worth, Texas.

Ethel Maude Steere, Joe's wife. Using information provided by Ethel's granddaughter Pat Washburn, we were able to find an entry for Ethel Mills in the *Social Security Death Index* (Source No. 10) which reports that Ethel was born on 25 August 1887 and died in December 1969 in Denver. Pat remembers that Ethel lived in the 1000 block of Downing Street in Denver and that when Pat visited, Ethel would feed her "massive amounts of food. I think she was still used to cooking for the Crags [a lodge in Estes Park owned by Joe Mills]."

Joe and Ethel had two children (Source No. 5):

11.1 **Eleanor Ann Mills.** According to her daughter Pat Washburn (Source No. 16), Eleanor died in 2001 just short of her 90th birthday.

11.2. **Mark Muir Mills.** Pat Washburn reports that Mark is also deceased (Source No. 16).

Parents and Siblings of Esther A. Burnell Mills

Arthur Tappan Burnell, father of Esther A. Burnell Mills. Arthur was born on 9 July 1863 in Davenport, Scott County, Iowa, and died on 13 March 1942 in Los Angeles, Los Angeles County, California (Source No. 11).

Mary Adaline Frayer, mother of Esther A. Burnell Mills. Mary was born on 15 November 1853 in Carson, Huron County, Ohio, and died in 1945 in Los Angeles, Los Angeles County, California (Source No. 11).

Unless otherwise noted, the information on Arthur and Mary's four children below comes from Source No. 11:

1. **Eugene E. Burnell.** Eugene was born in December 1884 in the state of Washington.

2. **Bessie Mae Burnell.** Elizabeth was born on 1 May 1887 (Source No. 14) in Kansas. According to Source No. 14, Elizabeth was born "Bessie Mae Burnell but later changed her names to 'Elizabeth B. Smith,' with the 'B' standing for 'Burnell.' She was known as 'Bessie' to her family and friends and was known as 'Elizabeth' professionally. "

As noted above, Elizabeth was present at Esther and Enos's marriage. She also lived with Esther for some time on Esther's homestead.

On page 156 of Source No. 3, Esther tells us that Elizabeth "soon became the most popular and versatile guide" at Longs Peak Inn, working as a guide for treks up Longs Peak and Twin Sisters and in Wild Basin. Esther ends her brief biographical information on her sister Elizabeth by saying that Elizabeth worked as a nature guide at Longs Peak Inn for 12 summers, received an M.A. from the University of Michigan, and taught higher mathematics. However, after her experiences with Enos Mills and her sister in the Rocky

Mountain National Park area, Elizabeth became the "supervisor of nature study in the Los Angeles City Schools."

Following Elizabeth's death on 9 April 1960 (Source No. 14), Enda Kiley told us (in August 2001) that Elizabeth's ashes were scattered on the Mills property south of Estes Park.

Norman Smith, Elizabeth's husband. Elizabeth and Norman were married some time in the 1950s (Source No. 14).

3. **Esther A. Burnell.** For genealogical details for Esther, see the entry for Enos A. Mills (Child No. 9) above.

4. **Bernice Imogene Burnell.** Bernice was born on 13 March 1892 in Lexington, Fayette County, Kentucky, and died on 22 May 1977 in Everson, Whatcom County, Washington.

Descendants of Enos A. Mills and Esther A. Burnell Mills

Enda Mills, daughter of Enos and Esther Mills. According to Enda's obituary (Source No. 8), she was born on 27 April 1919 "at Longs Peak." Specifically, she was born in the Mills Family Cabin at Longs Peak Inn, where Enos moved in 1909 (Source No. 14). Her obituary also reports that, after attending school at Cheyenne Mountain School in Colorado Springs and Estes Park schools, she graduated from high school in 1937 and then attended Colorado Women's College; the University of Colorado, where she was on the ski team; and Pomona College in California, from which she graduated (Source Nos. 7 and 8).

Again, according to Enda's obituary (Source No. 8), after graduation from college, she went to work for American Airlines and took flying lessons. However, when it was learned that she was blind in one eye because of a childhood accident, she had to quit taking lessons. During World War II, she joined the Navy WAVES and was serving in Rhode Island when she met her husband-to-be Robert Henry Bremer Kiley.

Robert and Enda were married on 27 February 1946 and moved to Denver, where Robert worked as an attorney. Enda worked as a secretary in Robert's law office and for the Colorado Mountain Club and the American Automobile Association. She also attended the University of Denver, from which she received a master's degree in education.

In 1966, Robert and Enda and their children moved to Estes Park, where, following Robert's death in 1993 (Source No. 10), Enda began leading 30-minute "walk a little, see a lot" nature hikes around her father's old cabin (Source No. 7), where she also told her visitors about the legacy of her father, just as she told us when we visited with her at her father's old homestead cabin on 16 August 2001. We are honored to have met her.

Enda died in Longmont on 13 January 2009, after having spent her last months at the Longmont Regent Retirement Communities. Her funeral service was held at the Episcopal Church of St. Bartholomew the Apostle in Estes Park on 21 January 2009.

Robert Henry Bremer Kiley, Enda's husband. Robert was born on 11 August 1919 and died on 16 February 1993 (Source Nos. 10 and 13). Because of his service as an enlisted radioman in the U.S. Navy during World War II, following his death he was buried at Ft. Logan National Cemetery in Denver, Colorado, in Site 276 of Section 3 (Source No. 13). Following World War II, Robert served as an officer in the U.S. Navy Reserves. By the time of his retirement from the Reserves, he had reached the rank of Commander (Source No. 14).

Enda and Robert had the following four children:

1. **Kathleen ("Koco") Patricia Kiley.** According to her obituary (Source No. 6), Kathleen was born on 19 October 1946 in Chelsea, Massachusetts, and died on 19 April 1991 in Sparks, Nevada. She received a bachelor's degree in biological sciences from Colorado

State University in 1968; a master's degree in biological science from Chapman College in Orange County, California; and pursued a course in nutrition at the University of California in Davis. She was a registered dietician. At the time of her death, she owned and operated a business called Body Time and was a member of the Board of Directors of the North Tahoe Fine Arts Council.

Graveside services were conducted in her honor at the "Enos Mills property on Highway 7" on Sunday, 28 April 1991. She is buried on the Mills property south of Estes Park.

2. **Still-living Son Kiley**.

3. **Still-living Daughter Kiley**.

4. **Patrick Vincent Kiley**. According to his obituary (Source No. 9), Pat was born on 22 November 1950 in Denver and died at his home in Longmont on 1 May 2010.

JULIA ANN MORRISSEY GRAVE

Location: Latitude 40° 16' 14" N, Longitude 105° 32' 59" W

Julia Ann Morrissey's grave is located on private property in a small grotto below the southwest side of a large granite outcropping known locally as Kirk's Knoll. Kirk's Knoll is behind the log summer cabin belonging to Warner Bass at 560 Longs Peak Road southwest of Estes Park. Longs Peak Road runs west from State Highway 7 and is the road that goes to the Longs Peak Ranger Station and the East Longs Peak Trailhead.

Description of Grave

Julia Ann Morrissey's ashes are in an urn that has been cemented into rocks in the middle of the above-described grotto. The urn can be seen between the rocks. A metal cross is affixed to the rock right above Julia's urn. Jim Pickering, who took us to the grave, told us that he had been told that the cross was at the grotto even before Julia's ashes were interred there.

Our use of dowser rods confirmed the presence of ashes in the urn.

Photo A: Grotto at Kirk's Knoll Showing Cross Above the Rocks Into Which the Urn Containing the Ashes of Julia Ann Morrissey Was Cemented

Ashes Possibly Scattered in Same Vicinity

Jim Pickering told us that he had been told but could not positively confirm that the ashes of Charles Edwin Hewes were also scattered in the area. In addition, when Charles Hewes's mother, Mary Catherine Palmer Kirkwood, died in January 1919, Charles brought her ashes back to the Hewes-Kirkwood Inn. Thus, they may also be scattered or buried somewhere in the same general area. (For additional information on Mary's and Charles's deaths, see "History of Julia Ann Morrissey" and "History of Charles Edwin Hewes" below.)

Finding the Grave

We first learned about Julia's grave from Pieter Hondius, Jr., following the presentation on "Guest Lodges in Rocky Mountain National Park" on 9 March 2002, in Estes Park. Pieter had been one of the panelists for the presentation. (For more information on Pieter; his father Pieter Hondius, Sr.; his mother Eleanor James Hondius; and the James family, see the chapter on the Elkhorn Lodge Cemetery.) Having learned that we were the couple doing a census of graves in Larimer County, Pieter told us that Jim Pickering knew about a grave south of Estes Park in the Longs Peak area. Pieter did not know whether the grave was in Boulder County or Larimer County.

Sybil Barnes, then the Local History Librarian for the Estes Park Public Library and the moderator for the March 9th presentation, told us that Jim was usually in the Estes Park area only in the summer but that she would contact him via email to find out which county the grave was in. A very short time later Jim replied to Sybil that the grave was indeed in Larimer County, that it was the grave of Julia Morrissey, and that, as mentioned above, he had also heard that the ashes of Charles Edwin Hewes were scattered in the same area. (For more information on Jim Pickering and Sybil Barnes and on all of the help that they provided during our research for this book, see the "Acknowledgments" section.)

In late May 2002, we talked to Jim on the phone. He told us that Warner Bass was the owner of the property and that Warner would be out of town until around July 4th.

On 6 July 2002, we talked to Warner's brother-in-law John Gregory, who gave permission for us to visit the grave with Jim Pickering and his wife, Pat.

Thus, on 12 July 2002, we met Jim and Pat at the Fern Lake Trailhead to take them to the grave of the Reverend Thornton R. Sampson about 350 feet down the Fern Lake Trail. Jim had written an article on Rev. Sampson for the Summer 2000 issue of *Colorado Heritage* and was very interested in visiting Sampson's burial site. (For more information on Reverend Sampson's grave and the history of his life, disappearance, death, and burial, see the chapter on the Reverend Thornton R. Sampson Grave. The information in Jim's *Colorado Heritage* article later became a chapter in his *The Ways of the Mountains*, both of which contributed greatly to the completeness of that chapter.) After we showed Reverend Sampson's grave to Jim and Pat, they took us to Julia Morrissey's grave.

A few days later, Jim sent generously sent us a draft of his book on Charles Edwin Hewes titled *In the Vale of Elkanah: The Tahosa Valley World of Charles Edwin Hewes* (See the "Bibliography" for a complete citation for this book, which was published in 2003.) The two "History" sections below are very brief summaries of the information on Julia Ann Morrissey and Charles Edwin Hewes contained in this very informative and readable book. Those interested in learning more about Charles Hewes, the Hewes-Kirkwood Inn, and the interactions of Charles Hewes, his family, and other members of the "Brigands" and the Front Range Settlers League, including Enos Mills, are encouraged to read *In the Vale of Elkanah*.

History of Julia Ann Morrissey

Julia Ann Morrissey was born in 1884 in Cork, Ireland. She immigrated to Cleveland, Ohio in 1907, where she was a housekeeper for a priest.

In April 1912, Mary Catherine Palmer Hewes Kirkwood, the twice-widowed mother of Charles Edwin Hewes and his younger brother Stephen Brown Hewes, Jr., suffered an emotional breakdown. Stephen took her to Cleveland, where he worked part of the year as an agent for Union Central Life. While in Cleveland, Mary Kirkwood hired Julia Morrissey as her maid. The next summer when Mary returned to the family's Hewes-Kirkwood Inn at the base of Longs Peak, she brought Julia with her. Julia remained with the Hewes-Kirkwood family for the rest of her life.

At Hewes-Kirkwood, Julia began as a chambermaid and laundress, but, over the years, became an invaluable adjunct to the family. Even after Mary Kirkwood died on 23 January 1919 (from suicide), Julia stayed on at the Hewes-Kirkwood Inn.

LARIMER COUNTY CEMETERIES

In April 2003, Jim Pickering kindly checked his copy of Charles Hewes's journal for entries after the date of Mary Kirkwood's death to see if it contained any clues as to the final disposition of Mary's ashes. As mentioned earlier, when we first visited Kirk's Knoll with Jim and Pat Pickering in July 2002, we all wondered if Charles Hewes's and Mary Kirkwood's ashes might have been scattered there.

After reviewing the applicable sections of Charles's 1919 journal, Jim sent us an email on 21 April 2003 containing information concerning Mary Kirkwood's death and cremation and Charles's activities after he returned to the Hewes-Kirkwood Inn with his mother's ashes. The information and quotes below are from Jim's April 21st email:

- Mary died of suicide on 23 January 1919.
- By January 25th, Charles was in Denver to attend his mother's funeral, which took place at "Moran's little private chapel" at 1527 Cleveland Place.
- On January 26th, Mary's body was cremated at the Riverside Crematory, with both Charles and his brother Steve in attendance.
- On February 2, Charles returned to Hewes-Kirkwood with his mother's ashes in a tin.
- "For the next week or so he recorded memories and dreams on several occasions. It was cold, but as usual he was out and about."
- "On February 16th, perhaps significantly, he went to Kirk's Knoll to worship, but without reference to anyone's ashes. Remember that Mary Kirkwood's second husband died before Charles and the family came to the mountains, so she would have been the first member of the family to have been interred there. But at least we know that by that date Charles saw Kirk's Knoll as a place for meditation and peace."
- "I next thought that perhaps Charles was waiting until his brother Steve returned from Cleveland for his usual summer at Hewes-Kirkwood. Steve returned on June 19th. Uncle Henry Palmer, age 75, also spent that summer at Hewes-Kirkwood, providing a perfect occasion for an internment or at least a reference. If it happened, it is not mentioned. Nor is it mentioned in Charles' year-end summary."
- "So, the mystery [of what happened to Mary Kirkwood's ashes] remains. I think if there was an explicit reference in the journals beyond 1919 to an internment, I would have recalled."

For several years following Mary's death, Julia Morrissey spent the off-season in Denver, where she worked as a domestic. She returned to the Hewes-Kirkwood Inn before the beginning of each tourist season to help open the hotel and then run the kitchen, where she was especially known for her homemade pies. By the middle of the 1920s, she began staying at the Hewes-Kirkwood Inn all year and would be Charles Hewes's only human companion during the winter months.

In spite of the considerable amount of time that they spent in each other's company, no evidence of any romantic relationship between Charles and Julia has surfaced. Given guests' descriptions of Julia, which include remembrances of her "white apron, large shapeless dress, and her size ten men's workshoes" and of personal hygiene that left something to be desired, this lack of a romantic relationship seems reasonable.

However, even though Charles began by recording in his journal in November 1914 that he was "considerably annoyed by the presence of Julia, mother's maid," later entries in his journal include descriptions of "long leisurely evening strolls with Julia over woods and field." In addition, each winter Charles and Julia would bake pudding and plum cakes, which they packed with fir boughs, and mailed to some 85 of "our friends all over the U.S.A."

Although the perpetual financial difficulties of the Hewes-Kirkwood Inn kept Charles from even being able to pay Julia for her considerable efforts on behalf of the Inn and his family, he kept track of the salary that he owed her. By 1931, the same year that Julia officially became an American citizen, her salary, on paper at least, had reached $150 a year.

Finally, in October 1944, Charles and his younger brother Steve at long last became outright owners of the Inn and the 80 acres of land remaining with it. At that point, Charles and Steve agreed to give Julia Morrissey, "our faithful helper," a new first mortgage on the property for $7,500 and another mortgage for $1,890 on the furnishings of the property in lieu of her 30 years of unpaid wages.

Julia continued to stay at the Inn, even after nursing Charles through his final illness, which ended in his death on 27 August 1947. "His remains were removed to Denver, cremated, and then returned to Hewes-Kirkwood where they were scattered not far from the Inn, among the rocks of a granite outcropping to the south, near the site of Steve's cabin, the place they called Kirk's Knoll."

Julia stayed on at the Inn following Charles' death. When Julia died on 25 August 1967 at the age of 83, the owner of the Hewes-Kirkwood Inn was Beth Miller Harrod. Beth had bought the property in 1951 and turned it into a summer music school named the Rocky Ridge Music Center. In Note 114 at the end of *In the Vale of Elkanah*, Jim Pickering refers his readers to pages 102-104 and 107-111 of the following book for an account of Julia Morrissey's final years at Hewes-Kirkwood Inn and her death: *Beth Miller Harrod: Master Teacher, Concert Pianist and Founder of Rocky Ridge* by Paul T. Rosewell, published in 2001 by Media Production and Marketing in Lincoln, Nebraska.

Following Julia's death, she was cremated and, as noted under "Location" above, "her ashes were interred at Kirk's Knoll."

History of Charles Edwin Hewes

As noted above, for a complete account of the life of Charles Edwin Hewes, see *In the Vale of Elkanah: The Tahosa Valley World of Charles Edwin Hewes* by James H. Pickering (complete citation in "Bibliography"). However, since it appears that Charles Hewes's ashes were scattered over the same granite outcropping, Kirk's Knoll, that includes the grotto containing Julia's ashes, a few words specifically about Charles seem in order here. (See also page 109 of *In the Vale of Elkkanah* concerning the final disposition of the ashes of Charles Hewes.)

Charles Edwin Hewes was born in Boone, Iowa, in October 1879 to Stephen Brown Hewes, Sr., and Mary Catherine Palmer. Both his paternal and maternal ancestors had patriotic roots and included a signer of the Declaration of Independence, Joseph Hewes, and a second lieutenant who fought and died for the Union during the Civil War, John Edgerton Palmer the Fifth.

Charles's father, Stephen Hewes, Sr., was a good salesman but was not good at handling his finances, a trait he seems to have passed on to his sons. On 7 January 1879, he shot himself in a bank in Ogden, Iowa, where he had gone in an unsuccessful attempt to collect a sizable debt owed him.

Charles's mother, Mary Catherine Palmer Hewes, supported 9-year-old Charles and his 5-year-old brother Steve by operating a millinery and dress-making shop until February 1899, when she married Thomas J. Kirkwood, a Civil War veteran and widower whom Mary had known since she was a girl.

By 1900, Charles's brother Steve and his uncle Henry Palmer were living in Denver, where they were joined by Mary Kirkwood; her second husband, Thomas Kirkwood; and Charles himself. While in Denver, Charles worked for Wells Fargo. On 24 April 1906, Thomas Kirkwood died of arteriosclerosis.

Following Thomas's death, a clairvoyant told Mary that Charles should depart for Estes Park and apply for a job at a hotel. To please his mother, on 17 June 1907, he left for Estes Park and went to Enos Mills's Longs Peak Inn, where he asked Enos's brother Joe for a job.

By the end of that summer, Charles, his mother Mary, and his brother Steve together filed for 480 acres of homestead claims and took advantage of other federal land acts to acquire an addition 480 acres. These 960 contiguous acres were in the Tahosa Valley not far from Longs Peak Inn. The family departed Denver for their new home on 22 September 1907.

What began as Bleak House, a 20 by 25 foot cabin for Mary Kirkwood, ended up, beginning on 4 July 1914, becoming the Hewes-Kirkwood Inn.

Charles Hewes's "job" at the Inn was "general utility man" and handler of the finances. During the winters and other time he could spare, he turned his attention to his real love—writing his journals, poems, and one novel.

The Inn remained in financial difficulties throughout its existence. Such well-known Estes Park figures as Clem Yore; Pieter Hondius, Sr.; and Pieter's wife Eleanor James Hondius all figured in various efforts to try to save Hewes-Kirkwood Inn and the associated family members from financial catastrophe.

Charles Hewes's most important contribution to his world seems to have been himself. Guests remembered him as a small, bald-headed man who "habitually dressed in leather putties, riding britches, and sweater, ever-ready to greet them with smiling face and blue twinkling eyes or to engage in conversation."

Jim Pickering ends his book on Charles Hewes with the following quote from Charles's friend Siegfried Wagener, who said that Charles was "the most beloved man I have known, a humble man of contagious satisfaction for whom it all was, 'Wonderful, simply wonderful.'"

On page 89 of Volume I of *Over Hill and Vale*, written by Harold Marion Dunning and published in 1956, Dunning offers the following opinion of Charles Hewes: "He is my most unforgettable character. He was the nearest Christlike character I have ever known."

Indeed, Dunning's three volumes of *Over Hill and Vale* are liberally sprinkled with quotes from Charles Hewes's poems and other information about Charles and other members of his family. For example, Volume III, published in 1971, contains Charles's ode to Rocky Mountain National Park on page 32; an obituary type of paragraph on page 108; a photograph of Charles taken on 24 September 1924 in front of the ever-roaring fireplace at the Hewes-Kirkwood Inn on page 355; a poem, *Park Hill,* about Rocky Mountain Jim Nugent, on page 345; and the story of Steve Hewes's encounter with a gun-toting rancher on pages 169 and 170. (See the "Bibliography" for complete citations for all three volumes of *Over Hill and Vale*.)

The photo of Charles in front of the Hewes-Kirkwood fireplace is also on page 112 of Jim Pickering's *In the Vale of Elkanah*.

BOB OZMEN GRAVE

Location: Latitude 40° 20' 56" N, Longitude 105° 34' 11" W

The grave of Bob Ozmen is located in a nature walk area in the campground in the north corner of the Estes Park Center of the YMCA of the Rockies south of Estes Park. The nature walk area and campground are west of Larimer County Road 69B (formerly Colorado Highway 66), west of the junction of the Wind River with the Big Thompson River, and just north of the junction of Glacier Creek and the Big Thompson River. The Big Thompson runs west to east at the north end of the area. The Swiftcurrent Lodge is just to the north of the grave.

The grave is located just south of Nature Walk Sign No. 10 on the east side of a big pine tree in which a number of large nails were driven at some time in the not-too-recent past. The grave and the pine tree are almost immediately west of the nearby bridge over the Big Thompson on CR 69B. (Jack Melton, the Director of the Lula Dorsey Museum at the Estes Park Center, told us on 28 October 2004 that the numbered signs in the area are for a self-guided nature walk.)

Photo A shows the grave at the foot of the pine tree, with Nature Walk Sign No. 10 in the background to the left of the pine tree.

Photo A: Grave of Bob Ozmen in a Campground at the North End of the Estes Park Center of the YMCA of the Rockies, With Nature Walk Sign No. 10 in the Left Background

Description

The headstone of Bob Ozmen's grave is a local gray-beige granite boulder that appears to have already been in place when Bob Ozmen was buried immediately east of it. The top of the boulder was flattened off, and the following words were carved into the flattened-off area, probably with a chisel:

BOB OZMEN

**JULY 3 TO AUG
19**

As Photo B shows, no year appears on the headstone. However, close observation of the headstone inscription indicates that the person who carved the inscription ran out of space for the August date. The "19" on the third line of the headstone could be either the date in August when the little boy died or it could be the first two digits of the year in which the child died, with the carver "running out of steam" before finishing the inscription. Carving in the granite with a chisel must have been hard going.

Photo B: Close-up View of Headstone on Bob Ozmen's Grave

The grave is in an east-west orientation, with the headstone on the west end of the grave. Our use of dowser rods confirm that, as the headstone suggests, a child is buried in the grave.

Finding the Grave

Truman L. Nicholas, a member of the Estes Park Genealogical Society, told us about Bob Ozmen's grave. We first met Truman in August 2001 when we made a presentation to the Estes Park Genealogical Society about the results of our grave-search efforts in Rocky Mountain National Park and the Estes Park area. (See the "Acknowledgments" section for information on all of the help that Truman provided to our grave-search efforts.)

Early in the summer of 2004, Truman contacted us for an update on our grave-search efforts in both the Park and the Estes Park area, which we provided him. He then made an effort to find some of the graves and cemeteries on the list that we sent him that we had not, at that point, been able to locate. After an unsuccessful attempt to find the grave of Unknown Child No. 3, which is nearby on the north side of the Big Thompson River, Truman stopped in at the Swiftcurrent Lodge to see if the folks there knew anything about the grave of Unknown Child No. 3. They did not, but they did know about the grave of Bob Ozmen and took Truman and his wife Beverly to see it.

On 30 August 2004, Truman sent us an email telling us about Bob Ozmen's grave. On 1 October 2004, we met Truman at his and Beverly's summer home in Estes Park, and Truman took us to the grave.

History of Bob Ozmen

We have not been able to learn anything definite about Bob Ozmen or his parents. Even before we came to Estes Park to visit the grave with Truman, we asked Sybil Barnes, then the Local History Librarian for the Estes Park Public Library, to see if she could find anything in the Library's files about a Bob Ozmen dying in Estes Park. She could not.

To be thorough, since the grave was on YMCA property, she talked to Jack R. and Lulabeth Melton, who wrote *YMCA of the Rockies; Spanning a Century* (published in 1992 under the auspices of the Lula W. Dorsey Museum at the YMCA of the Rockies) to see if they recalled anything about a child burial in the nature walk area described above. They did not. However, they told Sybil that there had once been some "sweat lodge/spirit quest" kind of activity in that area. Given that information, Sybil hypothesized that the carved rock might not have been a headstone at all and could be referring to someone "named 'Bob' who was with a group of people calling themselves 'Oz men' who camped there. Probably illegally." In other words, the rock could have been carved to commemorate a visit, not to mark a grave.

After having received the first draft of this chapter Jack Melton called us on 28 October 2004 to say that he and his wife planned on visiting the grave later that same day and that they had their doubts about it really being a grave and pretty much subscribed to Sybil's theory. On 5 November 2004, Jack sent us an email in which he said:

> "I went down to look at the site by the river. The patina on the rock and letters show that the lettering is not contemporary. It is 50 or 100 years old? I have no clue. The main thing that concerns me is that the edges of the letters are still very sharp."

If the site is indeed a burial, as our use of dowser rods indicates that it is, and if that burial occurred after the YMCA owned/occupied the property, it would have had to have occurred during or after 1908. According to page 37 of the Meltons' book, the YMCA held the "First Estes Park Conference" in the area of the Wind River Lodge in Estes Park between 31 July and 10 August 1908. Interestingly, these dates are close to the birth and death dates of Bob Ozmen, which were July 3 to August 19 (?) of some unknown year.

Those interested in a complete and very readable account of the history of the YMCA of the Rockies should consult the *YMCA of the Rockies; Spanning a Century*. The information on the YMCA below comes from that book. Page 37 of the book tells us that the 1908 conference was "a sea of tents" near the already existing Wind River Lodge. In 1910 the Lodge was joined by a Dining and Social Hall, which was the first building built specifically for the YMCA of the Rockies. Indeed (pages 43 and 44), four buildings of the Wind River Lodge were moved from "the side of Bible Point" to the vicinity of the Dining and Social Hall. Tent cottages provided additional sleeping accommodations. In 1910 (page 44), the YMCA's second "Vacation Conference" was held from July 8 through July 17 (again close to the dates of Bob Ozmen's life).

Although it seemed unlikely, we were hoping that the Lula W. Dorsey Museum at the YMCA of the Rockies might have maintained records of the names of those who attended the YMCA summer conferences over the years, especially the names of families who attended during the early years when a child who was born and died during a summer conference would have been most likely to have been buried in the area without any official records. Unfortunately, when Jack Melton called us on 28 October 28 2004, he said that no such records were maintained. (As noted above, Jack is the Director of the Museum as well as the co-author of *YMCA of the Rockies*.)

Consequently, on 29 October 2004 we consulted an online version of U.S. Federal Census Records at heritagequestonline.com (available to holders of library cards at the Fort Collins Public Library) to see if "Ozmen" was a legitimate last name and if there were any Ozmen families in the 1910 Census who might have attended the 1908 and/or 1910 summer conferences. From heritagequestonline.com, we learned that, between 1860 and 1920, the U.S. Federal Censuses list nine Ozmen families, broken down as follows:

- 1860 Census: The family of George W. Ozmen in Ohio.
- 1900 Census: The Judd Ozmen and Nellie Ozmen families in Ohio, the William S. Ozmen family in South Carolina, and the William H. Ozmen family in Iowa.

LARIMER COUNTY CEMETERIES

- 1910 Census: The Burr Ozmen family in Missouri. As Burr and his wife Harriett are possible parents for the Bob Ozmen buried in the YMCA's nature walk area, we will provide more information on them below.
- 1920 Census: Burr and Harriett Ozmen do not reappear in the 1920 Census. However, the census does list three Ozmen families, one in Indiana and two in Tennessee. None of these individuals appear to be related to the Burr Ozmen of the 1910 Census.

Details of 1910 Census Entry for the Burr Ozmen Family of Missouri

On page 36 of the Meltons' *YMCA of the Rockies; Spanning a Century*, they quote a description that W. O. Fletcher of the *Loveland Reporter* provided of the encampment at the YMCA's 1908 "First Estes Park Conference." In that quote, Fletcher notes that many states were represented at the encampment and that, specifically, he "noted delegates from Arizona, Kansas, Missouri, Minnesota, Utah, Nebraska, Oregon, Texas, and Arkansas."

While the fact that individuals from Missouri attended the 1908 summer conference does not mean that individuals from that same state attended the 1910 summer conference, it seems likely that either the same individuals would have returned or others to whom they talked following their return home in 1908 would have made the trip themselves in 1910. Hence, when we found a teacher from the University of Missouri in the 1910 Census with the last name of Ozmen (Burr Ozmen), we felt that it was at least possible that he and his wife Harriett could have made the trip to Estes Park for the 1910 summer conference where Harriett might have given birth, possibly prematurely, to Bob Ozmen. The information in the 1910 Census for Burr and Harriett Ozmen follows:

- The information in the 1910 Census for Burr Ozmen and his wife Harriett was recorded on 30 April 1910.
- Burr and Harriett were living in Columbia City, Columbia Township, Boone County, Missouri.

As will become important later, Columbia City later became Columbia and both are the home of the University of Missouri, which was founded in 1839 and thus was very much in existence in 1910.

- The 1910 Census provides the following statistics for Burr Ozmen:
    ▶ He was 31, which means he was born about 1879.
    ▶ He was male, white, and born in Missouri.
    ▶ His marriage to Harriett was his first marriage.
    ▶ His father and mother were both born in the United States.

    This is an interesting entry. In all of the census work that we have done over the years while doing genealogy research for our own families and for families discussed in other chapters in this book, we have seldom seen entries that said just "United States" rather than the state in which the individual was born. This could mean that Burr was an orphan and did not know where his parents were born. However, it probably means that Harriett was the one who was home when the census taker arrived and that she did not know or recall in which state(s) her husband's parents were born.

    ▶ He spoke English.
    ▶ He was a teacher at the University.

Since the University of Missouri is in Columbia, Missouri, Burr probably taught there.

- The 1910 Census provides the following statistics for Harriett Ozmen:
    - ▶ She was 28, which means that she was born about 1882.
    - ▶ She was female, white, and born in Kentucky.
    - ▶ Her marriage to Burr was her first marriage.
    - ▶ Under the main heading "Mother of how many children," the entries for "Number born" and "Number now living" were both left blank, which most likely means that Harriett had not had a child as of 30 April 1910, the date of the 1910 Census was taken.

        Note that Harriett could have been pregnant at the time the census was taken and could have then given birth to a baby in Estes Park on 3 July 1910.
    - ▶ Her father was born in Ohio, and her mother was born in Illinois.
    - ▶ She spoke English.

Thus, if we assume that the inscribed granite rock in the nature walk area of the Estes Park Center of the YMCA of the Rockies is indeed a headstone from the grave of the infant Bob Ozmen, as our use of dowser rods indicates that it is, it is possible that Burr and Harriett Ozmen were Bob's parents. We will leave it for future history buffs to do the additional research that might prove whether or not this couple had a son who was born while they were in Estes Park to attend the YMCA's second summer conference in July 1910 and who died there shortly thereafter.

(For information on a second grave on the property of the YMCA of the Rockies, see the chapter on the Edwin Bradt Grave.)

HERBERT RICHARDS GRAVE

Location: Latitude 40° 19′ 26″ N, Longitude 105° 36′ 24″ W

The grave of Herbert Richards is located in Rocky Mountain National Park about 0.2 of a mile downstream of Glacier Livery and about 100 feet northwest of Glacier Creek. However, it looks like the creek bed has moved over the years and that the grave might have been as close as 50 feet northwest of the creek at the time that Herbert Richards was buried in 1880. The burial is north of the access road that runs to Sprague Lake and the Sprague Lake Trailhead from Bear Lake Road.

The grave is on the northeast side of a draw, which, following heavy rains or during spring run off, would carry water into Glacier Creek from the higher areas in the vicinity.

Description of Grave

As of our visit on 9 July 2001, the grave of Herbert Richards was marked by an oval of native rocks, each about the size of a child's head. There is a large pine tree immediately northeast of the grave, but it may well not have been there when Herbert Richards was buried in 1880. Our use of dowser rods confirmed the burial of a child at the grave site. As of 9 July 2001, there was not an inscribed headstone at the grave site.

Photo A: Probable Grave of Herbert Richards Just Southwest of a Large Pine Tree About 0.2 of a Mile Downstream of Glacier Livery and About 100 Feet Northwest of Glacier Creek

Description of Headstone

See "Finding the Grave" and "Search for Headstone" below for a history of our search for this grave and our efforts, finally successful, to locate its headstone.

Original Description: We interpreted the first description that we had of the headstone to mean that the name of the child buried there was "George" and that the complete headstone inscription was as follows:

> George
> Tis a little grave but O have care,
> For wild wide hopes are buried here.
> How much of light, how much of joy
> is buried with our darling boy.

Correct Description: When we finally found the headstone, we discovered that the correct inscription was as follows:

> **Herbert**
> **Son of William and Mary**
> **Richards**
> **Died Feb. 6, 1880**
> **Aged 3 yrs 5 mo.**
> **Tis a little grave but O have care.**
> **For wild wide hopes are buried here.**
> **How much of light, how much of joy**
> **is buried with our darling boy.**

Since the verses on the two versions of the headstone are identical and since the actual headstone stored in Rocky Mountain National Park's Museum Storage Facility has the second inscription, we now believe that our first assumption concerning the inscription on the headstone was incorrect, that there are only one headstone and only one grave, and that the headstone for that grave is inscribed with the text under "Correct Description" above. A photo of Herbert Richard's headstone in the Park's Museum Storage Facility follows:

Photo B: Headstone of Herbert Richards Photographed in Rocky Mountain National Park's Museum Storage Facility on 8 August 2001

Finding the Grave

We were looking for a grave near Glacier Creek about 0.2 of a mile north of the Glacier Livery because of information Dr. D. Ferrel Atkins provided us during the late summer of 2000. (For more information on Ferrel and all of the assistance he gave us during our search for graves in Rocky Mountain National Park, see his entry in the "Acknowledgments" section of this book.) As part of his interest in the history of Rocky Mountain National Park, Ferrel compiled information about "historical structures" in the Park, including graves.

Ferrel provided us with a copy of the sheet of paper that he found in the Park's records concerning the headstone of Herbert Richards. This page contained the following information:

1. A drawing of Herbert's headstone.

2. Above the drawing, a typewritten note that said:

LARIMER COUNTY CEMETERIES

"DWIGHT: With a little light treatment, we came up with the following:"

3. Immediately to the left of the top of the drawing, the typewritten name "George," which we assumed for a long time was the name of the child whose grave the headstone had originally marked.

4. Immediately to the left of the middle of the drawing, the following typewritten verse:

> "Tis a little grave but O have care,
> For wild wide hopes are buried here.
> How much of light, how much of joy
> is buried with our darling boy"

5. Handwritten on the same sheet of paper below the drawing of the headstone and the typewritten text was the following information:
   - Tombstone
   - Found by: John Clay (or Clag) - visitor
   - Reported to Logans (This later turned out to be Charles Logan.)
   - Date: 9/23/73 (1973)
   - Location: 0.2 mile below Glacier Livery in Glacier Creek

Based on the information on that sheet of paper, on 1 July 2001, we went to Glacier Livery and took a GPS reading. We then returned home and used our computerized topographical maps of Colorado to determine the GPS reading for 0.2 of a mile below the Glacier Livery. Then, on 9 July 2001, we returned to the area and began looking for the grave at the GPS reading for 0.2 of a mile below the Glacier Livery.

We began our search on the northwest side of Glacier Creek rather than the northeast side because a road was being constructed on the northeast side and the considerable excavation work done there would have uncovered any bodies buried on the northeast side. Between July 1st and July 9th, we had checked with Sybil Barnes, then the History Librarian at the Estes Park Public Library and the Librarian for the Park's Library, to see if any bodies had been found during the road construction. She knew of none. (For more information on all of the assistance that Sybil provided us during our search for and research on graves and cemeteries in the Rocky Mountain National Park and the Estes Park area, see her entry in the "Acknowledgments" section of this book.)

After considerable searching on the northwest side of Glacier Creek, we finally found the rock pattern described under "Description of Grave" above for which dowser rods confirmed a child's burial. (See Photo A above.) Since the grave was on the side of a draw, heavy rains or spring run off between 1880 (when Herbret Richards was buried) and 1973 (when his headstone was found in Glacier Creek) could have uprooted Herbert's headstone from his grave and, either in one event or over time, washed it into Glacier Creek.

While we have no way of knowing for sure that the grave we found is actually the 1880 grave of Herbert Richards, we are fairly confident that it is Herbert's grave because:

- His headstone was found in Glacier Creek about 0.2 of a mile downstream from the Glacier Livery.
- The grave that we found was in a draw about 100 feet northwest of Glacier Creek, also about 0.2 of a mile downstream of Glacier Livery.

- We did not find any evidence that a Herbert Richards was later reburied in Grandview Cemetery or Roselawn Cemetery in Fort Collins, in Loveland Burial Park or Lakeside Cemetery in Loveland, or in the Bingham Hill Cemetery in Laporte.

Search for the Gravestone

The information provided by Ferrel Atkins gave no indication of what happened to Herbert Richards's headstone. We again went to the always helpful Sybil Barnes for assistance and asked her how we might go about trying to find both Herbert's headstone (which, at that point, we were erroneously still calling the "George" headstone) and the "FAJ" headstone found at Aspenglen Campground. (For more information of the "FAJ" headstone, see chapter on the Aspenglen Campground Cemetery.) Sybil passed our question on to Christy Baker. As of August 2001, Christy was in charge of Rocky Mountain National Park's Museum Storage Facility and was thus in a position to possibly determine if the Park had any record of these two headstones, both of which were found within the Park's boundaries.

On 30 July 2001, Christy got back to us to let us know that what we had been erroneously calling the "George" headstone was really the headstone of Herbert Richards and that it was indeed in the Park's Museum Storage Facility. Her email provided the inscription for the headstone reported as the "Correct Description" under "Description of Headstone" above. (She had no record of the "FAJ" headstone being in the Park's care.) She also confirmed that the headstone was found on 23 September 1973, which agrees with the date provided for the headstone's discovery on the sheet of paper that Ferrel had copied for us.

On 8 August 2001, we visited Christy and the Museum Storage Facility and photographed Herbert's actual headstone. (See Photo B above.)

Concerning the "George" on the typewritten part of the page of information on this headstone that Ferrel Atkins found in the Park's records, we have concluded that "George" was the name of the individual sending the note to "Dwight," not the name on the headstone as we had originally, and erroneously, assumed. (See Nos. 1-5 under "Finding the Grave" above, especially No. 3.)

Search for Information on Herbert Richards and His Parents

Herbert's headstone provides just this information:

- His parents were William and Mary Richards.
- He was born in September 1876, which is 3 years and 5 months before this death date.
- He died on 6 February 1880.

However, based on the information on the headstone, including the verse, we feel we can also make the following assumptions:

- Herbert's parents were probably well educated for the time and place. They had to be fairly literate to have either written the verse on his headstone or to have found it and had it copied on his headstone.

- Given the amount of time it would have taken to make such a relatively complex headstone, his parents were probably not just traveling through. If they were visitors to the area, they at least had enough income to have arranged for the headstone to be created and placed on Herbert's grave, either during their visit or after they departed.

A very similar headstone was found on the grave of Katya Whitcomb in the Buckeye Ranch Cemetery. Katya died in 1867. Her headstone came from Omaha, Nebraska. (See the chapter on Buckeye Ranch Cemetery.)

LARIMER COUNTY CEMETERIES

Neither the 1870 Colorado State Census nor the 1880 United States Census, which Sybil Barnes found for us, contained any Richards living anywhere near where Herbert's headstone was found.

The *Larimer County, Colorado, 1885 State Census*, transcribed and compiled into a book by the Larimer County Genealogical Society that was published in September 2000, does not contain any Richards with the first names William or Mary. Indeed, there are no Richards reported in that census in the Estes Park area.

In early June 2003, we checked the Bureau of Land Management's General Land Office Records at www.glorecords.blm.gov to see if any Land Patents had ever been issued to a William Richards in the Estes Park area in and around 1880. There were no Land Patents issued to any William Richards in Larimer County during the applicable time period. The only possibly applicable Land Patent was issued to William Richards and Sally Jackson in Weld County on 10 December 1867. Unless this William Richards later remarried a woman with the first name of Mary, this is probably not the William Richards who was Herbert's father. Recall that Herbert was born in September 1876.

The Glacier Basin area in which Herbert Richards was buried is strongly associated with Abner E. Sprague. Sprague was one of Estes Park's pioneers, known both as a rancher and as a resort owner. He built the Sprague Lodge in Glacier Basin after selling his 1,000-acre Moraine Park Ranch/homestead to J. D. Stead in 1904. (Source: Page 102 of *Rocky Mountain National Park; A History*, written by C. W. Buchholtz and published by the University Press of Colorado in 1983.) Thus, even though the area is associated with Sprague, it is unlikely that Herbert's parents had anything to do with Abner Sprague or his resort business.

However, page 83 of Buchholtz's book provides the following information: "The exact number of tourists arriving in Estes Park during the summers of the 1870s and 1880s is unknown, yet there is plenty of evidence of the region's growing popularity among vacationers." So William and Mary Richards could have been tourists, but that seems unlikely, especially since Herbert died in February!

Those interested in learning more about Abner Sprague, in his own compelling words, should read *My Pioneer Life; The Memoirs of Abner E. Sprague* published in 1999 by the Rocky Mountain Nature Association.

By February 2012, we had a online subscription to Ancestry.com. Thus, we searched Ancestry.com to try to find any evidence of a Herbert Richards who was born about September 1876 to William and Mary Richards and who died on 6 February 1880. Again, we did not find any evidence of his existence. This is not surprising as the most likely historical record in which Herbert would have appeared would be a U.S. Federal Census. However, the 1880 U.S. Census for the area where Herbert lived may well have been taken after February 1880 and would thus not include Herbert.

Hopefully, someday a future Larimer County historian will solve this perplexing mystery.

ROCKY MOUNTAIN NATIONAL PARK SCATTERED CREMAINS

The list below contains information on cremains scattered within Rocky Mountain National Park that a) the Park was aware of when we started our search for graves and cemeteries in Larimer County in the fall of 1999 or b) we later became aware of as the result of our research. It is surely not a complete list!

Chuck Collins

Chuck Collins's ashes were scattered near Fern Lake Lodge in 1966 or 1967.

As per retired Rocky Mountain National Park Ranger and Naturalist Ferrel Atkins, Chuck Collins's ashes were scattered near Fern Lake Lodge because that is where his daughter, the folk singer Judy Collins, got her start as a singer. (For additional information about Ferrel, see the "Acknowledgements" section.)

Retired Ranger Bob Haines told us in October 2000 us that he and other members of the Thursday Hiking Club found the metal container to which a label was affixed indicating that it had once contained the ashes of Judy's father, Chuck Collins. They found the container empty on the mantel above the fireplace in Fern Lake Lodge after it had been closed and before the Park tore it down. (For more information on Bob Haines, see the entry for Bob's brother William Walter Haines below and the "Acknowledgments" section.)

Bob remembers hearing Judy singing at the Lodge. When he first met her, she was at the Lodge with her husband and child, where she was making meals for hikers and campers. Sometimes in the evenings when campers came to the Lodge to warm themselves by the fire, Judy would take out her guitar and sing for them.

Bob also remembers that Chuck Collins was a blind pianist who had a morning radio program called "Collins Calling." After our presentation to the Estes Park Genealogical Society in August 2001 on our Larimer County grave search, an Estes Park resident, Larry E. Carpenter, then Secretary of the society, learned about our interest in Chuck Collins. He found a website providing information on Judy Collins at www.swinginchicks.com/judy collins.html. This website said that Chuck hosted a radio show called "Chuck Collins Calling" that was broadcast from Denver.

George Frederick Dick III and Betty Dick

The ashes of George Frederick ("Fred") Dick III were scattered by his family and friends on Father's Day, 20 June 1993 on the Trail River Ranch, which Fred and his wife Betty owned until his death and where Betty still lived during a large part of each year until her death on 14 November 2006. The ranch is within the Park and became Park property following Betty's death.

On 14 September 2001, John Gubbins took us to Trail River Ranch so that Betty could show us where Fred's ashes were scattered. (For more information on John and the considerable assistance he gave us during our grave-search efforts on the western side of Rocky Mountain National Park, see the "Acknowledgments" section.) The following information on Fred was provided by his wife Betty:

Fred Dick was born on 6 March 1919 in Bloomington, Illinois. He died on 20 November 1992 at his home in Scottsdale, Arizona.

According to his obituary published in the *Sky-High News* in Grand Lake, Colorado, Fred received his law degree from the University of Illinois and was admitted to the Illinois Bar in 1947. He was a flight instructor during World War II. In 1981, Fred retired from the People's Bank of Bloomington, Illinois, where he was President and Chief Executive Officer.

LARIMER COUNTY CEMETERIES

In 1961, Fred acquired Trail River Ranch, where he and his wife Betty resided while in Grand Lake. Even though his business was in Illinois and his winter home was in Arizona, the *Sky-High News* states that "his heart was always in Grand Lake, where he and Mrs. Dick have a host of friends."

Fred was survived by his wife Betty; two sons, George Frederick IV ("Tad") of Canada (died in the summer of 2005) and James of Boulder (since deceased); a step-son, Carl of Denver; three step-daughters, Dianne Mickelson and Elizabeth Tietz of Decatur, Illinois, and Deborah Swan of Eau Claire, Wisconsin; a sister, Helen Dick of Scottsdale; and 10 grandchildren.

Following Fred's death Betty had to resist the National Park Service's efforts to evict her from the Trail River Ranch, as described in the following article by Claire Martin and Steve Lipsher on Betty's death that was published on pages 1B and 4B of the 15 November 2006 issue of the *Denver Post*:

> "Betty Dick, who died of cancer at age 84 on Tuesday [14 November 2006], summered at one of the world's most exclusive—and, for a while, controversial—addresses: 20631 Trail Ridge Road, a cabin deep inside Rocky Mountain National Park.
>
> "She caused an international sensation two summers ago, when she resisted an attempt by the National Park Service to evict her from the cabin and 23 acres on the park's west side near the Colorado River.
>
> "The modest cabin 'meant everything' to Dick," said her daughter, Betsy Tietz.
>
> "'She enjoyed the hiking and all. But the thing about it was she didn't have to hike. The elk just came down in the meadow, and the moose came right to her door, and it was just there and she could enjoy it.'
>
> "Public sympathy overwhelmingly was on the side of Dick, who once described herself as 'a little old lady who won't live much longer anyway.'
>
> "The saga began with the dissolution of George 'Fred' Dick's first marriage. The divorce settlement gave Dick's ex-wife ownership of the cabin but with the stipulation that Fred Dick retained the first right to buy the property if she decided to sell.
>
> "In 1977, without telling her ex-husband, Marilyn Dick sold the property to the Park Service.
>
> "When Fred Dick learned about the deal, he immediately complained to the Park Service.
>
> "In late 1979, after what Betty Dick termed 'interminable' legal squabbles, the Dicks negotiated a 'life estate,' allowing them to continue summering on their 23 acres until they died. But the final wording identified the deal as a 25-year lease. "Tired of fighting, and believing that neither he nor Betty would live that long, Fred Dick signed the agreement, Betty Dick testified before Congress in April 2005.
>
> "'Fred was right about one thing. He would not live so long that there would be a difference between a life estate and a term of 25 years. But I am still here. And it does make a difference to me,' she said in that testimony.
>
> "Last May, U.S. Rep. Mark Udall, D-Colo.—with assistance from Sen. Wayne Allard, R-Colo., and Sen. Ken Salazar, D-Colo.—persuaded Congress to pass the Betty Dick Residence Protection Act, allowing her to stay in the cabin for the rest of her life before the property would revert to park ownership.

"'In late August, I presented Betty with a framed copy of the signed law,' said Udall in a statement. 'She was surrounded by friends and family who were gathered around the campfire outside the cabin. All around us was the beauty and splendor of the Rocky Mountains, and Betty got to enjoy her last days there secure in knowing that she had a right to enjoy and care for this property that meant so much to her and the community.'

"Even through the legal battles, Dick and the park staff maintained cordial relationships.

"'Betty Dick was a good neighbor to Rocky Mountain National Park,' park superintendent Vaughn Baker said.

"A former board president of the Rocky Mountain Repertory Theater in Grand Lake, Dick was honored this year by having her name placed on the permanent housing she helped secure for the actors.

"She died in Scottsdale, Ariz., where she spent her winters.

"Dick was divorced from Carl Dick, Jr., who preceded her in death, and she later married his first cousin, Fred.

"She is survived by four children: Carl Dick III, Dianne Mickelson, Deborah Swan and Elizabeth 'Betsy' Tietz; stepdaughter Emily Dick; and brother Don Marmon. She had 10 grandchildren and four great-grandchildren."

In emails dated 29 and 30 November 2006 (which included a very good photo of Betty in a cowboy hat and white sweater), John Gubbins told us that Betty's family and Colorado friends were planning a memorial service for her at the Trinity Church in the Pines in the Grand Lake area during the summer of 2007. Since Betty once told John that "she wanted to be by Fred" following her death, he and we are assuming that her ashes were laid to rest in the vicinity of Fred's at what is now officially the property of Rocky Mountain National Park.

Howard S. Gudgel

During a 23 August 2005 phone conversation with John G. Holzwarth III, he told us that some of the ashes of one of his best friends, Howard S. Gudgel, were scattered just north of the "utility area" for the west side of Rocky Mountain National Park in a location that had once been part of the Harbison Ranch. In a letter received from John dated 2 February 2006, he added that the remainder of Howard's ashes were buried in the Harbion's plot in the Grand Lake Cemetery. (For more information on John G. Holzwarth III, his family, and the Never Summer Ranch, also on the west side of the Park, see the entry for his father, "John G. Holzwarth II," below. For more information on the Grand Lake Cemetery, see the applicable chapter.)

Howard was born in Denver on 8 March 1932 and died on 3 August 2003. He was raised on the Harbison Ranch, which is why he chose to have some of his ashes scatted there. Since Howard and John III were of similar ages and grew up on nearby ranches, they became friends at a young age and remained friends until Howard's 2003 death. Howard and John even attended Colorado State University together.

Howard was quite an inventor. One of the things he invented was the large pavement-breaking equipment that we frequently see tearing apart worn-out highways.

Howard's parents were Clyde Gudgel and Mary Schnor. When Mary's mother died, her father, Henry Schnor, was left with two young girls, Mary and her sister Beatrice. He wanted to marry Kitty Harbison. At the time, Kitty and her sister Annie were running the Harbison Ranch. (The two Harbison sisters lived next to each other on the contiguous portions of two adjoining homesteads.) However, Kitty did not wish to get married and leave Annie. But the two sisters agreed to take Henry's two daughters.

Annie and Kitty were evidently not only good looking women but were also hard workers. The combination of their good looks, work ethic, and property put Annie and Kitty Harbison high on the marriage possibilities list of many a Grand Lake bachelor. But they never married. Instead, they raised Mary and Beatrice Schnor as they had promised Henry they would, and, along with running their ranch and other considerable efforts, they served meals to travelers on Trail Ridge Road.

William Walter Haines

His ashes were scattered by his nephew Mike Franklin from the top of Longs Peak following his death on 7 September 1985 in San Antonio, Texas. He was born in Liverpool, England, on 16 April 1919. He is the brother of Robert Haines, a now-deceased Rocky Mountain National Park Ranger.

William served as a dispatch rider for the U.S. Army between 1935 and 1947. After his Army career, William was involved with the manufacture of metal plating.

William's brother Robert John ("Bob") Haines held various positions at Rocky Mountain National Park between 1959 and 1980, including caretaker/first aid person at Hidden Valley (1959-67), Ranger (1967-69), and West District Naturalist (1969-80). Bob met his wife Theodora ("Teddie") Ann Mereness while working as a seasonal naturalist at Wild Basin. They were married on 9 December 1967 in the Park.

Bob was born in Omaha, Nebraska, in 1921. Teddie was born in Houston, Texas, to Harry Albert Mereness, Jr., and Mary Thomas Shreve in 1942. Harry was born in 23 July 1913 in Knoxville, Tennessee, and died in 25 August 2002 in Boulder, Colorado. Mary was born on 5 September 1917 in St. Louis, Missouri, and died 21 June 1985 in Estes Park. Teddie and Bob scattered Harry and Mary's ashes in the aspen grove at the Estes Valley Memorial Gardens and placed a plaque for them on a rock on the eastern edge of the cemetery. (For information on Bob's parents, see the chapter on the Lily Georgina Fearnly Haines Cremains.)

Teddie taught English in Strasburg, Colorado; in California; and in Estes Park for several years. Bob retired from his duties at Rocky Mountain National Park on 1 April 1980. Sadly, he died on 12 May 2008.

Doris Noreen Hamilton Hale

The ashes of Doris Noreen Hamilton Hale were scattered on Sundance Mountain on 11 September 1999. (For the exact location of where her ashes were scattered, see the entry below for her father Dwight Hamilton.) She was born in Longmont, Colorado, on 11 May 1924 and died on 16 July 1999, also in Longmont.

She was daughter of Dwight and Inez Jeannette C. Hamilton and the sister of retired Chief Park Naturalist Dwight L. Hamilton.

William Alfred Hale

The ashes of William Alfred Hale were scattered on Sundance Mountain on 19 August 2006. (For the exact location of where his ashes were scattered, see the entry below for his father-in-law Dwight Hamilton.)

According to his obituary in the *Estes Park Trail-Gazette*, Bill was born on 23 December 1918 in Stockton, Kansas, and died on 10 December 2005. He grew up in Englewood, Colorado, where he met his wife, Doris Noreen Hamilton Hale.

"At the outbreak of World War II, Bill joined the Army Air Corps and served in the Philippines until the war's end. He lived in Estes Park for the past 31 years where he enjoyed golf and hiking with family and friends.

"He is survived by a daughter, Carol Pride of Lakewood, Colo.; a son, Bill Hale of Colorado Springs; three grandchildren, Dawn, William, and Reggie. Two great-grandchildren also survive him, Ethan and Paulina."

Dwight Hamilton

His ashes were scattered on Sundance Mountain on 15 August 1971. (Sundance has two summits. The ashes of the members of the Hamilton and Hale families are scattered on the summit that lies "a bit northwest": Elevation of 12,495 feet, 40° 24' 30" N, 105° 42' 38" W.) According to GPS readings, it is the higher of the two summits.

Dwight was born in San Francisco on 23 December 1902. He died in Salida, Colorado, on 8 January 1971. (He did not have a middle name.)

He was the father of Dwight L. Hamilton, a Rocky Mountain National Park Chief Park Naturalist, whose ashes were also scattered in the Park. (See entry for "Dwight Linton Hamilton" below.)

Dwight Linton Hamilton

On 8 August 2005, we learned of the death of Dwight Linton Hamilton in a phone conversation with John G. Holzwarth III. (See the entry for "John G. Holzwarth II" below.) We then corresponded with Dwight's daughter, Leslie Hamilton Spurlin, who told us that her father had died in Hilo, Hawaii, on 23 April 2002 and that some of his ashes were scattered on Sundance Mountain on 23 August 2003, as he had requested. (For the exact location of where his ashes were scattered, see the entry above for his father Dwight Hamilton. Also, see the quote from Dwight below from our email correspondence with him in early December 2000.) Dwight's wife, Mickey, still has some of his ashes with her at their home in Hilo.

Leslie told us that on the day that Dwight's family and friends scattered his ashes on Sundance, "an eagle flew overhead as we finished." She also told us that her father was born in Longmont, Colorado, on 27 June 1926 and that his middle name was Linton.

In email correspondence received from, at the time, retired Chief Park Naturalist Dwight L. Hamilton in early December 2000, Dwight provided the following information about his family's involvement with Rocky Mountain National Park:

> "My father [Dwight Hamilton] chose Sundance [as the place to have his ashes scattered] as it overlooked so many of the mountains he'd climbed including Longs Peak, which he first climbed in 1916. He rode from Lyons to Estes Park in a Stanley Steamer and then walked and hitchhiked to the Longs Peak Trailhead. I'm not sure how many times he climbed Longs, but would guess a couple of dozen. He also climbed the East Face once.

> "He was a climber, not in the technical sense, but loved the hikes and sometimes scrambles to the summits of Colorado's Fourteeners. He was the 38th person to ascend them all. He also climbed Pikes Peak from every angle and in every month of the year. He loved the outdoors and no doubt influenced me in my choice of becoming a Park Ranger.

> "Mother often accompanied him on the easier climbs, but maybe gave it up after we traversed Forest Canyon. Dad had returned to Trail Ridge Road, and Mom, my sister, my uncle, and I were to go down Forest Canyon, and he was to drive around, hike up the Fern Lake Trail and meet us at Forest Inn. Good idea, but it took us 3 days to make the trip. Dad was getting a bit frantic by the

time we showed up. Without my uncle, who was probably 15 years old, we never would have made it.

"My sister [Doris Noreen Hamilton Hale] loved hiking as well. She lived in Estes until her death on 16 July 1999 and hiked whenever possible. Her husband, Bill Hale, still lives there.

"My wife and I have chosen to have our ashes scattered on Sundance when our time comes. Think we've talked our two daughters into carrying us there. It's a lovely spot, even in foul weather. Where else but in the wilds can you have a personal landscaper continually provide you with fields of wild flowers (in season)?"

Dwight L. Hamilton worked as a seasonal Park Ranger in Glacier and Rocky Mountain National Parks while attending Colorado State University (then Colorado A & M). His first permanent job as a Park Ranger was on the Natchez Trace Parkway in Mississippi. Dwight then served as a Park Ranger at Mount Rainier National Park, Colorado and Dinosaur National Monuments, Black Canyon of the Gunnison National Park, Hawaii Volcanoes National Park, and Glen Canyon National Recreation Area and as an Instructor/Trainer at the Horace M. Albright Training Center at Grand Canyon National Park before returning to Rocky Mountain National Park as Chief Park Naturalist in 1971. He retired on 31 March 1980. When we last corresponded with Dwight in December 2000, he and his wife Vada Maxine ("Mickey") Holloway Hamilton resided in Hilo, Hawaii. Their daughter Leslie Hamilton Spurlin told us that, following Dwight's death in April 2002, Mickey continued to live in their home in Hilo.

Inez Jeannette Carson Hamilton

The ashes of Inez Jeannette Carson Hamilton were scattered on Sundance Mountain in August 1978. (For the exact location of where her ashes were scattered, see the entry above for her husband Dwight Hamilton.) She was born Inez Jeannette Carson near Iuka, Illinois, on 27 October 1904. She died in Colorado Springs on 27 January 1978.

She was the wife of Dwight Hamilton and the mother of former Chief Park Naturalist Dwight L. Hamilton.

Allyn Frank Hanks

In 1973, his ashes were scattered on the Cub Lake Trail, about 1 mile past the Cub Lake Trailhead at the point the trail turns from south to west. Coincidentally, this is also the approximate location of the home of Ransom S. Kendall, an early homesteader in what later became Rocky Mountain National Park. (See the chapter on the Ransom S. Kendall Grave.)

Allyn Frank Hank's obituary on page 8 of the 12 January 1973 issue of *Estes Park Trail* provides the following information:

- Allyn was born on 3 March 1906 in Logan, Utah, to Frank and Lou Hanks. [His son Allyn Williams ("Bill") Hanks said that he thought Allyn was born in 1908. Bill Hupp (the son of the sister of Allyn Frank's wife's father) said that he though that Allyn was born on 23 March 1903.]

- He died on 11 January 1973 in Estes Park.

- In 1934, he married Hazel Williams (daughter of Frank Williams, whose sister Pearl Williams was the mother of the Bill Hupp mentioned in the first bullet).

- He was survived by Allyn Williams ("Bill") Hanks of Estes Park (see first bullet) and one sister, Mrs. Mary Israelson of Salt Lake City, Utah. He served in the U.S. Coast Guard in World War II.

- He began working for the National Park Service in 1928 as a Park Ranger at Yellowstone National Park.
- In September 1932 he was promoted to Chief Park Ranger at Grand Teton National Park and was made Superintendent of the Theodore Roosevelt National Monument in September 1947.
- He was Superintendent of the Everglades National Park and Cape Hatteras before becoming Chief of Visitor Protection for the National Park Service in Washington, D.C., in November 1957.
- He served as Superintendent of Rocky Mountain National Park from April 1961 until he retired in June 1964. Another article in the *Estes Park Trail* said that he was Superintendent from 10 May 1961 through 6 June 1964.
- Allyn was elected to the District 6 School Board of Estes Park in May 1967 and served on the Board until May 1971. He was elected Treasurer of the Board in 1969.
- He was a member of St. Bartholomew's Episcopal Church, the Masonic Lodge, The Colorado Consistory, the Rotary Club of Estes Park, and the National Association of Retired Federal Employees.

(For more information on the relationship between the Hanks and the Hupps and for information on the part that Allyn Frank Hanks played in allowing a headstone to be erected at the Hupp Family Cemetery in Rocky Mountain National Park, see the "History of Cemetery and Headstone" section of the chapter on the Hupp Family Cemetery.)

Hazel Williams Hanks

In 1990, her ashes were scattered on the Cub Lake Trail, about 1 mile past the Cub Lake Trailhead at the point the trail turns from south to west.

Hazel was born 4 June 1910 in Jackson Hole, Wyoming, and died on 11 November 1990 in Estes Park.

Hazel was a self-employed realtor with Becker Real Estate in Estes Park. She was a member the Eastern Star and St. Bartholomew's Episcopal Church.

Hazel's father Frank Williams started the Double Diamond Guest Ranch on Jenny Lake Road in Jackson Hole, Wyoming. The ranch now has a different name and serves as the headquarters for mountain climbing and hiking trips. Frank's sister Pearl married John Ervin Hupp, a grandson of the John T. and Eliza Hupp buried in the Hupp Family Cemetery. (For more information on the relationship between the Hanks and the Hupps, see the "History of Cemetery and Headstone" section of the chapter on the Hupp Family Cemetery.)

Frank and Pearl's father was Otho E. Williams, who moved his family to Jackson Hole, Wyoming, in 1900, where he homesteaded on the Snake River near Wilson. Their mother was Josephine Sullivan Williams.

A letter written by Pearl Williams Hupp to the City Clerk of Loveland in 1972 claimed that her and Frank's maternal grandfather James Sullivan donated part of his farm to the City of Loveland for the Lakeside Cemetery. (The purpose of Pearl's letter was to give Hazel Williams Hanks and her husband Allyn F. Hanks plots in the Lakeside Cemetery that Pearl had inherited from her parents. However, since Hazel and Allyn were cremated and their ashes were scattered in Rocky Mountain National Park, they did not use these plots.)

John G. Holzwarth II

In May 2005, John Gubbins told us that all or, possibly, just some of the ashes of John G. ("Johnnie") Holzwarth II were scattered at Never Summer Ranch on the west side of Rocky

LARIMER COUNTY CEMETERIES

Mountain National Park following his death. (For more information on John Gubbins, see the "Acknowledgments" section.) In an 8 August 2005 phone conversation with John G. Holzwarth III (Johnnie's son), we learned that all Johnnie's ashes were scattered on the Never Summer Ranch, for it was John III who personally scattered them! Specifically, Johnnie's ashes were scattered directly across the North Fork of the Colorado River (west) from where Johnnie's house (built in 1951) once stood, which was not far from the Never Summer Ranch Lodge. John III also told us that the "G" in his, his father's, and his grandfather's names stands for "Gotlieb."

A cenotaph for Johnnie was erected by his family in the Grand Lake Cemetery. According to the transcription of Johnnie's cenotaph available at http://ftp.rootsweb.com/pub/usgenweb/co/grand/cemeteries/grandlake.txt (which includes the transcription of all of the markers in the Grand Lake Cemetery), Johnnie was born on 7 November 1902 and died on 1 April 1983.

Two other members of the Holzwarth family have headstones in the Grand Lake Cemetery:

- Caroline Pratt Holzwarth (Johnnie Holzwarth's first wife), who was born on 15 September 1907 and died on 21 November 1965. Her middle name was Lyman. Johnnie and Caroline were married on 25 September 1931.

- Virginia Lyman Holzwarth (Johnnie and Caroline's daughter), who was born on 5 March 1935 and who died on 10 March 1952. According to John III, both Caroline's and Virginia's headstones mark actual burials and are not cenotaphs.

The information below on Johnnie Holzwarth and his family comes from:

1. Page 168 of *Grand Lake: The Pioneers* by Mary Lyons Cairns, published in 1946.

2. The section on "The Holzwarth Ranch" taken from Volume II of *Rocky Mountain National Park's Historic Structures*, which Sybil Barnes, then the Local History Librarian of the Estes Park Public Library, sent us on 31 May 2005. Most of the information on the Holzwarths' Never Summer Ranch in this section of Volume II came from the transcription of an interview that Johnnie Holzwarth gave on 18 August 1965. (For more information on Sybil, see the "Acknowledgments.")

3. A copy of the documentation submitted by Rocky Mountain National Park to the U.S. Department of Interior's National Register of Historic Places on 1 August 1975 to nominate the Holzwarths' Never Summer Ranch as the "Holzwarth Historic District." This documentation was prepared by the Park's unofficial historian Dr. D. Ferrel Atkins. (For more information on Ferrel, see the the "Acknowledgments" section.)

4. Phone conversations with John G. Holzwarth III on 8 and 23 August 2005 and 14 September 2005 and a letter from him dated 9 February 2006. John III was living in Grand Junction, Colorado, at the time. When the data provided in the above three references and the information provided by John III disagreed, we used the information provided by John III.

5. Emails from Leslie Hamilton Spurlin dated 15 and 16 August 2005 and 12 September 2005. Leslie is the daughter of Dwight L. Hamilton, a now-deceased National Parks employee. (See his entry elsewhere in this chapter.) We were given her name and contact information by John III in early August 2005. She provided some corrections to our original information on John G. ("Johnnie") Holzwarth II as well as information on a number of other individuals (both family and friends) whose ashes were also scattered in the Park. In her 12 September 2005 email, Leslie provided information that she obtained from John III during a visit with him in Grand Junction earlier that month.

Johnnie's father, John G. Holzwarth I, came to the United States from Germany in 1879 when he was only 14 years old. In return for his passage to the United States, he was originally bonded as an indentured servant to a baker in St. Louis. When the baker turned out to be cruel, John I escaped to Texas, where, according to Johnnie, "he helped a man drive 100 stolen horses across the Staked Plains, worked as a cook for some sheep herders, and served as a Texas Ranger."

In 1881, John I left Texas for Fraser, Colorado, where his brother had a homestead and drove a stage. John I first kept the mail-stage horses. Then, in 1883, he homesteaded the Stillwater Ranch, which is now under Granby Reservoir in the Upper Grand River Valley south of Grand Lake. Later that same year, John I left Stillwater Ranch for Denver, relinquishing his homestead to Tom Johnston, who continued to develop the ranch.

In Denver John I met Sophia Lebfromm, a domestic servant from Germany, who became his wife on 19 May 1894 (according to the Park's nomination form) or 1896 (according to the 1965 interview with Johnnie Holzwarth). On 23 August 2005, John III confirmed that his grandparents were married on 19 May 1894.

On 26 June 1895, John I and Sophia's first child, Christina Holzwarth, was born. Unfortunately, Christina lived less than 7 months, dying on 8 December 1895.

Within 10 years, John I and Sophia were operating a small saloon and boarding house in Denver. While they were in Denver, their remaining four children were born. The birth and death dates for those children follow:

- Julia K. Holzwarth: Born 4 September 1896, died 4 January 1967.
- Maria K. Holzwarth: Born 2 July 1898, died 1 July 1919.
- Sophia K. ("Sophia II") Holzwarth: Born 16 September 1900, died 3 March 1972.
- John G. ("Johnnie") Holzwarth II: Born 7 November 1902, died 1 April 1983.

With the arrival of Prohibition in Colorado on 1 January 1916, the Holzwarths' Denver business became unprofitable. Remembering John I's previous experiences in the Upper Grand River Valley, in the summer of 1917, John I and Sophia built a homestead cabin on land that would eventually become part of their Never Summer Ranch. John I did not actually file on their 160-acre homestead until 1 March 1919, which Ferrel Atkins says was "not [an] uncommon practice in the region at that time." The patent on the homestead (the NW 1/4 of Section 25, Township 5 North, Range 76 West) was issued on 13 January 1923.

On 22 July 1918, John I and Sophia purchased the adjacent Fleshuts-Leeman property (NE 1/4 of Section 25). (Joe Fleshuts had received his final homesteading patent on 29 July 1909.)

During the summer of 1919, John I and Johnnie worked on the ranch, returning to Denver in the winter. The family permanently moved to the homestead cabin in June 1920. By early 1922, they had already begun taking in tourists at a group of tourist cabins built on the family's original homestead and near the present location of Never Summer Ranch buildings (on the west side of the North Fork of the Colorado River).

Later, the Holzwarths' "dude ranch" operation was moved to a group of buildings built about a quarter mile south of the original Fleshuts cabin, which was about 100 feet west of what is now Trail Ridge Road and about a quarter mile east of the North Fork of the Colorado River. At first, the Holzwarth family maintained their own home on their original homestead. Later, in 1931 after Johnnie married Caroline Pratt, they moved their home to the guest ranch. The Holzwarths originally referred to their entire operation as the "Holzwarth Trout Lodge." In the 1940s, they changed the name to the "Holzwarths' Never Summer Ranch."

After the National Park Service purchased all of the Holzwarths' land for inclusion in Rocky Mountain National Park, they torn down the dude ranch buildings but left the buildings on the Holzwarths' homestead ranch, which became the Never Summer Ranch in the Holzwarth Historic District, a popular site for visitors on the west side of the Park.

When he was interviewed in 1965, Johnnie Holzwarth recalled that, "in those early days, it was not at all unusual to have 100 people sleeping around the ranch, sprawled on the ground, or huddled under trees. They built the "Girls' House" in 1924 and the "Skunk House" in 1925. (Johnnie doesn't explain in his 1965 interview how the "Skunk House" building got its name, but his son John III did. See below.)

In a letter from John III dated 9 February 2006, he told us that the "Girls' House" started life as the larger of three cabins, the one that contained the incipient dude ranch's kitchen and dining room where food was cooked and served to the guests before the ranch's "Lodge" was built. Later, one of the two smaller cabins was added to the "Girls' House" to make a home for Johnnie, his wife Caroline, and their children. (More information about Caroline and Johnnie and Caroline's children is provided below.) Later yet, when the Holzwarth family had moved into other quarters, it became the "Girls' House." And, finally, it became a recreation facility and known as the "Rec House."

In phone conversations with Johnnie's son, John III, on 23 August 2005 and 14 September 2005, John III recalled that the "Skunk House" got its name from the family of skunks that spent their winters under the building and had to be "evicted" each spring. John III also recalled that he lived in the "Skunk House" for awhile "when it was on the ranch." (It has since been moved to the "utility area" on the west side of the Park.) Indeed, John III told us that many of the buildings that made up the pre-Park version of the Never Summer Ranch still exist in other locations in Grand County—locations to which they were moved "whole" or where they were rebuilt after having first been dismantled.

The main ranch buildings began to assume their current shape when the main Lodge was built in 1929. That building was provided with indoor plumbing, which was soon added to the pre-existing buildings as well.

Concerning his first wife, Caroline Lyman Pratt, Johnnie said that she was first brought to the Grand Lake area from Kansas City "in a basket" in 1908 by her parents and grandparents, who "always vacationed in this area." (Recall that Caroline's headstone says that she was born on 15 September 1907.) Johnnie and Caroline were married on 25 September 1931 and spent their honeymoon on an 8-day pack trip through the Never Summer Range and over the Continental Divide to Estes Park.

Johnnie officially took over the operation of the Never Summer Ranch following the death of his father (John I) in 1932, for neither of his two then-living sisters, Sophia K. Holzwarth Geeck (Sophia II) and Julia K. Holzwarth, were interested in assuming responsibility for actually running the ranch. (Both sisters were living in Denver at the time of the 1965 interview.)

For all practical purposes, Johnnie had probably actually been handling the day-by-day running of the ranch ever since John I was severely injured "when a wagon overturned on him soon after moving to the Kawuneeche Valley." Realizing that his participation in the ranch would henceforth be limited, John I "studied taxidermy by mail and soon became quite proficient in the art." Both quotes are from page 8 of the Park's nomination form.

In our 14 September 2005 phone conversation with John III, he said that his father's mother, Sophia I, did most of the cooking for the dude ranch operation until John I died in 1932. Johnnie's sister (and John III's aunt), Sophia II, then cooked for the dude ranch operation from about 1933 through the end of 1942. After she quit cooking for the dude ranch operation, Sophia II helped her mother on the family's homestead ranch. She then took over management of the homestead ranch in 1952, before Sophia I's death on 15 October 1953.

Sophia II married Andrew ("Andy") Geeck. They had two daughters: Avalone, who was born on 19 May 1923 and who married Gene Clark on 3 July 1948, and Charlene, who was born on 15 June 1926.

Concerning his Aunt Julia, John III told us that she had an important job at Hilb & Co., a wholesale clothing company, in Denver and that she stayed active in the financial operations of the ranch, providing it with a number of timely loans.

Johnnie and Caroline had three children: John G. Holzwarth III (the John III quoted frequently in this section), who was born in 1933; Virginia, who was born on 5 March 1935, died on 10 March 1952, and is buried in Grand Lake Cemetery with her parents' grave markers; and Mary Francis, who was born in Denver in October 1945 and who was living in Phoenix, Arizona, when we received John III's 9 February 2006 letter.

According to the 1965 interview, while Johnnie wanted to modernize the ranch enough to make it reasonably comfortable for his guests, he also wanted to keep it authentically a ranch: "This is a ranch; it smells like one and should be like one. A man walking into my dining room has got to kick the manure out of the road, by God, before he can get there."

At the time of that 1965 interview, negotiations had been under way for a number of years between the Holzwarth family and the National Park Service for the government to purchase the Never Summer Ranch and include it in Rocky Mountain National Park. Some of Johnnie's comments on the subject (from the 1965 interview) follow: "Many people don't realize that the Park Service has done a wonderful job—in a damned slow way. But the country is just as wild as when I came. I feel normally, knowing the valley as I do, [that] eventually [it] should all belong to the Park."

By 1972 the negotiations were completed for the Park to purchase the homestead portion of the Holzwarths' Never Summer Ranch, which (as noted above) the National Park Service is preserving as the Holzwarth Historic District, a living history site to help teach the Park's visitors about the ranching history of the area prior to the establishment of the Park. (See section below on "Howard and Gretchen Wignall" for related information.)

Included in the information in the Park's archives on Never Summer Ranch is a copy of a letter that Johnnie sent to the ranch's "guests and friends" on 1 March 1972 in which he invited them to come to the ranch one more time during the summer of 1972 because "Neversummer Ranch will cease to operate as a guest ranch at the end of the season of 1972" since it had been sold to the National Park Service. A "P.S." on Johnnie's 1 March 1972 letter tells his quests and friends that "Wanda and I were married Christmas eve!" So on 24 December 1971, Johnnie remarried after the death of his first wife Caroline in 1965.

In our 8 August 2005 conversation with Johnnie's son, John III, we learned that Wanda's full name was Wanda V. Beck, that "Beck" was her maiden name, that she had been married previously, and that she and Johnnie were married in Wanda's apartment in Denver. John III also told us that Wanda, as of the date of our August 2005 conversation with him, lived in Arkansas near a granddaughter named Kim and that he called Wanda almost every week.

Jacqueline Jaye Johnson

Jackie's family scattered her ashes in the Park in August 2001 following her death in Estes Park on 18 August 2001.

A personal note about Jackie before we continue with details of her life: Jackie provided us with invaluable help in our efforts to find and document remote graves in the Estes Park area in Rocky Mountain National Park. Specifically, Jackie told us about, helped us find, and/or provided information about:

LARIMER COUNTY CEMETERIES

- Ransom S. Kendall's grave in Beaver Meadows in the Park. She is the one who took us to this grave and provided us with all of the information we have on Kendall. (See the chapter on the Ransom S. Kendall Grave.)
- The grave of Harris Wellcome, a Civil War veteran, is southeast of the YMCA. Elaine Hostmark also helped us find this grave and got us permission to visit the site, which is on private property. (See the chapter on the Harris Wellcome Grave.)
- One or more graves in Tuxedo Park, now part of Rocky Mountain National Park. (See the chapter on the Tuxedo Park Cemetery.)
- A possible grave marked by a large rock cross above the Beaver Ponds in Hidden Valley not far from Trail Ridge Road. We have not found this location. (See "Large Rock Cross in Hidden Valley in Rocky Mountain National Park" in the chapter on Graves and Cemeteries Not Found.)
- A ground-level cross on Sundance Mountain north of Trail Ridge Road that marks a burial. (See the chapter on the Sundance Mountain Graves.)
- A transcription in the Estes Park Public Library of a 1972 interview with Jack Moomaw, an early Park Ranger. This particular interview contained information about both the Sampson and the Chitwood graves in the Park. Jackie called on 26 March 2001 to tell us about the transcription. (See the chapters on the J. P. Chitwood Grave and the Reverend Thornton Rogers Sampson Grave.)

Jackie arranged for us to make a presentation on our Larimer Country grave research to the Estes Park Genealogical Society on 8 August 2001. Unfortunately, she was then unable to attend because of her failing health. The next Monday, August 13th, we received a handwritten note from Jackie saying she was sorry she missed the August 8th meeting and mentioning some of the graves searches with which she had been helping us.

Thus, not knowing that Jackie was seriously ill, we were saddened and shocked to learn of her death on August 18th, just 5 days later.

According to her obituary in the 24 August 2001 issue of the *Estes Park Trail*, Jackie was born on 29 January 1931 in St. Paul, Nebraska, to Nicholas Jay Paul II and Alyce Nelsen Paul. On 29 January 1951 (her birthday), she married Donald Johnson in St. Paul, Nebraska.

After having visited Estes Park and Allenspark since her early childhood, Jackie became a summer resident of Estes Park in 1967, a part-time resident in 1971, and a permanent resident in 1984.

Jackie volunteered at the Rocky Mountain National Park, the Rocky Mountain Nature Association, and the Dorsey Museum at the YMCA of the Rockies. She was a 50-year member of the P.E.O. Sisterhood and was the local chapter's AV at her death. She was also a member of the Estes Park Area Historical Museum Advisory Board and a former member of the Friends of the Museum Board; a member of the Colorado Mountain Club; a member of the Estes Park Genealogical Society; a member of the Howard County, Nebraska, Historical Society; and a former member of the St. Paul, Nebraska, Public Library Board.

She was survived by her husband, Don Johnson, of Estes Park; her mother, Alyce N. Paul, of St. Paul, Nebraska; two daughters, Kris Holien and her husband Bernie of Estes Park and Kelly Jacobs and husband Craig of Oakley, Utah; two sisters, Colleen Hoerner and her husband Vic of Niwot, Colorado, and Virginia Brooks and husband Jeff of Minneapolis, Minnesota; grandsons Nicholas, Matthew, and Alexander Jacobs of Oakley, Utah; and a cousin Kathleen Cotten of Estes Park. She was preceded in death by her father, Nicholas Jay Paul II, and her brother, Nicholas Jay Paul III.

Charles and Agnes Levings

Charles and Agnes Levings of Chicago were the parents of Louis R. Levings, who is buried on Ypsilon Mountain. (See the chapter on the Louis R. Levings Grave for details on Louis, his death, and his grave.) Charles and Agnes had their ashes scattered on Twin Sisters Peaks, where their family had a summer home, in line of sight with Louis's grave on Ypsilon Mountain.

Page 153 of Volume II of *Over Hill and Vale* (complete citation in "Bibilography") provides some additional information on Charles Levings. After describing his correspondence with Charles Levings concerning the reburial of his son Louis, correspondence which is detailed in the chapter on the Louis R. Levings Grave, Harold Dunning tells us the following about the Levings family and their neighbors:

> "The Levings home is up on the side of the Twin Sisters north of Longs Peak Inn. Here the Levings family lived for many years. He [Charles] was a retired architect from Chicago, I believe. The Levings and the Babcocks and the Charles Hewes and others were for many years the best friends in the Valley of Elkanah. Here was a very talented group and they produced many valuable things and works for the country. There were funny things too, that happened, and when one got something on another, it was great fun. It seems that Charles Levings was a great fisherman and could catch fish when no one else could. He boasted of having a secret bait that was accountable for his catching so many fish. What it was no one could find out, but one day some one followed him and found a red gum drop he had dropped. Immediately they thought he was using gum drops for bait. But on further investigation they thought he was eating them. And they also found out he bought them from Montgomery Ward by the bucket."

Harold Dunning then went on to quote a short poem that Charles Edwin Hewes wrote on the subject.

The most complete information we could find on Charles and Agnes Levings occurs on pages 47-49 of the "New Neighbors" chapter and in Note 27 (pages 117-118) in James H. Pickering's *In the Vale of Elkanah* (complete citation in "Bibliography").

Charles Levings was born in 1852 and died in 1935. He graduated from Cornell University in 1873 as a member of the university's first 4-year civil engineering class. As an architect he is known for having "laid out Chicago's Michigan Avenue [the "Magnificent Mile" as it was later known], constructed dams and parkways, built the north entrance to Yellowstone National Park, engineered the first railroad into Texas, and worked on the plans for the Texas state capitol in Austin."

Charles and his wife Agnes McCall were married on 20 November 1877. Agnes was the sister of Josephine McCall Babcock, the wife of William Babcock, Jr., and the mother of Dean Babcock.

Their sons were Louis Raymond Levings (1884-1905) and Mark McCall Levings (1881-1957). By the time that the Levings family moved to Tahosa Valley south of Estes Park (evidently in 1908, the same year as the Babcocks), Mark was already a successful architect, with practices in Chicago and Omaha. The first name of Mark's wife was Mary.

"Graystone," the Levings family's summer home on the lower slopes of Twin Sisters Peaks, was an "imposing house built of native granite." In 1909, the Levings family added to their holdings in Tahosa Valley 160 acres that had belonged to a neighbor named Moffat.

The Levings family maintained a summer home in the Estes Park area for many years. During this time, Charles "became deeply interested in the affairs of town and region."

LARIMER COUNTY CEMETERIES

Elbert ("Bert') Arthur McLaren I

In emails that we received from her on 17 September and 18 October 2005, Shirley Epperson McLaren told us that, on 16 June 2002, part of the ashes of her husband Elbert ("Bert") Arthur McLaren I were scattered along a beaver pond that is southeast of the McLarens' private inholding in the Kawuneeche Valley and near the previous site of the Buena Vista Park Service Cabin (about half way between the west entrance to the Rocky Mountain National Park and the Holzwarths' Never Summer Ranch). (For more information on Never Summer Ranch, see the entry above for "John G. Holzwarth II.") On the same day that some of his ashes were scattered in the Kawuneeche Valley, the remainder of Bert's ashes were buried at the foot of his parents' graves in the Grand Lake Cemetery. (See the chapter on the Grand Lake Cemetery.) Bert's parents were Fred Douglas and Iva Montgomery McLaren. A small stone memorializing Bert stands at the foot of his parents' graves.

The exact geographical location where part of Bert's ashes were scattered is as follows: Elevation 8772 feet, 40° 19' 25" N, 105° 51' 12" W.

Both of Bert's parents were born on farms near Lyons, Colorado, in 1892. Fred died in 1992, and Iva died in 1966. (Their birth and death dates are from the transcription of the headstones in Grand Lake Cemetery) available at http://ftp.rootsweb.com/pub/usgenweb/co/grand/cemeteries/grandlake.txt.)

Two of Bert's sisters, Phyllis McLaren Johnson and Dorothy McLaren Howard, are also buried in the Grand Lake Cemetery. According to the just-referenced transcriptions of the headstones in Grand Lake Cemetery, Phyllis was born in 1928 and died in 1973, and Dorothy was born in 1920 and died in 1997.

Bert was born on 29 November 1929 in Longmont, Colorado. He died in Grand Junction, Colorado, on 2 November 2001.

Bert's family chose to scatter ashes at the site of the Buena Vista Park Service Cabin because that is where he lived with his wife Shirley and their two children, Cyndy and Rusty, during 7 of the 14 years that he was stationed with the Park Service on the west side of Rocky Mountain National Park.

Bert's first wife was Rebecca Thompson, whom he married in 1950. Bert and Rebecca had two children: Charles ("Chuck"), who was born in 1951, and Victoria, who was born in 1954. Shortly after Victoria's birth, Bert and Rebecca were divorced.

Bert's second wife was Shirley Epperson of Gardiner, Montana, whom he married on 29 March 1958 in Livingston, Montana. Their first child, Cynthia ("Cyndy" or "Cyd") Lyn, was born in Jackson Hole, Wyoming, in 1961. Their second child, Elbert ("Rusty") Arthur II, was born in Kremmling, Colorado, in 1965.

Bert's father, Fred, was one of the first rangers in the Park. Bert's brothers Doug and Dick were also career Park Service employees. Between the three brothers and their father, they amassed over 150 years of service with the National Park Service. Dick's ashes were also scattered in the Park. (See entry for "Richard Cecil McLaren" below.)

In a letter he sent us dated 9 February 2006, John G. Holzwarth III provided the following reminiscences on Bert McLaren and his family:

> "As for Bert McLaren, our families were good friends for many years. Dick and Doug McLaren were some of my early heroes as skiers and later in the 10th Mountain Division. Dick or Doug often helped my dad [John G. (Johnnie) Holzwarth II] on snow surveys and checking Grand River Ditch Company buildings. Bert was 4 years ahead of me in Grade School. Bert's kids Cyd [Cynthia] and Rusty [Elbert] are the same age as our youngest kids. Bert spent part of one winter with us [John III and his wife Mary] here in

Grand Junction. Cyd stayed with us for a while before Bert died. Bert and Shirley often took care of our youngest kids after school before we came home from work."

Richard Cecil McLaren

In an email dated 17 September 2005, Shirley McLaren told us that part of the ashes of her brother-in-law Dick McLaren were scattered on the top of Mount Craig, also known as Mount Baldy, in the Park. On 28 November and 14 and 19 December 2005, Dick's daughter Pam Buchnoff of Fresno, California, sent us three emails containing the additional information provided below.

Richard ("Dick") Cecil McLaren passed away on 23 January 1991 in Fresno, California. In June 1991 a portion of his ashes were scattered over Mount Craig (also known as "Mount Baldy") in the Park near Grand Lake, Colorado. The remainder of his ashes were buried along with those of his wife Lady Dee McLaren in Fresno, California, after she passed away on 13 March 1992. Dick requested that his ashes be scattered on Mount Craig because he grew up in the area and spent some of the happiest times of his life there.

In an email dated 30 August 2006, McLaren family friend Leslie Hamilton Spurlin told us the following: "I asked Bert and Dick McLaren's niece, Martha Lee Boehner, Thursday, the 17th of August, (when I was hiking with her in Rocky) how they got Dick's ashes on top of 'Baldy,' and she said it was done by airplane! To which I replied, 'Well, MY family would never have thought of that; we just climb the darn mountain! [referring to the scattering of the ashes of various members of the Hamilton and Hale families on Sundance Mountain in Rocky Mountain National Park]"

Dick was born on 4 October 1921 in Longmont, Colorado, and grew up in Grand Lake, Colorado. During World War II, he served in Italy with the 10th Mountain Division of the U.S. Army, where he was wounded.

After the War, Dick returned to Grand Lake, where he joined the National Park Service on the west side of Rocky Mountain National Park. It was there that he met Lady Dee Shelton from Denver, who had a summer job at the Grand Lake Lodge. They were married in 1949, and in 1950 their first daughter Kathleen Adair was born in Kremmling, Colorado.

Shortly thereafter, the Park Service transferred Dick to Olympic National Park in Washington, where he was stationed for about 2 years. It was there that Dick and Dee's second daughter, Pamela Lynn, was born in 1952. Two weeks later, Dick was transferred to Yosemite National Park in California. Dick and Dee remained there for about 10 years. Dick was then transferred to Kings Canyon National Park and then to Sequoia National Park, both in California.

Dick ended his Park Service career at Grand Canyon National Park in Arizona. During Dick's four-decade career with the National Park Service, he held the following positions: Park Ranger, Supervisory Park Ranger, Assistant District Ranger, District Ranger, Area Ranger, Assistant Chief Ranger, Emergency Operations Specialist, Fire Management Officer, Fire Chief, and Air Operations Officer. When Dick retired in 1980, he and Dee moved to Fresno, California, to be near their daughters. Sadly, they both passed away before being able to spend much time with their grandchildren Mark and Sarah Buchnoff.

Enos A. Mills

Enos A. Mills was the driving force behind the founding of Rocky Mountain National Park in 1915. Indeed, his obituary on page 1 of the 22 September 1922 issue of the *Estes Park Trail* said that he was "the father of Rocky Mountain National Park, the most popular National Park in America today, and established Longs Peak Inn, a hotel near the base of Longs Peak, that proved quite popular with tourists."

LARIMER COUNTY CEMETERIES

As per Ferrel Atkins, while Enos Mills's ashes were definitely scattered in the Park, his daughter Enda Mills Kiley and her husband Robert Kiley disagreed as to where his ashes were scattered. One says that they were scattered behind the Mills family's home on Twin Sisters, and the other says that they were scattered on Longs Peak. In addition, Mrs. Joe Mills, the wife of Enos's younger brother, agreed that Enos's ashes were scattered on Longs Peak, specifically on the boulder field right under "The Dove." Since Enda was too young to remember her father's death and burial and since her husband would not have even been around at the time, Joe Mills's wife's recollection would have the best chance of being correct as she was both an adult and around at the time of Enos's death.

On page 232 of Volume I of *Over Hill & Vale* (complete citation in "Bibliography"), Harold Dunning said that Enos Mills was "buried by his little log cabin built in 1886 but due to souvenir hunters his grave became in danger of being unearthed so his remains were cremated and the ashes scattered from an airplane on the Longs Peak area."

The 8 June 1923 issue of *Estes Park Trail* confirms that Enos's body "was placed in a grave hewn out of solid rock [on] Sept. 24, 1922, two days after Mr. Mills' death." The article says that it had been reported that, during the week before the article was published, Enos Mills's body had been taken to Denver to be cremated and that his ashes would be "taken to the top of Longs Peak and thrown to the winds, but Emerson Lynn, manager of the Mills property, said that has not been determined."

As per Enos Mills's daughter, Enda Mills Kiley, Enos Mills was born 22 April 1870 and died on 21 September 1922. His 22 September 1922 obituary in the *Estes Park Trail* says that Enos was born in Kansas, came to Colorado at 14, and "secured his first job in the Park washing dishes at Elkhorn Lodge."

Also according to his obituary, he married Miss Esther A. Burnell, "a homesteader on the Fall River Road." The couple's only child, Enda Mills Kiley, was quite young when her father died. On 16 August 2001, we visited with Enda Mills Kiley and her granddaughter Eryn Mills at the family's property on the south side of Colorado Highway 7 across from where Longs Peak Inn once stood and where its current incarnation stands today. Enda showed us around Enos's famous cabin and told us about his life, especially his early days as a miner in the Boise, Idaho, area and his talent for helping those he took on hikes in what later became Rocky Mountain National Park really appreciate and understand the spectacular scenery that they were seeing. Enda is, of course, very proud of the work her famous father did and of the very important part that he played in ensuring that Rocky Mountain National Park was created to preserve the area it encompasses. The view of Longs Peak from Enos's cabin is indeed breathtaking. The day we were there, a light dusting of snow had just fallen of the mountain's peaks.

Enda told us that the ashes of her mother Ester Burnell Mills and her mother's sister Elizabeth Burnell Smith were both scattered somewhere on the family's property on the south side of Colorado Highway 7. (See the chapter on the Mills and Kiley Grave and Scattered Cremains.)

The same obituary quoted above attributes Enos Mills's death to a number of causes, starting with an injury sustained in a subway wreck the winter before he died, continuing with a "severe attach of influenza" that occurred when he returned to his home in Estes Park in January 1922, and ending with apparent blood poisoning following severe abscesses of his jaw and several teeth.

When Enos Mills died, there were many who held him and his contributions to the preservation of nature in general and the creation of Rocky Mountain National Park in particular in high regard. Indeed, the Appendix to *Enos Mills of the Rockies*, written by

Hildegarde Hawthorne and Esther Burnell Mills (Enos's wife) and published in 1935, contains 16 tributes to him following his death. The tributes were written by individuals and organizations ranging from Colorado Governor Oliver Shoup and Denver-area newspapers to the *American Boy Magazine* and the Colorado Mountain Club, of which he was a member.

Evidently, there were also those who, because of Enos's reportedly fiery temper and possibly because of feelings that Enos's role in the creation of Rocky Mountain National Park had been exaggerated, disliked him just as much. Among these latter individuals were Roe Emery of the Rocky Mountain Transportation Company and Horace Albright. Horace Albright and Steve Mather were the two individuals largely responsible for the creation of the National Park Service in 1916. Mather became the first Director of the NPS, with Albright serving as his Assistant Director. After several stints as Acting Director when Mather was incapacitated, Albright then became the NPS Director in his own right in 1929.

Ellsworth Bethel of the State Historical and Natural History Society of Colorado may have summed up Enos Mill's contributions the best: "The cause of nature protection sustains an irreparable loss in the death of its ablest and most ardent advocate. The stimulus which Enos A. Mills gave to Nature-study and a promotion of the love of all that is beautiful in scenery, in plant and animal life, is beyond estimate" (from page 254 of *Enos Mills of the Rockies*). [For an informative summary of Enos Mills's life after he moved to Colorado up through the dedication of Rocky Mountain National Park on 4 September 1915, see of James H. Pickering's "*This Blue Hollow,*" especially pages 156-158 and 220-225. (See the "Bibliography" for a complete citation.) For genealogical information on the Mills family, see the chapter on the Mills and Kiley Grave and Scattered Cremains.]

Enoch Josiah ("Joe") Mills

As per Ferrel Atkins, Joe's granddaughter, Pat Washburn, reported that his ashes were scattered on Trail Ridge Road. Joe was Enos Mills's younger brother.

According to his obituary on page 1 of the Friday, 4 October 1935 issue of *Estes Park Trail*, Joe's full name was Enoch Joseph Mills.

However, on 14 February 2011, Pat Washburn told us that Joe's correct middle name was "Josiah," not "Joseph." He was born in Kansas in 1880. He came west when he was 10 "and spent practically the remainder of his life in the west." In 1908 while he was coaching at Baylor University in Waco, Texas, Joe married Ethel Steere. The couple had two children, Eleanor Ann Mills and Mark Muir Mills.

Page 220 of Volume II of *Over Hill and Vale* (complete citation in "Bibilography") provides the following information about Joe Mills, some of which repeats information provided earlier:

> "Enoch 'Joe' Mills was born on a farm near Pleasanton, Kansas, July 23, 1880; and died in a head-on collision with a street car, in Denver, Oct. 3, 1935. He was a great lover of athletics, and became a coach at both the State College at Fort Collins, Colorado, and Fort Worth, Texas University. Later he became Director of Physical Culture at Baylor University, Waco, Texas, and Director of Athletics at the University of Colorado. For several years, in his younger years, he was manager of Longs Peak Inn, and later built and operated the Craigs Hotel [Crags Lodge], 'The House on the Hill,' just south of Estes Park, Colorado, village. On May 18, 1908, he married Ethel Maude Steere. They had two children, Eleanor Ann Mills and Mark Muir Mills. The Craigs Hotel [Crags Lodge] was built in 1913 soon after he gave up the proprietorship of the Forks Hotel on the Loveland road.

> "While Joe was at Longs Peak Inn, he homesteaded land over in what folks up there call Peaceful Valley, or The Promised Land. This is a valley that comes down from the saddle between the Twin Sisters and extends to the south. The

> rocky ridge that separates this valley from Elkanah Valley has a great high rock directly across to the east of Longs Peak Inn. Joe Mills built a log cabin just behind this rock and since then the rock has been called Cabin Rock. . . ."

Dunning ends his entry on Joe Mills and his cabin with a poem about the cabin by Charles Edwin Hewes.

Ferrel Atkins provided the following information about Joe and about his relationship with his famous brother:

> "Joe Mills, younger brother of Enos, willingly ran the Longs Peak Inn while Enos lectured around the country. Their relationship was severed when Enos apparently became resentful of Joe's declaration of independence by establishing his own homestead and marrying. From that time on, there was little or no relationship between the two. Joe built the Crags Lodge, now known as the Golden Eagle Resort, lying above the base of the Prospect Mountain Tramway."

Another take on the Mills-Mills falling out appears in "The Wars of the Elkanah Valley" chapter in James H. Pickering's *In the Vale of Elkanah. (*See the "Bibliography" for a complete citation.) On pages 53-54 of that chapter, Pickering refers to "the quarrel that erupted in the summer of 1908 between [Enos] Mills and his brother Joe":

> "Though the precise causes of their dispute are obscure there is no question that Joe Mills, who was widely-liked and who had spent years trying to emulate, without visible hint of jealousy, the accomplishments of his older brother, was deeply hurt. The psychological wounds were so great, in fact, that it was not until 1916 that Joe Mills could bring himself to revisit his boyhood haunts and friends in the Tahosa Valley."

In Note 36 (page 123) referring to this same paragraph, Pickering adds:

> "The wound was never closed, for when Enos Mills died in 1922, Joe Mills would deliberately absent himself from his brother's funeral. The reasons for the original quarrel and the estrangement that resulted remain unclear. We do know that it occurred during the summer of 1908 and seems to have been connected in some way with the building of Timberline House in Jim's Grove below the Boulder Field [on Longs Peak], a small shelter cabin used for 17 years by climbers bound for the peak as an overnight way-stop. According to one story, repeated by Alex Drummond in his biography of Enos Mills, Joe had the building half-complete when his brother intervened with a court order to stop construction, only to finish and operate it in his own name. Whatever the story, it was, in Drummond's words, 'a sorry episode, which can only have been the outward sign of deeper problems.'"

Pickering refers his readers to pages 213-220 of Alexander Drummond's *Enos Mills: Citizen of Nature* (published by the University of Colorado Press in 1995) for a discussion of the brothers' relationship and their quarrel.

Note that, if the quarrel between Enos and Joe Mills began during the summer of 1908, it could have indeed resulted from Joe telling Enos about his plans to marry Ethel Steere, which he did on 18 May 1908 while coaching at Baylor University in Waco, Texas.

As part of their joint oral history project, on 12 August 1979, the Estes Park Area Historical Museum and the Estes Park Public Library held a program titled *The Thirties in Estes Park.* One of the speakers that day was Pat Washburn, the granddaughter of Joe Mills.

During the program, after talking about her grandfather managing the Forks Hotel in Drake, where her mother Eleanor Ann Mills was born, Pat discussed a taped conversation that she had with her mother in which Pat asked Eleanor, "Tell me about your Uncle Enos." Eleanor's response was "I was not allowed to talk to my Uncle Enos because there was a family feud." Pat then goes on to explain two possible reasons for the feud, the same two reasons given by Jim Pickering and Ferrel Atkins:

> "The family feud occurred for two reasons. One was the Boulderfield Cabin, and those of you who climb Longs know about the cabin at the Boulderfield, half of which my grandfather built! Uncle Enos decided that he didn't want my grandfather to build it and got a permit from Larimer County to stop construction. The next summer Uncle Enos went up and finished building the cabin in the Boulderfield. So that was the beginning of the feud.

> "The second part of the feud was that my grandfather got married, and for any Mills to marry was anathema. For years there were no women working at Longs Peak Inn. Most of the staff at Longs Peak Inn were male because Uncle Enos did not like women very much. I judge that Ester [Esther A. Burnell, his wife] changed his mind, but my grandfather's marrying exacerbated the feud so that my grandmother never spoke to Mrs. Mills. The two 'Mrs.'s' Mills never spoke to each other, and my mother's story of the one time she saw her Uncle Enos was that she got the Babcock kids and—let's see, who else?—the Levings kids, all those folks from over there on that side, to sort of sneak over and peer at Longs Peak Inn, where they whispered, 'That's Enos Mills!' But she never met him!."

No matter what his older brother may have thought of Joe Mills, the residents of Estes Park seemed to think very highly of him! The following is a direct quote from Joe Mill's obituary in the *Estes Park Trail* cited above:

> "Entire Region Mourns Tragic Passing of Joe Mills, Who Died Yesterday From Injuries Incurred in Denver Tram Crash

> "Joe Mills, 55, one of the greatest and best loved citizens of Estes Park, died in the Presbyterian hospital in Denver Thursday morning from fatal injuries incurred in a head-on collision between his automobile and a Denver tram car last Friday afternoon.

> "The crash fractured his skull and severely lacerated his scalp, and he died without regaining consciousness after the collision.

> "The accident occurred at E. Colfax Avenue and Pontiac Street in Denver, and he was driving alone at the time. . . .

> "Since late Friday afternoon, when the staggering report of the possibly fatal accident reached the village, the question on the lips of every man and woman was, 'How is Joe Mills?' The final report of his death left Estes Park grief-stricken and subdued, slowly comprehending the significance of the irreparable loss of Joe Mills. . . .

> "Most of the Estes Park business houses will be closed tomorrow afternoon from 1 to 3 o'clock in honor of Joe Mills."

The editorial page (page 4) of the same issue recorded many of the same sentiments, with perhaps the most telling being this one:

> "Estes Park could not afford to lose him because he was one of her truest champions. He put personal advancement as a secondary consideration and labored in the interests of the region for its own sake, no less."

(For genealogical information on the Mills family, see the chapter on the Mills and Kiley Grave and Scattered Cremains.)

William Luther Spurlin

In an email dated 15 August 2005, William's wife, Leslie Hamilton Spurlin, told us that William's ashes were scattered near the bridge over the Colorado River at the Holzwarth Historic Site on 14 June 1992. (See entry for "John G. Holzwarth II.") In August 2006, Leslie provided the exact geographical location where William's ashes were scattered: Elevation 8895 feet, 40° 22' 16" N, 105° 51' 32" W.

William was born in Henderson, Kentucky, on 17 September 1925 and died in Grand Junction, Colorado on 23 April 1992. (His wife Leslie is the daughter of Dwight L. Hamilton and Maxine ("Mickey") Hamilton. See the entry for "Dwight Linton Hamilton" above.)

William was a career school teacher for the Denver Public Schools. During World War II, he fought with the U.S. Marines at Iwo Jima and Roi-Namur, Saipan, Tinian. He was also a veteran of the Korean conflict, having made the amphibious landing at Inchon.

Ken and Betty Suher

On 10 October 2001, their niece Trudy Yeros told us that Ken and Betty Suher's ashes were scattered together from the last overlook/car pull off on the northeast side of Highway 34 between Deer Ridge Junction and the parking lot on the north side of Highway 34 that contains the interpretative plaque for Horseshoe Inn.

Howard and Gretchen Wignall

Their ashes were scattered in Wild Basin. They were residents of Estes Park who died in the late 1970s. When retired Chief Park Naturalist Dwight L. Hamilton provided the above information about the Wignalls in December 2000, he also mentioned that Howard did a great dealing of filming for the Park, including a documentary on Johnnie Holzwarth and the Never Summer Guest Ranch. (The homestead portion of the ranch has been preserved as a living history site near the Grand Lake entrance to the Park. For more information on Johnnie Holzwarth, see the earlier entry for "John G. Holzwarth II.")

Gretchen's obituary appeared in the 8 September 1978 issue of the *Estes Park Trail-Gazette*. According to that obituary, she was born on 17 October 1916 in Isenach, Germany, and died on 6 September 1978 while hiking in Rocky Mountain National Park. Her obituary goes on to say the following:

> "She was very active as a volunteer in RMNP, an activity she began before her retirement as credit manager for the May D&F Department Stores in Denver two years ago. With her husband, Mrs. Wignall helped make several films for RMNP, including a documentary on the Holzwarth Ranch and a movie about the opening of Trail Ridge Road called 'The Roar of the Plows.'

> "Mrs. Wignall is survived by her husband Howard, of Estes Park; three sons, Dennis Lee of Denver, David Craig of Littleton, and Frederick H. of Estes Park; and one daughter, Theresa Lynn of Estes Park.

> "She is also survived by two grandchildren, one brother, and two sisters."

Howard's obituary appeared in the 3 August 1979 issue of the *Estes Park Trail-Gazette*. According to that obituary, he was born on 7 November 1919 in Payson, Utah, and was raised in Salt Lake City. He died on 28 July 1979 at the Swedish Medical Center in Denver from complications following surgery for a brain tumor. His obituary says that he and his wife retired to Estes Park in 1976 and that he was a Volunteer in the Park (VIP) at Rocky Mountain National Park, "taking wildlife photographs and doing other naturalist work until the time of his death."

Jack Woods

His ashes are reported to have been scattered from Trail Ridge Road during the winter of 1965-66.

Frank Wright and Ann Wright Senior

During a phone conversation with him on 14 September 2005, John G. Holzwarth III told us that the ashes of Frank Wright and his wife Ann Wright Senior were scattered on the east bank of the Colorado River due west of the old Phantom Valley Trading Post, which Ann had leased from the ranch and operated. Frank's ashes were scattered in the late 1980s, and Ann's were scattered in about 1990. Sometime following Frank's death, Ann remarried a gentleman with the last name of "Senior."

Frank and Ann's youngest son, James H. Wright, lives in Greeley, Colorado. Another of their sons, Dick Wright, lives in Anhim Lake in British Columbia, Canada.

(For information on John G. Holzwarth III, see the entry for "John G. Holzwarth II" above.)

Clement Yore

Clem's headstone is currently in the front yard of the home of Dave Schutz at 710 Tanager Road in Estes Park. However, Clem's ashes were scattered in what later became part of Rocky Mountain National Park. (For information on how this came to be and on Clement Yore himself, see the chapter on the Clement Yore Headstone.)

CEMETERY OF THE EPISCOPAL CHURCH OF ST. BARTHOLOMEW THE APOSTLE

Location: Latitude 40° 23' 13" N, Longitude 105° 31' 23" W

The Episcopal Church of St. Bartholomew and its cemetery are at 880 MacGregor Avenue in Estes Park just south of the Black Canyon Restaurant on the east side of MacGregor Avenue. The cemetery is on the east side of the church.

Description of Cemetery

According to information contained in a letter dated 9 April 2007 from Diane Weyl, then the Parish Administrator for St. Bartholomew's, the cemetery includes two body burials and 50 cremain interments. One of the body burials is of an infant, and the other is of an adult. (See table below for details.)

Some of the cremain burials have their own headstones rather than being buried in the church's columbarium because, when we visited the cemetery in the fall of 1999, we saw six headstones.

To the right of these headstones (right when one is facing east) is a plaque on the rock cliff commemorating Dorothy Stearns Stacey. (See table below.) The 2-acre lot on which the church and its cemetery or "churchyard" are located was given in the memory of Dorothy Stearns Stacey and Allison Stacey von Wedel by the Wayne Stacey family, which also gave money to help with the building of the church itself.

Photo A: Cemetery of the Episcopal Church of St. Bartholomew the Apostle

In June 2007, Diane Weyl provided the following information on the ashes and bodies interred in what St. Bartholomew's refers to as the "Upper Unit" of the cemetery to distinguish it from the formal columbarium for ash interments established in 1983.

SAINT BARTHOLOMEW

Name of Deceased	Age at Death	Birth Date	Death Date	Officiant	Date of Interment	Marker Type	Other Data
Stacey, Dorothy Stearns	73	12/28/1885	1958	Fred King	1958	Plaque on rock cliff	Ashes are behind the plaque.
Johnson, Darrin Lee	8 mo.	2/10/1966	10/22/1966	Jon Marr Stark	10/26/1966	Grave stone	From Oklahoma; body burial
Price, Harriet Elizabeth	69	3/21/1898	9/27/1967	Jon Marr Stark	9/30/1967	Grave stone	Rector Stark's housekeeper; body burial
Chapman, Dwight Bate	72	1896	2/11/1968	Jon Marr Stark	2/13/1968	Grave stone	Ash burial; wife's ashes are in columnbarium.
Lloyd, Flora	75	12/7/1895	8/7/1970	Fred King	1970	Grave stone	Ash burial
Newson, Hamilton S.	74	7/28/1898	2/2/1973	Fred King	1973	Grave stone	Ash burial located far up the hill separate from the rest
Stacey, Wayne	84	7/13/1891	1/25/1975	Fred King	1975	Plaque installed 9/21/1984	Ashes under small statue
Lloyd, Frank	85	7/31/1891	4/16/1976	Fred King	4/21/1976	Grave stone	Ash burial

Finding the Cemetery

This cemetery is one of the first ones we found when we began our search for graves and cemeteries in Larimer County in the fall of 1999. We looked for a cemetery near St. Bartholomew's just on the chance that the church might have one, which it did.

Brief History of the Episcopal Church of St. Bartholomew the Apostle and Its Cemetery

The letter that Diane Weyl, the Parish Administrator for St. Bartholomew, sent us on 9 April 2007 and a second letter that she sent in June 2007 contained information that we had requested on the history of that church and its cemetery. We had originally asked Sybil Barnes, then the Local History Librarian of the Estes Park Public Library, if the library had any information on the history of St. Bartholomew's. When she could not find any such information in the Library's files, Sybil passed our request on to a member of the church with whom she was acquainted, and he passed our request on to Diane.

Sources of Information on the History of the Parish Church of St. Bartholomew and Its Cemetery

Diane Weyl kindly provided us with the following information, which is the source of the following history of St. Bartholomew's and its cemetery:

1. *The History of the Parish Church of Saint Bartholomew the Apostle* by Chris Benight, undated.

2. A list of questions and answers concerning St. Bartholomew's, which includes several questions relating to the church's cemetery, undated.

3. Information on "St. Bartholomew's Churchyard" from what appears to be a bound booklet about the church, undated.

4. Letter to Joseph H. Minnis, the Bishop of the Episcopal Church of Colorado, from the "Estes Park Church Committee" dated 20 December 1955 petitioning to become an organized mission of the Episcopal Church.

5. Letter to Frank H. Shafroth, the Chancellor of the Episcopal Diocese of Colorado, from the Reverend Jon Marr Stark dated 18 October 1967 concerning the establishment of a formal cemetery at St. Bartholomew's.

6. *Brief History of St. Bartholomew's Episcopal Church in Estes Park, Colorado* by Janice M. Woods. This history is the transcript of a talk that Ms. Woods gave at a meeting of the Church Women on St. Bartholomew's in about 1982.

Brief History of the Episcopal Church of St. Bartholomew the Apostle of Estes Park

The earliest verified Episcopalian services in the Estes Park area were held in the Elkhorn Lodge sometime prior to 1914. Those services were led by the Reverend Walter Bonnell of the Trinity Church in Greeley and by Bishop Johnson, the Bishop of the Episcopal Church of Colorado, and continued on an irregular basis until World War II.

After the War, Mr. and Mrs. William Frank Jackson got permission from Bishop Ingley to resume services, which were held in both the Music Room of the Stanley Hotel and at the home of Mr. and Mrs. Wayne Hackett in Rocky Mountain National Park. The efforts of these early Estes Park Episcopalians to form a church were aided by the Venerable Eric A. Smith, the Archdeacon of the Episcopal Diocese of Colorado, and the Reverend Charles V. Young of the Trinity Church in Greeley. According to Chris Benight (Source No. 1), these two gentlemen "took a strong interest in the struggling group and conducted services, secured visiting priests, and started a nest egg which was to help the group progress toward official status."

Some of the early members of the church were Juanita Ashby, Goldie Bezold, Wayne Hackett, Meredith and Richard Montony, Ann and Charles Wilson, and Janice M. Woods. Summer members were Ted Finger and Mrs. Anne Welch.

In the fall of 1955, the group began its efforts to establish an official Episcopalian Mission Church. At the time, they were meeting at the old Grade School, which was at the 1982 location of the First National Bank. On 20 December 1955, the group petitioned Bishop Joseph H. Minnis (Source No. 4) to become a Mission Church. The petition was signed by 14 members of the group. As of early 1956, the incipient church had 24 members, with a budget of $1,200. The Reverend Charles V. Young was the priest in charge.

Bishop Minnis granted the group's petition, thus officially establishing the Mission Church of Saint Bartholomew the Apostle. In March 1956, the first confirmations of seven Estes Park people took place in the Trinity Church in Greeley, with Reverend Young presenting and Bishop Minnis confirming. On 25 March 1956, 14-year-old Juleen Kay Hossack became the first Episcopalian baptized in Estes Park. In September 1956, Mr. and Mrs. Milton R. Hayes of Estes Park, who owned the Ramshorn Cottages on Spur 66, donated 1 acre of land for a church site. However, before the church could be built, Rocky Mountain National Park expressed an interest in the land for the location of the current Beaver Meadows entrance; consequently, the Hayes family's land donation was sold to the Park.

As noted above, Mr. and Mrs. Wayne Stacey gave both the land on which the current St. Bartholomew's is located and money to help build the church. This was in May 1957. The church, which was designed by Dudley Smith and Casper Hegner, was begun in September 1957. Assisted by Father Warner, the Right Reverend Daniel Corrigan, who was the Suffragan Bishop of Colorado, conducted the first service at the church on 15 May 1958. The first wedding was held on 21 July 1958. On St. Bartholomew's Day in 1958, Bishop Minnis dedicated the new building.

The Reverend John Marr Stark was appointed vicar of St. Bartholomew's from June 1959 until 1967. He was the church's first resident priest. He was succeeded by the Reverend Fred F. King in March 1968. Reverend King served until 1978, when he was succeeded by the Reverend Thomas Long, who served until 1984.

On 29 September 1975, during the tenure of Reverend Long, the Right Reverend William C. Frey elevated St. Bartholomew's to an official Episcopalian parish.

The church's current parish hall was constructed and dedicated in 1988-1989.

The Reverend Edward J. Morgan became rector of the parish in 1985 and served until 1996. The rector of St. Bartholomew's as of July 2007, the Reverend M. Paul Garrett, began serving the church in August 1997.

As of April 2012, the Reverend Seth Richmond was the rector of St. Bartholomew's.

Brief History of St. Bartholomew's Cemetery

Because burial near parish churches is an ancient tradition, St. Bartholomew's established the burial ground immediately east of the church and makes it available to all professing Christians. The cemetery, which St. Bartholomew's refers to as its "churchyard," was blessed by Bishop Frey in May 1983. However, the first ashes were actually buried in St. Bartholomew's cemetery in 1958, constituting what the church believes was the first church-associated interment of ashes in Estes Park. (See the table above for more information on the first eight body and ash interments at the cemetery between 1958 and 1976.)

ST. FRANCIS OF ASSISI ANGLICAN CHURCH CEMETERY

Location: Latitude 40° 19' 35" N, Longitude 105° 30' 09" W

The St. Francis of Assisi Anglican Church and its cemetery are at 3490 St. Francis Way in Estes Park. St. Francis Way and the church are southeast of Estes Park and southeast of Fish Creek Road. To reach the church and cemetery, take Fish Creek Road south from U.S. Highway 36, take Blue Valley Drive southeast from Fish Creek Road, take Little Valley Drive southwest from Blue Valley Drive, and finally take St. Francis Way west from Little Valley Drive.

Description of Cemetery and Cremain Markers

As of 21 July 2000 when we visited the cemetery, it contained 21 cremain burials, 15 of which were of humans and 6 of which were of animals. (St. Francis of Assisi is the patron saint of animals.) Most of the burials of animal cremains are in a separate portion of the cemetery around a statue of St. Francis on a rise to the south of the church. The burials to the north of the church are only human cremains. Along the Stations of the Cross path, burials are of both human and animal cremains. (We assume that the one animal buried on the Stations of the Cross path as of 21 July 2000 is buried next to the person whose pet it was.)

Photo A: Two Cremain Burials on the Stations of the Cross Path at the St. Francis of Assisi Anglican Church

Cremain Markers North of Church

Ardyce Liddell
May 6, 1959-March 19, 1994

Warren C. Van De Veere
March 15, 1934-April 12, 1990

To the left of Warren Van De Veere's cremains is a place for cremains. As of our visit on 21 July 2000, there were no ashes interred in this site.

Emalu Swain Pointer
Dec. 22, 1920-May 27, 1987

ST. FRANCIS

Gladys Maude Swain
Aug. 12, 1894-March 14, 1987

Jack Richard Swain
June 3, 1919-Jan. 21, 1981

Dorothy Swain Pratt
Nov. 17, 1929-June 22, 1994

Elizabeth Eckstein
June 27, 1906-January 4, 2000

Laura Elizabeth Evans
March 27, 1906-February 25, 1994

Cremain Markers Along the Station of the Cross Trail
To the left of the large cross of Jesus between Stations 11 and 13:

Roscoe Reed, Priest
May 9, 1911-May 10, 1996

East of Father Reed's marker were several stakes with names on them and no signs that cremains had been buried. We assumed that these were probably reservations for the burial of cremains in the future:

Nagit and Judy Rao.
("Rao." is probably an abbreviation.)

Wayne and Betty Huff

Between Stations 2 and 3:

Richard E. Heiny
April 4, 1932-March 2, 1987

CANE
(Burial of Pet Cremains)

Gail S. Johnson
Feb. 2, 1917-Feb. 15, 1999

Cremains in Pet Cemetery (40° 19' 35" N, 105° 30' 04" W)
Markers for the following pets are listed clockwise starting to the left of the statue of St. Francis: JOSIE, BINGO, ROCKY, SUSIE, and BUSTER.

Finding the Cemetery
We were told about the cemetery associated with the St. Francis of Assisi Anglican Church in Estes Park by Lawrence Kern, an Anglican priest in Fort Collins. Father Kern had worked with Kay Merril of the Colorado Council of Genealogical Societies to produce the Ourey County and Delores County sections of the 1985 edition of Colorado Council of Genealogical Societies' *Colorado Cemetery Directory*. We met him through his sister Barbara Tuttle, whose now-deceased husband Arthur did research for the Larimer County Genealogical Society on graves and cemeteries in Larimer County about 15 years before 2000.

On 21 July 2000, following Father Kern's directions, we found the cemetery at the St. Francis of Assisi Anglican Church in Estes Park.

LARIMER COUNTY CEMETERIES

REVEREND THORNTON R. SAMPSON GRAVE

Location: Latitude 40° 21' 17" N, Longitude 105° 37' 58" W

The grave of the Reverend Thornton Rogers Sampson is about 350 feet west and north of the Fern Lake Trail Trailhead in Rocky Mountain National Park. (For more detailed information on the exact location of the grave, see "Finding the Grave" below.)

Description of Grave

As of 1 October 2000, there was no marker of any kind on Rev. Sampson's grave. The only sign of his grave is a flat, triangular area at the base of the diamond described by Hal Tecker under "Finding the Grave" below. On 1 October 2000, a dead tree stood on the cliff directly above the diamond. Our use of dowser rods confirmed a burial at this location. From Rev. Sampson's grave, the land slopes downward to the Fern Lake Trail. See Photo A below for the photograph we took of Rev. Sampson's grave on 1 October 2000.

Finding the Grave

We began looking for Rev. Sampson's grave because it was included on a list of graves in Rocky Mountain National Park provided to us by Dr. D. Ferrel Atkins. (For information on Ferrel and all of the help he gave in our efforts to find and document all of the graves and cemeteries in Rocky Mountain National Park, see the "Acknowledgments" section.) The typewritten information on Ferrel's list concerning Rev. Sampson's grave follows:

> "Sampson left Grand Lake on September 2, 1915 for Estes Park and vanished from sight. His remains were found on July 8, 1932 by a trail crew and were reinterred at the end of the Fern Lake Trail."

Handwritten notations (in two different handwrittings) accompanying the typewritten notes provided the following additional information:

- The word "end" in "at the end of the Fern Lake Trail" was circled, and the following handwritten note was "attached" to the circle: "i.e., under cliffs N. of Fern L. Trailhead."
- Written under the typewritten note was the following: "Bob Haines has infrared film of original wooden grave marker. Actual site no longer visible."

Based on the information above, we made a trip to the Fern Lake Trailhead in late September 2000. We looked for signs of a grave north of the trail. We located several possible burial sites, but our dowser rods indicated that none of these locations contained human or animal remains.

When we then talked to Ferrel Atkins again, he remembered that on 20 May 1997 he had interviewed Hal Tecker and his mother Inas Tecker, an interview which Ferrel thought contained information that might help us in our search for Rev. Sampson's grave. Ferrel loaned us the tape of the interview, which we listened to and from which we transcribed the following pertinent information:

> Ferrel: "Could you describe again how one would find it [Rev. Sampson's grave] starting at the Fern Lake Trailhead?"
>
> Hal: "Go up from the Fern Lake Trailhead until the trail makes a little curve and then comes right back around the curve and then a dip beside the river."

Ferrel: "I believe that [earlier] you said to the right, around and then it comes to a little dip."

Hal: "And then a little rise, like a 4-foot rise in the trail. On the right-hand side there's a place in the wall of the mountain—the rock—that just kind of diamonds in. It's [Sampson's remains are] buried right in front of that diamond."

Hal was a member of the family who owned the former Forest Inn, which, until it was bought out by Rocky Mountain National Park and subsequently demolished, was several hundred feet west and uphill from "The Pool" on the Fern Lake Trail.

Using the above information from Ferrel's interview of the Teckers, we returned to the Fern Lake Trailhead on 1 October 2000 and found a burial site (confirmed by our use of dowser rods) in the exact location described by Hal Tecker. (See "Location" and "Description of Grave" above.)

On 6 October 2000, retired (and now sadly deceased) Rocky Mountain National Park Ranger Bob Haines kindly gave us a copy of the photograph he had taken of Rev. Sampson's grave before the grave marker was removed. (The story of Bob's involvement with this grave marker is included under "History of Reverend Sampson's Disappearance, Death, Discovery, and Burial" below.) The diamond-shaped rock in the photograph that we took of the grave on October 1st (Photo A below) matches exactly the diamond-shaped rock in the photograph of the grave that Bob provided us (Photo B). The lower edge of the diamond-shaped rock is seen in the upper right corner of the Haines photo. Thus, the accuracy of our use of dowser rods to locate burials has been confirmed, even when those burials are only partial as was Rev. Sampson's. (See "History of Reverend Sampson's Disappearance, Death, Discovery, and Burial" below. For information on all of the help that Bob Haines provided our grave-search efforts in Rocky Mountain National Park, see the "Acknowledgments.")

Photo A: Photograph of Rev. Sampson's Burial Site Taken on 1 October 2000

LARIMER COUNTY CEMETERIES

Photo B: Photograph of Rev. Sampson's Burial Site Taken by Bob Haines in 1961 Before the Grave Marker Was Removed (Courtesy of Robert J. Haines)

Sources of Information on Reverend Thornton Rogers Sampson, His Death, and Burial

1. Oral Interview of Jack Moomaw by William Ramaley conducted on 22 January 1972 as part of the Estes Park oral history project. The tape of the interview and its transcription are available in the Local History Section of the Estes Park Public Library.

2. *Rocky Mountain National Park; A History*, written by C. W. Buchholtz. (See the "Bibliography" for a complete citation.) Page 142 contains a brief mention on the search for Reverend Sampson following his disappearance.

3. "The 17-Year Mystery of Thornton R. Sampson," chapter in *The Ways of the Mountains*, written by James H. Pickering and published in 2003. (See the "Bibliography" for a complete citation.)

4. "Explorer's final trip ended with fatal snowstorm," written by Ken Jessen, *Loveland Reporter-Herald*, 24 May 2009, page B4. The article reports on Reverend Sampson's final hike, death, discovery, and burial and contains photos of "Squeaky" Bob Wheeler and his dog at Camp Wheeler on the Colorado River and of Fern Lake Lodge.

History of the Reverend Thornton Rogers Sampson

The following brief summary of Rev. Sampson's life up to the time of his disappearance on 3 September 1915 is taken from considerably more detailed information provided on pages 27-30 of a chapter entitled "The 17-Year Mystery of Thornton R. Sampson" in James H. Pickering's *The Ways of the Mountains* (Source No. 3).

Thornton Rogers Sampson was born on 9 October 1852 in Hampden-Sidney, Prince Edward County, Virginia, where "his father, the Reverend Francis S. Sampson, was professor of Hebrew at Union Theological Seminary."

Thornton entered Hampden-Sidney College when he was only 16. Having graduated from that college in only 3 years, he taught for a year to earn money and then, before he was 20, entered the University of Virginia, where he studied moral philosophy and Greek and from which he graduated in July 1873.

Beginning in November 1874, Thornton went to Europe, where he studied in Edinburgh, Leipzig, and Beirut until he had mastered Greek, Arabic, and several other languages.

In April 1878, he both married a distant cousin Ella Royster and was ordained as a Presbyterian minister. In August 1878, the now Reverend Sampson and his wife were sent to Athens, Greece, to serve as missionaries, where they remained for 14 years.

In 1894, Rev. Sampson became President of Fredericksburg College in Texas. In 3 years he freed that institution from the considerable debt with which it had been encumbered at the beginning of his tenure.

He next became President of Austin College in Sherman, Texas, north of Dallas, where things did not go as well and from which "he was invited by the Board to resign" in May 1900. From Austin College in Sherman, he went to Austin, Texas, where he became the founding President of a new Presbyterian theological seminary. After Rev. Sampson raised a sufficient endowment, the Austin Theological Seminary accepted its first six students on 1 October 1902. On 30 June 1905, Rev. Sampson gave up the presidency of the seminary for reasons of health, but remained its Professor of Church History and Polity.

On 1 April 1914, he also bravely took on the added responsibility of the executive secretary for the Conference of Education in Texas. One of the most important accomplishments of this privately financed organization was to get the Texas legislature to pass the first compulsory school attendance law in the state's history. (We use the word "bravely" above advisedly. Author Susan Briles Kniebes grew up in Texas, where her ancestors go back to before Texas was a republic. Her reading of Texas history leads Susan to believe that the early Texans, unlike the folks living there currently, did not always take public-supported education as seriously as they should have.)

Then, in August 1915, Rev. Sampson and his wife traveled to Denver, Colorado, where Mrs. Sampson stayed while Rev. Sampson set out for the soon-to-be Rocky Mountain National Park and one of the mountain treks he had come to enjoy during his time in Europe and Asia.

History of Reverend Sampson's Disappearance, Death, Discovery, and Burial

After we had completed our own research on Rev. Sampson's disappearance and death in what is now Rocky Mountain National Park, on the belated discovery of his body, and on his final burial, we met James ("Jim") H. Pickering and his wife Pat. On 12 July 2002, we took them to Rev. Sampson's burial site, and they took us to the grave of Julia Ann Morrissey southwest of Estes Park on Longs Peak Road. (See the chapter on that grave for information on Julia Ann Morrissey and her employer Charles Edwin Hewes. See the "Acknowledgments" section for more information on Jim Pickering and all of the help he and his books provided to our efforts to find and documents graves and cemeteries in the Rocky Mountain National Park and the Estes Park areas.)

For a very complete and compelling account of Rev. Sampson's last days, the all-out search for him after his disappearance, and the final discovery of his body and the subsequent burial of his remains, see pages 31-53 of Jim Pickering's *The Ways of the Mountains* (Source No. 3). We do not attempt to summarize Jim's account below but, instead, provide the results of our own, much more limited research and include information from Jim's book only when it provides specific information missing from our results.

According to Ferrel Atkins and the records in the Park's Library, Rev. Sampson left Grand Lake on 12 September 1915 to hike from there to Estes Park to witness the official ceremony marking the creation of Rocky Mountain National Park, which was to take place in Horseshoe Park on September 4th. He never made it to Estes Park. (According to page 37 of *The Ways of*

LARIMER COUNTY CEMETERIES

the Mountains, Rev. Sampson was last seen on September 3rd "by a party of three women and their guide who were returning to Grand Lake from a trip into the mountains.")

While on his way to the dedication ceremony, he encountered a man on horseback also heading toward Estes Park. Pages 35 and 36 of *The Ways of the Mountains* tell us that this man was Clifford Higby, "a licensed guide and part owner of Fern Lake Lodge." Higby reported that he had told Rev. Sampson that he would put a marker (cairn marked with a red bandana) at the location on the Flattop Trail where Rev. Sampson was to turn downhill to the north to intersect the Fern Lake Trail. Rev. Sampson was then to take the Fern Lake Trail to reach Moraine Park. (He evidently knew how to get from there to Horseshoe Park, his final destination.) Once Rev. Sampson reached the marker, he was to take it apart so it would not confuse those traveling down the trail at a later date.

When Rev. Sampson did not arrive in Estes Park as planned, there was no immediate consternation because he was known to be an experienced mountaineer and to have frequently and successfully spent time alone in mountains both in the U.S. and abroad. Consequently, a search for him was not begun until September 13th. According to Ferrel Atkins and the information in the Park Library, the first thing the searchers did was to go to the cairn marker left on Flattop Trail to see if Rev. Sampson had reached and dismantled it. He had not.

According to page 46 of *The Ways of the Mountains*, by 3 October 1915, all hope of finding Rev. Sampson alive had evaporated and a memorial service was held for him at the University Presbyterian Church in Austin, Texas.

On page 142 of *Rocky Mountain National Park: A History* (Source No. 2), Curt Buchholtz makes a brief mention of the search "for a Dr. R. T. Sampson" in his discussion of C. R. Trowbridge, the Acting Supervisor of the Park between 1 July 1915 and 16 September 1916. In that account, Buchholtz quotes someone as saying that a whole squad spent "considerable time searching for a Dr. R. T. Sampson reportedly lost along the Continental Divide."

Rev. Sampson's body was finally found in a crevice above Odessa Lake on 8 July 1932 by a trail crew. [Interestingly, Shep Husted had predicted that Sampson's remains would be found in Odessa Gorge (Source No. 4).] The probable cause of Sampson's death was starvation or exposure; he had badly broken his leg when he apparently fell into the crevice and could not crawl out. His remains were identified by a number of artifacts accompanying them that had been with him in a photograph someone had taken of him on 28 August 1915 at Camp Wheeler at the base of Milner Pass on the North Fork of the Colorado River, which was known as Grand River in 1915.

At the request of his wife, Rev. Sampson's remains were buried in the Park at the above-described location near the Fern Lake Trail Trailhead. According to page 52 of *The Ways of the Mountains*, the internment of Rev. Sampson's remains took place on 17 July 1932, with Rev. Sampson's son Frank Sampson and representatives of the Estes Park Rotary Club present.

Some additional details concerning the discovery of Rev. Sampson's body are found in a transcription of William Ramaley's 22 January 1972 interview of Jack Moomaw (Source No. 1). Jackie Johnson of Estes Park, who helped us with a number of other Rocky Mountain National Park and Estes Park area graves, told us about this interview on 26 March 2001. (For additional information about Jackie, see the "Jacqueline Jaye Johnson" entry in the chapter on Rocky Mountain National Park Scattered Cremains.)

Jack Moomaw was a well-known Rocky Mountain National Park Ranger. He began working for the Park as a trail foreman in 1921, retired from active duty in 1945, and died on 10 January 1974. The pertinent parts of William ("Bill") Ramaley's interview of Jack follow:

Bill: "I know that some people, like Reverend Sampson, are buried [in the Park]. He disappeared."

Jack: "I know. It went all these years [looking for Sampson's body], and then I had a crew working up there and [had] gone within 10 feet of where the fellow was, and I never did see him. I had a fellow by the name of Adams (?), one of the boys who worked on the trail. I don't know whether he went over there to take a leak or what—all the way from where he was working, which wasn't as far as from here to that door—and found Rev. Sampson over there. There was a dollar watch more or less protected by his clothing or him or something, and it still worked."

Ferrel Atkins's 20 May 1997 interview with Hal Tecker and his mother provided the following additional information about Rev. Sampson's grave and the search for and eventual discovery of Rev. Sampson's remains:

Ferrel: "When you walked past it [Rev. Sampson's grave] yesterday, there was no marker of any kind?"

Hal: "I didn't climb up there to see. The only marker that would be left. . . . It was just a wooden stake, and I think it was a steel sign with some of his obituary on it."

Ferrel: "We've got a picture. I remember when I first came here about 1952 or '53 I was intrigued about it [Rev. Sampson's disappearance and the subsequent discovery and burial of his remains]. Very early when I came I saw a picture in the file. As we were talking about the other day, it was a green sign with white lettering on a board which has undoubtedly rotted by now because that's been over 40 years ago, and I don't know how old the picture was when I saw it. Now I found in our file (which I was looking at before I came here to refresh my memory) that in 1947 the members of the family wanted to put a little brass plaque up there and Chief Ranger Barton Herschler had said 'Well, you know you're not really supposed to do that [place memorial markers] within a National Park, but, since it's off the trail, if they did it inconspicuously, we might let them do it.'"

Inas: "I remember meeting some of them."

Hal: "I don't remember it [putting up a plaque] being done."

Ferrel: "The file that I had didn't go on to say whether anything ever happened to it or not."

Hal: "Well, there could be. Like I say, I'd known where it was and it wasn't any big interest since I knew the history behind it: He [Rev. Sampson] was a fellow that fell in a crevice above Odessa [Odessa Lake north of Flattop Mountain] and, when they put a new trail through, they found his pipe and watch and a few artifacts and that identified his bones. His family came up for 4 or 5 years [after he disappeared] looking for him."

Ferrel: "I think, as you and I talked about the other day, we have somewhere in our files (I don't know whether I could locate it now) a picture that was taken [at Grand Lake] on the morning that he disappeared, and, when he disappeared, whoever took this picture hung on to it because he thought it might help sometime. We've also got a picture of what they found with him: his fishing rod and so on. If you look at these two pictures, it looks exactly the same. This memo that I was reading said that the watch that he was carrying still ran."

Hal: "As I remember, the pipe, watch, and fishing rod or something, just a few things, and maybe a bone or two but the animals had taken care of most of it."

LARIMER COUNTY CEMETERIES

After having gathered the above information (minus the quotes from Jim Pickering's book, which we had not yet seen), on 6 October 2000, we visited with Bob Haines, as noted above, another retired Rocky Mountain National Park Ranger, and his wife "Teddie." Bob was able to provide the following additional information about Rev. Sampson's burial and his grave. (For more information on Bob and Teddie, see the "William Walter Haines" and "Mary Thomas Shreve Mereness" entries in the chapter on Rocky Mountain National Park Scattered Cremains, the chapter on the Lillian Georgina Fearnly Haines Cremains, and the "Acknowledgments" section.)

In 1961, Bob was hiking on the Fern Lake Trail when he "discovered" the sign marking Rev. Sampson's grave (Photo B above). As of 1961, both the sign and the stake to which it was attached were made out of wood. The sign was very hard to read. Bob recalled that all that he could read was "Rev. Thornton" at the top left of the sign and the words "He loved children" farther down on the sign. At that point, Bob could not read the "Sampson" following "Thornton" on the sign so was not aware that this was Rev. Sampson's grave.

Bob, who had always been quite a photographer, photographed the sign in its original position at Rev. Sampson's grave and then took both the sign and its stake to Park Headquarters and locked them in a walk-in safe while he went to search for some infrared film. His hope was that, if he photographed the sign with that film, he would be able to read all or at least most of what it said.

By the time he returned with the film several days later, some other industrious Park Ranger had thrown the sign away, thinking that it was junk cluttering up the walk-in safe!

In an email that he sent us in late October 2000, Ferrel Atkins said that he remembers a slide in the Park's records that shows a green sign with white lettering at Rev. Sampson's grave. He suggested that we ask the people in McLaren Hall to let us look for it. We talked to Lashelle Lyman, who, as of August 2001, was a Park Ranger. Lashelle had helped us several times previously. Lashelle contacted Joan Childress, who, as of the fall of 2000, was the Park Ranger in charge of the Park's slide and photo archives. On 1 November 2000, LaShelle told us that Joan said that she very much doubted that the slide that Ferrel described still existed.

On page 53 of *The Ways of the Mountains*, Jim Pickering reports that Rev. Sampson's grave marker/sign contained white lettering on a green background, just as Ferrel Atkins recalled, and that the wording on the sign was as follows:

REV. THORNTON ROGERS SAMPSON
DD 1852-1915
MISSIONARY EDUCATOR

A RUGGED MAN OF GOD WHO
PASSED AWAY AMID THESE
RUGGED MOUNTAINS THAT HE
LOVED SO WELL AND WHICH
INSPIRED HIS MANY ACHIEVEMENTS
IN THE WALKS OF MEN AND
WHERE IT WAS HIS WANT TO SO
OFTEN RETURN FOR CLOSE
COMMUNION WITH HIS MAKER

Jim was more persistent in his efforts to mine the Park's photography files than our informants were, for he cites as his source for the text of the above grave marker "Photograph, Rocky Mountain National Park Library"!

DONALD AND DOROTHY SANDBURG SCATTERED CREMAINS

Location: Latitude 40° 21' 12" N, Longitude 105° 29' 50" W

The cremains of Donald Irving Sandburg and Dorothy Allen Sandburg are scattered under a large pine tree southeast of the cabin on private property belonging to Walter and Carolyne Boettger at 1460 Flower Lane, which runs east from Fish Creek Road, in Estes Park. Rose petals are frequently seen at the site.

Finding the Site

We learned that the ashes of Donald and Dorothy Sandburg had been scattered at the location described above from Dell and Sharon Jo Babbitt, whose home is immediately east of the Boettgers' cabin. (For more information on the Babbitts, see the chapter on the Horseshoe Park Graves.) On 20 October 2001, Jo Babbitt took us to visit the site so that we could photograph it and obtain its GPS reading.

Description of Site

On 3 March 2002, Jo Babbitt provided us with the following description of the site where Donald and Dorothy Sandburg's ashes are scattered:

> "The upper branches of a tree, south of the cabin at 1460 Flower Lane, are dead, but deer, elk, and birds keep the place lively. This is a gathering place for large species of roosting birds and small birds that burrow holes into the top branches. The spot is located on private property, but it can be viewed from Fish Creek Road. Family members visit, to leave red rose petals amongst the native bushes beneath the tree, where the ashes of Dorothy and Donald Sandburg are scattered."

Photo A: Pine Tree at 1460 Flower Lane Under Which the Ashes of Donald and Dorothy Sandburg Are Scattered

History of Site Where Donald and Dorothy Sandburg's Ashes Are Scattered

The cabin at 1460 Flower Lane that now belongs to Walter and Carolyne Boettger had originally belonged to Dorothy Sandburg's parents, John Worth Allen and Josephine Shedd Allen, who bought the property in 1948. The Allens' granddaughter Chris Sandburg Spohn spent many weekends and summer vacations at the cabin.

In her 3 March 2002 email to us, Chris told us that her parents' ashes were scattered at the Boettgers' cabin "amongst the beauty of the mountains as they always requested." In a second email dated 8 March 2002, Chris added that her parents had specifically requested that their ashes be scattered "below the swing tree at The Cabin" and she thanked the Boettgers for making the family able "to provide them that wish."

Biographical and Genealogical Information of Donald Irving and Dorothy Allen Sandburg and Their Descendants

The following information on Donald and Dorothy Sandburg and their children and grandchildren was provided by their daughter Chris Sandburg Spohn, who gave it to Walter and Carolyne Boettger, who passed it on to the Babbitts. Jo Babbitt sent it to us via email on 3 March 2002, along with the site description provided above. Chris also provided some of the information below directly to us in an email dated 3 March 2002.

Donald Irving Sandburg. Donald I. Sandburg, the **son of Frank A. and Eda Hultman Sandburg**, was born 7 June 1921 in Denver. Donald graduated from South High School in 1939 and Denver University in 1943. He served in the European Theater during World War II. He managed the Joslins Department Store in Greeley, Colorado, between 1960 and 1972. He retired in 1983.

Donald passed away in Greeley on 8 April 2000 at the age of 78. As of March 2002, in addition to his children and grandchildren listed below, he was survived by one brother, Richard Sandburg of Littleton, Colorado. His parents and his sister Elaine were deceased at the time of his death.

Dorothy Allen Sandburg, Donald's wife. Dorothy Allen, the **daughter of John Worth and Josephine Shedd Allen**, was born on 1 December 1921 in Greeley, Colorado. Dorothy graduated from East High School in Denver in 1939 and from Denver University in 1944. She married Donald Sandburg on 22 January 1944. They moved to Greeley in 1960. Dorothy passed away in Greeley on 7 August 2000. Like her husband, she was 78 years old at her death.

Donald and Dorothy had the following two children:

1. **Christine Sandburg.** Chris and her **husband Larry Spohn** live in Eaton, Colorado. Chris is the one who places dried rose petals at the site where her parents' cremains were scattered.

    Chris and Larry have the following two children:

    1.1. **Brian Lawrence Spohn.**

    1.2. **Michelle Christine Spohn.**

2. **Kirk Sandburg.** Kirk and his **wife Jan** live in Bend, Oregon.

    Kirk and Jan have the following two sons:

    2.1. **Kyle Allen Sandburg.**

    2.2. **Luke Allen Sandburg.**

SUNDANCE MOUNTAIN GRAVES

Location

Information available to us as of February 2014 indicated that there are three graves of unknown adults very near each other on Sundance Mountain on or just north of the Ute Trail and north of Trail Ridge Road in Rocky Mountain National Park. (See the "Finding the Graves" below.)

The map below shows the locations of these three graves.

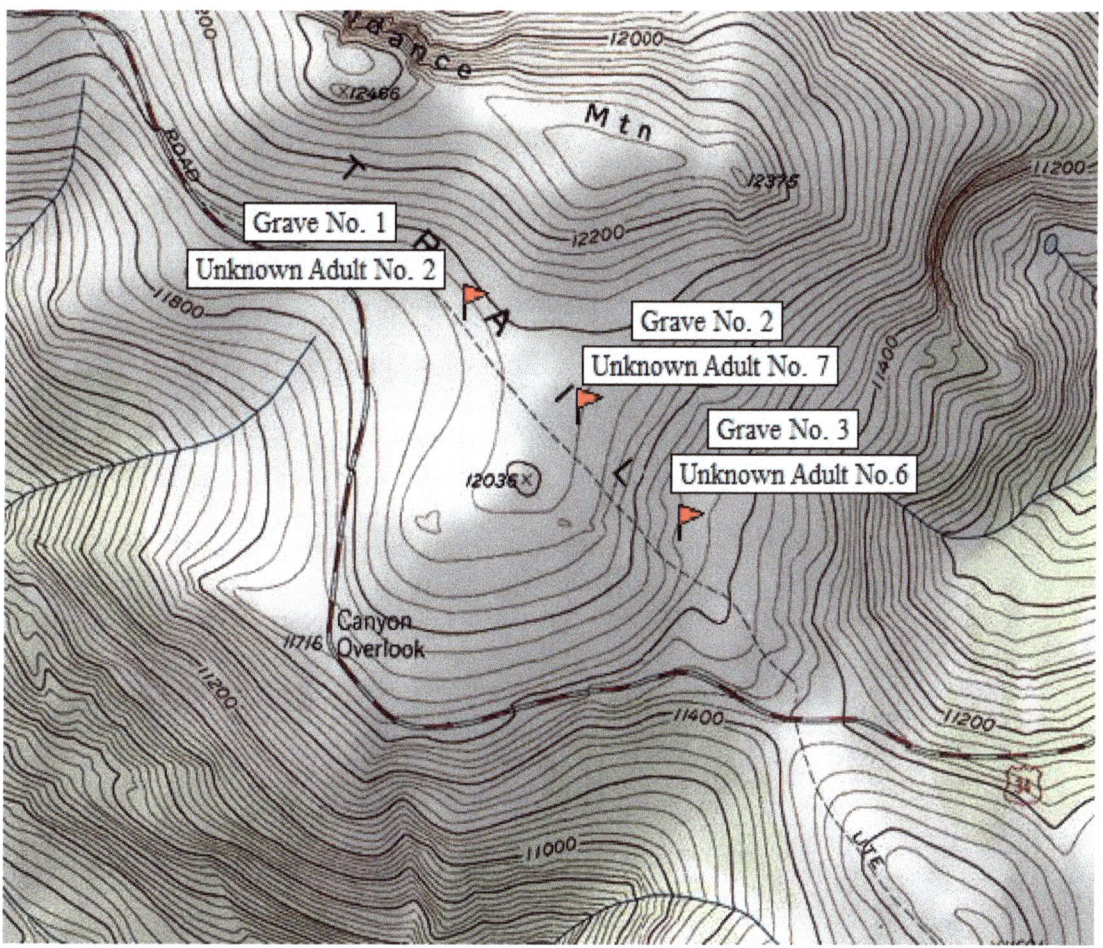

Portion of the U.S. Geological Survey's Trail Ridge Quad Map Showing the Three Graves on Sundance Mountain on or Just North of the Ute Trail

Details on the locations of these three graves follow. (For the information sources referred to in this section, see "Sources of Information on the Sundance Mountain Graves" below.)

Grave No. 1 (Grave of Unknown Adult No. 2)

Latitude 40° 24' 10" N, Longitude 105° 42' 24" W

This grave is officially "Unknown Adult No. 2 Grave" in the records of the Colorado Council of Genealogical Societies. As noted under "Finding the Graves" below, we found Grave No. 1 in October 2000 while looking for Grave No. 2. Grave No. 1 is about 0.2 of a mile due east of the pull off on the left side of Trail Ridge Road when heading from the Forest Canyon Overlook to the Rock Cut Parking Lot. The grave is directly on the Ute Trail, almost equidistance between the northwest (12,486-foot) and northeast (12,375-foot) summits of Sundance Mountain. (See Photo A below.)

On 1 October 2000, our GPS provided the above latitude and longitude information for Grave No. 1. In addition, it indicated that the grave was at an altitude of 11,997 feet. Our use of dowser rods indicated the burial of an adult body at this location. When Larry Carpenter, Fred Henkin, and Fred's wife Sharon Henkin used dowser rods at Grave No. 1 on 1 August 2008 (Source Nos. 7 and 8), all three of them got results indicating a body burial at the location. (We had taught Larry how to use dowser rods, and he taught Fred and Sharon.)

Grave No. 2 (Grave of Unknown Adult No. 7)

Latitude 40° 24' 01" N, Longitude 105° 42' 10" W

This grave is officially "Unknown Adult No. 7 Grave" in the records of the Colorado Council of Genealogical Societies. Its existence was reported to us by Ferrel Atkins (Source No. 1). It is also identified in the Colorado Historical Society's "Isolated Find Record 5LR7054" (Source No. 2), which included a copy of the Trail Ridge Quad Map that showed the grave as being on the northeast side of the Ute Trail.

Grave No. 2 is about 300 feet northeast of the Ute Trail and 1,600 feet southeast of Grave No. 1. (See Photos B, C, and D below.)

We were unable to find Grave No. 2 on either of our two trips to Sundance Mountain in October 2000 and July 2001. However, on 1 August 2008, Larry Carpenter, Fred Henkin, and Fred's wife Sharon found it during a third grave-hunting trip to Sundance Mountain (Source Nos. 6 and 8) and provided the latitude and longitude information above. (See "Finding the Graves" below.)

When Larry, Fred, and Sharon used dowser rods at this location, two out of three of them got results indicating that there is a body burial "a few feet to the left of the cross in Photo C [below] looking towards Longs Peak" (Source Nos. 6 and 9). Consequently, we are assuming that it is indeed a grave and not just a memorial marker, as has been suggested.

Grave No. 3 (Grave of Unknown Adult No. 6)

Latitude 40° 23' 51" N, Longitude 105° 42' 58" W

This grave is officially "Unknown Adult No. 6 Grave" in the records of the Colorado Council of Genealogical Societies.

Grave No. 3 is about 150 feet northeast of the Ute Trail and 1,300 feet southeast of Grave No. 2. (See Photo E below.)

As noted under "Finding the Graves" below, on 22 July 2008, Larry Carpenter, Fred Henkin, and Sharon Henkin found Grave No. 3 during their first grave-hunting trip to Sundance Mountain to find Grave Nos. 1 and 2 (Source Nos. 4 and 8). They provided the latitude and longitude information above (Source No. 5). When the three of them used dowser rods at this location, all three of them got results indicating that there is a body burial at the location (Source No. 7).

See "Finding the Graves" below for details of our discovery of Grave No. 1 while trying to find Grave 2; Kris Holien's visit to Grave No. 2; our second unsuccessful attempt to find Grave No. 2; Larry Carpenter's, Fred Henkin's, and Sharon Henkin's finding Grave No. 3 while looking for but not finding Grave Nos. 1 and 2; and their eventual successful efforts to find Grave Nos. 1 and 2.

See "Who's Buried in the Sundance Graves?" below for our thoughts on that subject.

Sources of Information on the Sundance Mountain Graves

1. Copy of a black and white photograph of a wooden cross marking a possible grave (identified as Grave No. 2 in this chapter) on Sundance Mountain in Rocky Mountain National Park and

a portion of the USGS's Trail Ridge Quad Map on which the location of the cross was marked. These two items were given to us by Ferrel Atkins, a retired (and now sadly deceased) Rocky Mountain National Park Ranger and Naturalist, in late September 2000. (For more information on the all of the help that Ferrel provided to our efforts to find the graves and cemeteries in Rocky Mountain National Park, see his entry in the "Acknowledgments" section.)

2. Colorado Historical Society, Office of Archaeology & Historic Preservation, "Colorado Cultural Resource Survey, Isolated Find Record 5LR7054," Revised September 1998, which reports on a "heavily weathered wooden cross" (Grave No. 2) on Sundance Mountain in Rocky Mountain National Park.

   When we received this record from Jackie Johnson after 1 October 2000, it was accompanied by a) a map titled "Upper Trail Ridge Survey Area Site" and dated 1999 that shows the location of a number of "cultural resources" in the vicinity of Sundance Mountain and b) photocopies of two black and white photographs of the "heavily weathered wooden cross." The map is based on the applicable portion of the U.S. Geological Survey's Trail Ridge Quad Map. One of the photos shows a closeup of the wooden cross, and the other photo shows the cross with a mountain (which turned out to be Longs Peak) in the background.

   See the Appendix to this chapter for the information contained in *"Isolated Find Record 5LR7054."*

   (For more information on all of the help that Jackie Johnson provided to our grave-search efforts in Rocky Mountain National Park and the Estes Park area, see her entry in the "Acknowledgments" section.)

3. Photograph (Photo D below) of the "heavily weathered wooden cross" (Grave No. 2) on Sundance Mountain taken by Kris Holien, the daughter of Jackie Johnson, in late October 2000 and given to us in early December 2000.

4. Email from Larry Carpenter dated 23 July 2008 in which he reports on the 22 July 2008 effort of himself, Fred Henkin, and Fred's wife Sharon to find Grave Nos. 1 and 2 on Sundance Mountain. They were unable to find either of those graves on 22 July but found Grave No. 3 instead. (On that date, Larry had with him an early draft of this chapter describing our finding Grave No. 1 on Sundance Mountain during our unsuccessful effort to find Grave No. 2, the "heavily weathered wooden cross" described in Source No. 2 above.)

5. Email from Fred Henkin dated 21 October 2008 in which he provides the GPS reading and photographs of Grave No. 3 that he and his companions found on 22 July 2008.

6. Email from Fred Henkin dated 22 October 2008 in which he provides the GPS reading and photographs of Grave No. 2, which he and his companions found on their third visit to Sundance Mountain on 1 August 2008.

7. Second email from Fred Henkin dated 22 October 2008 in which he provides photographs of Grave No. 1, which he and his companions found on their third visit to Sundance Mountain on 1 August 2008.

8. Email from Fred Henkin dated 14 November 2008 in which he provides the names of the individuals who made the three grave-search trips to Sundance Mountain during the summer of 2008 and the dates of those three trips.

9. Email from Larry Carpenter dated 5 December 2008 in which he provides his and Fred Henkin's answers to questions to them that we had included with a 17 November 2008 draft of this chapter.

Description of Graves

Grave Nos. 1 and 2 are marked with several pieces of wood (logs) fastened together with nails. Grave No. 3 is marked with several log pieces inside of a pile of largish boulders.

LARIMER COUNTY CEMETERIES

The wood from which all of these logs are made could not have been found naturally in the vicinity of the graves but would have had to have been carried to the area.

Grave No. 1 (Grave of Unknown Adult No. 2)

When we found this grave on 1 October 2000, it was marked by two logs with nails in them. We noted that the two logs could have easily have been put together to make a cross. Under the logs was a bed of relatively flat stones that had been stood on their edges in a groove over the grave.

Photo A: Grave No. 1 on Sundance Mountain in Rocky Mountain National Park (Officially "Unknown Adult No. 2 Grave") (Photo taken by Duane Kniebes on 1 October 2000)

Grave No. 2 (Grave of Unknown Adult No. 7)

The logs marking this grave are nailed together to form a cross that is lying on top of a flat bed of stones. In the photo below, the logs appear to have been painted white, but they are actually just sun- and weather-bleached (Source No. 9).

Photo B: Closeup View of Grave No. 2 on Sundance Mountain in Rocky Mountain National Park (Officially "Unknown Adult No. 7 Grave") [Photo Taken by Fred Henkin on 1 August 2008 (Source No. 6) and Used With His Permission]

Photo B is virtually a duplicate of the closeup photo of Grave No. 2 included with Source No. 2.

Photo C: View of Grave No. 2 on Sundance Mountain in Rocky Mountain National Park With Longs Peak in the Background (Officially "Unknown Adult No. 7 Grave") [Photo Taken by Fred Henkin on 1 August 2008 (Source No. 6) and Used With His Permission]

Photo C is virtually a duplicate of the photo of Grave No. 2 with Longs Peak in the background included with Source No. 2. Since Longs Peak is in the background, Fred was looking toward the southeast when he took the photo.

Photo D: View of Grave No. 2 on Sundance Mountain in Rocky Mountain National Park With Northwestern Peak of Sundance Mountain in the Background (Officially "Unknown Adult No. 7 Grave") [Photo Taken by Kris Holien in Late October 2000 (Source No. 3) and Used With Her Permission]

LARIMER COUNTY CEMETERIES

Grave No. 3 (Grave of Unknown Adult No. 6)

This grave is marked by a pile of boulders with several log pieces inside the pile (Source No. 9).

Photo E: View of Grave No. 3 on Sundance Mountain in Rocky Mountain National Park With the Northeastern Peak of Sundance Mountain in the Background (Officially "Unknown Adult No. 6 Grave") [Photo Taken by Fred Henkin on 22 July 2008 (Source No. 5) and Used With His Permission]

Finding the Graves

In late September 2000, Ferrel Atkins, a retired Rocky Mountain National Park Ranger and Naturalist who collected information on the Park's history including its graves, gave us (Source No. 1) both 1) a black and white photocopy of a photograph of a possible grave on Sundance Mountain that was marked by a weathered log cross and 2) a copy of a portion of the Trail Ridge Quad Map that had been marked with an X to show the approximate location of the cross/grave, which we refer to as Grave No. 2 in this chapter.

Then, on 30 September 2000, Ferrel told us that he and several other retired Park Rangers were discussing the grave on Sundance Mountain marked by a log cross. Their thought was that it might have been put there as a memorial by the family of a young man who flew his government training plane into Sundance Mountain and died, probably sometime between 1948 and 1950.

However, when we mentioned this possibility to Fred Henkin in October 2008, he told us (Source No. 6) that "the plane crash that you are referring to was a few miles west of Sundance Mtn. It occurred on the north side of Trail Ridge Road between Iceberg Pass and the Tundra Curves."

But back to 2000: On 1 October 2000, we made a trip to Sundance Mountain in an effort to find the wooden cross marked by an X on the portion of the Trail Ridge Quad Map that Ferrel Atkins gave us (Source No. 1). Instead, we found the Grave No. 1 described above and shown in Photo A. During that trip, we did not find the grave (Grave No. 2) marked with an X on the Quad Map that Ferrel Atkins had given us.

On our next visit to the Park a little later in October 2000, Jackie Johnson of Estes Park gave us a copy of the Colorado Historical Society's *"Isolated Find Record 5LR7054"* describing and providing location information for what we are calling Grave No. 2 (Source No. 2). That record was accompanied by two black and white photocopies of photographs of the grave and a map showing the approximate location of the grave.

In late October 2000, Jackie Johnson's daughter, Kris Holien (who had earlier accompanied Jackie on a visit to Grave No. 2), returned to Sundance Mountain and found an intact cross (apparently Grave No. 2) at the location she and her mother had visited earlier. She took a photograph of the cross (Photo D above). In early December 2000, Jackie then sent us that photograph.

On 30 July 2001, we made a return trip to Sundance Mountain to try to find Grave No. 2 ourselves. We immediately went to the location indicated by the GPS reading provided by the X on the Trail Ridge Quad Maps given us by Ferrel Atkins and Jackie Johnson. We looked and looked, but we never found the cross shown in Photos B, C, and D above.

We had originally met Larry Carpenter when we made a presentation on our Larimer County grave-search efforts to the Estes Park Genealogical Society on 8 August 2001. (At that time, Larry was the secretary of that organization.) In addition to his interest in genealogy, Larry is interested in old plane wrecks in Colorado. In his email of 9 December 2008 (Source No. 9), he described his interest this way:

> "I consider myself an aviation archaeologist who delves into air crashes dating back to WWII, attempting to pinpoint these old crash sites before everyone who might remember them has passed on. I document the aircraft type, date of occurrence, names, ranks, and hometowns of the men and women involved. I have been responsible for the placement of memorial markers at three bomber crash sites and have participated in the placement of two others."

We next encountered Larry when we made a similar presentation at the Estes Park Area Historical Museum on 20 April 2007. At both meetings, we taught the attendees, including Larry, how to use dowser rods to determine whether possible grave sites contain actual burials.

At the April 2007 meeting, we mentioned that we had never been able to find the "heavily weathered wooden cross" (Grave No. 2) on Sundance Mountain during our two attempts and were no longer physically able to make yet a third attempt. Larry volunteered to try to find the cross for us, so we gave him the then-current draft of this chapter and a pair of dowser rods.

Thus, we were very pleased to learn from Larry's 23 July 2008 email that he, Fred Henkin, and Fred's wife Sharon had made an attempt to find the cross on Sundance Mountain on 22 July 2008 (Source No. 4). While they were not able to find either the cross (Grave No. 2) or the grave that we had found on 1 October 2000 while looking for the cross ourselves (Grave No. 1), they found a third grave (Grave No. 3) just north of the Ute Trail on Sundance Mountain, photographed it, obtained a GPS reading for it, and successfully used dowser rods to confirm that the rock-log formation they found actually marked a body burial.

From later email exchanges with Larry Carpenter and Fred Henkin (Source Nos. 5-8) on 21 and 22 October and on 14 November, we were further gratified to learn that, during a third trip to Sundance Mountain on 1 August 2008, they and Fred's wife Sharon had found, photographed, and obtained GPS readings for both Grave No. 1 and Grave No. 2 and had also used dowser rods to confirm body burials at those two locations. (On 26 July 2008, Larry, Larry's wife Vi, Fred, and Fred's wife Sharon had made a second, unsuccessful trip to Sundance Mountain to try and find Grave Nos. 1 and 2.)

LARIMER COUNTY CEMETERIES

Who's Buried in the Sundance Graves?

Native Americans?

We have found no historical records indicating that anyone was ever buried on Sundance Mountain. When considering who might be buried in the graves on Sundance Mountain, one of the first possibilities that comes to mind is that one or more of the graves might contain the burial of a Native American. While this remains a possibility, the Native American graves that we've found in Larimer and the part of Rocky Mountain National Park in Grand County were all covered with a mound of more or less fist-size rocks and certainly weren't marked with crosses or any kind of wooden marker.

The pieces of log associated with Grave No. 3 are included within the pile of rocks over the grave, so they may not have ever been configured as a cross. However, as noted immediately above, we have not encountered wood of any kind used to mark other Native American graves in Larimer and Grand Counties.

(For information on other possible Native American burials that we have documented in Larimer County and in the part of Rocky Mountain National Park that is in Grand County, see the "Native American Graves" section of the "Introduction.")

Trappers or Early Settlers?

The three graves could possibly contain the remains of trappers or other early settlers. There are surely a number of graves of trappers yet to be found and identified as such in Larimer County. The only grave in Larimer County that we have been able to positively identify as the grave of a trapper is the Cabin Creek Grave in the Rawah Wilderness in the Laramie River Valley. (See the Cabin Creek Grave chapter for details.)

We have been told of at least one other possible trapper's grave: On 10 November 2001 following a presentation on our grave-search efforts in Larimer County to the Fort Collins Pioneer Association, Chuck Peterson of Livermore told us about a grave on Cameron Pass that might be the grave of an early Poudre Canyon trapper named Robert Chambers.

Then, on 15 October 2003 at the dedication ceremony for "Cap" Williams's grave marker in Poudre Canyon, Charles Gates told us about the "Lone Pine Grave," which might well be the same grave. (See the chapter titled Charles E. Williams Grave for information on "Cap" Williams and his grave.) According to Charles Gates, the grave is under a solitary pine tree on a road about 4 miles from Chambers Lake near the Skyline Campground, which is in the lower left section of the Boston Peak Quad Map near Two and One Half Creek. We made numerous efforts to get Chuck or Charles to take us to the grave, but their busy schedules never allowed them to help us.

Pages 18 and 19 of *The Poudre: A Photographic History*, written by Stanley R. Case and self-published in 1995, provide the following information on the death of trapper Robert Chambers:

> "In 1858 Robert Chambers and his son set up a trappers camp near a lake in the upper reaches of the canyon [Poudre Canyon]. While Robert Jr. was away from the camp one day, Indians killed and mutilated his father. Nine years later when the Union Pacific Railroad was laying track west of Cheyenne, Wyoming, Robert [Jr.] told a tie contractor about the timber available on the upper Poudre. The contractor established a camp by the lake, and its workers there gave it the name 'Chambers' in honor of the trapper who had lost his life."

The above quote does not mention Robert Jr. burying Robert Sr., but he surely must have buried his father near their trappers camp.

More Contemporary Individual?

While all three of the graves on Sundance Mountain could contain the remains of a more contemporary individual, the "heavily weathered wooden cross" that marks what we have identified as Grave No. 2 in this chapter is the most likely candidate. The cross was first identified in 1999 during "Surveys of Rocky Mountain National Park" conducted by the University of Northern Colorado (Source No. 2, Appendix to chapter). Of course, the cross could easily have been there much longer than that!

However, compare the appearance of the cross in Photos B and C, which were both taken in August 2008, with its appearance in Photo D, which was taken in October 2000. Notice that while in Photo D the cross appears to be flush with its "small boulder support base," in Photos B and C it is lying on top of that base. It seems that some person or persons are caring for the cross and its grave, which would indicate that it is of a more modern origin.

LARIMER COUNTY CEMETERIES

Appendix: Information Concerning Grave No. 2 From the Colorado Historical Society's *"Isolated Find Record 5LR7054"*

The information in this record is part of the Colorado Historical Society's Colorado Cultural Resources Survey. This survey, which identifies the cross on Sundance Mountain that we are calling Grave No. 2, was conducted in 1999 by the University of Northern Colorado in Greeley and is recorded in its Report on 1999 *Surveys in Rocky Mountain National Park by the University of Northern Colorado*. This particular "Isolated Find" was recorded by Robert Brunswig on 22 November 1999.

The Colorado Historical Society's *"Isolated Find Record 5LR7054"* provides the following information:

Location Information:
- County: Larimer
- Legal Location: Prime Meridian, 6th; Township, 4N; Range, 74W [all of which agree with the GPS reading for Grave No. 2 provided above]
- USGS Quad Name: Trail Ridge Date: 1957

Archaeological Data:
- Artifacts: Heavily weathered wooden cross with small boulder support base
- Dimensions: 0.7 m X 0.5 m
- Inferred Function: Memorial Marker
- Cultural Affiliation/Time Period: Historic Euro-American, c. 1950-1960

Environmental Data:
- Elevation: 11,962 feet, 3,646 meters
- Soil: Inceptsol/Aridisol
- Topography: The site lies on a mountain top in alpine tundra.
- Slope: Site: 10°; Surroundings: Same
- Nearest Water: Name/Nature: Unnamed stream; Elevation: 11,781 feet; Distance: 823 meters; Direction: West
- Vegetation: Alpine willow, alpine bluegrass, alpine lily, wheat grass, sorrel, alpine daises

TUXEDO PARK CEMETERY

Location: Latitude 40° 20' 43" N, Longitude 105° 34' 52" W

The Tuxedo Park Cemetery is located in Rocky Mountain National Park about 8 feet east of a cabin that is now used as summer housing for Park Rangers and was once a private vacation cabin. The cabin is one of a number of similar cabins that are southeast of the Bear Lake Road. This particular cabin is at the end of the second dirt road that leaves Bear Lake Road going south after you cross the bridge over the Big Thompson River heading toward Bear Lake. The cabin and its cemetery are about 400 feet south of Bear Lake Road and about 150 feet north of Glacier Creek.

Even though this cemetery is in Rocky Mountain National Park, it is, as noted above, in the area of the Park where Park Rangers live. Thus, you should not enter the area without the permission of either the Park Ranger living in the cabin or some other Park official.

As will be important later, Tuxedo Park Cemetery is in the Southwest Quarter of the Northwest Quarter of Section 4 of Township 4 North, Range 73 West.

Description of Cemetery

This small cemetery contains three graves within a circle of local rocks. As noted above, the cemetery is surprisingly close to a cottage. Our use of dowser rods indicated that the cemetery contains three adult burials.

Photo A: Rock Ring Containing Three Adult Burials East of Ranger Cabin in Tuxedo Park in Rocky Mountain National Park

Finding the Cemetery

We were originally told about the possibility of graves in Tuxedo Park in Rocky Mountain National Park by Jackie Johnson. However, since Jackie could not provide any specific details and since Tuxedo Park covers such a large area, by August 2001, we had not made any effort to actually find the graves. (Unfortunately, Jackie died on 18 August 2001. For more information on Jackie, who was immensely helpful to us in our efforts to find and document remote graves in the Estes Park area and Rocky Mountain National Park, see the section for "Jacqueline Jaye Johnson" in the chapter on Rocky Mountain National Park Scattered Cremains.)

LARIMER COUNTY CEMETERIES

Then, without our ever having mentioned the possibility of graves in Tuxedo Park to them, in late August 2001 Ira Goldfarb and his then fiancée (now wife) Joan Feder, who were living in the cabin just 8 feet west of the cemetery, discovered it and emailed us to report their finding. Now, just how were they able to find the cemetery when the generations of Park Rangers who had lived in the cabin before them had not? Read on!

Earlier that summer on Monday, 2 July 2001, we visited the Aspenglen Campground in Rocky Mountain National Park to look for the grave associated with a headstone found in the area that Dr. D. Ferrel Atkins, at the time a volunteer ranger and the Park's de facto historian, had told us about. We immediately encountered Ira Golfarb, then a first-year ranger, making his morning rounds of the campers. (Sadly, Ferrel died on 16 September 2011. For more information on Ferrel and the considerable help he provided us during our search for graves and cemeteries in Rocky Mountain National Park, see "Atkins, D. Ferrel" in the "Acknowledgments" section.)

We explained our grave-search project to Ira. He began by helping us find what turned out to be two graves in the Aspenglen Campground. (See the chapater on the Aspenglen Campground Cemetery.) Then he and Joan Feder ended up providing considerable help with our efforts to locate, GPS-pinpoint, and photograph remote graves in the Park that are at too high of an altitude for us to visit. (For details on the assistance that Ira and Joan provided, see "Goldfarb, Ira and Joan Feder" in the "Acknowledgments" section.)

So that Ira and Joan could help us, we provided them with a hand-held GPS and a couple of pairs of dowser rods, both of which we taught them how to use. After having used the dowser rods on a couple of occasions while searching for graves for us, Ira and Joan got to thinking about the circle of rocks just east of their cabin and wondering if one or more graves might be associated with it. When they used their dowser rods to search the area of the circle, they found three burials within the rock ring.

They informed us of their find by email at the end of August 2001 while we were at our family cottage in Michigan. On our return, we visited Ira and Joan at their cabin and used our dowser rods to confirm their findings: three adult bodies buried inside the rock ring.

On 12 July 2002, we returned to the cottage with Jim and Pat Pickering. On that return trip, we were able to again use dowser rods to detect the presence of three adult burials, and Jim was able to use the rods we had given him to confirm our findings. (For more information on Jim Pickering and all of the help we received from him and his books on the history of the Rocky Mountain National Park area, see "Pickering, James H." in the "Acknowledgments" section.)

Sources of Information on the Area Containing the Tuxedo Park Cemetery

1. The 1900 U.S. Census for Aspen, Pitkin County, Colorado, enumerated on 1 June 1900, which contains information on William Walsh and his family.

2. The 1910 U.S. Census for Aspen, Pitkin County, Colorado, enumerated on 21 April 1910, which contains information on William Walsh and his family.

3. The 1920 U.S. Census for Aspen, Pitkin County, Colorado, enumerated on 20 February 1920, which contains information on William Walsh and his wife Kate.

4. *"This Blue Hollow,"* written by James H. Pickering and published in 1999. (See the "Bibliography" for a complete citation.) Chapter 3 of this very readable and information-packed book discusses the Earl of Dunraven's "Land Grabbing in Estes Park."

5. *The Larimer County, Colorado, 1885 State Census With Index,* transcribed and published by the Larimer County Genealogical Society in September 2000.

6. Email received from Truman Nicholas on 25 August 2001 in which he recalls having been told about burials "in the forest just beyond the new bridge leading out of Moraine Park on the way to Bear Lake."

7. Email received from Sybil Barnes on 24 August 2004 following a meeting she had recently had with Truman Nicholas about the burials "in the forest just beyond the new bridge leading out of Moraine Park on the way to Bear Lake." In this email, she states that she does think that the area Truman described is Tuxedo Park and that this was the general vicinity of some old tourist cabins known as the "Bowen/Woods cottages."

8. Emails received from Sybil Barnes on 17 and 18 January 2013 in which she reports that Albin Griffith homesteaded along Mill Creek, which isn't far from Tuxedo Park; that Albin's son John married Virginia Cleave; and that Virginia's parents John and Margaret Cleave were originally buried on Albin Griffith's Mill Creek homestead. (These graves were later moved to the Cleave-Griffith Family Cemetery. See that chapter for details.) The information that Sybil provided in these two emails and in Source No. 10 below comes from her notes of a "field trip" to these areas that she attended with Don Griffith and Jackie Johnson on 8 July 1999.

9. Online homestead property records of the Bureau of Land Management at www.glorecords.blm.gov as of 19 January 2013. These records contain details on the following land parcels that either include the Tuxedo Park Cemetery or are nearby and that were either homesteaded or purchased from the U.S. Government between 1876 and 1896:

   a. On 5 February 1876, William Tempest purchased three land parcels containing a total of 170.34 acres. Two of these parcels are in the Northeast Quarter of the Northwest Quarter and the contiguous Northwest Quarter of the Northwest Quarter of Section 4 of Township 4 North, Range 73 West. Interestingly, the BLM records say that the third land parcel that Tempest purchased was the North Half of the Northwest Quarter of the same Section 4. However, the North Half of the Northwest Quarter of Section 4 and the Northeast and Northwest Quarters of the Northwest Quarter Section 4 are legal descriptions for the same land.

   b. On 3 March 1876, James Thorne purchased three land parcels containing a total of 170.96 acres. Two of these parcels are in the Northeast Quarter of the Northeast Quarter and the contiguous Northwest Quarter of the Northeast Quarter of Section 4 of Township 4 North, Range 73 West. Interestingly, the BLM records say that the third land parcel that Thorne purchased was the North Half of the Northeast Quarter of the same Section 4. However, the North Half of the Northeast Quarter of Section 4 and the Northeast and Northwest Quarters of the Northeast Quarter Section 4 are legal descriptions for the same land.

   c. On 30 January 1885, William L. Walsh received land patents for 160 acres on the following two land parcels, which he had homesteaded: the South Half of the Northeast Quarter of Section 4 of Township 4 North, Range 73 West and the South Half of the Northwest Quarter of the same Section 4. **The Tuxedo Park Cemetery is in this latter land parcel, specifically in the Southwest Quarter of the Northwest Quarter of the same Section 4.**

   d. On 6 November 1896, Albin Griffith received a land patent for 160 acres on the following two land parcels, which he homesteaded: the North Half of the Southeast Quarter of Section 34 of Township 5 North, Range 73 West and the North Half of the Southwest Quarter of Section 35 of the same Township and Range. The first parcel is along Mill Creek, and both parcels are north of Gianttrack Mountain and a little more than a mile northeast of the Tuxedo Park Cemetery.

10. Email received from Sybil Barnes on 22 January 2013 to which was attached a map of the area around Tuxedo Park on which she labeled two possible locations of the Griffith family's home,

LARIMER COUNTY CEMETERIES

the location where John and Margaret Cleave were originally buried, and the location where the Griffiths skidded their lumber down from Birestadt Lake to what is now Bear Lake Road.

11. Email received from Jim Pickering on 30 January 2013 in which he provided his thoughts on William Tempest (Source No. 9a) and James Thorne (Source No. 9b) having purchased land from the U.S. Government both near the Tuxedo Park Cemetery and in the areas along Fish Creek, the Big Thompson River, and Fall River (pages 37-38 and 40 of Source No. 4) where the Earl of Dunraven was acquiring land for a cattle ranching operation.

History of Area Containing the Tuxedo Park Cemetery Including Possible Occupants of Its Graves

Folks Buried in the Forest

As arranged by Jackie Johnson, on 8 August 2001, we gave a presentation on our grave-search efforts in Rocky Mountain National Park and the Estes Park area to the Estes Park Genealogical Society. On August 25th, we received an email from Truman L. Nicholas (Source No. 6), a member of the Society, in which he said that he remembered being told about "folks being buried in the forest just beyond the new bridge leading out of Moraine Park on the way to Bear Lake in the Rocky Mountain National Park." This may have been close to the road that once lead into the Park commencing from the Dunraven Inn, on Colorado Highway 66, and entering the road on the way to Bear Lake just beyond the somewhat new bridge I mentioned above." (For information on the help that Truman gave us with our grave-search efforts in the Rocky Mountain National Park and Estes Park areas, see "Nicholas, Truman" in the "Acknowledgments" section.)

At that point, we had not heard from Ira Goldfarb and Joan Feder about the graves that they had found near their cabin in Tuxedo Park, but it did occur to us that the graves Truman was talking about could be the same graves that Jackie Johnson mentioned as possibly being in Tuxedo Park. Thus, we filed Truman's email in our "Tuxedo Park Graves" research folder.

In August 2004, Truman again contacted us on another subject. At that point, we asked him if he had ever figured out how he had learned about the graves "in the forest just beyond the new bridge leading out of Moraine Park." As of January 2013, he had not been able to determine how he heard about these graves.

Previously, in September 2001, we had contacted Ferrel Atkins to see if he could figure out who might have once owned the cabin near the Tuxedo Park Cemetery. On 1 October 2001, he emailed us back that the cabin was once owned by a school teacher from Michigan but that the graves could certainly pre-date the school teacher's ownership of the cabin.

On 24 August 2004, when Truman Nicholas and Sybil Barnes, then the Local History Librarian of the Estes Park Public Library, were discussing the Tuxedo Park Cemetery, they were able to use the Library's resources to determine that the cabin may be one of the cabins in the general vicinity of the "Bowen/Woods cottages" (Source No. 7). In her email about the cottages, Sybil also reported that she thought that the area that Truman was discussing in his 25 August 2001 email to us (Source No. 6) was indeed Tuxdeo Park. (For information on all of the help that Sybil provide with our grave-search efforts in Rocky Mountain National Park and the Estes Park area, see "Barnes, Sybil" in the "Acknowledgements" section.)

The Cleave and Griffith Families

That was all we knew about Tuxedo Park and its cemetery until January 2013 when we started doing some additional research in preparation for creating the final draft of this chapter. The first thing we did to contact Sybil Barnes and Truman Nicholas to see if they had ever discovered anything else about the graves in Tuxedo Park. As mentioned above, Truman did not have any additional information. However, Sybil recalled a field trip that occurred on 8 July 1999 when Don Griffith took her and Jackie Johnson to areas in and around Tuxedo Park associated with his Griffith and Cleave ancestors (Source Nos. 8 and 10). (For more information about Don Griffith and the Griffith and Cleave families, see the chapter on the Cleave-Griffith Family Cemetery.)

This opened the possibility that there might be some connections between the Griffith and Cleave families and the Tuxedo Park Cemetery. Combining the information from Source Nos. 8 and 10 with the Bureau of Land Management's homestead property records for Albin Griffith (Source No. 9d), this is what we know about the activities of the Griffith and Cleave families in the general vicinity of Tuxedo Park:

On 6 November 1896, Albin Griffith (the grandfather of Don Griffith) received a land patent on 160 acres north of Gianttrack Mountain, with Mill Creek flowing through some of it. This land was a little more than a mile northeast of the Tuxedo Park Cemetery (Source No. 9d).

Albin or other members of his family must have purchased additional land that most likely included what is now the Tuxedo Park Cemetery because Don Griffith showed Sybil Barnes and Jackie Johnson the following locations on 8 July 1999 (Source No. 10):

- The original Griffith family house was located *either* about 4/10th of a mile northeast of the Tuxedo Park Cemetery on the north side of Mill Creek *or* about 3/10th of a mile southeast of the Tuxedo Park Cemetery on the south side of Mill Creek.
- Allbin Griffith's son John married Virginia Cleave. Before their bodies were moved to the Cleave-Griffith Family Cemetery (now located on the property of Beaver Brook Resort in Estes Park on 1700 Colorado Highway 66, about 150 feet east of the highway), Virginia's parents John and Margaret Cleave were buried about ½ mile almost due west of the Tuxedo Park Cemetery on the north side of Bear Lake Road and about 1.1 miles from the Big Thompson Bridge in "a flat area up the hill and to the east" of "some chokecherry buses by the side of the road" (Source No. 8).

Don also told Sybil and Jackie that the Griffith family kept cattle in the meadows of Hollowell Park (about 1 and 3/10th miles slightly southwest of Tuxedo Park Cemetery) and kept fish ponds on Mill Creek.

Thus, it seems clear that the Griffith family owned at least some of the land in this area, certainly the areas on which their home was located and on which John and Margaret Cleave were originally buried. Consequently one cannot help but wonder if the graves in the Tuxedo Park Cemetery might contain the remains of members of these families. However, since the Griffith and Cleave families moved John and Margaret Cleave's remains from ½ mile west of the Tuxedo Park Cemetery to the Cleave-Griffith Family Cemetery, one would think if any additional members of the families died while the families were living in the vicinity of the Tuxedo Park Cemetery, their remains would have been moved as well.

In addition, as the "Sources of Information" in the chapter on the Cleave-Griffith Family Cemetery make clear, Don Griffith was an inveterate recorder of his family's history. So if any members of the Cleave or Griffith families were occupants of the Tuxedo Park Cemetery, Don would certainly have reported it. But he might not have recorded the burial of neighbors or employees.

Native Americans

Considering that the ring of rocks surrounding the graves in the Tuxedo Park Cemetery certainly resembles teepee rings that we have seen elsewhere in Larimer County (west of County Road 21), another possibility is that Native Americans might have buried deceased members of their tribe inside the teepee ring to keep the graves from being obvious. Travelers along western trails such as the Overland Trail frequently buried deceased members of their group under the trail itself with no markers to keep the Native Americans from finding and desecrating the graves and the remains they contained. It is certainly possible that the Native Americans themselves might have employed the same strategy in Tuxedo Park.

Homesteaders of Land Containing the Tuxedo Park Cemetery

Finally, we searched the online homestead property records of the Bureau of Land Management to find out if anyone had either homesteaded the area that includes the Tuxedo Park Cemetery or purchased land there from the U.S. Government. Source No. 9 reports that results of that search, which told us that a William L. Walsh (Source No. 9c) had homesteaded the 16th section containing the Tuxedo Park Cemetery (Southwest Quarter of the Northwest Quarter of Section 4, Township 4 North, Range 73 West) and the three 16th sections immediately east of the 16th section containing the cemetery and that he received the land patent on that land on 30 January 1885.

Thus, one might think that members of the William L. Walsh family could have been buried in the Tuxedo Park Cemetery. Given that Colorado conducted its own census in 1885 (Source No. 5), the first thing we did was to see if we could find a William Walsh listed in that census who was living in the general area of Estes Park. Unfortunately, the only Walshes reported as living in Larimer County in 1885 were single man named James Walsh working as a quarry man in the Masonville area and a Robert Walsh who was farming in the Fort Collins area and living with a wife and son. Both of these gentlemen were born in Ireland. Consequently, the census taker either missed William Walsh or he sold this land in and near Tuxedo Park shortly after he received the land patent on it on 30 January 1885 and was out of the area by the time the census taker arrived.

So the next thing we did was to see if we could find a William Walsh living anywhere else in Colorado in post-1885 U.S. Censuses. Sure enough, a William Walsh, who was born in Ireland in June 1854, and his family were living in Pitkin County, Colorado, in 1900 and 1910 (Source Nos. 1 and 2). By 1920, William and his wife Kate, who was born in Ireland about 1865, were still living in Pitkin County, but their children had moved on (Source No. 3).

As of 1 June 1900, this 45-year-old William Walsh was working as a town marshal in Aspen in Pitkin County and was living with his wife Kate, whom he had married in 1883 (Source No. 1). Living with William and Kate were nine children, all born in Colorado between 1885 and 1899. Kate reports that she was the mother of 10 children, of whom 9 were still living. Thus IF this is the same William Walsh who homesteaded land in Tuxedo Park containing the Tuxedo Park Cemetery, the child who died could have passed away while the family was homesteading the land in Tuxedo Park, which would have been between 1883, when the couple was married, and 1885, when they left that area for Pitkin County. However, all of the burials in the Tuxedo Park Cemetery were of adults, and this child would have been no older that 3.

As was also the case with the Cleave and Griffith families, it is certainly possible that neighbors of the William Walsh family or people who lived on that land before the Walsh Family or between the Walsh family and the Griffith family could have died and been buried in the Tuxedo Park Cemetery.

Two of the Land Filers Involved With the Earl of Dunraven's Land Grab

William Tempest and James Thorne, two men who bought land near the Tuxedo Park Cemetery from the U.S. Government in February and March 1876 (Source Nos. 9a and 9b), provide an interesting side light even though there is no reason to think that they or any members of their families are buried in the Tuxedo Park Cemetery. These two men each bought from the U.S. Government about 170 acres of land immediately north of the land that was later (1885) homesteaded by William L. Walsh.

Tempest and Thorne also appear in the table on pages 37 and 38 of Jim Pickering's *"This Blue Hollow"* (Source No. 4) that lists the original 31 individuals who bought land from the U.S. Government and then (secretly) sold it to Theodore Whyte in May 1874. Whyte was an agent for the Earl of Dunraven, who sought to establish a cattle ranch in prime areas near Estes Park but who couldn't buy U.S. Government land directly since he was a foreigner (page 36 of Source No. 4). The land that Dunraven acquired in 1874 was located primarily "on both sides of Fish Creek, in a strip as much as a mile wide along five miles of the Big Thompson, and something less than a mile up Fall River from its point of confluence" (page 40 of Source No. 4).

Thus, the land just north of Tuxedo Park that Tempest and Thorne bought in 1876 was not in the area of particular interest to Dunraven. In addition, Dunraven's land grab efforts were pretty much over by 1876. In his email to us on 30 January 2013 (Source No. 11), Pickering's provided his thoughts on why Tempest and Thorne bought the two 170-acre parcels in Tuxedo Park after having previously sold (indirectly) their first two 170-acres parcels to Dunraven in 1874:

> "Having made easy money by turning over their initial earlier claims, the two went back for more—filing on land that was available but which they had never seen. The fact that the Big Thompson runs next to Tuxedo Park and Mill Creek empties into it simply follows on the original pattern of claiming land along rivers and known springs. That would explain why they were there—perhaps expecting that Whyte and Dunraven would buy them out and not realizing that running cattle in Tuxedo Park [because it is so heavily forested] was not an option."

So Who's Buried in the Graves in Tuxedo Park Cemetery?

At this point, we do not know and may never know. A considerable number of lumbering and sawmill operations took place in this area. (See the chapter on the Cleave-Griffith Family Cemetery for information on those families' lumbering activities in what is now Rocky Mountain National Park.) Perhaps those inherently dangerous activities might account for one or more of the burials in the Tuxedo Park Cemetery?

UNKNOWN ADULT GRAVES

Since all of the graves of unknown adults do not have their own chapters, below is a list of those graves accompanied by information on the chapters in which those unknown adult graves are discussed:

Unknown Adult No. 1 Grave: This chapter is in Volume I; the grave is on private property belonging to Grant D. McWilliams on Bull Mountain east of the Laramie River Valley.

Unknown Adult No. 2 Grave: See the chapter in Volume III on the Sundance Mountain Graves in Rocky Mountain National Park.

Unknown Adult No. 3 Grave: This chapter is in Volume I; the grave is on private property belonging to Donn G. And Shirley A. Decoursey at 180 Rams Horn Mountain Court in the Glacier View Meadows subdivision west of Livermore.

Unknown Adult No. 4 Grave: This chapter is in Volume I; the grave is on the part of the Roberts Ranch on the east side of U.S. 287 north of Livermore.

Unknown Adult No. 5 Grave: This chapter is in Volume I; the grave is just east of the former Poudre Canyon School.

Unknown Adult No. 6 Grave: See the chapter in Volume III on the Sundance Mountain Graves in Rocky Mountain National Park.

Unknown Adult No. 7 Grave: See the chapter in Volume III on the Sundance Mountain Graves in Rocky Mountain National Park.

Unknown Adult No. 8 Grave: This chapter is in Volume II; the grave is on private property belonging to Teri Jurgens Lefever and George Lefever about 1/3 mile northeast of the point at which Buckhorn Creek enters the Big Thompson River.

UNKNOWN CHILD GRAVES

Since all of the graves of unknown children do not have their own chapters, below is a list of those graves accompanied by information on the chapters in which those unknown child graves are discussed:

Unknown Child No. 1 Grave: This chapter is in Volume I; the grave is on private property belonging to the Abbey of Saint Walburga across U.S. Highway 287 from the old "town" of Virginia Dale.

Unknown Child No. 2 Grave: This chapter is in Volume I; the grave is on the private ranch belonging to the Wahl family on the west side of U.S. Highway 287 right before the rock cut at Owl Canyon.

Unknown Child No. 3 Grave: This chapter is in Volume III; the grave is on the north side of what is now a private road running west from the current Dunraven Inn but what was originally the south entrance road to Rocky Mountain National Park.

Unknown Child No. 4 Grave: See chapter in Volume III on the Horseshoe Park Graves in Rocky Mountain National Park.

Unknown Child No. 5 Grave: See chapter in Volume III on the Horseshoe Park Graves in Rocky Mountain National Park.

Unknown Child No. 6 Grave: This chapter is in Volume I; the grave is in the Roosevelt National Forest on Seven Mile Creek Road about 3 miles west of that road's intersection with Pingree Hill Road.

LARIMER COUNTY CEMETERIES

UNKNOWN CHILD NO. 3 GRAVE

Location: Latitude 40° 21' 01" N, Longitude 105° 34' 17" W

The Unknown Child No. 3 Grave is located on private property belonging to Dunraven Ltd. of Denver. The property is north of the Big Thompson River in Estes Park and west and a little north of the Dunraven Inn (2470 Colorado Highway 66, Estes Park) on the north side of an unnamed (as far as we could determine) private and gated road that passes Swiftcurrent Lodge (2512 Colorado Highway 66) before running northwest toward Rocky Mountain National Park. As will be important later, former Rocky Mountain National Park Ranger-Naturalist Ferrel Atkins told us that about 1930 this road lead to a south entrance to the Park. (For more information about Ferrel and all of the help that he provided with our grave-search efforts in and near Rocky Mountain National Park, see the "Acknowledgments.")

The grave itself was on the north side of this unnamed road immediately across that road from the west end of a log cabin that used to be the "original RMNP checking station" according to a letter dated 25 October 2001 that we received from Sybil Barnes, at the time the Local History Librarian of the Estes Park Public Library. (For more information about Sybil and all of the help that she provided with our grave-search efforts in and near Rocky Mountain National Park, see the "Acknowledgments.")

As of our 13 April 2002 visit to the grave, this "checking station," which had been converted into a home, was being rented by Pat Washburn, at the time a priest at St. Bartholomew's Episcopal Church in Estes Park. [For more information on Pat, see the chapter on the Mills and Kiley Grave and Scattered Cremains and the "Enoch Josiah ('Joe') Mills" section of the chapter on Rocky Mountain National Park Scattered Cremains. Joe Mills was Pat's grandfather.]

Description of Grave

The grave is at the base of a medium-sized pine tree and is covered with a number of almost head-sized rounded granite rocks that had probably come from the banks of the nearby Big Thompson River. Even though this grave was immediately across the road from Pat Washburn's home, she had never noticed it because it was blocked from her view by a number of small trees and a big granite boulder.

Our use of dowser rods confirmed that a child is buried in this grave.

Photo A: Unknown Child No. 3 Grave Northwest of the Dunraven Inn and Swiftcurrent Lodge and on the North Side of the Big Thompson River in Estes Park

UNKNOWN CHILD NO. 3

Finding the Grave

We were told about this grave by a lady attending the 9 March 2002 presentation on "Guest Lodges in Rocky Mountain National Park" that had been organized by Sybil Barnes. This lady, whose name we sadly forgot to record, told us that there was a "well-marked child's grave" north of the Big Thompson and west of the Dunraven Inn and that, as far as she could tell, none of the rocks marking the grave contained any inscriptions. The lady had noticed the grave when the teacher of an art class in which she participated took the students to the area near the grave because it contained so many potential subjects.

On 13 April 2002, Dell Babbitt and his wife Sharon Olson Babbitt, whom we had met earlier because of our mutual interest in graves in the Horseshoe Park area of Rocky Mountain National Park, accompanied us on our successful attempt to find the child's grave that the art student had told us about. It was Dell who first spotted the grave. All of us were able to use dowser rods to confirm a child's burial at the location. (For more information on the Babbitts and their research on the family of Willard Ashton and on Horseshoe Park, see "Finding the Graves in Horseshoe Park" and Source No. 21 in "Sources of Information on the Horseshoe Inn and the Willard Ashton Family" in the chapter on the Horseshoe Park Graves.)

History of Area Around the Grave of Unknown Child No. 3

We have not been able to learn the identify of this child. We have just two pieces of information that might provide a clue:

First of all, when we visited with Pat Washburn on 13 April 2002, she told us that the property on which the log house in which she was living "had been owned by the Grant family since the 1890s." Thinking that the same Grant family might still own the stone house and the nearby grave, in February 2013 when we were preparing this chapter for publication, we used the Larimer County Assessor's Office land ownership database at www.larimer.org/assessor to try to find the then-current owner of that property. At that point we were not able to determine the current owners of the property, but we did find all of the property in Estes Park owned by anyone with the last name of "Grant"; none of that property was located anywhere near the Dunraven Inn and the north side of the Big Thompson River just west of the Inn. When we tried the Assessor's Office database again on 27 February 2014, we learned that the property belonged to Dunraven Ltd. of Denver as of at least that date.

Secondly, when we were doing research on who had homesteaded or purchased land near Tuxedo Park in Rocky Mountain National Park, we learned that on 3 March 1876 James Thorne purchased land from the U.S. Government that included the land containing the Unknown Child No. 3 Grave. (See Source No. 9b in the chapter on the Tuxedo Park Cemetery.) However, James Thorne was one of 31 individuals who participated in the Earl of Dunraven's "land grab" in the Estes Park area and who evidently almost immediately sold their land to Dunraven through an agent without sticking around the area; when a few years later the U.S. Marshall "attempted to serve them with summonses for perjury. . . the men were not to be found" (pages 37-39 of Jim Pickering's *This Blue Hollow*; see the "Bibliography" for a complete citation). Apparently, none of them actually lived on the property they acquired from the U.S. Government under false pretenses. (For more information on this subject, see "Two of the Land Filers Involved With the Earl of Dunraven's Land Grab" in the chapter on the Tuxedo Park Cemetery.)

Consequently, the parents of the child buried in the Unknown Child No. 3 Grave probably lived on or near that land after the late 1870s and might even have been visitors to the Rocky Mountain National Park area before or after it became a park. (For information on graves of other children whose parents might have been visitors to the same area, see the chapters on the Bob Ozmen Grave and the Herbert Richards Grave, both of which are in the general vicinity of the Unknown Child No. 3 Grave.)

CARL WILBUR WEAVER GRAVE

Location: Latitude 40° 21' 45" N, Longitude 105° 32' 40" W

The ashes of Carl Wilbur ("Webb") Weaver are buried on private property about 50 yards west of the home of his wife, Jean Weaver, on the west side of Mary's Lake Road at 1021 Mary's Lake Road in Estes Park. Jean buried Webb's ashes in front of a clump of willow bushes 10-15 yards north of a pool on the north bank of the Big Thompson River where Webb frequently caught fish in the evening after returning home from work.

Description of Grave

As of January 2001, Webb's grave did not have a marker. It can be located by its GPS reading and the location information above.

Photo A: Location of Ash Burial of Webb Weaver on North Bank of Big Thompson River and West of Mary's Lake Road

Finding the Grave

We learned about this grave from Webb Weaver's wife, Jean, when we contacted her at the suggestion of her friends Bob and Teddie Haines. Bob and Teddie thought Jean would be able to get us contact information for Bill Robinson, a wrangler at the former Fall River Lodge in Horseshoe Park in Rocky Mountain National Park, which indeed she could. (For more information on Bob Haines, a former Rocky Mountain National Park Ranger and his wife Teddie, see "Haines, Robert" in the "Acknowledgments." For more information on Bill Robertson, see "Finding the Graves in Horseshoe Park" in the chapter on the Horseshoe Park Graves.)

When Jean learned that we were researching graves and cemeteries in Larimer County, she asked us if we wanted to include the ash burial of her husband Webb Weaver on her property in Estes Park. So on 15 January 2001 we visited Jean and recorded the above information on Webb's burial location.

Biographical Information on Carl Wilbur ("Webb") Weaver

The following information on Webb Weaver comes from his wife, Jean, and from his obituary in the *Estes Park Trail-Gazette* newspaper (date of obituary not recorded).

Carl Wilbur Weaver had been known as "Webb" ever since he was a child, and it was by that name that his family members and his friends in Estes Park knew him. He was born on

19 September 1915 in Shobonier, Illinois. He died unexpectedly at his home on Mary's Lake Road on 4 April 1971.

Webb moved to Estes Park from California 25 years before his death. While there, he met his wife, Jean, who had relocated to Estes Park from New Jersey.

From 1958 until his death, Webb worked as a mechanic with the Estes Park Power and Light Department. He loved the outdoors and was an avid sportsman, hunter, and, as noted above, fisherman. He was a member of the Estes Park Gun and Archery Club, and, about 2 months before his death, he became a member of the Estes Park Lions Club.

His wife, Jean, shared Webb's love of the outdoors. She is one of the "charter members" of the informal Thursday Hiking Club (so named because practically the only day they don't go on hikes is Thursday). She and other members of the Thursday Hiking Club including former Rocky Mountain National Park Ranger Bob Haines were the ones who discovered the empty metal can that had once contained the cremains of Chuck Collins, the father of folk singer Judy Collins. (See the entry for "Chuck Collins" in the chapter on Rocky Mountain National Park Scattered Cremains.)

HARRIS P. WELLCOME GRAVE

Location: Latitude 40° 20′ 03″ N, Longitude 105° 33′ 41″ W

The grave of Civil War veteran Harris P. Wellcome is on private property belonging to William G. Dietrich/the Gale Revocable Trust. To reach the grave site, take Colorado Highway 66 south out of Estes Park past the entrance to the YMCA (on west side of Highway 66) to Tunnel Road, which leaves Highway 66 running southeast. (As of our last visit on 17 September 2000, there was NOT a street sign marking Tunnel Road.) Take Tunnel Road 0.2 of a mile past several older wooden buildings on the northeast side of the road. Right after these buildings, there is a private road running north. The grave is northeast of the intersection of Tunnel Road and this private road. You can see the back of the Dietrichs' natural wood house on the hill above and about 200 feet beyond the grave.

Description of Grave

The grave is marked by a native-rock headstone and footstone, neither of which is inscribed. What looks like a large squaw bush was growing on the grave when we last visited it on 17 September 2000.

Photo A: Grave of Harris P. Wellcome Near Tunnel Road South of Estes Park

Finding the Grave

Jackie Johnson of Estes Park told us about Harris Wellcome's grave and put us in touch with Elaine A. Hostmark, also of Estes Park. Elaine was a friend of the William G. Dietrich family and talked to a member of the family to get permission for us to visit the grave.

To the great loss of many interested in the history of Estes Park and Rocky Mountain National Park, Jackie died on 18 August 2001. Her ashes were scattered in the Park. (For more information on Jackie and all of the valuable assistance she gave us in our grave-search efforts, see the section for "Jacqueline Jaye Johnson" in the chapter on Rocky Mountain National Park Scattered Cremains.)

Sadly, Elaine Hostmark (8 May 1913-1 July 2008) also passed away (Source No. 7 below) after helping us get permission to access the Harris P. Wellcome Grave, which she, author

Duane Kniebes, and Jackie Johnson visited together on 16 August 2000. We visited a second time on 17 September 2000 so author Susan Briles Kniebes could see Wellcome's grave.

Sources of Information on Harris P. Wellcome and His Grave

1. Information on Harris P. Wellcome's Civil War Service from the Record and Pension Division of the U.S. War Department, dated 5 October 1891. Debbie Pierson of Larimer County Veterans Services provided us with these records in April 2004.

2. Article containing information on Civil War Veteran "H.P. Welcome [sic]," *Estes Park Trail*, 3 June 1921, page 1. Jackie Johnson gave us this article.

3. Oral Interview of Dan Griffith by Ferrel Atkins conducted on 6 August 1966 as part of the Rocky Mountain National Park Oral History Project. The tape and its transcription of this interview are available in the Local History Section of the Estes Park Public Library.

4. *The Griffith Family in Estes Park;* Museum Talk presented by Don Griffith on 20 January 1977 at the Estes Park Area Historical Museum. The tape and its transcription of this interview, which were made as part of the Estes Park Oral History Project, are available in the Local History Section of the Estes Park Public Library. Jackie Johnson told us about the information on Harris P. Wellcome on pages 9-10 of the transcription of this talk.

5. "Memoirs of the Twenties in Estes Park," written by Elaine Hostmark, *Museum Pieces*, Vol. 13, No. 4, Fall 1993, page 3, published by the Estes Park Area Historical Museum. Jackie Johnson gave us this article.

6. Online homestead property records of the Bureau of Land Management at www.glorecords.blm.gov as of 8 April 2004. These records provide a legal description of the 160 acres on which Harris P. Wellcome's grave is now located and for which he received a land patent on 26 May 1905.

7. *Social Security Death Index* as of 3 March 2013 as transcribed by Ancestry.com.

Biographical Information of Harris P. Wellcome

As noted immediately above, Jackie Johnson provided us with copies of several publications containing biographical information on Harris P. Wellcome and the location of his grave (Source Nos. 2, 4, and 5). Interestingly enough, one of the articles Jackie gave us (Source No. 5) was written by Elaine A. Hostmark.

The first article that Jackie gave us (Source No. 2) reports that Harris Wellcome was a Civil War veteran:

> "Mrs. J. E. Macdonald this year decorated the grave on Memorial Day of Estes Park's only soldier of the Civil War, H. P. Welcome [sic], who was one of the early settlers in the Park and owner of the ranch now owned by Mrs. Springer and who died about 11 years ago and was buried on the place owned by him."

Note that in this article, Harris Wellcome's middle initial is correctly given as *P* but that his last name is incorrectly spelled "Welcome."

The second article we received from Jackie contained Elaine Hostmark's reminiscences of "The Springer Place" (Source No. 5) and provides some additional information about Wellcome:

> "Mrs. Ida Springer's place at the foot of the hill was homesteaded by a relative, Harris B. Wellcome. He died about 1910 and his body is buried on the property. My memory says he was an army colonel, but I find no corroboration of this. Likewise, we always say Mrs. Springer but her obituary in the *Estes Park Trail* in 1956 calls her Miss Ida Springer. [As noted below, Wellcome's records from the U.S. War Department (Source No. 1) indicate that

he actually died on 4 February 1911 and that he was a sergeant in the Union Army during the Civil War.]

"The property was called Wellcome Lodge. So many people stopped to tell Mrs. Springer that the name was misspelled that she changed it on the sign. One could see where the two l's were painted out and one l inserted. Mrs. Springer was a Christian Scientist and held church in her living room each summer Sunday. This property had in the twenties and still has some of the most beautiful silver spruce trees in the Park. Tradition has it that the reason the trees were so beautiful was that Mrs. Springer sat in their shade and read Mary Baker Eddy to them. An autochrome photo of them by Fred Clatworthy appeared in a 1928 issue of the *National Geographic Magazine*."

Note that this article incorrectly gives Harris Wellcome's middle initial as *B* and but correctly spells his last name as "Wellcome."

The third article provided by Jackie was a presentation by Don Griffith on *The Griffith Family of Estes Park* (Source No. 4) and carries the history of the Wellcome/Springer property one more generation toward the present:

"The first place they [the Griffith family] set up this mill was on what used to be the Springer property. As you go up Tunnel Road to where the rock cut is, there's a road that takes off to your left through a big grove of blue spruce—that's the Springer property. It's on Wind River and that's where their [the Griffith family's] first mill site was.

"The property at that time where they had the mill belonged to Harris Wellcome, who Dad [Dan Griffith] said is buried somewhere up there."

Note that the transcriber of Don's presentation correctly gives Harris's last name as "Wellcome." (For more information on the Griffith family and their lumber operations, see the chapter on the Cleave-Griffith Family Cemetery.)

We next encountered an oral interview of Dan Griffith, the father of the Don Griffith quoted above (Source No. 3), conducted by Ferrel Atkins on 6 August 1966 as part of the Rocky Mountain National Park oral history project.

Pages 9 and 10 of the transcription of this interview provide the following exchange concerning Harris Wellcome:

Question from Ferrel: "We got some pictures in the file that show your old sawmill up at Bierstadt Lake. Was that the first sawmill that you had in this part of the country?"

Dan Griffith's Answer: "Yes, I think it was. We had a—we sawed on a little setting up on Harris Welcome's. That was up on Wind River, and then we moved it up there [to Bierstadt Lake]."

Note that the transcriber of Ferrel's interview of Dan gives Harris's last name as "Welcome."

We were resigned that this was all we would learn on Harris Wellcome, but we were wrong. In August 2003 we saw an article in the *Denver Post* about Debbie Pierson, an assistant at the Larimer County Veterans Services office in Fort Collins. The subject of the article was Debbie's effort, much of which was done on her own time, to ensure that all veterans' graves in Larimer County receive an applicable military marker. Thus, we felt that Debbie would want to know about Harris Wellcome's grave and the remote graves of other veterans that we had found. Consequently, on 31 August 2003, we met with Debbie in her office in Fort Collins to explain our grave-search efforts and provide her with information on remote graves of veterans, both marked and unmarked, that we had found during our grave-search efforts.

When Debbie learned about Harris P. Wellcome's grave in Estes Park and the belief of Estes Park residents that he was a veteran of the Civil War, she contacted the U.S. Department of Veterans Affairs to find out if he was really Civil War veteran. If he was, she could request a marker for his grave, assuming that William G. Dietrich, the owner of the property on which Wellcome's grave is located, would allow such a marker to be placed on Wellcome's grave.

In early April 2004, Debbie called us to let us know that she had received proof from the Department of Veterans Affairs that Harris P. Wellcome was indeed a Civil War Veteran: He served as a sergeant in Company B of the 41st Wisconsin Infantry in the Union Army from 1 May 1864 through 10 September 1864. Debbie then sent us all of the information on Harris that the Department of Veterans Affairs had sent her. The data that could be gleaned from that information (Source No. 1) follow:

- Wellcome's middle initial is indeed *P*, not *B*.
- He was born on 24 May 1843 in Freeman Township, Franklin County, Maine, and died on 4 February 1911 in Estes Park, Larimer County, Colorado.
- At the time that Wellcome entered the Union Army, the Army's records say that he was 23 years old, was 5 feet 9 inches tall, and had a light complexion, gray eyes, and light hair.
- Before he enlisted in the Union Army, Wellcome had lived first in Maine and then in Wisconsin, where he was a farmer. At the time of his enlistment, Wellcome was living in Markesan, Wisconsin.
- He was discharged from the Union Army at Milwaukee, Wisconsin.
- Following his discharge in September 1864, he lived in Wisconsin until 1868, when he moved to Kansas.
- In 1868 in Kansas, Wellcome married Elizabeth Ann Corning. They were married by a Reverend Simpson. He and Elizabeth never had any children.
- They lived in Kansas until 1891, when they moved to California because of Elizabeth's poor health.
- Following Elizabeth's death, Wellcome moved to Estes Park, where he took up a homestead.
- In 1905, when he was 62, Harris applied for a pension for his Civil War service, listing as the reason: "He is now unable to earn a support by manual labor by reason of disability due to age."
- He then received a pension of $12 a month until his death on 4 February 1911.

Since the above information indicates that Wellcome homesteaded land in the Estes Park area, we searched the online homestead property records of the the Bureau of Land Management's General Land Office (Source No. 6) to try to find the exact legal description of his homestead. The BLM website shows that on 26 May 1905 Harris P. Wellcome received a land patent for the following 160 acres:

LARIMER COUNTY CEMETERIES

Aliquot Parts:	West Half of the Southwest Quarter
	North Half of the Northwest Quarter
Section:	3
Township:	4N
Range :	73W
Meridian:	6th PM
State:	Colorado
County:	Larimer

This means that Harris P. Wellcome's grave is, as one would expect, on land that was part of his original 160-acre homestead.

The information that Debbie Pierson sent us in April 2004 included a form to be completed to request a headstone for Harris's grave from the U.S. Department of Veterans Affairs. On 8 April 2004, Elaine Hostmark graciously agreed to contact William G. Dietrich, the owner of the land on which Harris is buried, to ask for his permission to obtain and erect a headstone on Harris's grave. Unfortunately Elaine's health deteriorated so, on 8 February 2005 we sent William Dietrich a letter requesting permission to obtain a headstone for Harris's grave and install it there. We never received a response.

CLEMENT YORE HEADSTONE

Location: Latitude 40° 22' 05" N, Longitude 105° 33' 39" W

Clement Yore's headstone is under a pine tree on private property in the front yard of Dave Schutz at 710 Tanager Road in Estes Park.

Photo A: Headstone of Clement Yore in Front Yard of 710 Tanager Road in Estes Park

Headstone Inscription

The marble headstone appears to be a standard U.S. Military issue headstone of the time to which Clem's years of birth and death and "A man so loved will not be forgotten" were added.

CLEMENT YORE

COLO
1 WASH. INF.
SP. AM. WAR

1875-1936

A MAN
SO LOVED
WILL NOT BE
FORGOTTEN

Finding the Headstone

We started looking for Clement Yore's "grave" because that is how it was listed in the 1985 edition of the Colorado Council of Genealogical Societies' *Colorado Cemetery Directory*, which provided the following information: "Location: Southwest of Estes Park, in yard of his [*sic*] home (NE1/4 Sec. 35, T5N, R73W, 6th P.M.); Type: Single grave; and History: d. 1936."

Armed with this information, in the fall of 1999 we talked to one of the Rangers on duty at Rocky Mountain National Park's Beaver Meadows Visitor Center. The Ranger referred us to Dave Schutz. We called Dave and made an appointment to meet his at his home, with the results reported below.

History of Yore Headstone

When we visited Dave Schutz and Clem Yore's headstone during the fall of 1999, Dave described for us the following set of events that lead to Clem's headstone being in the front yard of Dave and Cheryl Schutz's home in Estes Park:

1. Clem died on 24 October 1936. He had requested that he be cremated and his ashes be scattered near the studio of Dave Stirling, who was Dave Schutz's maternal grandfather. At that time, Stirling's studio was outside Rocky Mountain National Park. The land on which the studio was located later became part of the Park and was just inside what is now the Fall River Road entrance to the Park. (Since Clem's ashes were eventually scattered in the Park, this fact is briefly mentioned in the "Clement Yore" section of the chapter on Rocky Mountain National Park Scattered Cremains.)

2. When Clem died, there were no nearby cremation facilities. So he was buried in his own front yard with the headstone that is now in the Schutzs' front yard.

3. Clem and his headstone were later moved to a Loveland cemetery.

4. When local cremation facilities became available in the 1940s, Clem's widow Alberta McCauley Yore had Clem's body exhumed and cremated. Mrs. Yore then came to Dave Stirling's studio and scattered Clem's ashes on the path leading to the studio as per Clem's wishes. When she left after scattering Clem's ashes, she also left Clem's headstone with Dave Stirling with the comment, "You have Clem now, so you might as well have the stone."

5. In the 1960s, Dave Schutz noticed Clem's headstone behind the studio/house of his grandfather Dave Stirling. That was when Dave and Cheryl Schutz learned the story of Clem from his grandfather and when Dave Schutz and a friend then moved the headstone to the yard in front of Dave Stirling's studio/house where Dave Schutz and his family were then living.

6. After Dave Stirling's death in June 1971, the art studio and property reverted to the National Park Service. In the fall of 1972, Dave and Cheryl Schutz moved to 710 Tanager Road in Estes Park and took Clem's headstone with them and placed it in their front yard, where it remains to this day.

However, right after Dave and his family moved to Tanager Road, Dave offered Clem's headstone to the Estes Park Area Historical Museum. The ladies in charge didn't want a headstone around them, so they turned down Dave's offer. Since then the Museum has asked for the headstone, but, Dave told us, "They will have to wait till I'm gone to get it now."

Biography of Clement Yore

Details of Clem's biography below come from the handwritten copy of the obituary given at Clem's memorial service by Dave Stirling and from pages 96-98 of Volume I of Harold Dunning's *Over Hill and Vale*. (See the "Bibliography" for a complete citation.) Page 96 of Volume I of *Over Hill and Vale* contains a photo of Clem Yore as a Deputy Sheriff of Larimer County. (Dave Schutz gave us a copy of the handwritten obituary and eulogy that Dave Stirling gave at Clem's funeral, which was held on Wednesday, 28 October 1936 in Estes Park.

Those copies are available in our research files in the Local History Archives of the Fort Collins Museum of Discovery.)

Clem was born in St. Louis, Missouri, on 6 May 1875 to James H. and Virginia Yore, "a pioneer family" according to Dave Stirling. Clem attended public school in St. Louis and in Rock Island and Canton, Illinois, and the Augusta Military Academy in Fort Defiance, Virginia. His formal education ended when he received a Bachelor of Laws Degree from Washington University Law School in St. Louis in 1896. Although he passed the Bar, he practiced law for only 1 year.

His headstone tells us that Clem was a member of the Colorado contingent of the 1st Washington Infantry during the Spanish-American War, which took place between 1898 and 1899.

He was a reporter for newspapers in Seattle, San Francisco, New York, Boston, and St. Louis before serving as the city editor of the *Chicago American* for 7 years (according to Dunning) or 12 years (according to Stirling).

After Clem married Alberta McCauley Plondke in St. Louis on 3 June 1915, he and Alberta moved to Estes Park, where Clem wrote more than 600 stories and 300 poems, most with a western theme or location, which were published in leading magazines. He also wrote and published two novels and two books of poetry, some of his books being published in four languages. His poem *Colorado* became the official poem of the State of Colorado. (See page 97 of Volume I of *Over Hill and Vale* for the text of this poem.)

Clem's professional memberships include serving as President of the Colorado Author's League, an Honorable Life Member of the Chicago Press Club, and a member of the Denver Press Club, the Author's League of America, and the League of Western Writers. Outside of his profession, Clem was a member of the Masonic Lodge, the Sons of the Revolution, and the Christian Science Church.

Following the second of two heart attacks in the same week, Clem died on 24 October 1936. In addition to his wife, Clem was survived by one daughter, Juanita Yore Farris of Santa Monica, California; three brothers, J. Hanley Yore of St. Louis, Norris W. Yore of Clayton, Missouri, and Frank Yore of Chicago; two sisters, Byrd Ann Yore and Barbara Yore of Clayton, Missouri; and one 96-year-old aunt, Nancy Caroline Hanley of St. Louis.

LARIMER COUNTY CEMETERIES

GRAVES AND CEMETERIES NOT FOUND

In spite of our best efforts, we were not able to find 43 burial sites (in some cases *possible* burial sites) in Larimer County that we learned about during the 14 years (1999-2013) we were searching for and documenting burial sites there. This chapter includes the eight burial sites not found in the areas covered by this volume (Volume III) of this book (Estes Park and its surrounding area and the Rocky Mountain National Park, including the part of it in Grand County). These sites are listed in alphabetical order by the last name of the person or persons buried therein when that name is known or by the location of the burial site when the person's name or persons' names are not known. We have provided information on how we learned about these burial sites, where they are reported to be located, and what we were able to learn about them in the hope that, in the future, individuals researching Larimer County history will be able to find and document at least some of these burial sites.

Additional information about some these sites is available in our research folders in the Local History Archives of the Fort Collins Museum of Discovery.

Burial Sites on Private Land

While most of the eight burial sites discussed below are in Rocky Mountain National Park, a couple are on private property. Those searching for such sites in the future should not enter private property without first getting the permission of the current owners of that property. To determine the name and contact information for current property owners, consult the Larimer County Assessor's Office land ownership database at http://www.larimer.org/assessor.

Memorial to Pilots Who Died Fighting the Big Elk Fire

How We Learned About This Memorial/Its Location

Our neighbor Paul Albright told us about an article by Mary Bulter in the 20 July 2003 issue of the *Boulder Daily Camera* about a memorial being erected on that date that was dedicated to the three pilots who had died fighting the Big Elk Fire, which burned 4,413 acres in northwest Boulder County and southeast Larimer County during the summer of 2002. Slurry bomber pilots Rick Schwartz and Milt Stollak died when their plane (a PB4Y-2 Privateer) lost its left wing and crashed when they were delivering a load of fire retardant. Gordon Knight died 12 days later when the helicopter he was piloting crashed when he was dumping water on hot spots in the then largely extinguished Big Elk Fire.

The memorial, donated and carved by Paul Frysig, the owner of Western Stone in Lyons, was placed in front of the Big Elk Meadows fire station.

Efforts to Visit This Memorial

Since the Big Elk Meadows fire station is in the gated community of Big Elk Meadows, we needed permission to enter the community to visit the memorial. The memorial's website said that those wishing to visit the memorial should contact Michael Tipton, an officer of the Big Elk Meadows Fire Department. On 10 July 2005, we sent Tipton an email explaining why we wanted to visit the memorial and asking for permission to do so. (We were also personally interested in visiting the memorial since Chris Kniebes, the brother of author Duane Kniebes, is a slurry bomber pilot.) Tipton never got back to us.

Grave on Deer Ridge Junction Trail in Rocky Mountain National Park

How We Learned About This Grave/Its Location

On 5 October 2001, Ferrel Atkins, a former Ranger-Naturalist at Rocky Mountain National Park and, as of that date, a volunteer ranger, sent us an email saying that while he was about his duties in the Park, he met a young woman from Denver who told him the following:

"She found a flat tombstone, level with the ground, which was south and east of Deer Ridge Junction (below the road [U.S. 36 east of its junction with U.S. 34, Trail Ridge Road]). It was 3 or 4 years ago that she saw it and could not be more specific. . . . It had only a first name, no family name but had the year of birth/death. She passed it by thinking it was probably just a pet since there was no family name."

(For more information about Ferrel Atkins, see the "Acknowledgments" section.)

Deer Mountain is between Beaver Meadows on its south and Horseshoe Park on its northwest.

Efforts to Find This Grave

Later that October, we hiked the part of the Deer Ridge Junction Trail described in Ferrel's email but were not able to find the tombstone/grave.

Large Rock Cross in Hidden Valley in Rocky Mountain National Park

How We Learned About This Rock Cross/Its Location

In 2000 Jackie Johnson of Estes Park told us about a large rock cross that might mark a body or ash burial. The cross is above the beaver ponds in Hidden Valley not far from Trail Ridge Road (U.S. 34) in Rocky Mountain National Park. (For more information on Jackie, see "Johnson, Jacqueline Jaye" in the "Acknowledgments" section.)

Efforts to Find This Cross

We made at least one attempt to find this cross on our own. When we were not able to find it, we were going to talk to Jackie again to see if she could take us there. However, before we could contact Jackie, we learned that she had died (on 18 August 2001).

Indian Burial Ground North of Glen Haven

How We Learned About This Indian Burial Ground/Its Location

On 9 October 2004, we received an email from Truman Nicholas telling us that "a friend with a Bobcat" had told him about a possible Indian burial ground north of Glen Haven. (For more information on Truman and the other graves he helped us find, see the "Acknowledgments" section.)

Efforts to Find This Burial Ground

Truman wrote the owners of the property to get permission to visit the area with us. However, the owners said that they wouldn't be comfortable with our visiting the property until they became permanent residents there in 2006. Neither we nor Truman ever contacted the owners again.

Grave of Mount Olympus Climber

How We Learned About This Grave/Its Location

On page 179 of his *History of Larimer County*, Ansel Watrous reports the following in a discussion of early deaths in the Estes Park area:

"Later [after the 1871 death of Charles Miller] a climber of Mount Olympus accidentally shot and killed himself. He was buried on the south side of the Thompson, just below the mouth of Fall river."

(For a complete citation of Watrous's book, see the "Bibliography")

Efforts to Find This Grave

On 3 April 2001, we followed Watrous's directions above and looked for this gentleman's grave in Estes Park. Because of the construction of both roads and buildings in the area and the extensive reconstruction in that area following the 1976 Estes Park flood, a number areas where the climber could have been buried were not places we could look. The few places we could use dowser rods did not yield any results. Our conclusion was that the grave is probably either under or behind 120 East Riverside. (In April 2001, a used book store named "Fine Old Books" was at that address.)

Possible Grave Under Rock Cairn and Cross on Sprague Pass in Rocky Mountain National Park

How We Learned About This Possible Grave

Bob Haines, a retired Rocky Mountain National Park Ranger, told us about a large beehive-shaped cairn of rocks with a wooden cross on top of it on Sprague Pass that he thought might be a grave. (For more information about Bob, see the "Acknowledgments" section.) Bob had heard that the cairn might mark the burial of an "old miner." He also wondered if it might have been built by workers building the Eureka Ditch during "their spare time."

Photo A: The Rock Cairn on Sprague Pass (Courtesy of Bob Haines)

Its Location

Bob Haines told us that you should be able to see the cairn against the sky if you looked west from Moraine Park with a good pair of binoculars toward the pass (the V between Gabletop Mountain and Sprague Mountain).

Efforts to Find This Cairn/Grave

Rocky Mountain National Park Rangers Ira Goldfarb and Joan Feder were going to climb to Spraque Pass and use dowser rods to see if there was a burial under the cairn. However, they never had a chance to do this. (For information on the significant help that Ira and Joan provided to our efforts to locate other graves in Rocky Mountain National Park, see "Goldfarb, Ira and Joan Feder" in the "Acknowledgments" section.)

Disappearance of H. F. Targett Near Chasm Lake on Longs Peak

How We Learned About Targett's Disappearance/Where He Disappeared

We first learned about H. F. Targett's disappearance from somewhere near Chasm Lake at the foot of Longs Peak on 21 June 1921 from page 323 of Volume III of Harold Dunning's *Over Hill and Vale*. (See the "Bibliography" for a complete citation.) Targett was from Los Angeles.

Efforts to Learn More About Targett and His Disappearance

While we were doing research for this book, we kept our eyes open for additional information about Targett and whether his remains were ever found. While reading Jim Pickering's *The Ways of the Mountains* to learn more about the deaths and burials of J. P.

Chitwood, Louis Levings, and Reverend Thornton Sampson in Rocky Mountain National Park, we encountered the following in Note 9 on page 102 of that book:

> "[H. F.] Targett, of Los Angeles, on September 21, 1921, told Emerson Lynn, manager of Longs Peak Inn, that he was going to hike to Chasm Lake, and never returned. Nineteen years later, a skull, presumably belonging to Targett, was found near Peacock Pool, below Chasm Lake."

We have never been able to learn the final disposition of Targett's skull.

(For more information on Jim Pickering and the help that he and his books have been during our search for and research on graves in the Rocky Mountain National Park area, see "Pickering, James H." in the "Acknowledgments" section. See the "Bibliography" for a complete citation for *The Ways of the Mountains*.)

Memorial to Roger Wolcott Toll on Trail Ridge Road in Rocky Mountain National Park

How We Learned About This Memorial

We learned about this memorial to Roger Wolcott Toll (1883-1936), the third superintendent of Rocky Mountain National Park (1921-1929), from page 460 of Volume III of Harold Dunning's *Over Hill and Vale*. We later encountered a fairly detailed telling of Toll's time as Park Superintendent on pages 158-170 of C. W. Buchholtz's *Rocky Mountain National Park: A History*. (See the "Bibliography" for complete citations for both books.)

Its Location

The memorial to Roger Toll is located at the end of a 0.5-mile paved path from Trail Ridge Road (U.S. 34) to an elevation of 12,310 feet on Sundance Mountain. The trailhead for this path is on the north side of Trail Ridge Road, with the associated parking area being about 13 miles west of Deer Ridge Junction between the Forest Canyon Overlook and the Alpine Visitor Center.

Efforts to Visit This Memorial

We saw this memorial several times during our two visits to the Sundance Mountain in October 2000 and July 2001 to find the graves there. (See the chapter on the Sundance Mountain Graves.) However, after each of these trips we were so tired following prolonged hiking about 11,000 feet that we just didn't have the energy to climb to the Roger Toll Memorial to get its GPS reading and take a photograph.

ACKNOWLEDGMENTS

The most rewarding aspects of the 14 years we spent conducting the research that resulted in this book were meeting and spending time with Larimer County residents who both helped us find the graves, cemeteries, and memorials discussed in this book and provided us with a great deal of the information on the history of the folks buried in or memorialized at those sites, their families, and their property. A number of those individuals have become highly valued friends.

Below we have provided information on the individuals who have been especially helpful to our efforts to both find and document as many of the graves, cemeteries, and memorials in Larimer County as possible. The many, many other individuals who helped us with specific sites are discussed in the chapters on those sites.

Atkins, D. Ferrel: Dr. D. Ferrel Atkins was born on 15 February 1924 in Clark County, Illinois. Between 1952 and 1958, Ferrel was an Assistant Professor, Associate Professor, and Department Chairman at the University of Richmond in Virginia. From 1958 through his retirement in 1988, he was a Professor of Mathematics and Computer Sciences at Eastern Illinois University. During the summers between 1952 and 1984, he was a Ranger-Naturalist at Rocky Mountain National Park. Then, between 1986 and 2009, he was a volunteer ranger and the "de facto historian of Rocky Mountain National Park." (See page iv of Ferrel's Foreword to *My Pioneer Life: The Memoirs of Abner E. Sprague*. See the "Bibliography" for a complete citation.)

Ferrel was so well thought of by his contemporaries that he was one of the four individuals to whom C. W. Buchholtz dedicated his 1983 *Rocky Mountain National Park: A History*. (See the "Bibliography" for a complete citation.)

In his capacity as the Park's historian, Ferrel researched and created a list of "historical structures" in the Park, which included burials, memorials, and cremain scatterings. For details on the burial and memorial sites of which Ferrel made us aware, see the following chapters: Aspenglen Campground Cemetery (3-year-old child with the initials of "F.A.J."), J. P. Chitwood Grave, Carrie Cassedy Fuller Grave, Bruce William Gerling Memorial, Horseshoe Park Graves (child of Willard H. Ashton and his second wife Cora Bush Ashton and other graves), Hupp Family Cemetery, Louis R. Levings Grave, Herbert Richards Grave, Reverend Thornton R. Sampson Grave, and the Unknown Child No. 3 Grave.

Ferrel's list also included information on the cremain scatterings of the following individuals: Chuck Collins (father of folk singer Judy Collins), Enos A. Mills, Joe Mills, and Jack Woods. (See the chapter titled Rocky Mountain National Park Scattered Cremains for information on all of the cremains scattered in the Park of which we are aware.)

Sadly, Ferrel died in Mattoon, Illinois, on 16 September 2011.

Barnes, Sybil: Sybil was an immense help to us with a number of graves and cemeteries in Rocky Mountain National Park and the Estes Park area, both with finding them and by providing information about them. For details on the graves and cemeteries with which Sybil provided assistance, see the following chapters: Alpenglen Campground Cemetery, Bootyroyd-Hutchinson Cemetery, Edwin Bradt Grave, J. P. Chitwood Grave, Cleave-Griffith Family Cemetery, Elkhorn Lodge Cemetery, F.H.R. Cemetery, Herbert Richards Grave, Horseshoe Park Cemetery, Mary Jane James Grave, Bob Ozmen Grave, Cemetery of the Episcopal Church of St. Bartholomew the Apostle, Tuxedo Park Cemetery, and Unknown Child No. 3 Grave.

Sybil was the Local History Librarian at the Estes Park Public Library between 1994 and 2008 and was a part-time librarian at the Rocky Mountain National Park Library between 1993

ACKNOWLEDGMENTS

and 2012. She is also the author of *Images of America, Estes Park,* which was published in 2010. (See the "Bibliography" for a complete citation.)

In April 2014 Sybil took time to meet with us in Estes Park to provide us with advice on this book's index, title, and other issues concerning its publication.

Brinkhoff, Mike: When we met with Mike at his home west of the Manhattan Cemetery in April 2000 and later at the Manhattan Cemetery on 14 May 2000, he provided information about a number of graves and cemeteries in the Poudre Canyon and areas north of Poudre Canyon, including the Manhattan Cemetery, the Campbell Cemetery, the grave of Kitty Lyon, the grave of Unknown Child No. 6, the crater/"burial site" of the men transporting dynamite to the west portal of the "Larimie-Poudre Diversion Tunnel following an explosion," graves at Eggers, a grave or graves on Old Baldy near the "last Yockey sawmill,", and two possible Native American burial sites. We found the first four of these burial sites but not the last four.

For more information on Mike and his family, see the chapter on the Manhattan Cemetery, especially the sections titled "Description of Cemetery and Its Grave Markers," "History of Manhattan Cemetery," and "More on the Brinkhoff Family." For more information on the graves we did not find, see "Graves at Eggers," "Grave(s) in Vicinity of 'Last Yockey Sawmill' on Middle Bald Mountain ('Old Baldy')," and "Indian Burials Reported by Mike Brinkhoff" in the Graves and Cemeteries Not Found chapter. Since we did not get a GPS reading for the crater/"burial site," it is also included in the Graves and Cemeteries Not Found chapter; see "Crater/'Burial Site' at West Portal to the Laramie-Poudre Diversion Tunnel."

Brinks, Rose L.: Rose is the author of the *History of the Bingham Hill Cemetery,* which gives the history of the cemetery itself and of those buried there and their families. (See the "Bibliography" for a complete citation.) See the chapter on the Bingham Hill Cemetery for information about Bingham Hill that Rose provided to us in addition to that found in her very interesting and well-researched book. Rose also told us about two modern but remote family cemeteries of which she was aware: the Bania Family Cemetery and the Reu Family Cemetery.

Carpenter, Larry E.: Larry was the Secretary of the Estes Park Genealogical Society when we first met him on 8 August 2001 while making a presentation to that group on our grave-search efforts in Larimer County. Since then he has helped us locate the plaque that had originally marked the grave of Carrie Cassedy Fuller and—with the help of his friends Fred and Sharon Henkin of Westerville, Ohio—find three graves on Sundance Mountain in Rocky Mountain National Park. Then, in August 2009—with the help of Detective Rick Life of the Estes Park Police and Rick's father Richard Life of Fort Collins—he found the long-elusive grave of J. P. Chitwood on Flattop Mountain in the Park.

Carpenter, Philip ("Phil") J.: Phil Carpenter was Superintendent of Cemeteries for Fort Collins from at least the time we started our Larimer County grave research in 1999 until his retirement in March 2010. Indeed, we took him out to lunch to celebrate his retirement. Phil and his staff, especially Alyce Nierman, his Administrative Aide, were particularly helpful to us during the period before Fort Collins put the records for its cemeteries online, when they answered our numerous questions concerning whether or not particular individuals were buried in Grandview Cemetery or Roselawn Cemetery. (See "Online Records of Fort Collins's Grandview and Roselawn Cemeteries" in the "Bibliography.")

Damschroder, Cecilia ("Ceil"): Ceil was the President of the Larimer County Genealogical Society when we first started our research that resulted in this book. In addition to providing specific help during our research on graves and cemeteries in southern Fort Collins, Ceil gave us a list of remote Larimer County graves and cemeteries originally

LARIMER COUNTY CEMETERIES

created by Arlene Davis. (For more information on this list, see "Davis, Arlene" in the "Bibliography.) We learned about many of the graves and cemeteries that we found in Larimer County because they were on this list. For details on the graves and cemeteries with which Ceil provided specific assistance, see the chapters on the Bardwell Family Cemetery, Harmony Cemetery, and Williamson Cemeteries Nos. 1 and 2.

Danhauer, Sharon: Sharon was very helpful with our research on graves and cemeteries in the Loveland area, especially the Langston Family Cemetery, the Medina Family Cemetery, and Unknown Adult No. 8 Grave near the mouth of Buckhorn Creek. Sharon is one of the most active members of the Loveland Historical Society, especially the subcommittee working to preserve and restore the Medina Family Cemetery. She offers her service as a tour guide for places of historical interest in the Loveland area, using either a step-on bus or the client's own car. She also has several slide-show programs she can present and is fully equipped to do oral history interview and tape transcriptions.

Last but most certainly not least, Sharon proofread this book for us. However, any remaining errors are our responsibility, not hers.

Figgs, Daylan: Daylan is the Land Manager of Fort Collins's Natural Areas. In May 2005 and May 2006, he took us to Fort Collin's 18,728-acre Soapstone Prairie Natural Area, which is 25 miles directly north of Fort Collins, about 5 miles west of I-25, and immediately south of the Colorado-Wyoming border. The purpose of the trip was to see if we could find any burial sites at any of the numerous old ranches and homesteads in the area. We did find one burial: See the chapter on the Guy Place Child's Grave.

In July 2005, Daylan also took us to the graves of two children of the Hyatt family located on the east-central edge of the 2,606-acre Bobcat Ridge Natural Area, which in the southwest quarter of Section 15 and just southwest of Masonville at the head of Buffum Canyon. See the chapter on the Hyatt Family Cemetery.

Goldfarb, Ira and Joan Feder: In 2001, Rocky Mountain National Park Rangers Ira Goldfarb and his wife Joan Feder Goldfarb (his fiancée at the time) were immensely helpful to us in our search for graves and memorials in parts of the Park that were at heights beyond our ability to reach. For details on the sites with which they provided help, see the following chapters: Aspenglen Campground Cemetery, J. P. Chitwood Grave, Carrie Cassedy Fuller Grave, Bruce William Gerling Memorial, Louis R. Levings Grave, and Lulu City Graves.

Ira and Joan also found three graves next to the cabin in Tuxedo Park that they were living in during the summer of 2001, graves that we had been told existed but that we had made not attempt to find because Tuxedo Park is such a large area. For more information on these graves, see the chapter on the Tuxedo Park Cemetery.

Gubbins, John: John is very familiar with the Grand County (west) side of Rocky Mountain National Park because his family is the in-holder of a summer home there that is surrounded by the Park. Consequently, he is quite knowledgeable about the historical features in the area, including graves and cemeteries. On 14 September 2001 he told us about the graves at Lulu City and took us to the Grand Lake Cemetery, the Gaskill Cemetery, and the location where the ashes of George Frederick Dick III were scattered on his family's Trail River Ranch—all on the west side of the Park. In turn, we taught John how to use dowser rods.

In May 2005 John later told us about the ashes of John G. Holzwarth II being scattered near Never Summer Ranch, also on the west side of the Park. For more information on all of the help that John provided, see the chapters on the Gaskill Cemetery, Grand Lake Cemetery, and Lulu City Graves, and the sections on George Frederick Dick III and Betty Dick and on

ACKNOWLEDGMENTS

John G. Holzwarth II in the chapter on Rocky Mountain National Park Scattered Cremains.

Haines, Robert ("Bob"): Bob was a retired Rocky Mountain National Park Ranger who helped us with our research on a number of burial sites in Rocky Mountain National Park and the Estes Park area. Unfortunately, Bob died in Estes Park on 12 May 2008. For additional information on Bob Haines and Bob's wife Teddie, see the entry for "William Walter Haines" (Bob's brother) in the chapter on Rocky Mountain National Park Scattered Cremains.

For details on the graves, cemeteries, and cremain scatterings in Rocky Mountain National Park and Estes Park with which Bob provided help, see the following chapters: Gaskill Cemetery, Grand Lake Cemetery, Lillian Georgina Fearnly Haines Cremains, Louis R. Levings Grave, Lulu City Graves, and Reverend Thornton R. Sampson Grave. Also see the entries for Chuck Collins and William Walter Haines in the chapter on the Rocky Mountain National Park Scattered Cremains.

Johnson, Jacqueline ("Jackie") Jaye: Jackie was extremely helpful to us in our efforts to find and document graves in Rocky Mountain National Park and the Estes Park area. Indeed, she was helping us right up to her death on 18 August 2001. For more information on Jackie, see the section for "Jacqueline Jaye Johnson" in the chapter on Rocky Mountain National Park Scattered Cremains.

Kestrel, Steve: Steve Kestrel is a sculptor who works in stone, among other media, to produce exquisite animal sculptures, which are displayed in a number of galleries and museums around the county. He was chosen the 1997 Gilcrease Rendezvous sculptor and is a frequent contributor to the Coor's Western Art Exhibit at Denver's annual National Western Stock Show. His familiarity with rock and stone turned out to be especially useful when he went with us to find the "Baby Brown Grave" and when we ended up finding the Lory State Park Cemetery instead. (See the chapter on the Lory State Park Graves for information on both the Lory State Park Cemetery and the grave of Baby Brown, which we eventually did find.)

The grave of Nicholas Patterson is on the property that Steve and his wife Cindi own in the Redstone Canyon area. Indeed, we first met them while we were looking for that grave. Steve also helped us find the Bardwell Family Cemetery, which is also in the Redstone Canyon area, and told us where to find the Boyd Family Cemetery. (See the chapters on the Bardwell Family Cemetery, the Boyd Family Cemetery, and the Nicholas Patterson Grave.)

Meirath, Bill: Bill is the Chairman of the Subcommittee of the Loveland Historical Society working to preserve and restore the Mariano Medina Family Cemetery. Indeed, it is through Bill's considerable efforts that the Loveland community became aware of the abandoned and destroyed Medina Family Cemetery and succeeded in preserving it. Bill accompanied us on our original or follow-up visits to the following graves or cemeteries and/or helped us with our research on their history: Chance Family Cemetery, Clark Family Cemetery (which Bill told us about in the first place), Edward Lennis Hurd Grave (which Bill also told us about in the first place), Langston Family Cemetery, Little Thompson Crossing Grave, Alfred E. Mathews Grave, Medina Family Cemetery, Charles D. Miller Grave, H.L.W. Peterson Grave and "Mexican Joe" Grave in the Lakeside Cemetery, Unknown Adult No. 8 Grave, and the Virginia Dale Stage Station Cemetery.

Miller, Lafi and Juliana Jo: Lafi and his wife Juliana Jo Sloan Miller and Lafi's book *Those Crazy Pioneers* were an immense help to us in our efforts to find and document remote graves and cemeteries in the Red Feather Lakes, Prairie Divide, and Livermore areas. Lafi's *Those Crazy Pioneers*, self-published in 2001, provides a great deal of very interesting historical information about several sections of northern Larimer County, including especially

LARIMER COUNTY CEMETERIES

Livermore, Red Feather Lakes, and the Elkhorn district, with special emphasis on Lady Moon's escapades. The weekend of 13 July 2001 Lafi and Jo invited us to spend the weekend with them at their second home near Red Feather Lakes so they could take us to a number of the nearby graves and cemeteries. Over several grave-finding expeditions, the Millers took us to: the original site of the grave of Marietta Smith (now in Grandview Cemetery), the Jewett Family Cemetery, the Pickens' Point Memorials on Pingree Hill, the Robinson Ranch Cemetery, the Jessie N. Swan Grave, the Swanson Memorial Garden at the Chapel in the Pines at Red Feather Lakes, the Trail's End Ranch Cemetery, and the Levi Yockey Grave. They also provided us with information on the Black Mountain Ranch Cemetery.

Sadly, Lafi died on 8 February 2014, and Jo died on 7 September 2014, both dying in Fort Collins at the age of 97. Following their deaths, their ashes were interred in front of the memorial wall at the Swanson Memorial Garden at the Chapel in the Pines near Red Feather Lakes. (See the chapter on the Swanson Memorial Garden.)

Lafi was born on 2 September 1916 in Herford, Texas. His family moved to Fort Collins in 1920. Jo was born on 28 October 1916 in Fort Collins. She was raised on her family's cattle ranch 40 miles northwest of Fort Collins on Prairie Divide. In 1938 Lafi and Juliana Jo Sloan were married. The following year Lafi enrolled at Colorado A&M, now Colorado State University. Their son, John Dennis, was born between Lafi's sophmore and junior years. Seven days after he graduated in 1943, Lafi joined the U.S. Army. He trained with the Army's 10th Mountain Division in Camp Hale, Colorado, and was then assigned to the Army's first Rocket Field Artillery Battalion, with which he served in the Philippines, leaving the service after World War II with the rank of captain.

Lafi and Jo's daughter, René Lee, was born in 1947. Lafi had a number of interesting jobs, but he and Jo are probably best known for the Miller Manor Dance Studio, which they owned and operated between 1950 and 1985.

Nicholas, Truman: We first met Truman and his wife Beverly on 1 August 2001 when we made a presentation on our grave search efforts in Rocky Mountain National Park and the Estes Park area. For details on the help Truman provided and the graves and cemeteries he told us about and took us to, see the following chapters: F.H.R. Cemetery, Bob Ozmen Grave, and the Tuxedo Park Cemetery.

Pickering, James H.: Jim Pickering, now retired, was a professor of English at Michigan State University (where he served as Director of the Honors College) and at the University of Houston (where he served as dean, provost, and president). In 2006 he was named the Historian Laureate of the Town of Estes Park. He is the author-editor of 25 books on the history of the Estes Park area, including: *"This Blue Hollow": Estes Park, The Early Years, 1859-1915*, published in 1999; *Mr. Stanley of Estes Park*, published in 2000; and *America's Switzerland; Estes Park and Rocky Mountain Park: A History, 1903-1945*, published in 2006; *In the Vale of Elkanah: The Tahosa Valley World of Charles Edwin Hewes*, published in 2003; and *The Ways of the Mountains: Thornton Sampson, Agnes Vaille and Other Tragedies in High Places*, published in 2003. (For complete citations for the first and last two of these books, which we have used as research sources for several chapters in this book, see the "Bibliography.")

Jim and his books have been very helpful to us during our research on the following chapters: J. P. Chitwood Grave, Cleave-Griffith Family Cemetery, Elkhorn Lodge Cemetery, Joel Estes Memorial, Louis R. Levings Grave, Julia Ann Morrissey Grave, the section on Charles and Agnes Levings in Rocky Mountain National Park Scattered Cremains, and Reverend Thornton R. Sampson Grave.

ACKNOWLEDGMENTS

Roberts, Catherine: We first met Catherine and her husband Evan when we visited the Lamb Family Cemetery on a Sunday in 2000. Catherine was an immense help to us in our efforts to find and then research the history of a number of graves and cemeteries in the Livermore area. See the following chapters for details on the assistance that Catherine provided: Cherokee Stage Station Cemetery (which is on the Roberts Ranch north of Livermore), Alfred Arthur Fisk Grave, Elliott Ranch Cemetery, Livermore Cemetery, Robert O. and Mary E. Roberts Memorial, and Unknown Adult No. 4 Grave (which is also on the Roberts Ranch). Sadly, Evan passed away on 23 August 2002 and is buried in Grandview Cemetery.

Thiem, Jon: We first met Jon on 27 September 2003 when he gave a presentation to the Livermore Woman's Club on his research on John and Ida Elliott and Josephine Lamb for his then soon-to-be-published book *Rabbit Creek Country*. Catherine Roberts had kindly invited us to attend the presentation. (See the "Bibliography" for a complete citation for *Rabbit Creek Country*, which was published in 2008.) On 11 October 2006 Jon and his hiking buddy John Lee accompanied author Susan Kniebes to Lory State Park, where they successfully found the grave of "Baby Brown." (See the chapter on the Lory State Park Graves for details on this successful hike.) Both Jon's input and the contents of his *Rabbit Creek Country* helped us with our research on the Elliott Ranch Cemetery, John Shipman Grave, Livermore Cemetery, and Grandview Cemetery, especially the section titled "History of the Grave of Eugene Patrick Lamb." Finally, in the spring of 2014, Jon provided greatly appreciated advice concerning the appropriate contents of this book's Preface and Introduction.

Vannorsdel, Richard: We first met Dick over the Memorial Day weekend in 2000. At that point, he was the Laramie River District Maintenance Supervisor for the Larimer County Road & Bridge Department, and we were making our first visit to the Laramie River Valley to find, GPS pinpoint, and research graves there. During that visit, Dick told us about and took us to visit the burial of a son of David Usher on Pine Creek Ranch and told us about the memorial cairn for Ray Baugher on the Diamond Tail Ranch.

When we returned to the Laramie River Valley in August 2000 to visit Ray's memorial and several other graves in the valley, Dick told us about and arranged for us to visit the Wangnild Family Cemetery. Between those two visits, Dick also provided us with information on the members of the Vannorsdel family buried in the Vannorsdel Family Cemetery in Stove Prairie and in the Rhodes Family Cemetery in Masonville.

Following Dick's retirement in September 2004, Dick and his wife Carol moved to property they own on the Old Flowers Road south of Sky Corral Guest Ranch and northwest of the Vannorsdel Family Cemetery on the Colard Ranch. When they die, Dick and Carol plan to have their ashes scattered or buried on that property and have a memorial marker placed there.

For more information on the help Dick provided, see the following chapters: Ray Baugher Memorial, Rhodes Family Cemetery, Usher Child Grave, Vannorsdel Family Cemetery, and Wangnild Family Cemetery.

BIBLIOGRAPHY

Books, Pamphlets, and Other Paper-Based Publications

Ahlbrandt, Arlene and Stieben, Kate, Editors, *The History of Larimer County, Colorado, Volume II*. Compiled by the Larimer County Heritage Writers. Dallas: Curtis Media Corporation, 1987. For Volume I of this series, see Morris, Andrew J., below.

Ball, Clara, Editor, *Loveland-Big Thompson Valley, 1877-1977 Centennial*. Loveland, Colorado: Loveland-Big Thompson Valley Centennial Commission, Inc., 1975.

Barnes, Sybil, *Images of America, Estes Park*. Charleston, South Carolina: Arcadia Publishing, 2010.

Black III, Robert C., *Island in the Rockies: History of Grand County*. Boulder, Colorado: Pruett Publishing Company for the Grand County Pioneer's Society, 1969.

While we did not consult this book ourselves, it was highly recommended by John Gubbins as a resource for those researching the history of Grand County, Colorado, where the west side of Rocky Mountain National Park is located. (For more information on John Gubbins, see the "Acknowledgments" section.)

Bliss, Elyse Deffke, *Apples of the Mummy's Eye: The Dickerson Sisters*, Revised and Expanded 2nd Edition. Self-published. Boulder Colorado: Johnson Printing (printer), 1999.

Elyse Bliss wrote this book based on interviews with Alice Dickerson, one of the Dickerson sisters. Helen was the other sister. (For more information on the Dickerson sisters, see the chapter on the Dickerson Sisters' Memorial.)

Brinks, Rose L., *History of the Bingham Hill Cemetery, Laporte and Bellvue, Colorado*. Self-published. Fort Collins, Colorado: Citizens Printing (printer), May 1988, April 1990, and June 1998. (For more information on Rose Brinks, see the "Acknowledgments" section.)

Buchholtz, C. W., *Rocky Mountain National Park: A History*. Niwot, Colorado: University Press of Colorado, 1983.

Burgess, Harriet, *The MacGregor Ranch Story*, a Library Talk presented by Harriet Burgess on 16 July 1981 at the Estes Park Public Library.

The tape and its transcription by Lorraine Roberts, which were made as part of the Estes Park Oral History Project, are available in the Local History Section of the Estes Park Public Library. The Estes Park Oral History Project is a joint effort of the Estes Park Area Historical Museum and the Estes Park Public Library.

Burnett, Frank Jones, *Golden Memories of Colorado*. New York: Vantage Press, 1965.

Cairns, Mary Lyons, *Grand Lake in the Olden Days: A Compilation of Grand Lake, The Pioneers and The Olden Days*. Denver: The World Press, 1971.

Case, Stanley R., *The Poudre: A Photo History*. Self-published following Stan Case's death on 5 January 1995. Fort Collins, Colorado: Don-Art Printers (printer), 1995.

Cassell, Colleen Estes, *The Golden Pioneer: Biography of Joel Estes, The Man Who Discovered Estes Park*. Seattle: Peanut Butter Publishing, 1999.

Clark, Francis, *Early Sawmills in Larimer County*. Fort Collins, Colorado: Clark Associates, 1992.

BIBLIOGRAPHY

City of Fort Collins, *Walk Gently Through Fort Collins' Past: A Visit With Some of Grandview Cemetery's More Colorful Characters.* Fort Collins, Colorado: City of Fort Collins, 2005.

Colorado Council of Genealogical Societies, *Colorado Cemetery Directory*, 1985. A copy of the portion of this *Directory* containing information on the graves and cemeteries of Larimer County is available in our research files in the Local History Archive of the Fort Collins Museum of Discovery. The entire publication was distributed to Colorado libraries following its 1985 publication.

Coon, Waunita Clymer, *Mexican Joe's Grave*, a transcription of an interview of Waunita Coon by Zethyl Gates on 2 February 1975 and published by the Loveland Public Library as part of its Oral History Project.

Davis, Arlene Hinsey, a list of remote Larimer County graves and cemeteries prepared for us by Cecilia Damschroder (then the President of the Larimer County Genealogical Society). Ceil prepared this list from a set of 3 X 5 in. cards originally compiled by Arlene Davis from a search that she had conducted of newspapers and other documents containing information about deaths, graves, and burials prior to the establishment of Grandview Cemetery in 1887. (If Davis encountered information on more recent but remote graves or cemeteries during her search, she recorded it as well.)

A copy of the Davis's list is available in our research files in the Local History Archive of the Fort Collins Museum of Discovery.

Davis, Arleen Hinsey, Julianna Sloan Miller, and Mildred Payson Beatty, *Cemeteries of Larimer County, Colorado.* Fort Collins, Colorado: Cache la Poudre Chapter, Daughters of the American Revolution, 29 February 1972.

Dunning, Harold Marion, *Over Hill and Vale: In the Evening Shadows of Colorado's Longs Peak.* Volume I was published in 1956, Volume II in 1962, and Volume III in 1971. Boulder, Colorado: Johnson Publishing Company.

Ellerman, Gladys Ann Nauta, *Dale Tales: Virginia Dale, Colorado.* Self-published. Fort Collins, Colorado: Business Express (printer), 1999.

A copy of this out-of-print book is available in our research files in the Local History Archive of the Fort Collins Museum of Discovery.

Feneis, Jeff and Cindy Feneis, *Exploring Loveland's Hidden Past: The People and Places of Early Loveland, Colorado.* Loveland, Colorado: Loveland Museum and Gallery, 2007.

Fickel, Helen McCarty and Frances Bunyan Nielson, Compilers, *Heritage of Berthoud and The Little Thompson Valley, 1867-1910.* Self-published by Helen McCarty Fickel, 1992. Copies available from the Berthoud Historical Society.

Fletcher, Patricia K. A., Jack Earl Fletcher, and Lee Whiteley, *Cherokee Trail Diaries, Volume I—1849 A New Route to the California Gold Fields and Volume II—1850 Another New Route to the California Gold Fields.* Sequim, Washington: Fletcher Family Foundation, 1999.

Fletcher, Jack E. Fletcher and Patricia K. A. Fletcher, *Cherokee Trail Diaries, Volume III—1851-1900 Emigrants, Goldseekers, Cattle Drives, and Outlaws.* Sequim, Washington: Fletcher Family Trust, 2001.

Fry, Norman Walter, *Cache la Poudre—"The River" as Seen From 1889 to 1954.* Self-published in 1955 following Norman Fry's death on 30 July 1954.

LARIMER COUNTY CEMETERIES

Galvin, James, *The Meadow.* New York: Owl Book Division of Henry Holt and Company, 1992.

This very readable and frequently poetic book is the history of the area of northern Colorado just east of the Laramie River Valley and some of its more interesting inhabitants, especially Lyle Van Waning, during the first nine decades of the 20th century. That the book contains some poetic turns of phrase isn't surprising since Galvin has published several volumes of poetry and is a member of the permanent faculty of the University of Iowa's Writers' Workshop.

——, *Fencing the Sky.* New York: Henry Holt and Company, 1999; New York: Picador USA, 2000.

This novel, a reverse murder mystery about the disappearance of the American West, also takes place east of the Laramie River Valley and in nearby areas of Wyoming.

Gates, Zethyl, *Mariano Medina: Colorado Mountain Man.* Boulder, Colorado: Johnson Publishing Company, 1981; Loveland, Colorado: Loveland Museum and Gallery, 1992.

Griffith, Dan, a transcription of an interview of Dan Griffith by Ferrel Atkins on 6 August 1966 at Dan Griffith's home in Estes Park.

The transcription of the interview tape by Lorraine Roberts and the tape itself were made available on 19 February 1985 as part of the Estes Park Oral History Project and are available in the Local History Section of the Estes Park Public Library. The Estes Park Oral History Project is a joint effort of the Estes Park Area Historical Museum and the Estes Park Public Library.

Griffith, Don, *The Griffith Family in Estes Park,* a transcription of interview of Don Griffith by Dave Hieb on 20 January 1977 at the Estes Park Area Historical Museum.

The transcription of the interview tape by Lorraine Roberts and the tape itself were made available on 6 October 1981 as part of the Estes Park Oral History Project and are available in the Local History Section of the Estes Park Public Library. The Estes Park Oral History Project is a joint effort of the Estes Park Area Historical Museum and the Estes Park Public Library.

Hawthorne, Hildegarde and Esther Burnell Mills, *Enos A. Mills of the Rockies.* Long's Peak, Colorado: Temporal Mechanical Press, 1935.

Hickman, Lyn, *The Elkhorn Lodge,* a transcription of a historical walk conducted by Lyn Hickman on 18 August 1977 at the Ellkhorn Lodge in Estes Park, Colorado.

The transcription of the historical walk tape by Lorraine Roberts and the tape itself were made available on 5 April 1984 as part of the Estes Park Oral History Project and are available in the Local History Section of the Estes Park Public Library. The Estes Park Oral History Project is a joint effort of the Estes Park Area Historical Museum and the Estes Park Public Library.

Hondius, Eleanor E., *Memoirs of Eleanor E. Hondius of Elkhorn Lodge.* Boulder, Colorado: Pruett Press, 1964.

Jessen, Kenneth, *Ghost Towns Colorado Style, Volume One, Northern Region.* Loveland, Colorado: J. V. Publications, 1998.

Larimer County Genealogical Society, *Larimer County, Colorado, Index to Marriages, Volume I: 1858-1910.* Fort Collins, Colorado: Larimer County Genealogical Society, 1986. Also published as a CD.

——, *Cemeteries in Larimer County, Volume I: Mountain Home, Post, Grandview.* Fort Collins, Colorado: Larimer County Genealogical Society, 1989.

BIBLIOGRAPHY

———, *Cemeteries in Larimer County, Volume II: Roselawn, Resthaven.* Fort Collins, Colorado: Larimer County Genealogical Society, 1991.

———, *Cemeteries in Larimer County, Volume III: Greenlawn Cemetery, Berthoud.* Fort Collins, Colorado: Larimer County Genealogical Society, 1992.

———, *Cemeteries in Larimer County, Volume IV: Lakeside Cemetery, Loveland, Colorado.* Edited by Albert L. Boswell. Fort Collins, Colorado: Larimer County Genealogical Society, 1993. Updated in 2002 and published as a CD in 2003.

———, *Larimer County, Colorado, 1885 State Census With Index.* Fort Collins, Colorado: Larimer County Genealogical Society, September 2000.

———, *Cemeteries in Larimer County, Volume V: Loveland Cemetery, Loveland, Colorado.* Edited by Albert L. Boswell. Fort Collins, Colorado: Larimer County Genealogical Society, 2001. Published as a CD in 2003.

———, *Cemeteries in Larimer County, Volume VI: Highland Cemetery, Wellington and Other Small Cemeteries.* Fort Collins, Colorado: Larimer County Genealogical Society, 2005.

Larimer County Stockgrowers' Association and Livermore Woman's Club, *Ranch Histories of Livermore and Vicinity, 1884-1956.* Livermore, Colorado: Larimer County Stockgrower's Association, originally published in 1956.

The Livermore Woman's Club did historians a great service by republishing this book in its entirely in 1993 and again in 2003. In spite of its title, *Ranch Histories of Livermore and Vicinity, 1884-1956* covers ranches in all parts of Larimer County.

Livermore Woman's Club History Committee, *Among These Hills: A History of Livermore, Colorado*, First Edition. Compiled by the Livermore Woman's Club. Published by Double DJ Enterprises and printed by Citizens Printing Company, 1995.

———, *Among These Hills: A History of Livermore, Colorado*, Revised Second Edition. Complied by the Livermore Woman's Club. Published by Ink and Scribe and printed by United Graphics, 2009.

Mefford, Jack, Janet Sanders-Richter, and Jan Weir, Compilers, *Hardships & Hope: Fascinating Frontier Women of Northern Colorado.* Published by Midland Federal Savings to commemorate Colorado's 100-year centennial, 1976.

Miller, Lafi, *Those Crazy Pioneers With the Life and Times of Lady Moon & Vignettes of History.* Self-published, 2001. (For more information on Lafi and Jo Miller, see the "Acknowledgments" section.)

Morris, Andrew J., Editor, *The History of Larimer County, Colorado, Volume I.* Compiled by the Larimer County Heritage Writers. Dallas: Curtis Media Corporation, 1985. For Volume II of this series, see Ahlbrandt, Arlene and Kate Stieben above.

Noel, Thomas J. with Ron D. Sladek, *Fort Collins & Larimer County: An Illustrated History.* Carlsbad, California: Heritage Media Corporation, 2002.

Pedersen, Henry F., Jr., *Those Castles of Wood: The Story of Early Lodges of Rocky Mountain National Park and Pioneer Days of Estes Park, Colorado.* Self-published, 1993.

Pickering, James H., *"This Blue Hollow": Estes Park, the Early Years, 1859-1915.* Niwot, Colorado: University Press of Colorado, 1999.

LARIMER COUNTY CEMETERIES

———, *In the Vale of Elkanah: The Tahosa Valley World of Charles Edwin Hewes*. Estes Park, Colorado: Alpenaire Publishing Company in cooperation with the Estes Park Historical Museum, 2003.

———, *The Ways of the Mountains: Thornton Sampson, Agnes Vaille and Other Tragedies in High Places*. Estes Park, Colorado: Alpenaire Publishing Company in cooperation with the Estes Park Historical Museum, 2003.

(For more information on Jim Pickering, see the "Acknowledgments" section.)

Rottenberg, Dan, *Death of a Gunfighter: The Quest for Jack Slade, the West's Most Elusive Legend.* Yardley, Pennsylvania: Westholme Publishing, 2008.

Rottenberg provides a very readable and more balanced account of Joseph Alfred "Jack" Slade than is otherwise easily available to students of the history of Overland Trail.

Sprague, Abner E., *My Pioneer Life: The Memoirs of Abner E. Sprague* with Introduction by Edgar M. Stopher. Estes Park, Colorado: Rocky Mountain Nature Association, Rocky Mountain National Park, 1999.

Swan, Wesley, *Memoires of an Old Timer.* Self-published, 1972.

We were given our copy of this out-of-print book by Lafi and Jo Miller. (Wesley is Jo's uncle.) That copy is in our research files in the Local History Archive of the Fort Collins Museum of Discovery.

Swanson, Evadene Burris, *Fort Collins Yesterdays.* Fort Collins, Colorado: George and Hildegarde Morgan (publishers) and Don-Art Printers (printers), 1993.

Thiem, Jon with Deborah Dimon, *Rabbit Creek Country: Three Ranching Lives in the Heart of the Mountain West.* Albuquerque: University of New Mexico Press, 2008.

This eminently readable and informative biography of the lives of John William Elliott, John's wife Ida Meyer Elliott, and Josephine Lamb also contains historical information on the parts of Larimer County west of Livermore and in the Laramie River Valley that included the Elliotts' and Josephine Lamb's holdings. (For more information on Jon Thiem, see the "Acknowledgments" section.)

Thomas, Adam, *In the Hallowed Halls of Learning: The History and Architecture of Poudre School District R-1.* Prepared by HISTORITECTURE, L.L.C., Estes Park, Colorado, for the Advance Planning Department of the City of Fort Collins and Facility Services of Poudre School District, R-1. Fort Collins, Colorado: August 2004. As of 18 July 2008, the document was available online at http://fcgov.com/historicpreservation/pdf/historical-context-doc.pdf.

Watrous, Ansel, *History of Larimer County, Colorado.* Originally published in 1911. The 1972 edition we consulted was sponsored by the Cache la Poudre Chapter of the Daughters of the American Revolution. Fort Collins, Colorado: Miller Manor Publications, 1972.

Whiteley, Lee, *The Cherokee Trail: Bent's Fort to Fort Bridger.* Boulder, Colorado: Johnson Publishing Co., 1999.

Online Databases

Genealogy Records Available at Ancestry.com. To use http://www.Ancestry.com, one either needs to go to a public library that makes it available to its users or get an annual personal subscription to Ancestry.com. There are various levels of membership. For example, access to only U.S. records is less expensive than access to both U.S. and European records.

BIBLIOGRAPHY

For those who are serious about doing genealogy research on your own ancestors, Ancestry.com is an invaluable resource. We have used it extensively to learn about the Larimer County families whose family histories are included in this book as well as about the genealogy of our own ancestors.

Newspaper Articles in the Colorado Historic Newspaper Database as found at http://coloradohistoricnewspapers.org. The Colorado Historic Newspapers Collection (CHNC) currently includes more than 600,000 digitized pages, representing 160+ individual newspaper titles published in Colorado from 1859 to 1923. Due to copyright restrictions, CHNC does not generally include newspapers published after 1923. You would click "Search" on the left side of the home screen to begin your search for articles of interest to you. The user interface for this database is fairly self-explanatory.

Online Records of Fort Collins's Grandview and Roselawn Cemeteries as found at http://fcgov.com/departments. This database provides information on who is buried in Grandview and Roselawn and the location of each individual's grave. It also provides details on the individual's birth date, death date, burial date, name of funeral home, who authorized the person's burial, and the relationship between the authorizing individual and the deceased.

The user interface to this online database has changed several times since we started using it. Below we've provided instructions for the use of the database as of 4 November 2014. If you have difficulties using the database or if the user interface changes again, contact the Office of the Fort Collins Cemeteries at 970-221-6810 or Cemetery@fcgov.com for instructions for using this database or try to figure it out yourself, which we always managed to do.

1. Access the following URL: http://fcgov.com/departments

2. Scroll down to "Cemeteries" in the left-most column of the Home page and click on it.

3. Under "Cemeteries" in the right column on next screen, click on "Grandview" or "Roselawn" depending upon which cemetery's database you wish to search. However, the results displayed in Step 7 below will include individuals buried in BOTH Grandview and Roselawn no matter which cemetery you choose here.

4. Click on "Map of Cemeteries" below and to the right of the top photo on the next screen. (It will take a few moments for the cemetery's database to load.)

5. Click on "OK" in the lower right-hand corner of the "Disclaimer" popup.

6. In the Search box at the top right of the next screen, enter the last name of the person you are searching for (for example, "Andrews") and either press Return or click on the magnifying glass icon at the right end of the Search box.

7. A *non-alphabetical* vertical list of the people buried in Grandview and/or Roselawn with that last name you entered in Step 6 will display.

8. If you click on the headstone icon to the left of each person's name, a photograph of the applicable portion of the applicable cemetery will display with an overlay showing the grave numbers in the vicinity of the grave of the person you selected and highlighting that person's grave in yellow. Details of the burial of that person's death and burial are in a scrollable list below "Burial Plot" to the left of the cemetery photograph.

9. However, to get a more usable horizontal and *alphabetical* list of the individuals with that last name buried in Grandview and Roselawn, click on the Table icon to the left of the "Displaying X-Y" information at the bottom of the horizontal list displayed in Step 7.

LARIMER COUNTY CEMETERIES

10. The resulting table, which can be scrolled left or right, contains the following information for each individual listed in the table:

    Cemetery ID providing the following information: Cemetery (G=Grandview, R=Roselawn). Section Letter, Lot No., Grave No.
    Last Name
    First Name (If you click on the "First Name" heading, the table will be rearranged in alphabetical order by first names.)
    Age at Time of Death
    Sex
    Birth Date
    Death Date
    Burial Date
    Location of Death (If known)
    Funeral Director
    Next of Kin (Person who authorized the person's internment)
    Relationship (Relationship of person who authorized the deceased's internment to the deceased)

Online property records of the Bureau of Land Management as found at http://www.glorecords.blm.gov. You would click the "Search Documents" tab at the top of the home screen to begin your search for either the location of land homesteaded or purchased from the U.S. Government by a particular individual OR the name of the individual(s) who homesteaded or purchased a particular piece of land, provided you know the legal land description of that property. (For a discussion of what legal land descriptions entail, see "Legal Land Descriptions" in the "Introduction.") The user interface for this database is fairly self-explanatory.

Larimer County Assessor's Office Land Ownership Database as found at http://www.larimer.org/assessor. This database provides information on the current owners of property in Larimer County. Its interface is rather difficult to use (at least for us), but we've always been able to eventually find the ownership information we were searching for; it just sometimes took awhile.

INDEX

When a geographical location (town, mountain, creek, ranch, cemetery, etc.) in this Index is not followed by location information, it is in Larimer County. If the name of a town or other location is followed by a county but not a state, it is in Colorado.

A

Abdu'l-Baha Abbas, 1210, 1218
Alaska Railroad, 1152
Albertson, Cy, Rev., 1256
Albright families: Horace, 1323; Paul, 1374 (*see also* Vol. I and II)
Alderdyce, Zada. *See* MacGregor, Zada Alderdyce
aliquot parts, 1118
Allard, Wayne, 1308
Allen families: Dorothy (*see* Sandburg, Dorothy Allen); John Worth and Josephine Shedd, 1341-1342
Allison, Catherine. *See* Roberts, Catherine Allison)
American Revolution
  British forces veterans, 1271
Ancestery.com, 1388-1389
Anderson families: Glenda, 1113 (*see also* Vol. I and II); Terry R., 1113 (*see also* Vol. I and II)
Andrew, John D., 1209, 1220
Andrews families: Amanda Roseberry, 732; Charles ("Charley") B., 103-104, 183, 536-537; James, 289; Jimmy, 537; Julia Henderson, 537; Nelda Phyllis (*see* Griffith, Nelda Phyllis Andrews)
Armour Institute of Technology, 1251
Armstead family: Leah Jane Lee, 1235; Seth Abraham Armstead, Sr., 1235; Seth Abraham Armstead, Jr., 1235; Virginia June McCaffrey, 1235; Wilberta Ellen, 1235; William ("Bill") Ervin, 1226, 1235
Arnold families: Lois, 1167; Unknown, 1167
Art Institute of Chicago, 1272
Artman, Nancy Judith Patrick, 1211-1213, 1215-1216
Ashby, Juanita, 1330
Ashton
  child grave, 1202, 1207-1208, 1211-1212
  family: Alfred, 1209, 1222; Andrew, 1209, 1213, 1217; Annette, 1220, 1223; Bertha S., 1219; Carrie M., 1218; Catherine Colby, 1220; Cora E. Bush, 1209-1212, 1215-1216, 1218, 1220-1221, 1378 (*see also* Vol. I and II); Daughter of Willard H. and Cora Ashton, 1212 (*see also* Ashton, Annette); Frank J., 1218; Grace (daughter of Willard H. and Grace Jones Ashton) (*see* Carter, Grace Ashton); Grace Maggie Eure Jones (first wife of Willard H. Ashton), 1209-2011, 1218; Mary Johnson, 1217-1218; Willard Andrew, 1220; Willard Herbert, 1206, 1208-1212, 1214-1216, 1218-1219, 1378 (*see also* Vol. I and II); Ruth Elizabeth (*see* Nelson, Ruth Elizabeth Ashton); Son of Willard H. and Cora Ashton, 1206, 1212, 1221, 1223
  Ranch, 1207
Aspen Glen Art Studio, Hidden Valley Ranch, 1210
Aspenglen Campground, RMNP
  Cemetery, 1126-1128, 1253, 1305, 1354, 1378, 1380 (*see also* Vol. I and II)
  history, 1129-1130
Atkins, D. Ferrel, 1126-1127, 1133, 1143, 1165, 1194, 1207, 1226-1227, 1231, 1245, 1252, 1303, 1305, 1307, 1314-1315, 1323, 1325, 1334-1335, 1337-1340, 1344-1345, 1348-1349, 1354, 1356, 1362, 1367-1368, 1374, 1378, 1386. *See also* Vol. I and III
Attberry, Hildred. *See* Griffith, Hildred Attberry
Auburn, Grand County. *See* Gaskill, ghost town
Auraria, Arapahoe County, 1173

B

Babbitt family: Dell, 1208, 1212, 1341-1342, 1363; Sharon Jo Olson, 1208, 2010-2012, 1217, 1220-1222, 1341-1342, 1363
Babcock family, 1319: Adele Ramsey, 1257; Dean, 1251, 1254-1258; Evelyn (*see* Harn, Evelyn Babcock); Josephine McCall, 1251, 1257, 1319; Sylvia (*see* Tacker, Sylvia Babcock); William, Jr., 1257, 1319
Baby Brown Grave, 1381, 1383. *See also* Vol. I and II
Baha'i Faith, 1208, 1210, 1212, 1218-1219
Baha'a'llah, 1218
Baker families: Christy, 1128, 1305; Vaughn, Superintendent, RMNP, 1309; William, B. 1263, 1265
Baldy, Mount. *See* Craig, Mount
Ball, Clara, 1384. *See also* Vol. I and II
Balmer, H. M., 1135, 1137-1138, 1140-1141
Bania Family Cemetery, 1379. *See also* Vol. I and II
Bardwell Family Cemetery, 1380-1381. *See also* Vol. I and II

I-1

LARIMER COUNTY CEMETERIES

Barnes, Sybil, 1128-1129, 1131, 1140-1141, 1143, 1149-1150, 1156-1157, 1178-1179, 1208, 1228, 1241, 1293, 1298-1299, 1304-1305, 1314, 1329, 1355-1357, 1362-1363, 1378-1379, 1384. *See also* Vol. I and II
baseline, 1118
Bass families: Tom (*see* Bassford, Tom); Warner, 1292-1293
Bassford, Tom, 1244
Bates, Louis E. *See* Matthews, Louis E. Bates
Bauer, Mr., 1067
Baugher, Ray, Memorial, 1383. *See also* Vol. I and II
Bear Lake, RMNP, 1134, 1138, 1353, 1355-1356
Beatty, Mildred Payson, 1385. *See also* Vol. I and II
Beaver Brook Resort, 1165, 1357
Beaver Flats. *See* Lower Beaver Meadows, RMNP
Beaver Meadows, RMNP, 1165, 1231, 1243. *See also* Upper and Lower Beaver Meadows, RMNP
Beaver Point, RMNP, 1165
Beaver's Lumber, 1149
Beavis, Walter, 1285
Bellvue, 1384. *See also* Vol. I and II
Benett, Joyce, 1178
Berthoud
 churches, 1148
 Historical Society, 1385 (*see also* Vol. I and II)
 history, 1385 (*see also* Vol. I and II)
 Pass, 184
Bethel, Ellsworth, 1323
Bezold, Goldie, 1330
Bible Point, 1131-1132
Bierstadt Lake, RMNP, 1149, 1356, 1368
Big Elk Fire, pilots who died fighting, 1374
Big Elk Meadows fire station, 1374
Big Thompson River, 1145-1146, 1173, 1285, 1297, 1353, 1356, 1359, 1362, 1364, 1375. *See also* Vol. II
billiard table, first one in Colorado, 1190
Bingham Hill Cemetery, 1379. *See also* Vol. I and II
Bingo (pet burial), 1333
Bissell, Ky, 1267
Black Canyon, 1159-1160, 1270, 1272
 Creek, 1273-1274
 Hills, 1282
 of the Gunnison National Park, 1312

Black families: George, 1254, 1256-1257; John (*see* Black, George); Robert C., III, 1384 (*see also* Vol. I and II)
Black Mountain Ranch Cemetery, 1197, 1382. *See also* Vol. I and II
Blinn family: Augustus and Harry Elmer, 1229; Josephine ("Josie") Leach [*see* Hupp, Josephine ("Josie") Leach Blinn]
Bobcat Ridge Natural Area, 1380. *See also* Vol. I and II
Boehner, Martha Lee, 1321
Boettger, Walter and Carolyne, 1341-1342
Bonnell, Walter, Rev., 1330
Booth, Thomas, 1186, 1188, 1197-1199
Boothroyd-Hutchinson Cemetery, 1378. *See also* Vol. I and II
Boulder, Boulder County, 1230. *See also* Vol. I and II
Boulder Marble & Granite Works, 1228
Bowen Creek (near Gaskill), 1192
Bowen Gulch (near Gaskill), 1191
Bowen/Woods cottages, RMNP, 1355-1356
Bowker Club, 1191
Bowman families: Jack, 864; O. J., 1154
Boyd Family
 Cemetery, 1381 (*see also* Vol. I and II)
 Market, 1223
Bradford, Marshall, 1274
Bradley, H. C. (Mr. and Mrs.), 1209, 1215-1217, 1223
Bradt, Edwin, Grave, 1131-1132, 1378. *See also* Vol. I
Bradt, Gordon, 1132
brands. *See* cattle brands
Brandt, Lucas, 1285. *See also* Vol. II
Brennan, John R., 1266
Brinkhoff, Mike B., 1379. *See also* Vol. I and II
Brinks, Rose L., 1379, 1384. *See also* Vol. I and II
Brinwood Hotel, 1149
Bryant, Roy, 1285
Bryson, Charles E., 1130
Buchanan, Jennie L. *See* James, Jennie L. Buchanan
Buchholtz, Curt W., 1263, 1306, 1336, 1338, 1377, 1378, 1384. *See also* Vol. I and II
Buchnoff, Pamela Lynn McLaren, 1321
Buckeye Ranch Cemetery, 1115, 1120. *See also* Vol. I and II
Buckhorn Mountain, 1113. *See also* Vol. I and II
Buena Vista. *See* Bible Point
Buena Vista Park Service Cabin, west side of RMNP, 1320
Buffum Canyon, 1380. *See also* Vol. I and II

Bulter, Mary, 1374
Bunnell, Fred E., 1203, 1211
Bunyan, Frances. *See* Nielson, Frances Buynan
Bureau of Land Management. *See* U.S. Bureau of Land Management
Burgess, Harriet, 1270-1277, 1279-1282, 1384
Burnell family: Arthur Tappan, 1289; Bernice Imogene, 1290; Bessie Mae (*see* Smith, Elizabeth Burnell); Elizabeth (*see* Smith, Elizabeth Burnell); Eugene E., 1289; Esther A. (*see* Mills, Esther A. Burnell); Mary Adaline Frayer, 1289
Burnett family: Benjamin Franklin, Captain, 1263-1265 (*see also* Vol. I); Frank Jones, 1263, 1384 (*see also* Vol. I and II); Lulu May, 1265; William N., 1263
Burnett's clothing store (in Lulu City), 1265
Bush family: Cora E. (*see* Ashton, Cora E. Bush); Henry, 1220
Buster (pet burial), 1333
Butler families: Bill, Archaeologist, RMNP, 1188; Sylvester, 1199

C

Cabin Creek Grave, 1121, 1350. *See also* Vol. I and II
Cabin Rock, 1324
Cache la Poudre River, 1384-1385. *See also* Vol. I and II
Cache la Poudre and North Park Toll Road Company, 1264
Cairns, Mary Lyons, 1186, 1189-1190, 1197, 1263, 1314, 1384
Cameron Pass, 184, 1264, 1350. *See also* Vol. I
Cammel, Scott, Grave, 1350. *See also* Vol. I
Campbell Cemetery, 1379. *See also* Vol. I and II
Camp Wheeler, 1336, 1338
Cane (pet burial), 1333
Capra, Judy, 1191
Carlson, Albion and Jane, 1282
Carpenter families: Larry E., 1134-1135, 1307, 1344-1345, 1349, 1379 (*see also* Vol. I and II); Philip ("Phil") J., 1183-1184, 1379 (*see also* Vol. I and II); Vi, 1349
Carran, Eva Jean Boothroyd, 1270. *See also* Vol. II
Carter
    Grace Ashton, 1210, 1219-1220
    Lake, 1270 (*see also* Vol. I and II)
Cascade Lake, RMNP, 1127
Cassedy, Carrie. *See* Fuller, Carrie Cassedy
Cassell, Colleen Estes, 1172, 1384. *See also* Vol. I and II

cattle brands
    XIX, 1275
Central City, Gilpin County, 1190
Chambers
    Lake, 1350 (*see also* Vol. I)
    family: Robert, Sr., 1350-1351 (*see also* Vol. I); Robert, Jr., 1350-1351 (*see also* Vol. I)
    Robert, Sr., Grave, 1350 (*see also* Vol I)
Chapel in the Pines, Red Feather Lakes, 1382. *See also* Vol. I and II
Chapin families: Frederick H., Mrs., 1256; Maria, 1163
Chapin Lake, RMNP, 1256
Chapman, Dwight Bate, 1329
Chasm Lake, RMNP, 1376-1377
Cherokee Stage Station Cemetery, 1383. *See also* Vol. I and II
Cherokee Trail, 1385. *See also* Vol. I and II
Cherry Creek, Arapahoe County, 443-444, 908, 1173. *See also* Vol. I and II
Cheyenne, Laramie County, Wyoming, 1136, 1238. *See also* Vol. I and II
Chimney Hollow, 1270. *See also* Vol. II
Chitwood, J. P.
    death certificate, 1135, 1137-1138
    death, discovery, burial, rediscovery, and reburial, 1135-1141
    grave location, 1133-1135, 1378, 1380, 1382 (*see also* Vol. I and II)
    his dog, 1137
Chrestensen, Jeff, Ranger, RMNP, 1258
Christian churches
    Baptist, 1179 (*see also* Vol. I and II)
    Catholic, 1154, 1247-1249 (*see also* Vol. I and II)
    Christian Science, 1368, 1373
    Episcopal, 1328-1331, 1378 (*see also* Vol I and II)
    Presbyterian, 11153-1154, 1337 (*see also* Vol. I and II)
    United Brethren, 1147, 1148 (*see also* Vol. II)
Civil War veterans, 1295, 1366-1369. *See also* Vol. I and II
Clark
    Family Cemetery, 143, 572, 669-670, 672-673, 1103, 1381 (*see also* Vol. I and II)
    Francis, 1384 (*see also* Vol. I and II)
Clay/Clag, John, 1304
Clear Creek (2 miles east of Golden, Jefferson County), 1172-1173
Cleave family. *See also* Cleave-Griffith Family Cemetery: John T., 1142, 1144-1145, 1355, 1357 (Cont. on next page)

INDEX

I-3

Cleave family, Cont.: Margaret May, 1142, 1144, 1355, 1357; Paul, 1144, 1146; Virginia (*see* Griffith, Virginia Cleave)

Cleave-Griffith Family Cemetery, 1142-1143, 1145-1147, 1149, 1152, 1355, 1357, 1378, 1382. *See also* Cleave family; Griffith family; Vol. I and II

Cleave, John T. and Margaret May, original burial location, 1145-1146, 1356-1357

Cobb family: A. L., 1164, 1240, 1242; Edna B. (*see* James, Edna B. Cobb Arnold Gray); Raymond R. ("Ty"), 1164

Colard Ranch, 1383. *See also* Vol. I and II

Collins
    Chuck, cremains scattered in RMNP, 1307, 1378, 1381 (*see also* Vol. I and II)
    family: Chuck, 1307, 1365 (*see also* Vol. I and II); Judy, 1307, 1365, 1378 (*see also* Vol. I and II)

Colona. *See* Laporte

Colorado A&M. *See* Colorado State University

Colorado Attorney-General, 1282

Colorado Cemetery-Location Project, 1114

Colorado College, Colorado Springs, El Paso County, 1281. *See also* Vol. I

Colorado Council of Genealogical Societies, 1114, 1117, 1197, 1239, 1252, 1284, 1333, 1343-1344, 1371, 1384. *See also* Vol. I and II

Colorado Department of Public Health and Environment, 1135

Colorado Historic Newspapers Collection, 1389. *See also* Vol. I and II

Colorado Historical Society. *See* History Colorado

Colorado Mountain Club, 1318, 1323

Colorado National Forest, 1265

Colorado Normal School. *See* University of Northern Colorado

Colorado River, 1190, 1264, 1326-1327
    headwaters of, 1264
    North Fork, 1314-1315, 1336, 1338

Colorado School of Mines, Golden, Jefferson County, 1276

Colorado State Supreme Court, 1281. *See also* Vol. I and II

Colorado State University, 1291, 1309, 1312, 1323, 1382. *See also* Vol. I and II

Colorado-Wyoming border, 1380. *See also* Vol. I and II

Community Church of the Rockies Columbarium, 1153-1154

Contor, Roger, Ranger/Management Assistant, RMNP, 1227, 1267

Cooley, Sid and Sadie Morrison, 940

Coon families: Marcus, wife, and child, 1263; Waunita Clymer, 1384 (*see also* Vol. I and II)

Cooper families: Mary A. (niece of Willard H. Ashton), 1209; Mrs. (sister of Willard H. Ashton), 1209, 1215; William S., 1257

Corrigan, Daniel, Suffragan Bishop, Episcopal Diocese of Colorado, 1331

Coughlin ("Kolbs"/"Kolbe"), Florence J., 1164

Craig, Mount, west side of RMNP, 1321

Crags Lodge, 1178, 1289, 1323, 1323-1324

CSU. *See* Colorado State University

Cub Creek, RMNP, 1244

Cub Lake, RMNP, 1245
    Trail, 1244, 1312-1313
    Trailhead, 1227, 1312-1313

Cut Bank, Glacier County, Montana, 1236-1237

D

Damschroder, Cecilia ("Ceil"), 1379, 1384. *See also* Vol. I and II

Danhauer, Sharon, 1380. *See also* Vol. I and II

DAR. *See* Daughters of the American Revolution

Daughters of the American Revolution
    Cache la Poudre Chapter, 1385 (*see also* Vol. I and II)

Davies family, 1151

Davis families: Arlene Hinsey, 1380, 1384 (*see also* Vol. I and II); Coral Ervin and Elizabeth Koebel, 1227, 1237; Earl Kenneth, 1237; Inez Ethel Hupp, 1237; Patricia Ann, 1237; Raymond ("Ray") Merritt, 1226, 1228, 1231, 1238, 1245 (*see also* Vol. II); Telpha LaVonne (*see* Foxhoven, Telpha LaVonne Davis); Thomas Earl and Carmela Catherine Vaticano, 1237; Wando Elizabeth Dunning, 1238

death, causes of
    Alzheimer's, 1278 (*see also* Vol. I)
    avalanche-related accidents, 1186-1187, 1197-1199
    asthma, 1277 (*see also* Vol. II)
    blood poisoning, 1322
    cancer, 1308, 1310 (*see also* Vol. I and II)
    drowning, 1271 (*see also* Vol. I and II)
    gun shots (accidental or murder), 1198, 1268, 1285, 1375 (*see also* Vol. I)
    heart conditions, 1232-1233, 1296, 1373 (*see also* Vol. I and II)
    horse-related accidents, 1211-1213 (*see also* Vol. I and II)
    Indian attacks, 1350 (*see also* Vol. I)
    (Cont. on next page)

INDEX

death, causes of, Cont:
    lightning, 1198, 1276 (*see also* Vol. I and II)
    mountaineering accidents, 1135-1141, 1194-1195, 1253-1258, 1338-1339
    peritonitis, 1281 (*see also* Vol. I)
    pneumonia, 1277 (*see also* Vol. I and II)
    suicide, 1293-1295 (*see also* Vol. I and II)
    tumors (cancer?), 1327 (*see also* Vol. II)
    typhoid fever, 1163 (*see also* Vol. I and II)
    vehicle accidents, 1323, 1325 (*see also* Vol. I and II)

Decoursey, Donn G. and Shirley A., 1360. *See also* Vol. I and II

Deer Mountain, RMNP, 1215

Deer Ridge, RMNP, 1215
    Junction Trail, grave on, 1374-1375

Delta Tau Delta, 1250-1251, 1256

Dennison, Charles W., 1284-1285

Denver, Denver County
    & Rio Grande Railroad, 1152
    University, 1342

Derby, William F. and Anna May, 1223

Derrick, Shirley, 1158, 1160

desecration of graves and cemeteries, laws concerning, 1187

Desert Land Act of 1877, 1120. *See also* Vol. I

Diamond Tail Ranch, 1383. *See also* Vol. I and II

Dick family
    cremains scattered in RMNP, 1197, 1263, 1307, 1309, 1380 (*see also* Vol. I and II)
    members: Betty and children by first marriage, 1307-1309, 1380 (*see also* Vol. I and II); Carl Dick, Jr., 1309; George Frederick ("Fred"), III, 1307-1308; George Frederick ("Tad"), IV, 1308; Helen, 1308; James, 1308; Marilyn, 1308

Dietrich, William G., 1366, 1370

Dimon, Deborah. *See* Sattler, Deborah Dimon

Dinosaur National Monument, 1312

Dona family: Kelee, 1177-1179; Scott, 1177

Dorr, Superintendent, RMNP, 1185

Dowdy Lake Grave, 1120. *See also* Vol. I and II

dowser rods
    how to construct, 1121
    use of to confirm burials, 1120-1121, 1126, 1184, 1202-1203, 1205, 1208, 1226, 1239-1240, 1243, 1247, 1259, 1261-1262, 1292, 1298-1299, 1301-1302, 1304, 1334-1335, 1344, 1349, 1353-1354, 1362 (*see also* Vol. I and II)

DMS (Degrees, minutes, seconds), 1116

Drake (the town), 1284. *See also* Vol. II

Drake, John, 1185

Dream Lake, RMNP, 1138

Drummond, Alex, 1324

Dry Gulch, 1159

Dudley, Bertha, 966

Dunning, Harold Marion
    general, 1143-1144, 1158-1159, 1163, 1169, 1183, 1207, 1253-1257, 1263, 1270, 1278-1279, 1285, 1286, 1296, 1319, 1322, 1372-1373, 1377, 1385 (*see also* Vol. I and II)
    graves for which he provided headstones, 1285 (*see also* Vol. II)
    his involvement in reburial of Louis R. Levings, 1255-1256

Duguay's Hardware and Drug Store, 1265

Dunraven
    Earl of (Windham Thomas Wyndham-Quin, the 4th Earl of Dunraven), 1144-1145, 1148, 1159, 1231, 1273-1274, 1354, 1356, 1358-1359, 1363
    home, 1183
    Inn, 1356, 1361, 1362-1363 (*see also* Vol. I and II)
    "Lord." *See* Dunraven, Earl
    Ltd., 1362-1363

Dunshee, Ben, 1265

Duty, Doc. *See* Duty, Edward R. ("Doc")

Duty, Edward R. ("Doc"), 1187, 1197-1199

E

E.J. Burton's Grocery, 1265

Eastern Stars, 1313

Eckstein, Elizabeth, 1333

Eggers graves, 1379. *See also* Vol I and II

Elkanah Valley. *See* Valley of Elkanah

Elkhorn
    Corporation, 1169
    District, 1382 (*see also* Vol. I and II)

Elkhorn Lodge (in Estes Park), 1144-1145, 1156, 1158, 1174, 1241, 1270, 1322, 1330, 1386. *See also* Vol. I and II
    & Guest Ranch, 1155
    Cemetery, 1155-1157, 1170, 1378, 1382 (*see also* Vol. I and II)
    creation of, 1160
    ghosts, 1169 (*see also* Vol. I)
    how it got its name, 1160
    James family's move to that area, 1160
    operation under James and Hondius families, 1160-1162
    operation after Eleanor Hondius, 1168

LARIMER COUNTY CEMETERIES

Elliott
    family: Ida Meyer, 1383, 1388 (*see also* Vol I and II); John William, 1383, 1388 (*see also* Vol I and II)
    Ranch Cemetery, 1383 (*see also* Vol I and II)

Ellwanger, Katherine Lloyd. *See* Griffith, Katherine Lloyd Ellwanger

Ely, Nancy ("Nan") Maria Hupp and Harold Mortimer ("Mort"), 1229-1230, 1235

Emery, Roe, 1323

English Hotel. *See* Estes Park Hotel

Enos Mills Cabin and Gallery, 1286-1288, 1290, 1322

Episcopal Church of St. Bartholomew the Apostle, Estes Park, 1290, 1313, 1328-1331, 1362
    Cemetery, 1328-1329, 1331, 1378 (*see also* Vol. I and II)

Estes Cone, 1257

Estes family, 1171-1174: 1927 reunion, 1174-1175; Charles F., 1174; Edwin, 1171; Francis Marion, 1171, 1173-1175; George, 1174; Hardin, 1172; J. W./Wesley Jasper, 1171, 1174; Joel, Sr., 1171-1175, 1384 (*see also* Vol. I and II); Joel, Jr., 1171, 1173-1174; Joel E., Judge, 1175; Joel S. (grandson of Joel Estes, Sr.), 1171; Mahalia Ring, 1172; Martha Ann ("Patsey") [*see* Hiatt, Martha Ann ("Patsey") Estes]; Martha Ann ("Patsy") Stollings, 1171-1172, 1174; Mary Jane, 1175; Mary Louise, 1174; Milton, 1171, 1174; Mollie, 1171; Newton, 1174; Peter H., 1172; Sarah, 1171, 1174

Estes Park, 1387. *See also* Vol. I and II
    Area Historical Museum, 1135, 1143-1144, 1158, 1271, 1318, 1324, 1349, 1367, 1372, 1384, 1386 (*see also* Vol. I and II)
    Chamber of Commerce, 1171
    Country Club, 1242
    first child (Charles F. Estes) born in, 1174
    first school, 1160
    floods, 1127, 1376
    discovery, 1173, 1384 (*see also* Vol. I and II)
    Genealogical Society, 1177, 1183, 1298, 1307, 1318, 1349, 1356, 1379 (*see also* Vol. I and II)
    graves, cemeteries, and memorials, 1153-1154, 1171, 1177-1178, 1239-1240, 1247-1248, 1328-1333, 1341-1342, 1362-1365, 1371-1372, 1378, 1381-1382 (*see also* Vol. I and II)
    Gun and Archery Club, 1365
    Historian Laureate, James Pickering, 1382
    Hotel, 1144, 1148
    lumber, 1149, 1242
    Lumber Yard, 1242
    Oral History Project, 1135, 1270, 1324, 1336, 1384, 1386 (*see also* Vol. I and II)
    Police, 1379
    Post Masters/Mistresses, 1144, 1230, 1234, 1274
    Power and Light Department, 1365
    Public Library, 1128, 1135, 1140, 1143, 1156, 1158, 1178, 1208, 1241, 1245, 1270, 1298, 1304, 1324, 1329, 1336, 1367, 1378, 1384, 1386 (*see also* Vol. I and II)
    School Board, 1280, 1313, 1362

Estes Valley Memorial Gardens, 1176
    individuals buried there, 1147, 1310

Eureka Ditch, RMNP, 1376

Evans, Laura Elizabeth, 1333

Everglades National Park, 1313

Ewart, William Dana, 1203, 1211

F

FAJ headstone, 1127-1128, 1305

F.H.J. tombstone, 1127

F.H.R. Cemetery, Estes Park, 1177-1178, 1378, 1382. *See also* Vol. I and II

Fall River, 1126-1127, 1144-1145, 1154, 1155, 1160, 1165, 1202, 1239, 1270. 1356, 1359, 1375
    Inn of the, 1239
    Lodge, 1185, 1207, 1364
    Pass, 1276
    Road, 1127, 1130, 1137, 1233, 1239 (*see also* Vol I)

Farris, Juanita Yore, 1373

Fearnly family: George, 1200; Lillian Georgina (*see* Haines, Lillian Georgina Fearnly)

Feder, Joan. *See* Golbfarb, Joan Feder

Feneis, Jeff and Cindy, 1385. *See also* Vol. I and II

Fenton, Mary Esther Griffith, Chester ("Ted") Le Roy, and Virginia Bell, 1152

Fern Lake, RMNP
    Lodge, 1307, 1336, 1338
    Trail, 1334-1335, 1338, 1340
    Trailhead, 1139-1140, 1293, 1334

Ficke, Helen McCarty, 1385. *See also* Vol. I and II

Figgs, Daylan, 1380. *See also* Vol. I and II

File, Kenneth A., 1251, 1256

Finger, Ted, 1330

Finn, Walter, Ranger, RMNP, 1256

Fish Creek in Estes Park area, 1144, 1173, 1183, 1282, 1356, 1359

Fisher-Davis single-surface planer, 1149

Fisk Alfred Arthur, Grave, 1383. *See also* Vol. I and II

Flattop
- Mountain, RMNP, 1133-1134, 1136, 1138-1139, 1194, 1339
- Trail, RMNP, 1133, 1137, 1338

Fleshuts, Joe, 1315
Fletcher, Jack Earl and Patricia K.A., 385. *See also* Vol. I and II
Flynn, Mike, 1198
Ford, Henry Crawford, 1271
Forest Canyon, RMNP, 1276, 1311
- Overlook, 1377

Forest Inn, 1335
Forks Hotel near Drake, 1323, 1325. *See also* Vol. II
Fort Collins (the town), 1264, 1380, 1382, 1384. *See also* Vol. I and II
- cemeteries [*see* Grandview Cemetery; Harmony Cemetery; Resthaven Memorial Gardens (Vol. II); Roselawn Cemetery, Williamson Cemeteries Nos. 1 and 2]
- Museum of Discovery, 1180, 1194, 1227, 1253, 1373, 1384-1385 (*see also* Vol. I and II)
- Natural Areas, 1380 (*see also* Vol. I and II)
- Pioneer Association, 1350 (*see also* Vol I)
- Superintendent of Cemeteries, 1379 (*see also* Carpenter, Philip, and Vol. I and II)

Fort Logan National Cemetery, Denver, 1290. *See also* Vol. II
Fort Lupton Bottom, Weld County, 1173-1174
Foxhoven, Telpha LaVonne Davis and Richard Earl, 1238
Franklin, Mike, 1310
Frazier, Deborah, 1286
Frey, William C., Rev., 1331
Front Range Settles League, 1293
Fry, Norman Walter ("Pah"), 1385. *See also* Vol. I and II
Frysig, Paul, 1374
Fuller, Carrie Cassedy
- and family, 1184-1185
- ash burial, 1184
- Grave, 1180-1183, 1378-1380 (*see also* Vol. I and II)
- plaque for original grave, current location, 1183-1184

G

Gabletop Mountain, RMNP, 1376
Gale Revocable Trust, 1366
Galliher, Andrea Koutonen, 1271-1272, 1276-1277, 1280, 1282-1283
Galvin, James, 1386. *See also* Vol. I and II
Garrett, M. Paul, Rev., 1331

Gaskill
- Cemetery, west side of RMNP, Grand County, 1120, 1186-1189, 1192, 1199, 1263, 1380-1381 (*see also* Vol. I and II)
- Creek, 1186
- ghost town on west side of RMNP, Grand County, 1186-1193, 1197
- L.D.C., Captain, 1190

Gates families: Charles, 1350 (*see also* Vol. I); Zethyl, 1116, 1384-1385 (*see also* Vol. I and II)
Geeck family: Andrew ("Andy") and children, 1317; Sophia K. Holzwarth, 1315-1317
Gem Lake and Gem Lake Trail, RMNP, 1267
Geographic Names Information System, 116
George
- Creek, 68
  - graves near, 68, 559-560
- Grace Nation (*see* Griffith, Grace Nation George)

Georgetown, Clear Creek County, 1190
Gerling
- Bruce William, Memorial for, 1194-1195, 1378, 1380 (*see also* Vol. I and II)
- family: Bruce William, 1194; William J., 1194-1195

ghosts
- at Elkhorn Lodge, 1117, 1156-1157 (*see also* Vol. I and II)
- on the Poudre, 1117 (*see also* Vol. I and II)

ghost towns, 1386. *See also* Cipango (Vol. II), Gaskill (Vol. III), Manhattan (Vol. I); Lulu City (Vol. III), Poverty Flats (Vol. III)
Gianttrack Mountain, RMNP, 1355, 1357
Gieck, Marjorie Louise Griffith, Robert Edward ("Ed"), and family, 1151
Glacier
- Basin, RMNP, 1306
- Creek, RMNP, 1297, 1302-1304, 1353
- Livery, 1128, 1302-1304
- Lodge, 1150
- National Park, 1312
- View Meadows Subdivision, 1360 (*see also* Vol. I and II)
- National Recreation Area, 1312

Glen Evans, 1271, 1274
Glen Haven, 1275
- possible Indian burial ground north of, 1375

Global Positioning System, 1116
GNIS. *See* Geographic Names Information System
gold mining. *See* mines
Golden, Jefferson County, 1172. *See also* Vol. I
Golden Eagle Resort, 1324

Goldfarb family: Ira, Ranger, RMNP, 1127, 1133-1134, 1180-1183, 1194, 1253, 1259, 1263, 1354, 1356, 1376, 1380 (*see also* Vol. I and II); Joan Feder, Ranger, RMNP, 1133-1134, 1180-1183, 1194, 1253, 1259, 1263, 1354, 1356, 1376, 1380 (*see also* Vol. I and II);

Goldwater, Barry, Senator, 1195

Gorenson, Florence. *See* Griffith, Florence Gorenson

GPS. *See* Global Positioning System

GPS readings, 1116. *See also* Vol. I

Graham, Mrs. C. H., 1171

Granby Reservoir, Grand County, 1315

Grand Canyon National Park, 1312, 1321

Grand County
    graves and cemeteries, 1186-1193, 1196-1199, 1259-1266, 1380-1381 (*see also* Vol. I and II)

Grand Lake, west side of RMNP, Grand County, 1136, 1138, 1190, 1196, 1259, 1308, 1334, 1337 (*see also* Vol. I and II)
    Cemetery, 1186, 1196-1198, 1263-1264, 1309, 1314, 1317, 1320, 1380-1381 (*see also* Vol. I and II)
    Mining and Milling Company, 1190
    Mining and Smelting Company, 1189

Grand River. *See* Colorado River

Grand River Ditch Company, 1320

Grand Teton National Park, 1313

Grandview Cemetery, Fort Collins, 1379, 1382-1383, 1384. *See also* Vol. I and II
    individuals buried there, 1382-1383, 1384 (*see also* Vol. I and II)
    online records database, how to use, 1389-1390

Grant family, 1363: Eliza A./E. (*see* Hupp, Eliza A./E. Grant); George and Nancy Brannin, 1228

graves, laws concerning, 10, 592, 1122, 1187

Gray families: D_ _lt E., 1168; Jeanne M. (*see* Seybold, Jeanne M. Gray); Marle S., 1168; Walter A., Sr., 1167-1168, 1242; Walter A., Jr., 1168

"Graystone," 1319

Greenacre, Sarah Metta (*see* Griffith, Sara Metta Greenacre)

Gregory, John, 1293

Griffith
    Albin, homestead, 1145, 1355
    families. *See also* Cleave-Griffith Family Cemetery: Albert, 1146; Albin, Rev., 1145-1146, 1148-1149, 1357; Anne (*see* Toft, Georgia Anne Griffith); Charles Leslie, 1151-1152; Dale Edward, 1152; Dan Braxton, 1143, 1146-1150, 1245, 1367-1368, 1386 (*see also* Vol. I and II); Daniel Arthur, 1150; Debra, 1150; Dennis Michael ("Mike"), 1152; Donald ("Don") Louis, 1143, 1146, 1148, 1150, 1355, 1357, 1367-1368 (*see also* Vol. I and II); Douglas Lee, 1150; Ellen Louise Jesser, 1147-1150; Estes Braxton, 1150; Florence Gorenson, 1152; Georgia Anne (*see* Toft, Georgia Anne Griffith); Grace Nation George, 1152; Harvey Ernest, 1152; Hildred Attberry, 1147; John N., 1142, 1145, 1147-1149, 1151, 1355, 1357; John Timothy ("Tim"), 1152; Katherine Lloyd Ellwanger, 1150; Marie, 2011-2012; Marjorie Louise (*see* Gieck, Marjorie Louise Griffith); Mary Esther (*see* Fenton, Mary Esther Griffith); Mary Lois, 1147, 1149; Mary Lucille (*see* Davies family); Mary Margaret Grimm, 1145-1146, 1148; Nelda Phyllis Andrews, 1150; Nellie, 1147; Norma Kay, 1151; Oma Katherine (*see* Miller, Oma Katherine Griffith); Orin, 1152; Richard Lawrence, 1151; Ruth Irene (*see* Mounts family); Sara Metta Greenacre, 1151; Sharyn, 1150; Virginia Cleave, 1142, 1144, 1147, 1151, 1355, 1357; William ("Billie") Dean, 1152

Gubbins, John, 1186-1191, 1197, 1259-1263, 1265-1266, 1307, 1309, 1313, 1380-1381, 1384. *See also* Vol. I and II

Gudgel
    family: Clyde, 1309; Howard S., 1309; Mary Schnor, 1309-1310
    Howard S., cremains scattered in RMNP, 1309

Guild, Eugene R., Ranger, RMNP, 1134, 1136-1138, 1140-1141

Gunderson, Diane, 1156-1157

H

Hackett, Wayne
    U.S. Commissioner, 1185
    Mr. and Mrs., 1330

Haines families: Lillian Georgina Fearnly, 1200-1201; Robert ("Bob") John, 1153, 1165, 1197, 1200, 1207, 1251-1253, 1257, 1307, 1310, 1334-1335, 1340, 1364-1365, 1376, 1381 (*see also* Vol. I and II); Theodora ("Teddie") Ann Mereness, 1153, 1200, 1207, 1310, 1340, 1364, 1381 (*see also* Vol. I and II); Walter Hunt, 1201; William Walter, 1201, 1310

Haines family scattered cremains, 1200, 1310, 1381. *See also* Vol. I and II

INDEX

Hale
- Doris Noreen Hamilton, 1310, 1312
  - cremains scattered in RMNP, 1310
- William Alfred, 1310-1312
  - cremains scattered in RMNP, 1310

Hamilton
- families: Doris Noreen (*see* Hale, Doris Noreen Hamilton); Dwight and Inez Jeanette Carson (parents of Doris Noreen and Dwight L. Hamilton), 1310-1312; Dwight Linton, Chief Park Naturalist, RMNP, 1310-1312, 1326; Leslie (*see* Spurlin, Leslie Hamilton); Vada Maxine ("Mickey") Holloway, 1311, 1326
- family cremains scattered in RMNP, 1311-1312

Hanks
- family cremains scattered in RMNP, 1312-1313
- family members: Allyn Frank, Superintendent, RMNP, 1226-1228, 1244, 1312-1313 (*see also* Vol. II); Allyn Williams ("Bill"), 1227-1228, 1312; Frank and Lou, 1312; Hazel Williams, 1226-1228, 1244, 1312 (*see also* Vol. II); Mary (*see* Israelson, Mary Hanks)

Harbison
- Kitty and Annie, 1309-1310
- Ranch, 1309-1310

Hardin, Cora Miller, 1285

Harmony Cemetery, 1380. *See also* Vol. I and II

Harn, Evelyn Babcock and Edward J., 1257

Harrod, Beth Miller, 1295

Hartmann, Joseph, Rev., 1247-1248

Hartong, Allan, Ranger, RMNP, 1185

Hawaii Volcanoes National Park, 1312

Hawthorne, Hildegarde, 1286, 1323, 1386. *See also* Vol. I and II

Hayden families: Albert (Mrs.), 1143, 1157, 1160; Julian (Mr. and Mrs.), 1244

Hayes, Milton R. (Mr. and Mrs.), 1331

Heeney family: Georgianna Needham, 1159-1160, 1270, 1272-1274, 1278; Marie Clara (*see* MacGregor, Marie Clara Heeney)

Hegner, Casper, 1331

Heiny, Richard E., 1333

Henkin, Fred S., Sharon, and Jennifer, 1134, 1344-1349, 1379. *See also* Vol. I and II

Henry, Jack, 1266

Herschler, J. Barton, Chief Ranger, RMNP, 1180-1185, 1227, 1339

Hewes family: Charles Edwin, 1229-1230, 1255-1257, 1292-1296, 1319, 1324, 1388 (*see also* Vol. I and II); Joseph, 1295; Mary Catherine Palmer (*see* Kirkwood, Mary Catherine Palmer Hewes); Stephen Brown, Sr., 1295; Stephen Brown, Jr., 1293-1296

Hewes-Kirkwood Inn, 1292-1294, 1296

Hiatt, Joseph and Martha Ann ("Patsey") Estes, 1172

Hickman, Lyn, 1158, 1386. *See also* Vol. I and II

Hidden Valley
- west of Horseshoe Park, RMNP, 1149, 1205, 1214, 1310,
  - beaver ponds, possible grave, 1318, 1375
  - Ranch, 1210
- southeast of Horseshoe Park), RMNP, 1214
- Creek, RMNP, 1214
- Ski Resort, RMNP, 1254

Higby families: Clifford, 1135, 1138, 1258, 1338; Nina, 1233

History Colorado, 1344-1345, 1348, 1352. *See also* Vol. I and II

Hitler, Adolph, Chancelor of Germany during World War II, 453

Hoerner, Vic and Colleen, 1318

Holien, Bernie and Kris Johnson, 1318, 1344-1345, 1347, 1349

Holley Ranch Graves, 1115, 1120. *See also* Vol. I and II

Hollowell Park, RMNP, 1357

Holmquist, Mollie, 1154

Homestead Act of 1862, 1119, 1231, 1273. *See also* Vol. I and II

Hondius
- family land owned in what is now Rocky Mountain National Park, 1165-1166
- family members: Eleanor/Ella Estes James, 1143-1145, 1158-1159, 1161-1162, 1165, 1170, 1232, 1241-1242, 1270, 1273, 1296, 1386 (*see also* Vol. I and II); Pieter ("Peter"), Sr., 1130, 1161, 1165-1166, 1170, 1232, 1296 (*see also* Vol. II); Pieter ("Peter"), Jr., 1161, 1166, 1292-1293; Peter, 1166, 1170
- Park, RMNP, 1165

Holzwarth, John ("Johnnie") Gotlieb III, cremains scattered in RMNP, 1197, 1313-1314, 1380-1381. *See also* Vol. I and II

Honstein, E. W., 1081

Horseshoe
- Inn, 1202-1211, 1231, 1233
  - history and ownership, 1213-1217
- Park, RMNP, 1166, 1202-1217, 1233, 1337, 1364. *See also* Little Horseshoe Park
  - Cemetery, 1202-1203, 1206-1208, 1211, 1213, 1222-1224 (Cont. on next page)

LARIMER COUNTY CEMETERIES

Horseshoe, Cont.:
   Park, Cont.:
      Graves, 1202-1208, 1222-1224, 1363, 1378 (*see also* Vol. I and II)
      land therein acquired from U.S. Government, 1203, 1211
   Ranch, 1209, 1215
Hossack, Juleen Kay, 1331
Hostmark, Elaine A., 1318, 1366-1367, 1370
Hot Sulfur Springs, Grand County, 1190. *See also* Vol. I
Howard, Dorothy McLaren, 1320
Howlett, William, Rev., 1249
Huff, Wayne and Betty, 1333
Humphries, Emma May Allison. *See* West, Emma May Allison Humphries
Hupp
   Annex, 1233
   family, 1166, 1174, 1243: Aaron and Mary Homan, 1228; Betty Jo (*see* Whitney, Betty Jo Hupp); Betty Lou King, 1228, 1236; Charles Richard, 1231-1232, 1233-1234; Doris Sidney (*see* Williams, Doris Sidney Hupp); Eliza A./E. Grant, 1166, 1225-1228, 1231, 1313; Ellen Truitt, 1229, 1233-1235, 1245; Frances ("Fannie") Ann, 1166, 1225-1226, 1228-1229, 1231-1232, 1245; Francis [*see* Hupp, Frances ("Fannie") Ann]; George Tipton, 1228; Grace Elizabeth Hunter, 1230, 1234; Henry Aaron, 1167, 1229, 1232-1235; Inez Ethel (*see* Davis, Inez Ethel Hupp); John Ervin, 1227-1228, 1235-1236, 1244, 1313; John T., Sr., and Catherine Stoutemeyer, 1228; John T., Jr., 1166, 1174, 1225-1228, 1231, 1313; John T. ("Wallace") (son of John T., Jr.), 1229; Josephine ("Josie") Leach Blinn, 1229, 1232-1234, 1245; Mary Elizabeth ("Mollie") [*see* Jones, Mary Elizabeth ("Mollie")]; Michael Ervin, 1236; Myral ("Mary") Heck, 1230; Nancy ("Nan") Maria [*see* Ely, Nancy ("Nan") Maria Hupp]; Pearl Etha Williams, 764-765, 1227-1228, 1235-1236, 1312-1313; Wilberta Ellen (*see* Armstead, Wilberta Ellen Hupp); William ("Bill") Ervin, 1226, 1228, 1231, 1234, 1236, 1312; William ("Bill") Horace, 1227, 1230, 1234
   Family Cemetery, 1121, 1225-1229, 1231-1232, 1236, 1243, 1313, 1378 (*see also* Vol. I and II)
   Family Ranch, 1166, 1231-1232
   Hotel, Estes Park, 1233
   hotels, Estes Park area, 1232-1233
   Livery, Estes Park area, 1231

Husted family: Clara, 1144; Shep, 1144, 1149, 1254, 1338
Hurd, Edward Lennis ("Lenny"), Grave, 1381. *See also* Vol. I and II
Hyatt Family Cemetery, 2203, 1380. *See also* Vol. I and II
Hyde, A. A., 1132
Hyde Memorial Chapel, YMCA of the Rockies, 1132
Hygiene, Boulder County
   churches, 1148

I

Illinois Institute of Technology, 1251, 1256
Indian Cemetery No. 1, 1120. *See also* Vol. I and II
Indian Cemetery No. 2, 1120. *See also* Vol. I and II
Ingley, Bishop, Episcopal Church of Colorado, 1330
Israelson, Mary Hanks, 1312

J

Jackson, William Frank (Mr. and Mrs.), 1330
Jackson, Teton County, Wyoming, 1235-1236
Jacobs, Craig and Kelly Johnson, 1318
James
   family, 1157-1158, 1240
      arrival in Estes Park, 1159
      move to what became Elkhorn Lodge, 1160
   family members: Ann, 1162, 1170; Baby, 1166, 1170; Charles ("Charlie") W., 1158-1160, 1163-1164, 1166-1167, 1170; Edna B. Cobb Arnold Gray, 1164-1165, 1167-1170, 1242; Eleanor/Ella Estes (*see* Hondius, Eleanor/Ella Estes James); Eleanore A. (*see* Owen, Eleanore A. James); Ella McCabe, 1159-1163, 1169-1170; Homer Edwin, 1129, 1149, 1157, 1159-1161, 1170, 1240-1241; Howard Perry, Sr., 1159-1162, 1164, 1167-1170, 1242; Howard Perry ("Bud"), Jr., 1164-1165, 1167-1169; Jane L., 1233; Jennie L. Buchanan, 1129, 1163, 1240-1241; Jesse, 1011; Libby, 977; Mary Jane, 1129, 1163-1164, 1240-1241, (*see also* James, Mary Jane, Grave); William (father of William Edwin James, Sr.), 1162, 1170, 1270; William Edwin, Sr., 1129, 1158-1163, 1167-1170, 1174, 1232, 1241; William ("Willie") Edwin, Jr., 1158, 1163, 1166-1167, 1170
   Mary Jane, Grave, 1115, 1164, 1239-1240, 1378. *See also* Vol. I and II
Jelsema, Ted, 1233

Jenkins, Phil, 1185
Jennings family: Arthur W., 1128-1129; Ed, 1128
Jessen, Kenneth, 1336, 1386. See also Vol. I and II
Jesser, Ellen Louise. See Griffith, Ellen Louise Jesser
Jewett Family Cemetery, 1382. See also Vol. I and II
Jim's Grove, 1324
Joe Wright Reservoir Grave, 1120. See also Vol. I and II
Joel Estes Memorial, 1171, 1173-1175, 1382. See also Vol. I and II
Johnson
    families: Bishop, Episcopal Church of Colorado, 1330; Charles and Edward, 1279; Darrin Lee, 1329; Donald, 1318; Gail S., 1333; Jacqueline ("Jackie") Jaye, 1140, 1243-1244, 1267-1268, 1317-1318, 1338, 1345, 1348-1349, 1353, 1355-1357, 1366-1367, 1375, 1381 (see also Vol. I and II); Mary (see Ashton, Mary Johnson); Phyllis McLaren, 1320; Richard and Helen, 1217
    Jacqueline ("Jackie") Jaye, cremains scattered in RMNP, 1317
Johnston, Tom, 1315
Jones
    families: Amelia Wright, 1219; Grace Maggie Eure (see Ashton, Grace Maggie Eure Jones); John W., 1219; Mary Elizabeth ("Mollie") and John J., 1229, 1232; Mrs. Walter, 1244
    Inn, 1229, 1232
Josephine, The, 1233
Josie (pet burial), 1333
Jurgens, Teri. See Lefever, Teri Jurgens

K

Kawuneeche Valley, 1191-1192, 1320
Kaye, Glen, 1127
Kemp, Patience, 1186
Kemper, Pat, 1113
Kendall
    Mrs. Orpha, 1282
    Ransom S., 1227, 1243-1246, 1312
Kerstien
    family: Frank, Julia, and family, 1248; Leo J., 1248
    Leo J., Grave, 1247-1248
Kestrel family: Cindi, 1381 (see also Vol. I and II); Steve, 1381 (see also Vol. I and II)
Kiley family: Enda Mills, 1286-1288, 1290, 1322; Kathleen ("KIoko") Patricia, 1286-1287; Patrick Vincent, 1286, 1291; Robert Henry Bremer, 1290, 1322

King, Fred, Rev., 1329, 1331
Kings Canyon National Park, 1321
Kirk's Knoll, 1292, 1294
Kirkwood family: Mary Catherine Palmer Hewes, 1292-1296; Thomas, 1295-1296
Kline, Chuck, 1127-1128
Knapp, Ira, Undersheriff, 1137, 1140
Kniebes family: Carrie. See Miller, Carrie Kniebes; Chris, 1374; Duane Van, 1208, 1240, 1251, 1284-1285, 1366-1367, 1374 (see also back of page before Table of Contents; Vol. I and II); Susan Briles, 1251, 1367, 1383 (see also back of page before Table of Contents; Vol. I and II)
Knight, Gordon, 1374
Knox, John, Rev., 1153
Koenig/Ramsey Ranch, 941, 951
Koontz family: Lurilla Veysey Hall, 1278; Minnie Maude (see MacGregor, Minnie Maude Koontz)
Korean War veterans, 1235, 1326. See also Vol. I and II
Kraut, Charlie, 1005
Kuykendall, William Floyd, Rev., 1154

L

Laddman, "Smoky" and Lorraine E. Hyatt, 737
"Lady" Catherine Moon. See Moon, Catherine Lawder, "Lady"
Lake Estes, 1171. See also Vol. II
Lakeside Cemetery, Loveland, 1120, 1313, 1381. See also Vol. I and II
    individuals buried there, 1229, 1381 (see also Vol. I and II)
Lamb
    families: Ann (see Mills, Ann Lamb); Elkanah J., Rev., 1153; Rose Cordelia Lamb, 1232, 1285; Eugene Patrick, 1383 (see also Vol. I and II); Josiah and Ruth, 1287; Jean ("Jeanie") E., 276; Josephine Agnes, 1383, 1388 (see also Vol. I and II)
    Family Cemetery, 1383 (see also Vol. I and II)
Land Ordinance of May 20, 1785, 1119
Langston Family Cemetery, 1120, 1380-1381. See also Vol. I and II
Laporte, 1384. See also Vol. I and II
Laramie-Poudre Diversion Tunnel
    crater/"burial site" at West Portal, 1379 (see also Vol. I and II)
Laramie River Valley, 1360, 1383. See also Vol. I and II
Larimer County
    1885 Colorado State Census for, 1128-1129, 1306, 1354, 1387 (see also Vol. I and II)
    (Cont. on next page)

LARIMER COUNTY CEMETERIES

Larimer County, Con.:
    Assessor's Office, 1390 (*see also* Vol. I and II)
    Coroners, 1135, 1137-1138, 1140-1141 (*see also* Vol. I and II)
    County Judges, 1275 (*see also* Vol II)
    Genealogical Society, 1128, 1158, 1162, 1379, 1385-1387 (*see also* Vol. I and II)
    Heritage Writers, 1384 (*see also* Vol. I and II)
    Marriages Index (1858-1910), 1386 (*see also* Vol. I and II)
    requirements concerning burials on private property, 1122 (*see also* Vol. I)
    Road & Bridge Department, 1383 (*see also* Vol. I and II)
    schools, 1388 (*see also* Vol. I and II)
    Sheriffs/Deputy Sheriffs, 1372 (*see also* Vol. I)
    Stockgrowers Association, 1387 (*see also* Vol. I and II)
    Veterans Services, 1367-1368 (*see also* Vol. II)
Larosh. *See* Snell and Larosh hotel in Gaskill
Lass. *See* Vol. II
    family: Kathleen Wacker (*see* Wacker, Kathleen Lass); Wilhelm Michael August, 1, 1113 (*see also* Vol. II)
    Family Cemetery, 1113 (*see also* Vol II)
Lawder, Catherine Gratton. *See* Moon, Catherine Lawder, "Lady"
Lawn Lake, RMNP, 1215, 1254
    Flood, 1126-1127, 1154
Leafgren, Marjorie. *See* Colard, Marjorie Leafgren
Leake, R. M. ("Dick") and Nelle, 431
Ledges, The, 1257
Lee families: John, 1383 (*see also* Vol. I and II); Leah Jane (*see* Armstead, Leah Jane Lee); René, 1382 (*see also* Vol. I and II)
Lefever family: George, 457, 1360 (*see also* Vol. I and II); Teri Jurgens, 1360 (*see also* Vol. I and II)
legal land descriptions, 1117-1118
Levings
    Agnes McCall and Charles, cremains scattered in RMNP, 1257, 1319, 1382 (*see also* Vol. I and II)
    family: Agnes McCall, 1251, 1319; Charles, 1255-1256, 1319; Louis Raymond, 1250-1255, 1257; Mark and Mary McCall, 1319
    Louis R., Grave, 569, 1250-1253, 1258, 1319, 1378. 1380-1382 (*see also* Vol. I and II)
Lewis, Will, 1184
Lewiston Hotels Company, 1233
Liddell, Ardyce, 1332

Life, Rick, Detective, and Richard, his father, 1134-1135, 1379. *See also* Vol. I and II
Lipsher, Steve, 1258
Little Horseshoe Park, RMNP, 1207, 1214
Little Thompson
    Crossing Grave, 1381 (*see also* Vol. I and II)
    River, 1173-1174 (*see also* Vol. II)
    Valley, 1385 (*see also* Vol. I and II)
Livermore, 1381-1383. *See also* Vol. I and II
    Cemetery, 1383 (*see also* Vol. I and II)
    Woman's Club, 1383, 1387 (*see also* Vol. I and II)
Lloyd families: Flora, 1329; James V., Superintendent, RMNP, 1194-1195
Lone Pine Grave, 1350. *See also* Vol. I
Long, Thomas, Rev., 1331
Longs Peak, RMNP, 1254, 1289, 1310-1311, 1321-1322, 1344, 1347, 1376, 1376-1377. *See also* Vol. II
    Boulder Field, 1324
    Inn, 1257, 1286, 1289-1290, 1296, 1319, 1321-1323, 1377
Lory State Park Graves, 1378, 1381, 1383. *See also* Vol. I and II
Losasso, Charley and Thelma, 1192
Loveland
    cemeteries [*see* All Saints' Episcopal Church Columbarium (Vol. II); Lakeside Cemetery; Langston Family Cemetery; Loveland Burial Park, Medina Family Cemetery]
    churches, 1146, 1148
    Historical Society, 1380-1381 (*see also* Vol. I and II)
    Museum and Gallery, 1385 (*see also* Vol. I and II)
    Public Library Oral History Project, 1384 (*see also* Vol. I and II)
Loveland Burial Park, 1120. *See also* Vol. I and II
    individuals buried there, 1146-1147, 1253 (*see also* Vol. II)
Lower Beaver Meadows, RMNP, 1231
Ludwig Ranch Cemetery, 1115. *See also* Vol. I and II
Lula W. Dorsey Museum, YMCA of the Rockies, 1132, 1299
Lulu City (ghost town), west side of RMNP, Grand County, 1190-1191, 1259-1260, 1263-1266. *See also* Vol. I
    Graves, 1197, 1259-1263, 1380-1381 (*see also* Vol. I and II)
    named for, 1265
Lulu Pass. *See* Thunder Pass

lumbering and sawmill operations, 1384. *See also* Vol. I and II
    Curtis sawmill, 1149
    in Estes Park/RMNP areas, 1148-1149, 1356, 1359, 1368
    in Gaskill area, 1193
    in Horseshoe Inn area, 1203
    in Lulu City, 1265
    MacGregor family sawmill, 1274
Lumpy Ridge, RMNP, 1160, 1267, 1275
    Skeleton, 1267-1268
Lyman, Lashelle, Ranger, RMNP, 1165, 1212, 1267, 1340
Lynn, Emerson, 1322, 1377
Lyon, Kitty, Grave, 1379. *See also* Vol. I and II
Lyons, Boulder County, 1274. *See also* Vol. II
    sandstone, 1239

M

MacDonald, J. E., Mrs., 1367
MacGregor
    Black Canyon homestead, 1272-1273
    family: Alexander ("Alex") Quiner, 1174, 1269-1272, 1274-1276; Alice C. Detzman, 1277; Bruce A., 1277; Cecil Malcolm, 1277; Clara (*see* MacGregor, Marie Clara Heeney); Ethel Michael and Beatrice Jean, 1278; Florence, 1278; Inez C., 1277; Donald, 1269-1270, 1277, 1279-1280, 1282; George Heeney, 1276-1277, 1282; Halbert, 1276, 1282; Marie Clara Heeney, 1159, 1272, 1274-1276, 1281; Maude (*see* MacGregor, Minnie Maude Koontz); Minnie Maude Koontz, 1269-1270, 1277-1280, 1282; Muriel Lurilla, 1269-1270, 1273, 1280-1282; Ronald, 1277; Zada Alderdyce, 1276-1277
    Family Cemetery, 1269-1270, 1277-1281
    post office/store, 1274
    Ranch, 1269, 1271, 1274, 1279-1280
        Historic District, 1283
        Museum, 1271-1272, 1275, 1283
    Toll Road, 1271, 1274
Madina, Mariano. *See* Medina, Mariano
Maguire family: Anna, 1158, 1161; Catherine, 1158, 1161, 1164, 1167-1168, 1170; James ("Mike"), 1158, 1161
Manford Hotel and John J., 1233
Manhattan Cemetery, 1279. *See also* Vol. I and II
Manske, Glen, 1177
Maps
    location of graves and building in town of Gaskill, 1187
    location of graves and homesteaded land in/near Horseshoe Park, 1203-1204
    location of graves, cemeteries, and memorials in Volume III, 1124-1125
    portion of Larimer County covered in Volume III, 1123
March family: Daniel, 1130; Minnie E., 1130
Markovich, Michael and Lola, 1284-1285
Mary's Lake, 1149, 1229, 1232
Masman, William C., 1067-1068. *See also* Mosman, William
Masonic Lodge, 1163, 1313, 1373. *See also* Eastern Star; Vol. I and II
Masonville, nearby graves and cemeteries, 1380, 1383. *See also* Vol. I and II
Mather, Steve, 1323
Mathews, Alfred E., Grave, 1381. *See also* Vol. II
Matthews families: Alfred C. and Ella M. Wright, 1254; Bryan, 1255; Lois E. Bates, 1254; Ted Ronald, 1250, 1252-1255
McCabe family: Ella (*see* James, Ella McCabe); James J., 1276
McCall family: Agnes (*see* Levings, Agnes McCall); Josephine (*see* Babcock, Josephine McCall)
McCormick, Dave and Pat, 1285
McCreery, W. H., 1160
McCrerry Springs, 1159
McDaniel, Ranger, RMNP, 1137, 1139-1141
McGeorge Tin Shop, 1255
McGraw Ranch, 1249
McGregor families: Alexander, 1271 [*see also* MacGregor, Alexander ("Alex") Quiner]; Clara (*see* MacGregor, Clara); Duncan, Sr., 1271; Duncan, Jr., and Elanor Burget/Burghardt, 1271; Duncan (son of Alexander and Margaret MacGregor), 1271; Margaret Goodwin, 1271; R. Q. [*see* MacGregor, Alexander ("Alex") Quiner]
McKelvey, Mr. and Mrs., 1185
McLaren
    Elbert ("Bert") Arthur I, cremains scattered in RMNP, 1320
    family: Charles ("Chuck"), 1320; Cynthia ("Cyndy"/"Cyd"), 1320-1321; Dorothy (*see* Howard, Dorothy McLaren); Doug, 1320; Elbert ("Bert") Arthur, I, 1320-1321; Elbert Arthur ("Rusty"), II, 1320; Fred Douglas and Iva Montgomery, 1320; Kathleen Adair, 1321; Lady Dee Shelton, 1321; Pamela Lynn (*see* Buchnoff, Pamela Lynn McLaren); Phyllis (*see* Johnson, Phyllis McLaren) (Cont. on next page)

LARIMER COUNTY CEMETERIES

McLaren family, Cont.:
: Rebecca Thompson, 1320; Richard ("Dick") Cecil, 1320; Shirley Epperson, 1320-1321; Victoria, 1320

McQuery, Dick, 1137

Medina
: Family Cemetery, 1380-1381 (*see also* Vol. I and II)
: Marianna (*see* Medina, Mariano)
: Mariano (Jesus Garcia Mariano), 1386 (*see also* Vol. I and II)

Medino, Mariano. *See* Medina, Mariano

Mefford, Jack, 1387. *See also* Vol. I and II

Meirath, Bill, 1381. *See also* Vol. I and II

Melton, Jack R. and Lulabeth, 1127, 1233, 1297-1299

Mereness family: Harry Albert and Mary Thomas Shreve, 1310; Theodora ("Teddie") Ann [*see* Haines, Theodora ("Teddie") Ann Mereness]

Merrian, Regional Director, National Park Service, 1185

Merril, Kay, 1333

Mexican burials, 547, 549, 709. *See also* "Mexican Joe" Grave

"Mexican Joe" Grave, 1120, 1381, 1384. *See also* Vol. I and II

Meyers, Andy, 1198

Michigan River, 1264. *See also* Vol. I

Middle Bald Mountain. *See* Old Baldy

Middle Park and Grand River Mining and Land Improvement Co., 1265

Mill Creek in Rocky Mountain National Park, 1145, 1149, 1355, 1357, 1359

Miller
: Charles D., Grave, 1284-1285, 1381 (*see also* Vol. I and II)
: families: Carrie Kniebes, 1208; Charles D., 1284-1285, 1381 (*see also* Vol. I and II); Cora (see Hardin, Cora Miller); John Dennis, 1382 (*see also* Vol. I and II); Juliana Jo Sloan, 1381-1382, 1385, 1388 (*see also* Vol. I and II); Lafi, 1381-1382, 1387-1388 (*see also* Vol. I and II); Oma Katherine Griffith, 1147-1148; Robert, 1147
: Manor Dance Studio, 1382 (*see also* Vol. I and II)

Milliken, Weld County, Colorado, 1237

Mills and Kiley Grave and Scattered Cremains, 1286-1288, 1290-1291

Mills
: Enoch Josiah ("Joe"), cremains scattered in RMNP, 1323
: Enos Abijah, cremains scattered in RMNP, 1322
: families: Abijah and Sarah Moon, 1287; Ann Lamb, 1287; Augustus E., 1287; Eleanor Ann, 1289, 1323, 1325; Elkanah F., 1287; Ellen ("Ella"), 1288; Enda (*see* Kiley, Enda Mills); Enoch Josiah ("Joe"), 1286, 1296, 1323-1326, 1378 (*see also* Vol. I and II); Enoch Josiah, Mrs., 1322; Enos, Sr., 1287; Enos Abijah, 1255, 1281, 1286, 1288, 1290, 1293, 1296, 1321-1322, 1324-1325, 1378 (*see also* Enos Mills Cabin and Gallery; Vol. I and II); Eryn, 1322; Esther A. Burnell, 1281, 1286-1290, 1322-1323, 1325, 1386 (*see also* Vol. I and II); Ethel Maude Steere, 1289, 1323-1324; Horace Greeley, 1288; Joe [*see* Mills, Enoch Josiah ("Joe")]; John G., Commissioner, 1198; Mark Muir, 1289, 1323; Mary E., 1287; Naomi Victoria (*see* Dodsworth, Naomi Victoria Mills); Paul N. ("Tiny"), 1168; Ruth, 1288; Sarah A. (*see* Winslow, Sarah A. Mills); Sabina Isabella ("Belle"), 1288

Miner, Mr. and Mrs Willard and baby, 1198

mines
: Carbonate, 1266
: Eureka Mine, 1266
: Garden City, 1265
: Georgianna Mine, 1265
: North Star Mine, 1264, 1266
: Ptarmigan Mine, 1265-1266
: Shipler's mine near Lulu City (*see* North Star Mine)
: Silver Heels Mine, 1265
: Southern Cross Mine, 1266
: Toponis Mine, 1186
:   snowslide, 1186-1187, 1198-1199
: Wolverine Mine, 1190, 1198, 1266

Minnis, Joseph H., Bishop, Episcopal Church of Colorado, 1330-1331

Modena Cemetery. *See* Medina Family Cemetery

Modena, Mariano/Marianna. *See* Medina, Mariano

Modeno, Mariano. *See* Medina, Mariano

Montgomery, Iva. *See* McLaren, Iva Montgomery

Montony, Richard and Meredith, 1330

Moomaw, Jack, Ranger, RMNP, 1133, 1135, 1140-1141, 1233-1234, 1318, 1336, 1338-1339

Moon, Catherine Lawder, "Lady," 1117, 1382, 1387. *See also* Vol. I and II

Moore, Robert ("Bobby") Thomas, Second Lieutenant, 1197. *See also* Vol. I

INDEX

Moraine Park, RMNP, 1244-1245, 1355-1356
  Ranch, 1306
Morgan, Edward J., Rev., 1331
Morris, Andrew J., 1387. *See also* Vol. I and II
Morrissey, Julia Ann, 1293-1295
  Grave, 1139, 1292-1293, 1295, 1337, 1382 (*see also* Vol. I and II)
Mosier Ranch Cemetery, 1197. *See also* Vol. I
mountain men, 1386. *See also* trappers; French fur trappers; Vol I and II
Mountain View
  Bible Fellowship, Estes Park, 1177-1179
  Cemetery, Longmont, Boulder County, 1129, 1157-1158
    individuals buried there, 1162-1167, 1170 (*see also* Vol. II)
  Memorial Park, Boulder, 1235
Mounts family, 1151
Mowry Brothers (of Gaskill), 1190
Mummy Mountain, RMNP, 1127, 1215
Muriel L. MacGregor Charitable Trust, 1269, 1271, 1275, 1282-1283
Myer's Barber Shop, 1265
Myler, Mrs. W. I., 1171

N

NAD. *See* North American Datum
Nash, Ella and daughter, 1212
National Park Service, 1134, 1141, 1185, 1206, 1213, 1257, 1282-1283, 1308, 1313, 1315, 1317, 1320-1321, 1323. *See also* Vol. II
National Register of Historic Places, 1283, 1286. *See also* Vol. I
National Western Stock Show, Denver, 1381. *See also* Vol. I and II
Native American graves, 1120, 1187-1188, 1350, 1357-1358, 1375, 1379. *See also* Vol. I and II
Nelson families: Aven/Evan/Even/, 1208-1209, 1211, 1219-1220; Cecila Alice Calhoun, 1209, 1220; Helen, 1209, 1220; Ruth Elizabeth Ashton, 1207, 1211, 1219
Never Summer
  Mountains, 1264, 1316
  Ranch, west side of RMNP, Grand County, 1197, 1313-1317, 1320, 1380 (*see also* Vol. I and II)
Newson, Hamilton S., 1329
Nicholas family: Beverly, 1178, 1298, 1382 (*see also* Vol. I and II); Truman L., 1177, 1298, 1355-1356, 1375, 1382 (*see also* Vol. I and II)
Nickerson, Winslow and Lillian, 1198
Nicky's Restaurant, 1239-1240

Nielson, Frances Buynan, 1385. *See also* Vol. I and II
Nierman, Alyce, 1279. *See also* Vol. I and II
Noel, Thomas J., 1387
North American Datum, 1116
North Park, Jackson County, 1264. *See also* Vol. I
Nugent, James, 1296. *See also* Vol. II

O

Oaks and Kellogg survey, 1273
Odessa Lake, RMNP, 1180-1185, 1338-1339
Old Baldy
  graves near "last Yockey sawmill," 1379 (*see also* Vol. I and II)
Old Church Shops, 1154
Old Flowers Road/Trail, 1383. *See also* Vol. I and II
organization of this book, 1115
Our Lady of the Mountains Catholic Church, 1247-1249
Overland Trail, 1358, 1388. *See also* Vol I and II
Owen, Eleanore A. James, 1165, 1168
Ozmen
  Bob, 1298-1299
    Grave, 1297-1298, 1378, 1382 (*see also* Vol. I and II)
Ozmen families, 1299-1301

P

P.J. Wade General Store, 1192
Palatines to America, 1114. *See also* Vol. I and II
Palmer family: Henry, 1294, 1296; John Edgerton, 1295; Mary Catherine (*see* Kirkwood, Mary Catherine Palmer Hewes)
Parker and Godsmark's Hotel, 1265
Park Hotel, 1233
Park Road Company, 1274
Patrick families: Esta Snedaker, 1216; C C, 2010-2013, 1215-1217, 1223; Nancy Judith (*see* Artman, Nancy Judith Patrick)
Patterson, Nicholas, Grave, 1381. *See also* Vol. I and II
Paul family: Nicholas Jay, II, and Alyce Nelsen, 1318; Paul, Nicholas Jay, III, 1318
Peaceful Valley, 1323-1324
Peacock Pool, RMNP, 1377
Pedersen, Henry F., Jr., 1210, 1212, 1387
Peterson
  Chuck, 1350 (*see also* Vol. I)
  H.L.W., Grave, 1381 (*see also* Vol. I and II)
Pettit, George W., 1203, 1211
Pickens' Point Memorials, 1382. *See also* Vol. I and II

I-15

LARIMER COUNTY CEMETERIES

Pickering family: James ("Jim") H., 1135, 1139, 1143-1144, 1158-1160, 1172, 1232, 1253-1255, 1257, 1271, 1292-1296, 1319, 1323-1325, 1336-1337, 1354, 1356, 1359, 1363, 1376-1377, 1382, 1387-1388; Pat, 1293, 1337, 1354 (*see also* Vol. I and II); Pat, 1293, 1337, 1354

Pierson, Debbie, 1367-1370. *See also* Vol. II

Pikes Peak, El Paso County, 1311

Piltz, Carl, 1255

Pine Creek Ranch, 1383. *See also* Vol. I

Pine Haven Resort, 1239

Pinewood Springs, 1174

Pingree Hill, 1264, 1382. *See also* Vol. I and II

Pioneer Museum. *See* Fort Collins Museum of Discovery

Pioneers' Mining Company, 1190

Platteville, Weld County, 1173. *See also* Vol. I and II

PLSS. *See* Public Land Survey System

Plummer, Robert, 1198

P.M. *See* Principal Meridian

Pointer, Emalu Swain, 1332

Pollock, Irene Matilda. *See* Williams, Irene Matilda Pollock

Poudre
    Canyon School, 1360 (*see also* Vol. I and II)
    School District R-1, 1388 (*see also* Vol. I and II)

Prairie Divide, 1381-1382. *See also* Vol. I and II

Pratt, Dorothy Swain, 1333

Preemption Act of 1841, 1119, 1273

Price, Hariet Elizabeth, 1329

Principal Meridian, 1118

private property
    respect for, 1115-1116 (*see also* Vol. II)
    regulations concerning burials on, 1122 (*see also* Vol. I)

Prospect Mountain Tramway, 1324

Public Land Survey System, 1117

R

Rabbit Creek, 1388. *See also* Vol. I and II

Ramaley, William ("Bill"), 1135, 1140-1141, 1336, 1338-1339

Ramsey, Adele. *See* Babcock, Adele Ramsey

Ramshorn Cottages, 1331

range, 1118

Red Feather Lakes, 1381-1382. *See also* Vol. I and II

Redstone Canyon, 1381. *See also* Vol. I and II

Reed, Roscoe, Priest, 1333

Reid families: John G., 1203, 1211, 1224; George D., 1145

remittance men, 1244. *See also* Vol. I

remote graves, respect for, 1116, 1187

Reu Family Cemetery, 1379. *See also* Vol. I and II

Rhodes Family Cemetery, 1115, 1383. *See also* Vol. I and II

Richards
    family: Herbert, 1303, 1305-1306; William and Mary, 1303, 1305-1306
    Herbert, Grave, 1302-1305, 1378 (*see also* Vol. I and II)

Richmond families: Edmond E. and Emma, 1211, 1213-1216, 1223; Seth, Rev., 1331

Ring, Mahalia. *See* Estes, Mahalia Ring

Ritters, Norma, 1171

Riverside Hotel, 1233

RMNP. *See* Rocky Mountain National Park

Roaring River, 1127

Robert O. and Mary E. Roberts Memorial, 1383. *See also* Vol. I and II

Roberts
    family: Catherine Allison (second wife of James Evan Roberts), 1383 (*see also* Vol. I and II); Evan (*see* Roberts, James Evan); James Evan, 1384, 1386 (*see also* Vol. I and II)
    Memorial. *See* Robert O. and Mary E. Roberts Memorial
    Ranch, 1360, 1383 (*see also* Vol. I and II)

Robinson
    Elbert Charles, 1117. *See also* Vol. I and II
    Ranch Cemetery, 1382. *See also* Vol. I and II

Rock Cut Parking Lot, RMNP, 1343

RockMount Cottages, 1150

Rocky (pet burial), 1333

"Rocky Mountain" Jim. *See* Nugent, James

Rocky Mountain National Park, 1126-1130, 1133-1141, 1180-1185, 1186-1189, 1194-1195, 1196-1198, 1202-1208, 1225-1228, 1250-1253, 1302-1303, 1307-1327, 1321-1322, 1334-1336, 1343-1351, 1353-1359, 1378-1383. *See also* Vol. II
    Library, 1128, 1139, 1180, 1194, 1207, 1257, 1304
    lodges, 1387 (*see also* Vol. I and II)
    Museum Storage Facility, 1128, 1133, 1303, 1305
    opening ceremony, 1337
    Oral History Project, 1143, 1367

(Cont. on next page)

Rocky Mountain National Park, Cont.:
    Rangers, 1127-1128, 1133-1138, 1140-1141, 1180-1185, 1194-1195, 1197, 1227, 1233-1234, 1256-1258, 1259-1261, 1320-1321, 1335, 1338-1340, 1353, 1371, 1378, 1380-1381 (*see also* Vol. I and II) (Cont. on next page)
    scattered cremains, 1307-1327, 1378, 1380-1382 (*see also* Vol. I and II)
    ski patrol, 1254
    Superintendents, 1136, 1138-1139, 1185, 1194, 1227, 1244, 1268, 1309, 1313, 1377 (*see also* Vol. II)

Rocky Mountain
    Nature Association, 1318
    Transportation Company, 1323

Rocky Ridge Music Center, 1295
Rogers, Pat, 1267
Rogerson House, The, 1186, 1189-1191
Rogerson, Joseph, 1186, 1189-1190
Rohrer, Carl, 1168
Roosevelt National Forest, 1361. *See also* Vol. I and II
Roselawn Cemetery, Fort Collins, 1379. *See also* Vol. I and II
    online records database, how to use, 1389-1390
Rosendro, José. *See* "Mexican Joe" Grave
Rosewell, Paul T., 1295
Rottenberg, Dan, 1116, 1388. *See also* Vol. I and II
Rowe, Mr., 1159
Royer, C. W., 1198
Ruffner, Harry, 1175
Ryder, Annie, 1200

S

Sagebrush Flat Cemetery, west side of RMNP, Grand County, 1198-1199
Saint Bartholomew Cemetery. *See* Episcopal Church of St. Bartholomew the Apostle Cemetery
Salazar, Ken, 1308
Sampson family: Ella Royster, 1337; Francis S., Rev., 1336; Frank, 1338; Thornton Rogers, Rev., 1140, 1336-1340, 1388 (*see also* Vol. I and II)
Sampson, Reverend Thornton Rogers, Grave, 1121, 1139, 1252, 1293, 1334-1335, 1378, 1381-1382. *See also* Vol. I and II
Sandburg, Donald and Dorothy, scattered cremains, 1341-1342
Sandburg family: Chris (*see* Spohn, Chris Sandburg); Donald Irving, 1341; Dorothy Allen, 1341; Elaine, 1342; Frank A. and Eda Hultman, 1342; Kyle and Jan and their children, 1342; Richard, 1342
Sanders-Richter, Janet, 1387
Santa Fe, Sante Fe County, New Mexico, 1172. *See also* Vol. I
Sattler, Deborah Dimon, 1388. *See also* Vol. I and II
Saurino
    family, 1180
    Judy, 1184
sawmills. *See* lumbering and sawmill operations
Schageman, Rita, 1271-1272, 1278-1280
Schnor family: Beatrice, 1309-1310; Henry, 1309-1310; Mary (*see* Gudgel, Mary Schnor)
Schutz family: Cheryl, 1372; Dave, 1327, 1371-1372
Schwartz, Rick, 1374
sections, types of, 1118, 1203
    half section, 1118
    half a quarter section, 1118
    quarter section, 1118, 1203
    quarter of a quarter (sixteenth section), 1118, 1203
Sequoia National Park, 1321
Seven Mile Creek, 1361. *See also* Vol. I and II
    Grave (*see* Unknown Child No. 6 Grave)
    Road, 1361 (*see also* Vol. I and II)
Seybold family, 1240: Dianne, 1240-1241; Jeanne M. Gray, 1167-1168, 1240-1241
Shadow Mountain Reservoir, Grand County, 1198-1199
Shafroth, Frank H., Chancellor, Episcopal Diocese of Colorado, 1330
Shelton, Lady Dee. *See* McLaren, Lady Dee Shelton
Sherwood Hotel, 1233
Shipler
    Joe, 1262-1265
    Mountain, 1264
Shipler's Cabin, 1262-1263
Shipman, John, Grave, 173-174, 210, 407-409, 563, 574, 1105, 1383. *See also* Vol. I and II
Shipp families: Elsie Myrtle (*see* Pennock, Elsie Myrtle Shipp); Mary Margaret (*see* Colard, Mary Margaret Shipp); Sam, 173-174, 407, 486
Shoup, Oliver, Governor of Colorado (1919-1923), 1323
Simmonds, Minerva, 1197-1198
Sky
    Corral Guest Ranch, 1383. *See also* Vol. I and II (Cont. on next page)

LARIMER COUNTY CEMETERIES

Sky, Cont.
    Land Ranch, 1210, 1219
Skyline Campground, 1350 (*see also* Vol. I)
Slade, Joseph Alfred ("Jack"), 1388. *See also* Vol. I and II
Sladek, Ron D., 1387. *See also* Vol. I
Sloan, Juliana Jo. *See* Miller, Juliana Jo Sloan
Slurry bomber pilots, 1374
Smith families: David Frank, 1117 (*see also* Vol. I and II); Dudley, 1331; Elizabeth Burnell, 1287-1289, 1322; Eric A., Archdeacon, Episcopal Diocese of Colorado, 1330; Norman, 1290
Smith, Marietta, Grave, 1382. *See also* Vol. I and II
Snedaker family: Esta (*see* Patrick, Esta Snedaker); James, 1216
Snell and Larosh's General Store (in Lulu City), 1265
Snell and Larosh's Hotel (in Gaskill), 1192
Soapstone Prairie Natural Area, 1380. *See also* Vol. I and II
Sorenson, Carol. *See* Vannorsdel, Carol Sorenson
Spanish-American War veteran, 1371, 1373
Spectacle Lakes, RMNP, 1250, 1255-1256, 1258
Spohn family: Brian Lawrence, 1342; Chris Sandburg, 1341-1342; Larry, 1342; Michelle Christine, 1342
Sprague
    Abner E., 1244, 1306, 1378, 1388 (*see also* Vol. I and II)
    Lake, RMNP, 1302
        Trailhead, 1302
    Lodge, 1306
    Mountain, 1376
    Pass, RMNP
        possible grave under cairn on pass, 1376
Springer
    Ida, 1367-1368
    Place/property, 1148, 1367-1368
Spurlin family: Leslie Hamilton, 1311-1312, 1314, 1321, 1325-1326; William Luther, 1326
Spurlin, William Luther, cremains scattered in RMNP, 1326
squaw bush, 1243, 1366. *See also* Vol. I
Stanley
    F. O., 1149
    Hotel, 1149, 1330
Stark, Jon Marr, Rev., 1329-1331
State
    Agricultural College. *See* Colorado State University
    Historical and Natural History Society of Colorado, 1323
Stead, J. D., 1306
Stead's Ranch, Estes Park, 1184-1185, 1207, 1244
Steere, Ethel Maude. *See* Mills, Ethel Maude Steere
Stephens, Ranger, 1137, 1140-1141
Stevens, Charles ("Charlie") P., Grave, 1270. *See also* Vol. II
Stewart families: Lulu, 1265; Samuel B., 1264 (*see also* Vol. I)
Stewart's Toll Road/Stewart's Road to the Mines, 1263-1265
Stieben, Kate, 1384
Stillwater Ranch, 1315
Stirling, Dave, 1372-1373
St. Francis of Assissi Anglican Church Cemetery, Estes Park, 1332-1333
Stock-Raising Homestead Act of 1916, 1120. *See also* Vol. I
Stokes, Mr., 1198
Stollak, Milt, 1374
Stollings, Martha Ann ("Patsy"). *See* Estes, Martha Ann ("Patsy") Stollings
Stone, John Timothy, 1127
Stonewall Creek, 111, 120, 290, 292, 293
    Ranch, 155, 279, 281-282, 288-289, 377
Stovall, Edward, 1169
Stove Prairie, 1383. *See also* Vol. I and II
St. Vrain
    River, Boulder County, 1274 (*see also* Vol. II)
    Road, 1174
St. Walter's Catholic Church, Estes Park, 1249
Suher, Ken and Betty, cremains scattered in RMNP, 1326
Sullivan, James, 1313. *See also* Vol. II
Sumonia, Duke, 1285. *See also* Vol. II
Sundance Mountain, RMNP, 1343, 1377
    Graves, 457, 570, 1310-1312, 1318, 1321, 1343-1352, 1360, 1379 (*see also* Vol. I and II)
    northeast summit, 1344, 1348
    northwest summit, 1344
Sunnyside Knoll, 1239
Susie (pet burial), 1333
Swain family: Gladys Maude, 1333; Jack Richard, 1333
Swan
    Jessie Nightingale, Grave, 1382 (*see also* Vol. I and II)
    Wesley Everett, 1388 (*see also* Vol. I and II)
Swanson Memorial Garden, 1382. *See also* Vol. I and II
Swiftcurrent Lodge, 1297-1298, 1362

INDEX

T

Tacker, Sylvia Babcock and Harold L., 1257
Targett, H. F., disappearance of on Longs Peak, 1376-1377
Tecker family: Hal, 1334-1335, 1339; Inas, 1334
Tempest, William, 1355-1356, 1358-1359
Texas Rangers, 1315
Theodore Roosevelt National Monument, 1313
Thiem, Jon, 1115-1116, 1383, 1388. *See also* Vol. I and II
Thomas, Adam, 1388. *See also* Vol. I and II
Thomassen, David and Ruth Brown, 453-454
Thompson Cemetery. *See* Thomson Ranch Cemetery
Thomson Ranch Cemetery, 1120. *See also* Vol. I and II
Thorne, James, 1355-1356, 1358-1359, 1363
Throckmorton, W. H., 1199
Thunder Pass, 1264
Thursday Hiking Club, 1267, 1307, 1365
tie hackers, 1350. *See also* Vol. I and II
Timber Culture Act of 1873, 1119. *See also* Vol. I and II
Timberline House, 1324
Tipton, Michael, 1374
Tip Top Guest Ranch, 1, 1113. *See also* Vol. II
Toft, Georgia Anne Griffith, 1144, 1150-1151
Toll, Roger Wolcott, Superintendent, RMNP, 1139, 1258, 1377
    Memorial on Trail Ridge Road, 1377
township, 1118
Trail's End Ranch Cemetery, 1120, 1382. *See also* Vol. I and II
Trail Ridge Road, RMNP, 1152, 1323, 1343
Trail River Ranch, west side of RMNP, Grand County, 1197, 1307-1308, 1380. *See also* Vol. I and II
trappers' graves, 1350. *See also* Vol. I
trappers. *See* Vol. I and II; mountain men
Travis, J. Mont, Rev., 1154
Trowbridge, C. R., Acting Supervisor, RMNP, 1338
Tuell, Mary Jane Williams and Harry A., 1234
Tuttle, Arthur and Barbara, 1333
Tuxedo Park, 1353-1354, 1356, 1359, 1363
    Cemetery, RMNP, 1115, 1318, 1353-1359, 1378, 1380, 1382 (*see also* Vol. I and II)
Twin Owls, 1273
Twin Sisters Peaks, RMNP, 1257, 1289, 1319, 1322, 1324
Tyndall Glacier, RMNP, 1133-1134, 1136-1138

U

Udall, Mark, 1308-1309
Union Pacific Railroad, 1350. *See also* Vol. I and II
University of Colorado, Boulder, 1235, 1281, 1290, 1323. *See also* Vol. I and II
    Medical School, 1241
University of Denver, 1290. *See also* Vol. I
    Law School, 1281
University of Northern Colorado, Greeley, Weld County, 1238, 1282, 1352. *See also* Vol. I and II
University of Wyoming, Laramie, Wyoming, 1236. *See also* Vol. I and II
Unknown Adult No. 1 Grave, 1360. *See also* Vol. I and II
Unknown Adult No. 2 Grave, 1343-1344, 1346, 1360. *See also* Vol. I and II
Unknown Adult No. 3 Grave, 1360. *See also* Vol. I and II
Unknown Adult No. 4 Grave, 1120, 1360, 1383. *See also* Vol. I and II
Unknown Adult No. 5 Grave, 1360. *See also* Vol. I and II
Unknown Adult No. 6 Grave, 1360. *See also* Vol. I and II
Unknown Adult No. 7 Grave, 1344, 1346-1347, 1360. *See also* Vol. I and II
Unknown Adult No. 8 Grave, 1360, 1380-1381. *See also* Vol. I and II
Unknown Child No. 1 Grave, 1361. *See also* Vol. I and II
Unknown Child No. 2 Grave, 1361. *See also* Vol. I and II
Unknown Child No. 3 Grave, 1361, 1378. *See also* Vol. I and II
Unknown Child No. 4 Grave, 1202-1203, 1205, 1207, 1211, 1361-1363. *See also* Vol. I and II
Unknown Child No. 5 Grave, 1202-1203, 1205, 1208-1211, 1213, 1220, 1223-1224, 1361. *See also* Vol. I and II
Unknown Child No. 6 Grave, 1361, 1379. *See also* Vol. I and II
unoccupied land acquisition acts, 1117, 1119-1120. *See also* Vol. I and II
Upper Beaver Meadows, RMNP, 1165, 1226-1226, 1231
Upsilon, Mount. *See* Ypsilon Mountain/Mount Ypsilon
U.S. Air Force, 1235, 1238. *See also* Vol. II
U.S. Army, 1235, 1254, 1310, 1382. *See also* Vol. II
    Tenth Mountain Divison, 1321, 1382 (*see also* Vol. I and II)

LARIMER COUNTY CEMETERIES

U.S. Army Air Corps, 1311. *See also* Vol. II
U.S. Army Air Forces, 1235. *See also* Vol. I and II
U.S. Bureau of Land Management, 1211, 1243, 1286, 1306, 1355, 1357-1358, 1367, 1369-1370, 1390. *See also* Vol. I and II
U.S. Department of Defense, 1116
U.S. Department of Veterans Affairs, 1369-1370
U.S. Fish and Wildlife Service, 176
USGS. *See* U.S. Geological Survey
U.S. Geological Survey, 1114, 1116-1117, 1214, 1252, 1345. *See also* Vol. I and II
U.S. Marine Corps, 1326. *See also* Vol. II
U.S. Navy, 1290. *See also* Vol. I and II
Usher Child Grave, 1383 (*see also* Vol. I and II)
Ute Trail, 1343-1344, 1349

V

Vaille, Agnes, 1388
Valhalla Cottages, Estes Park, 1150
Valley of Elkanah, 1319, 1324
Van Brunt, Theodore, 1128
Van De Veere, Warren C., 1332
Vannorsdel Family Cemetery, 1383. *See also* Vol. I and II
Venner, Robert C., 1169
Veterans of Foreign Wars, 646, 758, 1005
Vietnam War veterans, 1235. *See also* Vol. I and II
Virginia Dale Stage Station Cemetery, 1381. *See also* Vol. I and II
von Wedel, Allison Stacey, 1328

W

Wacker, Kathleen Lass, 1113. *See also* Vol. II
Wagener, Siegfried, 1296
Wagner, Richard E., Ranger, RMNP, 1136. 1140-1141
Walsh, William and Kate, 1354, 1355, 1358
Walz, Mike, 1150
Wangnild Family Cemetery, 1383. *See also* Vol. I and II
Wapiti Center, 45
Warner, Alfonzo R., 1197
Washburn, Pat, 1287, 1289, 1323-1325, 1362, 1363
Water Supply and Storage Company, 1138. *See also* Vol. I
Watrous, Ansel, 1143, 1157, 1159-1161, 1164, 1270, 1375, 1388. *See also* Vol. I and II
Way, Superintendent, RMNP, 1136, 1138
Weaver
    Carl Wilbur ("Webb"), Grave, 1364
    family: Carl Wilbur ("Webb"), 1364-1365; Jean, 1267-1268, 1364-1365
Weir, Jan, 1387
Weitzel, Tom, Rev., 1178
Wellcome
    family: Elizabeth Ann Corning, 1369; Harris P., 1367-1370
    Harris P., Grave, 1318, 1366-1367
    Lodge, 1368
Western Stone, Lyons, Boulder County, 1374
Weyl, Diane, 1328-1330
Wheel Bar, 1233
Wheeler families: Bob ("Squeaky"), 1336; H. N., Superintendent (first), Colorado National Forest, 1265
Whitcomb Katya, grave and death, 1305. *See also* Buckeye Ranch Cemetery and Vol. I
Whiteley, Lee, 1385, 1388. *See also* Vol. I and II
Whitney, Betty Jo Hupp and Gerald Gregg, 1236-1237
Whyte family: Theodore George William, 1144, 1273, 1359; Maude, 1144
Wignall, Howard and Gretchen, 1326-1327
    cremains scattered in RMNP, 1326
Wild Basin, RMNP, 1289, 1310, 1326
Williams
    Charles E. ("Cap"), 1350. *See also* Vol. I
    families: Frank (from Estes Park area) 1227, 1312-1313; Hazel (*see* Hanks, Hazel Williams); Jack, 1186, 1188, 1197, 1199; James Sidney ("Sid"), Sr., 1234; James Sidney, Jr., 1234; Martha Elizabeth and three husbands, 1234; Mary Jane (*see* Tuell, Mary Jane Williams); Otho Eli and Josephine Sullivan, 1236, 1313; Pearl Etha (*see* Hupp, Pearl Etha Williams); Thomas Ervin and Aileen Ann Popst, 1234-1235
Williamson Cemeteries Nos. 1 and 2, 1380. *See also* Vol. I and II
Wilson, Charles and Ann, 1330
Wind River, 1297, 1368
    Lodge, 1299
Winslow, Sarah A. Mills and Charles T., 1288
Woods
    families: Jack, 1327; Janice M., 1330
    Jack, cremains scattered in RMNP, 1327, 1378 (*see also* Vol. I and II)
World War I veterans, 1201, 1235. *See also* Vol. I and II
World War II, 1307. *See also* Vol. I and II
    plane crash sites in the Rocky Mountains, 1349
    veterans, 1254, 1290, 1310-1312, 1321, 1326, 1342, 1382 (*see also* Vol. I and II)

Worster Cemetery, 1120. *See also* Vol. I and II
Wright family: Frank and Ann Senior, 1327; James H., 1327
Wright, Frank and Ann Senior, cremains scattered in RMNP, 1327
Wyoming-Colorado border. *See* Colorado-Wyoming border

Y

Yellowstone National Park, 1313, 1319
Yeros, Trudy, 1207-1208, 1326
YMCA of the Rockies, 1126-1127, 1149-1150, 1233, 1297
    Dorsey Museum, 1318
      livery, 1207
Yockey Levi, Grave, 1382. *See also* Vol. I and II

Yore
    Clement, Headstone, 1371-1372
    family: Alberta McCauley Plondke, 1372-1373; Barbara, 1373; Byrd Ann, 1373; Clement, 1296, 1327, 1372-1373; Frank, 1373; J. Hanley, 1373; James H., 1373; Juanita (*see* Farris, Juanita Yore); Norris W., 1373; Virginia, 1373
Yosemite National Park, 1321
Young, Charles V., Rev., 1330-1331
Ypsilon
    Lake, RMNP, 1254
    Mountain (aka Mount Ypsilon), RMNP, 1250, 1252-1258, 1319

Z

Zahourek family: Carol, 1156-1158, 1161; Jerry, 1156-1157, 1165-1166, 1168-1170

Order Information

If you borrowed this copy from a library or would like to order a copy for a friend or family member, please send a check or money order to: Iron Gate Publishing, P.O. Box 999, Niwot, CO 80544. Our books are available online to institutions through Ingram, to individuals at Amazon.com and on our website:

www.irongate.com

Volume I
Cemeteries and Remote Burials in Larimer County, Colorado, Volume I: The Poudre and North, Including the Laramie River Valley and Livermore
Number of Pages: 632
ISBN 978-1-68224-010-6   softbound $44.95
ISBN 978-1-68224-011-3   hardbound $54.95

Volume II
Cemeteries and Remote Burials in Larimer County, Colorado, Volume II: South of the Poudre, Including Fort Collins, Loveland, and Berthoud
Number of Pages: 574
ISBN 978-1-68224-012-0   softbound $41.95
ISBN 978-1-68224-013-7   hardbound $51.95

Volume III
Cemeteries and Remote Burials in Larimer County, Colorado, Volume III: Estes Park Area and Rocky Mountain National Park, Including Park Property in Grand County
Number of Pages: 308
ISBN 978-1-68224-014-4   softbound $23.95
ISBN 978-1-68224-015-1   hardbound $33.95